Language Arts and Literature

Course 1

PEARSON

AGS Globe

Shoreview, MN

Reading Consultant

Timothy Shanahan, Ph.D., Professor of Urban Education, Director of the Center for Literacy, University of Illinois Chicago, Author, *AMP™ Reading System*

Acknowledgments appear on pages 548–551, which constitutes an extension of this copyright page.

Reviewers

The publisher wishes to thank the following educators for their helpful comments during the review process for *Language Arts and Literature, Course 1.*

Sherie J. Campbell, ESE Teacher, Ben Hill Middle School, Tampa, FL; **Stephanie Fetterolf,** Vice Principal, Hilltop Middle School, Toronto, Ontario, Canada; **Jayne O'Gorman,** 6th Grade Reading Teacher, Clifford Crone Middle School, Naperville, IL; **Jane McKenney,** K–12 English Coordinator, Smith Middle School, Troy, MI; **Michelle Richards,** Instructional Coordinating Teacher, Cochrane Middle School, Charlotte, NC; **Mary Alice Ross,** Content Coordinator for English/Language Arts, Flint Community Schools, Flint, MI; **Ellen Smith De La Cruz,** Teacher, Balboa Park Academy—Juvenile Court and Community Schools, San Diego, CA; **Lori Wells,** M.Ed., LSSP, LPA, Educational Diagnostician, Harlingen High School South, Harlingen, TX; **Alicia Wingard,** Special Education Teacher, Mountain Brook Junior High School, Birmingham, AL

PEARSON
AGS Globe

1-800-992-0244

www.agsglobe.com

Contents

Unit 2 Short Stories **78**

Unit 3 Types of Nonfiction **182**

Unit 4 Poetry **252**

Unit 6 Themes in Folk Literature 408

How to Use This Book: A Study Guide

This book is an anthology of literature. An anthology is a collection of literature written by different authors. The literature can be poems, plays, short stories, essays, parts of novels, folktales, legends, or myths. Sometimes an anthology contains selections from a certain country or continent. For example, you might have an anthology with great literature from around the world. Sometimes anthologies are organized around different genres, or types of literature. Then, you might have sections on poems, short stories, plays, essays, or folktales.

Reading a Literature Anthology

This anthology contains much enjoyable literature. An anthology helps you understand yourself and other people. Sometimes you will read about people from other countries. Sometimes you will read about people who lived in the past. Try to relate what the author is saying to your own life. Ask yourself: Have I ever felt this way? Have I known anyone like this person? Have I seen anything like this?

A literature anthology can also help you appreciate the beauty of language. As you read, find phrases or sentences that you particularly like. You may want to start a notebook of these phrases and sentences. You may also want to include words that are difficult.

This anthology is also important because it introduces you to great works of literature. Many times, you will find references to these works in everyday life. Sometimes you will hear a quotation on TV or read it in the newspaper. Great literature can come in many forms. On the next page are definitions of some kinds of literature genres in an anthology.

Genre Definitions

autobiography a person's life story, written by that person

biography a person's life story told by someone else (you will find biographies of many famous authors in this book)

diary a daily record of personal events, thoughts, or private feelings
- A diary is like a journal, but a diary often expresses more of the writer's feelings.

drama a story told through the words and actions of characters, written to be performed as well as read; a play

essay a written work that shows a writer's opinions on some basic or current issue

fable a short story or poem with a moral (lesson about life), often with animals who act like humans
- Aesop was a famous author of fables.

fiction writing that is imaginative and designed to entertain
- In fiction, the author creates the events and characters.
- Short stories, novels, folktales, myths, legends, and most plays are works of fiction.

folktale a story that has been handed down from one generation to another
- The characters are usually either good or bad.
- Folktales make use of rhyme and repetitive phrases.
- Sometimes they are called tall tales, particularly if they are humorous and exaggerated.
- Folktales are also called folklore.

journal writing that expresses an author's feelings or first impressions about a subject
- Students may keep journals that record thoughts about what they have read.
- People also keep travel journals to remind themselves of interesting places they have seen.

legend a traditional story that at one time was told orally and was handed down from one generation to another
- Legends are like myths, but they do not have as many supernatural forces.
- Legends usually feature characters who actually lived, or real places or events.

myth an important story, often part of a culture's religion, that explains how the world came to be or why natural events happen
- A myth usually includes gods, goddesses, or unusually powerful human beings.
- Myths were first oral stories, and most early cultures have myths.

nonfiction writing about real people and events
- Essays, speeches, diaries, journals, autobiographies, and biographies are all usually nonfiction.

novel fiction that is book-length and has more plot and character details than a short story

poem a short piece of literature that usually has rhythm and paints powerful or beautiful impressions with words
- Often, poems have sound patterns such as rhyme.
- Songs are poetry set to music.

prose all writing that is not poetry
- short stories, novels, autobiographies, biographies, diaries, journals, and essays are examples of prose.

science fiction fiction that is based on real or imagined facts of science
- Most stories are set in the future.
- Jules Verne was one of the first science fiction authors.

short story a brief work of prose fiction that includes plot, setting, characters, point of view, and theme
- Edgar Allan Poe was a great writer of short stories.

Different works of literature should be read in different ways. However, there are some basic methods you should use to read all works of literature.

Before Beginning a Unit

- Read the unit title and selection titles.
- Read the paragraphs that introduce the unit.
- Look at the pictures and other artwork in the unit.
- Think about what you already know about the unit.
- Think about what you might want to learn.
- Develop questions in your mind that you think will be answered in this unit.

Before Reading a Selection

- Read the selection's title.
- Look at the pictures and other artwork.
- Read the background material included in About the Author and About the Selection.
- Read the Objectives and think about what you will learn by reading the selection.

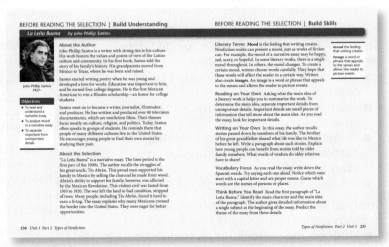

- Read the Literary Terms and their definitions.
- Complete the Before Reading the Selection activities. These activities will help you read the selection, understand vocabulary, and prepare for the reading.

As You Read a Selection

- Read the notes in the side margins. These will help you understand and think about the main ideas.

- Think of people or events in your own life that are similar to those described.

- Reread sentences or paragraphs that you do not understand.

- Predict what you think will happen next.

- Read the definitions at the bottom of the page for words that you do not know.

- Record words that you do not know. Also, write questions or comments you have about the text.

After Reading a Selection

- Reread interesting or difficult parts of the selection.

- Reflect on what you have learned by reading the selection.

- Complete the After Reading the Selection review questions and activities. The activities will help you develop your grammar, writing, speaking, listening, viewing, technology, media, and research skills.

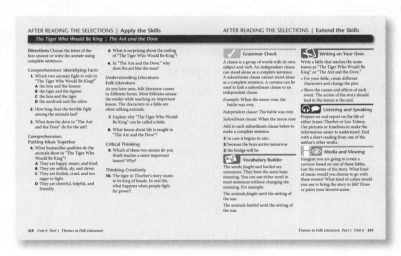

Reading Certain Types of Literature

The methods already described will help you understand all kinds of literature. You may need to use additional methods for specific types of literature.

Reading Poetry

- Read the poem aloud.
- Listen to the sounds of the words.
- Picture the images the author is describing.
- Reread poems over and over again to appreciate the author's use of language.

Reading Essays

- Review the questions in the After Reading the Selection before you begin reading.
- Use the questions to think about what you are reading.
- Remember that essays usually express an author's opinions. Try to understand why the author may have formed these opinions.

Reading Plays

- Picture the setting of the play. Since there usually is not much description given, try to relate the setting to something you have seen before.
- Pay attention to what the characters say. How does this give clues about the character's personality? Have you ever known anyone like this? Are you like this?

Tips for Better Reading

Literary Terms

Literary Terms are words or phrases that we use to study and discuss works of literature. These terms describe the ways an author helps to make us enjoy and understand what we are reading. Some of the terms also describe a genre, or specific type of literature. In this anthology, you will see white boxes on the side of the Before Reading the Selection pages. In these boxes are Literary Terms and their definitions. These terms are important in understanding and discussing the selection being read. By understanding these Literary Terms, readers can appreciate the author's craft. You can find the definitions for all of the Literary Terms used in this book in the Handbook of Literary Terms on page 516.

setting the place and time in a story

plot the series of events in a story

theme the main idea of a literary work

Using a Graphic Organizer

A graphic organizer is visual representation of information. It can help you see how ideas are related to each other. A graphic organizer can help you study for a test, organize information before writing an essay, or organize details in a literature selection. You will use graphic organizers for different activities throughout this textbook. There are 14 different graphic organizers listed below. You can read a description and see an example of each graphic organizer in Appendix A in the back of this textbook.

- Character Analysis Guide
- Story Map
- Main Idea Graphic (Umbrella)
- Main Idea Graphic (Table)
- Main Idea Graphic (Details)
- Venn Diagram
- Sequence Chain
- Concept Map
- Plot Mountain
- Structured Overview
- Semantic Table
- Prediction Guide
- Semantic Line
- KWL Chart

Six Traits of Writing

A *trait* is a quality or feature of something. Traits, or qualities, of good writing help students and teachers discuss writing using a common language. These traits will help you as you plan, draft, revise, and edit your writing. The Six Traits of Writing icons pictured below are used in the Writing Workshops at the end of each unit in this textbook. As you write, think about how you can use each trait to help make your writing better. You can also read more about each trait in Appendix C at the back of this book.

 **Six Traits of Writing:**
Ideas message, details, and purpose

 **Six Traits of Writing:**
Word Choice vivid words that "show, not tell"

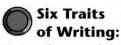 **Six Traits of Writing:**
Voice the writer's own language

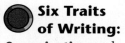 **Six Traits of Writing:**
Organization order, ideas tied together

 **Six Traits of Writing:**
Sentence Fluency smooth rhythm and flow

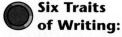 **Six Traits of Writing:**
Conventions correct grammar, spelling, and mechanics

Taking Notes

You will read many selections in this literature anthology. As you read, you may want to take notes to help remember what you have read. You can use these notes to keep track of events and characters in a story. Your notes may also be helpful for recognizing common ideas among the selections in a unit. You can review your notes as you prepare to take a test. Here are some tips for taking notes:

- Write down only the most important information.
- Do not try to write every detail or every word.
- Write notes in your own words.
- Do not be concerned about writing in complete sentences. Use short phrases.

Using the Three-Column Chart

One good way to take notes is to use a three-column chart. Make your own three-column chart by dividing a sheet of notebook paper into three parts. In Column 1, write the topic you are reading about or studying. In Column 2, write what you learned about this topic as you read or listened to your teacher. In Column 3, write questions, observations, or opinions about the topic, or write a detail that will help you remember the topic. Here are some examples of different ways to take notes using the three-column chart.

The topic I am studying	What I learned from reading the text or class discussion	Questions, observations, or ideas I have about the topic
Fiction	• one genre of literature • many different types of fiction—science fiction, adventure, detective stories, romance, suspense	• The book I am reading right now is fiction. It is an adventure story. • I wonder if poetry is part of the fiction genre.

Vocabulary Word	Definition	Sentence with Vocabulary Word
Premises	a building or part of a building	Students are not allowed on the school **premises** during the weekend.

Character	Character Traits Found in the Selection	Page Number
John Krakauer	Conflict, person against self—Krakauer wonders if he will run out of oxygen before returning to camp.	p. 355
	Determined—Krakauer is determined to make it back to camp even though his oxygen has run out and it is snowing on the mountain.	p. 358
	Thankful—After reaching camp, Krakauer is thankful that he is safe.	p. 360

Reading Checklist

Good readers do not just read with their eyes. They read with their brains turned on. In other words, they are active readers. Good readers use strategies as they read to keep them on their toes. The following strategies will help you to check your understanding of what you read.

- **Summarizing** To summarize a text, stop often as you read. Notice these things: the topic, the main thing being said about the topic, important details that support the main idea. Try to sum up the author's message using your own words.

- **Questioning** Ask yourself questions about the text and read to answer them. Here are some useful questions to ask: Why did the author include this information? Is this like anything I have experienced? Am I learning what I hoped I would learn?

- **Predicting** As you read, think about what might come next. Add in what you already know about the topic. Predict what the text will say. Then, as you read, notice whether your prediction is right. If not, change your prediction.

- **Text Structure** Pay attention to how a text is organized. Find parts that stand out. They are probably the most important ideas or facts. Think about why the author organized ideas this way. Is the author showing a sequence of events? Is the author explaining a solution or the effect of something?

- **Visualizing** Picture what is happening in a text or what is being described. Make a movie out of it in your mind. If you can picture it clearly, then you know you understand it. Visualizing what you read will also help you remember it later.

- **Inferencing** The meaning of a text may not be stated. Instead, the author may give clues and hints. It is up to you to put them together with what you already know about the topic. Then you make an inference—you conclude what the author means.

- **Metacognition** Think about your thinking patterns as you read. Before reading a text, preview it. Think about what you can do to get the most out of it. Think about what you already know about the topic. Write down any questions you have. After you read, ask yourself: Did that make sense? If not, read it again.

What to Do About Words You Do Not Know

- If the word is in bold type, look for the definition of the word at the bottom of the page.

- If the word is not in bold type, read to the end of the sentence and maybe the next sentence. Can you determine the meaning now?

- Look at the beginning sound of the unknown word. Ask yourself, "What word begins with this sound and would make sense here?"

- Sound out the syllables of the word.

- If you still cannot determine the meaning, see if you know any parts of the word: prefixes, suffixes, or roots.

- If this does not work, write the word on a note card or in a vocabulary notebook. Then look up the word in a dictionary after you have finished reading the selection. Reread the passage containing the unknown word after you have looked up its definition.

- If the word is necessary to understand the passage, look it up in a dictionary or glossary immediately.

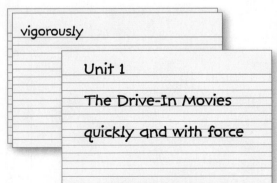

vigorously

Unit 1

The Drive-In Movies

quickly and with force

Word Study Tips

- Start a vocabulary file with note cards to use for review.

- Write one word on the front of each card. Write the unit number, selection title, and the definition on the back.

- You can use these cards as flash cards by yourself or with a study partner to test your knowledge.

Tips for Taking Tests

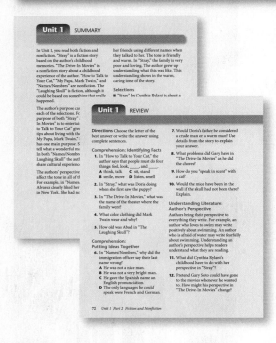

Before the Test Day

- Make sure you have read all of the selections assigned.
- Review the Literary Terms and definitions for each selection.
- Review your answers to the After Reading the Selection questions.
- Reread the Unit Summary and review your answers to the Unit Review.
- Review any notes that you have taken or graphic organizers you have developed.
- Ask your teacher what kinds of questions will be on the test.
- Try to predict what questions will be asked. Think of and write answers to those questions.
- Review the Test-Taking Tip at the bottom of each Unit Review page.

During the Test

- Come to the test with a positive attitude.
- Write your name on the paper.
- Preview the test and read the directions carefully.
- Plan your time.
- Answer the questions that you know first.
- Then go back and answer the more difficult questions.
- Allow time to reread all of the questions and your answers.

Tinkerbell Saving Peter Pan
Roy Best, 1931

F iction stories are made up by the person who writes them. Sometimes fiction stories are about things that really could happen. Other times, they are not possible in real life.

Nonfiction is writing that includes true facts instead of made-up ideas. It is based on real people, things, and experiences. Also, nonfiction usually has a purpose, such as to describe, explain, persuade, or entertain.

In this unit, you will read both fiction and nonfiction pieces. You will see that they are alike and different.

"Why do we continue to be enspelled by fairy tales, after all these centuries? . . . Because we all have encountered wicked wolves, faced trial by fire, found fairy godmothers. We have all set off into unknown woods at one point in life or another."

—Terri Windling
from *Women and Fairy Tales*

Unit 1 About Fiction and Nonfiction

Elements of Fiction

Fiction is writing that is imaginative and designed to entertain. The author creates the events and characters. All works of fiction share certain basic elements.

- They include people or animals called **characters.**

- The series of events in a story is called a **plot.**

- The time and place in a story is called the **setting.**

- The one who tells the story is the **narrator.**

- The main idea of the story is called the **theme.**

Fiction is told from a certain **point of view.** A point of view is the position from which the author tells the story. A **first-person point of view** is where the narrator is also a character, using the pronouns *I* and *we.* A **third-person point of view** is where the narrator is not a character, and refers to characters as *he* and *she.*

Types of Fiction

A **novel** is fiction that is book-length and has more plot and characters than a short story. Characters often face a problem in a certain time and place.

A **novella** is fiction that is longer than a short story but shorter than a novel.

A **short story** is a brief work of fiction. Like a novel, a short story has characters, a setting, and a plot. Unlike a novel, it has a single conflict and is meant to be read in one sitting.

Characteristics of Nonfiction

Nonfiction writing is different from fiction in a few important ways.

- Nonfiction writing is only about real people and events.

- Nonfiction is told from the author's point of view. Nonfiction writing has a **tone** that shows the writer's feeling toward a subject.

- Nonfiction tells an **author's purpose**, or reason for writing. This might be to explain, persuade, inform, or entertain.

WORLD of COW
By Stik

moo moo
moo moo
m

Cow Writers Block

www.CartoonStock.com

Types of Nonfiction

A **biography** is a person's life story told by someone else. A biography is usually told from the third-person point of view.

An **autobiography** is a person's life story, written by that person. An autobiography is told from the first-person point of view.

A **letter** is impressions or feelings written to a specific person. A letter might share information, thoughts, or feelings.

A **journal** or **diary** is writing that expresses an author's feelings or first impressions about a subject.

An **essay** is a written work that shows a writer's opinions on some basic or current issue.

Informational text is writing that we come across in everyday life, including instructions and newspaper articles.

A **speech** is a written work meant to be read aloud.

Part 1

Reading Strategy:
Predicting

Previewing a text helps readers think about what they already know about a subject. It also prepares readers to look for new information—to predict what will come next. Keep this in mind as you make predictions:

■ Make your best guess about what might happen next.

■ Add details about why you think certain things will happen.

■ Check your predictions. You may have to change your predictions as you learn more information.

Literary Terms

fiction writing that is imaginative and designed to entertain

plot the series of events in a story

exposition introduction of the setting, characters, and basic situation

conflict the struggle of the main character against himself or herself, another person, or nature

rising action the buildup of excitement in a story

climax the high point of interest or suspense in a story or play

falling action events that follow the climax in a story

resolution the act of solving the conflict in a story

narrator one who tells a story

point of view the position from which the author or storyteller tells the story

first-person point of view a point of view where the narrator is also a character, using the pronouns *I* and *we*

third-person point of view a point of view where the narrator is not a character, and refers to characters as *he* or *she*

author's purpose the reason(s) for which the author writes: to entertain, to inform, to express opinions, or to persuade

nonfiction writing about real people and events

Stray   by Cynthia Rylant

About the Author

As a child, Cynthia Rylant never imagined that she would be a writer. "I always felt my life was too narrow," she says. She thought she had "nothing to write about." At age 24, however, Rylant started writing. She found that her life did in fact contain the seeds of many stories. Her first book was called *When I Was Young in the Mountains*. The story tells about her childhood in the hills of West Virginia.

Unlike many writers, Rylant does not use a computer to write her stories. Instead, she writes by hand on yellow notepads. Since her first book came out, Rylant has written more than 60 children's books.

About the Selection

Cynthia Rylant lived with her grandparents for four years in a tiny house without running water. The difficulties she experienced are like those in "Stray." Now Rylant has two dogs and two cats of her own. They help her write about pets in a real way.

In "Stray," Doris Lacey and her parents are stranded at home following a winter storm. Doris notices a puppy on the snowy road and brings it indoors. She knows and is reminded by her parents that the family cannot afford a pet. They tell her that she can keep the puppy only until the roads are cleared. Doris grows close to the puppy. She is heartbroken when it comes time for her father to take it away. The events that follow show how the Laceys find a voice to express their feelings.

Cynthia Rylant
1954–

Courtesy of Cynthia Rylant.

Objectives

◆ To read and understand a work of fiction

◆ To identify parts of a plot including exposition, rising action, climax, falling action, and resolution

◆ To define conflict

Before Reading **continued on next page**

fiction writing that is imaginative and designed to entertain

plot the series of events in a story

exposition introduction of the setting, characters, and basic situation

conflict the struggle of the main character against himself or herself, another person, or nature

rising action the buildup of excitement in a story

climax the high point of interest or suspense in a story or play

falling action events that follow the climax in a story

resolution the act of solving the conflict in a story

Literary Terms "Stray" is a work of **fiction,** writing that is imaginative and designed to entertain. The **plot**, or series of events, in the story is made up of several parts. The **exposition** is the introduction of the setting, characters, and basic situation of the story. Every good story includes some main problem or **conflict**. This is the struggle of the main character against someone or something else. During the **rising action**, the excitement in the story builds. The high point of the story is the **climax**, when the story's outcome becomes clear. Events following the climax are part of the **falling action**. The **resolution** is the final outcome that solves the conflict of the story.

Reading on Your Own A prediction is a guess about what will happen next in a story. You can use prior knowledge to make predictions. For example, consider what it would be like to lose something special. If you have ever lost something important to you, you know how sad it feels. Think about these experiences to help you understand a character in the same situation.

Writing on Your Own In "Stray," a girl wants her parents to let her keep a homeless puppy. Make two lists about owning a dog. In one list, write good things about having a dog. In the other list, write possible problems. Use at least three of these words: *eat, share, buy, responsible.*

Vocabulary Focus Create word puzzles with your vocabulary words. Write each word on a sheet of paper. Then use the letters in each word to think of clues that help you identify the definition of the word.

Think Before You Read With a partner, make a list of expenses involved with taking care of a dog. As you read, think about the money the Laceys would need to own a dog.

Stray

In January, a puppy wandered onto the property of Mr. Amos Lacey and his wife, Mamie, and their daughter, Doris. Icicles hung three feet or more from the **eaves** of houses, snowdrifts swallowed up automobiles and the birds were so fluffed up they looked comic.

The puppy had been abandoned, and it made its way down the road toward the Laceys' small house, its ears tucked, its tail between its legs, shivering.

Doris, whose school had been called off because of the snow, was out shoveling the **cinderblock** front steps when she spotted the pup on the road. She set down the shovel.

"Hey! Come on!" she called.

The puppy stopped in the road, wagging its tail timidly, trembling with shyness and cold.

Doris trudged through the yard, went up the shoveled drive and met the dog.

"Come on, Pooch."

Reading Strategy:
Predicting

What do you think Doris will do about the puppy?

eaves the lower edges of a roof

cinderblock a block made of concrete and burned coal

What word gives a clue how Doris's mother feels about the puppy?

A *pound* is a place for dogs without owners. The word *shepherd* is short for German Shepherd, a large, muscular dog with medium-length hair.

Reading Strategy: Predicting

From what you know so far, do you predict that Doris's parents will change their minds?

"Where did *that* come from?" Mrs. Lacey asked as soon as Doris put the dog down in the kitchen.

Mr. Lacey was at the table, cleaning his fingernails with his pocketknife. The snow was keeping him home from his job at the warehouse.

"I don't know where it came from," he said mildly, "but I know for sure where it's going."

Doris hugged the puppy hard against her. She said nothing.

Because the roads would be too bad for travel for many days, Mr. Lacey couldn't get out to take the puppy to the pound in the city right away. He agreed to let it sleep in the basement while Mrs. Lacey **grudgingly** let Doris feed it table scraps. The woman was **sensitive** about throwing out food.

By the looks of it, Doris figured the puppy was about six months old, and on its way to being a big dog. She thought it might have some shepherd in it.

Four days passed and the puppy did not complain. It never cried in the night or howled at the wind. It didn't tear up everything in the basement. It wouldn't even follow Doris up the basement steps unless it was invited.

It was a good dog.

Several times Doris had opened the door in the kitchen that led to the basement and the puppy had been there, all stretched out, on the top step. Doris knew it had wanted some company and that it had lain against the door, listening to the talk in the kitchen, smelling the food,

grudgingly in an unwilling or resentful way

sensitive careful and uneasy

being a part of things. It always wagged its tail, eyes all sleepy, when she found it there.

Even after a week had gone by, Doris didn't name the dog. She knew her parents wouldn't let her keep it, that her father made so little money any pets were out of the question, and that the pup would definitely go to the pound when the weather cleared.

Still, she tried talking to them about the dog at dinner one night.

"She's a good dog, isn't she?" Doris said, hoping, one of them would agree with her.

Her parents glanced at each other and went on eating.

"She's not much trouble," Doris added. "I like her." She smiled at them, but they continued to ignore her.

"I figure she's real smart," Doris said to her mother. "I could teach her things."

Mrs. Lacey just shook her head and stuffed a forkful of sweet potato in her mouth. Doris fell silent, praying the weather would never clear.

But on Saturday, nine days after the dog had arrived, the sun was shining and the roads were plowed. Mr. Lacey opened up the trunk of his car and came into the house.

Doris was sitting alone in the living room, hugging a pillow and rocking back and forth on the edge of a chair. She was trying not to cry but she was not strong enough. Her face was wet and red, her eyes full of distress.

Mrs. Lacey looked into the room from the doorway.

"Mama," Doris said in a small voice. "Please."

Mrs. Lacey shook her head.

"You know we can't afford a dog, Doris. You try to act more grown-up about this."

Doris pressed her face into the pillow.

Outside, she heard the trunk of the car slam shut, one of the doors open and close, the old engine cough and choke and finally start up.

"Daddy," she whispered. "Please."

She heard the car travel down the road, and, though it was early afternoon, she could do nothing but go to her bed. She

What action up until this point in the story suggests a conflict? Explain.

Reading Strategy: **Predicting**
What prior knowledge do you have that helps you to understand the scene at the dinner table?

Doris's reaction to her father taking the puppy away is part of the rising action.

Are Doris's tears part of the rising action or the falling action?

Describe the setting at this point in the story.

Powdered milk is a dry dairy mixture that is added to water to create milk. It usually costs less than bottled milk.

Explain the mood shifts that Doris has gone through during this story.

What is surprising about the resolution of the conflict?

cried herself to sleep, and her dreams were full of searching and searching for things lost.

It was nearly night when she finally woke up. Lying there, like stone, still exhausted, she wondered if she would ever in her life have anything. She stared at the wall for a while.

But she started feeling hungry, and she knew she'd have to make herself get out of bed and eat some dinner. She wanted not to go into the kitchen, past the basement door. She wanted not to face her parents.

But she rose up heavily.

Her parents were sitting at the table, dinner over, drinking coffee. They looked at her when she came in, but she kept her head down. No one spoke.

Doris made herself a glass of powdered milk and drank it all down. Then she picked up a cold biscuit and started out of the room.

"You'd better feed that **mutt** before it dies of **starvation**," Mr. Lacey said.

Doris turned around.

"What?"

"I said, you'd better feed your dog. I figure it's looking for you."

Doris put her hand to her mouth.

"You didn't take her?" she asked.

"Oh, I took her all right," her father answered. "Worst looking place I've ever seen. Ten dogs to a cage. Smell was enough to knock you down. And they give an animal six days to live. Then they kill it with some kind of a shot."

Doris stared at her father.

"I wouldn't leave an *ant* in that place," he said. "So I brought the dog back."

Mrs. Lacey was smiling at him and shaking her head as if she would never, ever, understand him.

Mr. Lacey sipped his coffee.

"Well," he said, "are you going to feed it or not?"

---

mutt a dog that is made up of at least two breeds

starvation a health problem due to lack of food

Directions Choose the letter of the best answer or write the answer using complete sentences.

Comprehension: Identifying Facts

1. Why do the Laceys wait before taking the puppy to the pound?
   A They are deciding whether or not to keep the puppy.
   B They are waiting for a storm to pass.
   C They were thinking of a name for the puppy.
   D They did not know how to get to the pound.

2. During the nine days, how did the puppy behave? How do you know?

3. In your own words, describe what Mr. Lacey saw at the pound.

Comprehension: Putting Ideas Together

4. Which words best describe Doris's parents?
   A demanding and thoughtless
   B friendly and giving
   C cautious and kind
   D careless and rude

5. Do you think Mr. and Mrs. Lacey care about Doris's feelings? Explain.

6. Why do you think Doris did not know that her father had brought the puppy back?

Understanding Literature: Plot

The six main parts of the plot in a story are usually introduced in this order: exposition, conflict, rising action, climax, falling action, and resolution. By presenting the main parts in this set order, writers make stories easier for readers to follow.

7. Describe the conflict in this story.

8. What is the climax, or high point, in the story? Explain.

Critical Thinking

9. Imagine Doris's father had given the dog to someone else. Do you think the conflict would have been resolved in the same way? Explain.

Thinking Creatively

10. Think about your family. What do you think would happen if you wanted to keep a homeless puppy?

After Reading **continued on next page**

Stray   *by Cynthia Rylant*

 Grammar Check

All nouns are either common or proper. A common noun names any one of a group of people, places, or things. A proper noun names a certain person, place, or thing. Proper nouns need capital letters every time they are used. Common nouns only need capital letters at the start of a sentence or in titles.

Write five sentences using both common and proper nouns. Underline each common noun. Circle each proper noun. Then rewrite two of the sentences, replacing proper nouns for common nouns and common nouns for proper nouns.

 Vocabulary Builder

On a sheet of paper, rewrite each sentence below. The new sentence should include a vocabulary word from "Stray." It should express nearly the same meaning as the original sentence.

1 A loose branch is hanging off the edge of the roof.

2 Kay forces herself to say some kind words to the winner.

3 Juan blushes as he greets the new teacher.

 Writing on Your Own

Doris's father uses strong words to describe the area animal shelter. Write a news report about the rescue and decision to keep the dog. Use details from the story. Get the reader's attention by starting with a strong sentence. Include examples and points that support your main idea.

 Listening and Speaking

Prepare a speech about ways to improve conditions at the animal shelter in Doris's hometown. Begin by describing the current conditions at the shelter. Then, suggest ways to correct the problems. When you are finished, present your speech to the class.

 Research and Technology

With a group, create a brochure for new pet owners. Search the Internet and library for information on caring for dogs. Present to the class information about feeding and training puppies and dogs. Include ideas on how to keep dogs happy and healthy.

The Drive-In Movies   by Gary Soto

About the Author

As a child, Gary Soto loved the excitement and action of his Fresno, California, neighborhood. When Soto was six years old, however, a government program changed his neighborhood. Many rundown buildings were replaced with new ones. "It didn't work in our area," Soto declares today. "The houses were bulldozed, and in their place grew weeds." As he grew older, Soto continued to feel a sense of loss over his old neighborhood. Today, he believes that his pain and sadness led him to become a writer. When he put his feelings on paper, he could see and think about them. Today, Soto is a prize-winning author of fiction, short stories, poems, and children's picture books.

Gary Soto
1952–

Objectives

◆ To read and understand a short story

◆ To identify the point of view of a story and explain the difference between first person and third person

◆ To identify the narrator in a story

About the Selection

The first drive-in movie theater had three speakers near the screen to project sound. Anyone who parked near the screen could hear every word perfectly. Unfortunately, even people who lived close by could hear every word! This system was later replaced with a single speaker for each car. When the window was rolled down, the speaker could be placed on the car door. That way, everyone in the car could hear the sound, but the neighbors could not. This also made the drive-in movies a good place for family time.

In "The Drive-In Movies," a young Gary Soto wants to go to the drive-in movies. His plan is to be very good and impress his mother. Then, he hopes she will take the whole family to the movies. He does lots of chores one Saturday in order to please her. Some of his efforts backfire, however, and seem to ruin his hoped-for plans.

Before Reading **continued on next page**

The Drive-In Movies by Gary Soto

narrator one who tells a story

point of view the position from which the author or storyteller tells the story

first person a point of view where the narrator is also a character, using the pronouns *I* and *we*

third person a point of view where the narrator is not a character, and refers to characters as *he* or *she*

Literary Terms The **narrator** is the voice that tells a true or imagined story. **Point of view** is the position from which the story is told. In **first person,** the narrator is part of the action of the story and uses the pronouns *I* and *we*. Readers know only what the narrator sees, thinks, and feels. In the **third person,** the narrator is not a character in the story. The narrator is an outsider looking in and refers to characters as *he* or *she*. A third-person narrator can share information that the characters do not know. Most true stories about a writer's life are told in the first person.

Reading on Your Own A prediction is a best guess about what will happen next in a story. You can use details in a story and your own experiences to make predictions. Keep track of your predictions as you read. Then, read ahead to check each prediction. When you find details that show your prediction may be wrong, change your prediction.

Writing on Your Own Think about something special you would like to have or do. Make a list of ways that you could earn this special thing.

Vocabulary Focus Use the vocabulary words in the story to create a short crossword puzzle. Write clues for each numbered word, down and across. Trade puzzles with a partner and complete each other's crosswords.

Think Before You Read With a partner, create a list comparing drive-in movie theaters and indoor theaters. Include five ways they are similar and five ways they are different. Look for your ideas in the story while you read.

The Drive-In Movies

For our family, moviegoing was rare. But if our mom, tired from a week of candling eggs, woke up happy on a Saturday morning, there was a chance we might later scramble to our blue Chevy and beat nightfall to the Starlight Drive-In. My brother and sister knew this. I knew this. So on Saturday we tried to be good. We sat in the cool shadows of the TV with the volume low and watched cartoons, a **prelude** of what was to come.

prelude the lead-in to a main event

As you read, look for clues that show this story's point of view.

Candling eggs means examining uncooked eggs for freshness by placing them in front of a burning candle.

Why is the narrator being extra good?

One Saturday I decided to be extra good. When she came out of the bedroom tying her robe, she yawned a hat-sized yawn and blinked red eyes at the weak brew of coffee I had fixed for her. I made her toast with strawberry jam spread to all the corners and set the three boxes of cereal in front of her. If she didn't care to eat cereal, she could always look at the back of the boxes as she drank her coffee.

I went outside. The lawn was tall but too wet with dew to mow. I picked up a **trowel** and began to weed the flower bed. The weeds were really Bermuda grass, long stringers that ran finger-deep in the ground. I got to work quickly and in no time **crescents** of earth began rising under my fingernails. I was sweaty hot. My knees hurt from kneeling, and my brain was dull from making the trowel go up and down, **dribbling** crumbs of earth. I dug for half an hour, then stopped to play with the neighbor's dog and pop ticks from his poor snout.

Reading Strategy: Predicting

Do you think the narrator will give up working so hard and keep playing with the dog instead? Read ahead a little and check your prediction.

I then mowed the lawn, which was still beaded with dew and noisy with bees hovering over clover. This job was less dull because as I pushed the mower over the shaggy lawn, I could see it looked **tidier**. My brother and sister watched from the window. Their faces were fat with cereal, a third helping. I made a face at them when they asked how come I was working. Rick pointed to part of the lawn. "You missed some over there." I ignored him and kept my attention on the windmill of grassy blades.

Why might a trip to the drive-in movies be a reward for the narrator?

While I was emptying the catcher, a bee stung the bottom of my foot. I danced on one leg and was ready to cry when Mother showed her face at the window. I sat down on the grass and examined my foot: the stinger was **pulsating**. I pulled it out quickly, ran water over the sting and packed it with mud, Grandmother's remedy.

What does the narrator mean by *Grandmother's remedy?*

trowel a small hand-shovel for gardening	**dribbling** to fall in drops little by little	**pulsating** moving up and down quickly
crescents moon-shaped curved pieces	**tidier** neater	

Hobbling, I returned to the flower bed where I pulled more stringers and again played with the dog. More ticks had migrated to his snout. I swept the front steps, took out the garbage, cleaned the lint **filter** to the dryer (easy), plucked hair from the **industrial** wash basin in the garage (also easy), hosed off the patio, smashed three snails sucking paint from the house (disgusting but fun), tied a bundle of newspapers, put away toys, and, finally, seeing that almost everything was done and the sun was not too high, started waxing the car.

My brother joined me with an old gym sock, and our sister watched us while sucking on a cherry Kool-Aid ice cube. The liquid wax drooled onto the sock, and we began to swirl the white slop on the **chrome**. My arms ached from **buffing**, which though less boring than weeding, was harder. But the beauty was evident. The shine, hurting our eyes and **glinting** like an armful of dimes, brought Mother out. She looked around the yard and said, "Pretty good." She **winced** at the **grille** and returned inside the house.

We began to wax the paint. My brother applied the liquid and I followed him rubbing hard in wide circles as we moved around the car. I began to hurry because my arms were hurting and my stung foot looked like a water balloon. We were working around the trunk when Rick pounded on the bottle of wax. He squeezed the bottle and it sneezed a few more white drops.

We looked at each other. "There's some on the sock," I said. "Let's keep going."

We polished and buffed, sweat weeping on our brows. We got scared when we noticed that the gym sock was now blue. The paint was coming off. Our sister fit ice cubes into our mouths and we worked harder, more intently, more dedicated to the car and our mother. We ran the sock over

Reading Strategy: Predicting

Will the narrator get to enjoy the drive-in after a day of hard work? Read on to check whether you are correct.

filter a screen that stops unwanted materials from passing through	**chrome** bright metal trim	**winced** drew back slightly, as if in pain
	buffing polishing	**grille** a grate on a car
industrial big enough for a factory	**glinting** sparkling	

the chrome, trying to pick up extra wax. But there wasn't enough to cover the entire car. Only half got waxed, but we thought it was better than nothing and went inside for lunch. After lunch, we returned outside with tasty sandwiches.

Rick and I nearly jumped. The waxed side of the car was foggy white. We took a rag and began to polish **vigorously** and nearly in tears, but the fog wouldn't come off. I blamed Rick and he blamed me. Debra stood at the window, not wanting to get involved. Now, not only would we not go to the movies, but Mom would surely snap a branch from the plum tree and chase us around the yard.

Mom came out and looked at us with hands on her aproned hips. Finally, she said, "You boys worked so hard." She turned on the garden hose and washed the car. That night we did go to the drive-in. The first **feature** was about nothing, and the second feature, starring Jerry Lewis, was *Cinderfella*. I tried to stay awake. I kept a wad of homemade popcorn in my cheek and laughed when Jerry Lewis fit golf tees in his nose. I rubbed my watery eyes. I laughed and looked at my mom. I promised myself I would remember that scene with the golf tees and promised myself not to work so hard the coming Saturday. Twenty minutes into the movie, I fell asleep with one hand in the popcorn.

vigorously quickly and with force

feature something offered as special or important; a movie

The Drive-In Movies   by Gary Soto

Directions Choose the letter of the best answer or write the answer using complete sentences.

Comprehension: Identifying Facts

1. Which of the following chores does Soto not do on that Saturday?
   A wash the patio
   B sweep the front steps
   C pick up some toys
   D paint the dog house

2. How does Soto persuade his mother to take the family to the drive-in movies?

3. What two things does Soto promise himself?

Comprehension: Putting Ideas Together

4. What are the names of the narrator's brother and sister?
   A Rick and Debra
   B Jerry and Cindy
   C Chevy and Starlight
   D Gary and Patty

5. About what time of day does Soto start and stop doing chores?

6. What are two things that help you know this story took place in the past?

Understanding Literature: Predicting

Predictions about a selection can be made before you start reading. They can also be made one or more times while you are reading. You can also make predictions after you are finished reading. These after-reading predictions are about what would happen if the story kept going.

7. Do you think the narrator will remember that night for a long time? Explain.

8. Do you think the narrator's family was able to stay awake at the movie? Explain.

Critical Thinking

9. The children make a mess with the car wax. Why do you think their mother does not get angry at them?

Thinking Creatively

10. Pretend that, like the narrator, you worked all day and then went to the movies. How would you feel if you fell asleep?

After Reading continued on next page

The Drive-In Movies   *by Gary Soto*

 **Grammar Check**

Singular nouns are used for one person, place, or thing. Plural nouns are used for more than one person, place, or thing. The plural form of most nouns is made by adding *-s* or *-es* to the end. Other plurals have unusual spellings.

- *Singular Nouns:* bell, canyon, tax, woman, mouse, strategy
- *Plural Nouns:* bells, canyons, taxes, women, mice, strategies

Identify whether each of the following words is singular or plural. Then, use each word in a sentence.

1 approaches   **4** strategies

2 men   **5** prediction

3 causes

 Vocabulary Builder

Synonyms are words with similar meanings. For each word below, choose a synonym from the vocabulary words in this selection.

1 cringed _____

2 sparkling _____

3 moon-shaped _____

 Writing on Your Own

Gary Soto's story is packed with details about an event in his own life. Write a story about an event, a person, or a period in your life. Follow these steps:

- Brainstorm ideas from your life.
- Narrow your topic to a single idea.
- List the details of the chosen idea.
- Number the details in the order in which they happened.
- Use your list to write your story.

 Listening and Speaking

Pretend it is the day after their trip to the drive-in. With a partner, act out a conversation that Soto and his mother might have had. Use details from the story to invent an interesting dialogue.

  Media and Viewing

Search the Internet or library books for images of drive-in movie theaters. From what you can tell, when was this form of entertainment most popular? Work in small groups to create a poster showing the history of drive-ins. Be sure to include pictures with dates and descriptive information.

Web Sites

In Part 1, you are learning how to make predictions while reading literature. Making predictions is also important when you are using Web sites. Sometimes you need to find certain information fast. Predicting which buttons or tools to use will help you to search more quickly.

About Web Sites

Web sites are certain places on the Internet. Each Web site has an address, or Universal Resource Locator (URL). The ending of a URL gives information about who takes care of the site:

- .edu—site is cared for by a school
- .gov—site is cared for by a government office
- .org—site is cared for by a nonprofit body
- .com—site is cared for by a business

A Web site can have many Web pages. You can move from one page to another by clicking your mouse on a link.

Keep in mind that not all the information you find will be completely correct. For this reason, make sure that your details come from trusted places.

Reading Skill

Web sites have a special structure that helps you search for and find information quickly. The chart below shows some Web site parts that will help you use a Web site effectively.

Web Site Parts	
Link	A connection to another spot on • the same Web page • a different Web page on the same Web site • a different Web site A link can be underlined or highlighted text. It could also be a drawing or a photo. Links are what make the Web a "web."
Icon	A small photo or drawing that may appear by itself or with text. Icons are often links as well.
Graphics	Pictures, maps, tables, and other nontext things often found on a Web site. These graphics often give information, but they may also be links to other Web pages.

On the next two pages are examples from the Web site www.aspca.org. The Animaland pages provide information about pets.

This home page is a starting point that will lead you to further information on other pages. These pages may be within this site or on related sites.

The website for kids who love animals!

http://www.aspca.org/site/PageServer?pagename=kids_home

Brought to you by the **ASPCA**

ANIMALAND

| Nose for News | Pet Care | Ask Azula | Animal Careers | Animal ABCs | Real Issues | Cartoons | Activities | Pet of the Week | Home |

Welcome to ASPCA Animaland®—the website for kids who love

SPOTLIGHT ON...

SO, YOU WANNA BE AN ANIMAL COP?
Rescuing animals who have been abused and making sure that people follow laws about animal care is a very rewarding—and majorly demanding—career!

LET IT SNOW!
This beautiful and mysterious feline is one cool cat.

"RATS" ALL, FOLKS!
Learn all about how to care for these smart and loyal pets who love to hang out with their peeps.

PET OF THE WEEK

Meet Monty
Submitted by Sarah, age 10

Favorite trick: "Bullying other cats."
Why I love Monty: "He's a cool dude!!!!!"

Send in your pet's photo!

Each of these 10 buttons leads to more information about a particular topic. By clicking on the button, you will open up a new page.

To go deeper into a Web site, you can click on an underlined item. Like buttons, underlined items are links that take you to certain types of information.

http://www.aspca.org/site/PageServer?pagename=kids_pc_home

Brought to you by the **ASPCA**

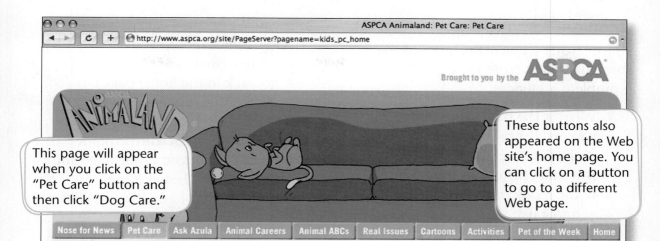

This page will appear when you click on the "Pet Care" button and then click "Dog Care."

These buttons also appeared on the Web site's home page. You can click on a button to go to a different Web page.

| Nose for News | Pet Care | Ask Azula | Animal Careers | Animal ABCs | Real Issues | Cartoons | Activities | Pet of the Week | Home |

PET CARE

Dog Care | Cat Care | Bird Care | Rabbit Care | Fish Care | Gerbil Care | Hamster Care | Guinea Pig Care | Mouse Care | Rat Care

This list has links that connect to the animals discussed in "Pet Care."

Dog Care: The 411

Scientific name: *Canis familiaris*

Size: XS, S, M, L, XL!! Dogs range in size from tiny four-pound tea cup poodles to Irish wolfhounds, the tallest dogs at almost three feet high.

Lifespan: As a rule, smaller dogs tend to live longer than larger ones. A compact Chihuahua can live to be 16, while giant breeds like bull mastiffs usually live to be about eight years old. And somewhere in the middle, the average, All-American mixed-breed pooch has a lifespan of about 12 to 14 years.

Colors/varieties: There are more than 400 different breeds of dogs —spotted Dalmatians, shiny black Labrador retrievers, brindle-coated boxers...to name just a few! But the most popular pooches of all are non-pedigree—that includes shaggy dogs, dogs with hairy ears, dogs with all-white socks, dogs with fluffy tails, and everything in between. You may have heard people call these dogs "mutts," but we prefer *one-of-a-kind*!

Parents and teachers, click here [link] for more dog care information to share with your students and children.

LEARN MORE
- The 411
- Chow Time!
- Home Sweet Home
- Fun & Games

These links will lead to more information about dogs.

CLICK HERE TO WATCH PET CARE CARTOONS!

Monitor Your Progress

Directions Choose the letter of the best answer or write the answer using complete sentences.

1. What is the first page you see when you open this Web site?
   A the pet care guide
   B a short history of the ASPCA
   C the home page, which has buttons and a list
   D the home page, which gives links to other Web sites

2. What would most likely appear if you clicked on a button marked "Animal Careers"?
   A a page explaining how to take care of your pet
   B a page with games and cartoons
   C a page giving information about jobs related to animal care
   D a page giving important information about pet diseases

3. If you are on the Pet Care page for "Dog," what should you do to get more information?
   A go back to the home page and click on the doghouse
   B go to the top of the "Dog" page and click on "Scientific name"
   C go to the bottom of the page and click under "Learn More"
   D go to the left-hand list and click on "Gerbil Care"

4. Why should you check out where information on the Internet comes from?

5. There are other groups that provide information about pets on the Internet. This could include an online pet store and a nonprofit group that encourages pet adoption. Which do you think would be a more trusted site for information on animal care? Explain.

Writing on Your Own

Review what you have learned about using a Web site. Write a letter to a friend telling how www.aspca.org works. Include details explaining how to use the site to find information about cat care.

COMPARING LITERARY WORKS | Build Understanding

How to Talk to Your Cat   by Jean Craighead George

About the Author

Jean Craighead George was born in Washington, D.C. She grew up in a family that enjoyed nature and animals. In third grade, George started writing poems and short stories. But she did not think of herself as a writer until she was out of college. In the 1940s, she was a writer for *The Washington Post* and sometimes worked at the White House. Since then, she has written over 80 books. Some of her most famous books are *My Side of the Mountain* and *Julie of the Wolves*. George learned about wolves during a summer she spent studying wolves in Alaska.

Jean Craighead
George
1919–

George loves animals and has given a home to over 170 pets over the years. That number does not include her cats and dogs. The animals usually spend the summer and leave in the fall when it comes time to migrate. While they are with her, she uses them as characters in her stories.

About the Selection

"How to Talk to Your Cat" shows and tells how to talk to a cat. This guide offers cat history as well as tips on understanding cat behavior. For example, it covers cats in ancient Egypt and how a cat says "hello." It also shows how to "read" a cat's whisker and tail positions. And, as the title suggests, there is much helpful advice for cat owners to follow.

The selection is a how-to guide that is written in a very friendly way. However, it is not a story. Look back at "Stray." Unlike that selection, "How to Talk to Your Cat" does not "tell a story."

Comparing continued on next page

Objectives

◆ To read and understand a how-to guide
◆ To compare fiction and nonfiction selections with related topics
◆ To identify an author's purpose in writing

How to Talk to Your Cat   *by Jean Craighead George*

author's purpose
the reason(s) for which the author writes: to entertain, to inform, to express opinions, or to persuade

nonfiction
writing about real people and events

Literary Terms An author always has a reason for what he or she writes. The **author's purpose** could be to entertain, to inform, to express opinions, or to persuade. A how-to guide is **nonfiction**—writing about real people and events. In a how-to guide, the author's purpose is to teach readers how to do something. In a short story, the author's purpose is to entertain or share experiences. Both a how-to guide and a short story can use cause and effect. This shows how one thing, a cause, brings about another thing, or effect. Some events have many causes. Some causes also lead to more than one event.

Reading on Your Own You have probably seen a cat before. As you read, try to match the cat faces and movements with your prior knowledge about the actions of a cat. Imagine yourself talking to a cat.

Writing on Your Own Think about the differences between explaining how to do something and sharing something that happened. Write two short paragraphs. Make one about how to send an e-mail and one about a funny e-mail.

Vocabulary Focus In English, the same letter can make different sounds. There are some rules that can help you understand the sounds. Other times, you must make your best guess based on what you know. In your vocabulary words, the letters *a* and *c* each make more than one sound. For each word with an *a* in it, write another word you know that has a similar spelling and sound. Then, try to do the same thing with the words that have a *c*.

Think Before You Read Think back to the story "Stray." How do you think the selection you are about to read will be similar to or different from "Stray"? Share your ideas with a classmate.

How to Talk to Your Cat

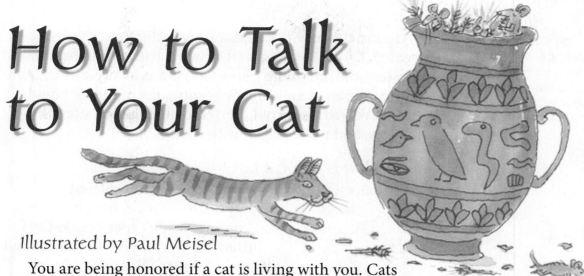

Illustrated by Paul Meisel

You are being honored if a cat is living with you. Cats are loners. They don't like company. They don't even like the company of another cat. They hunt by themselves. They are completely **self-sufficient** and can leave you at any time and go off and make a living. And yet cats can have warm and loving relationships with humans.

As you read, think about what you already know about cats.

What explains this contradiction?

The cat.

Humans did not **domesticate** the house cat as they did the dog. The cat domesticated itself. About 4000 B.C. the Egyptians began storing their wheat and rice in **granaries**. Mice settled in and ate the grain, and the wild Kaffir cat, *Felis sylvestris*, stole in from the desert and ate the mice. This wild cat slept by day and hunted by night. It caught fish and birds as well as mice, and it slipped into and out of homes with silent dignity. The Egyptians were charmed by its talents and beauty. They not only encouraged it to become a household pet, but they eventually **elevated** it to the rank of a goddess, the goddess Bast. Goddess or not, the cat remained wild. Just like wild animals today, the young of the wild Kaffir cats were friendly to humans but turned against them when they grew up.

Find Egypt on a map.

The *Kaffir cat* belongs to the animal group, or species, called *Felis sylvestris*. Today's common house cat belongs to the species called *Felis domesticus*.

self-sufficient able to take care of oneself

contradiction something that is both true and false

domesticate to tame

granaries bins for storing grains

elevated made greater

How would you feel if a wild cat were coming into and out of your home?

Around the year 2000 B.C. a slightly different species appeared among the wild Kaffir cats. It had shorter legs and a narrower head, but more important, it was as sweet as a kitten to humans even as an adult. *Felis catus*, the domestic house cat, had **evolved**. It purred, **flattered** humans with its silky touches, and **wooed** them with cat talk.

What is this cat talk?

Cat talk is a **complicated**, self-centered language. If you speak to your cat first, it probably won't speak back. Cats **initiate** conversations. To understand them, you have to feel, look, listen, and even smell. Cat talk is scent, touch, sound. It is movements of tail, ears, whiskers, and the pupils of the eyes. It is body language. It is **enchantment**.

There is no best age to learn language from a cat, and there is no best age to take one home. Kittens, **adolescents**, and adults all adjust quickly to life on beds, pillows, sunny windowsills, and warm fireplaces, and to cat snacks.

There is one thing to know about cats: The cat that picks you, the one that meows at your door asking to be taken in, makes the best pet. You have not forced yourself upon it. Of its own free will it has chosen you. That's what a cat is all about—free will.

---

evolved developed

flattered gave many compliments

wooed sweet-talked

complicated difficult

initiate to start

enchantment a state of delight

adolescents teenagers

Take only one cat. Cats are **solitary** animals. They dislike other cats and will fight at a whisker twist. If you want two cats, get them when they are kittens, **preferably** from the same litter. They will spar and tumble, but not **wage** war. They might even purr to each other and sleep side by side. Older cats brought together will occasionally work out a **truce** with each other but need space and time to do so.

You might be able to initiate a cat conversation by staying away for the day. When you return home, you'll probably get the "I missed you" talk. The cat runs to you. The fur is pressed lightly to the body with whiskers bowed forward. The pupils are large with pleasure, and the tail is held straight up like a flagpole. Sometimes the cat adds, "You've been gone a long long time," by rising on its hind legs and arching its shoulder and neck toward your hand. Stroke its head to say, "I'm glad to see you, too."

There is no such thing as a cat "good-bye." They do not need it. When you walk off, they go their independent way with no **sulking**. Only when you come back do they have something to say.

You and your cat are speaking in scent when you exchange touches.

A cat touch is silent talk. Scent glands lie along the flank and the lip, under the chin, on the top of the head, and along the tail of the cat. When you are rubbed by **flank**, lip, chin, head, or tail, you are being told, "You are my property."

Although you can't smell the message, you will probably answer by picking up or petting your cat. Now you have scent marked the fur. However, you have not said, "You are my property." You have said, "Yes, I am your property." That's cat talk. They own you. You cannot own a cat. Isn't it interesting that we license dogs to claim our ownership, but not cats?

What is a whisker twist? What does this phrase suggest about cats' tempers?

Reading Strategy: Predicting
Pretend you had a cat and you said "goodbye" as you were leaving for school. What do you think the cat would do?

Since cats do not have money, how can they "own" people?

---

solitary alone

preferably if possible

wage to carry on

truce a peaceful end to fighting

sulking to be moody and silent

flank the part of an animal or person that is on the side between the ribs and hip

The purr distinguishes the cat from all other animals.

No other animal can make such a sound. Never having heard it before, even a child knows that it says, "I'm content and happy." It is an **audible** smile; it is **luscious** satisfaction and the **witchery** through which cats charm people.

No one knows how the purr is made or what part of the **anatomy** it comes from. The cat can purr while breathing in and breathing out.

There are several kinds of purrs. The normal smoothly running purr means the cat has been **moderately** pleased by your petting it or the comfort of your lap. The three-part down-up-down purr announces that the cat is more than just comfortable, it is **divinely** content. This purr is often so loud, it can be heard across a room.

Amazingly, the purr is never given when the cat is alone. Sitting in the sun on a soft pillow will not turn on the purr; curled on the hearth before a toasty fire won't do it either. The purr is communication, and cats are too smart to talk to themselves.

It is possible for you to begin a purr talk by sitting down and making a lap. You may have to wait a long time, but eventually the **lure** works.

What is so unusual about cats purring while breathing in and out? Can you talk while breathing in and out? Try it!

audible able to be heard

luscious highly pleasing

witchery to act as though casting magical spells

anatomy body

moderately somewhat; kind of

divinely in a very good way

lure to draw attention to

The cat will decide when it has had enough and jump to the floor. If you try to hold it back, you'll hear tough cat talk. This is made up of the purr-snarl, claws out, whiskers bowed back, and tail whipping. The cat is saying, "Don't **restrain** me . . . or else." Wise people let their cat **depart**.

You, however, can end the purr session by standing up. The cat jumps to the floor with a loud thump of its feet—foot talk—which says, "I don't like this." A cat can land on its feet without making a sound, so listen for feet. You will know you have talked to your cat.

Moving whiskers are also cat communication.

Bent forward, they mean the cat is enclosing you, loving you. Bent backward, the cat is saying it is **alarmed**. It has thrust its whiskers out of the way to bite.

Watch whiskers. If they are forward, you can hug the cat. If back, get out of the way.

Also watch the tail, the silent communicator.

The cat is very honest. Its tail tells you just how it feels.

The tail held straight up says, "I like you."

When it is hanging down and loose from the body, the cat is saying, "All is well."

Straight up but bent over at the tip means "I am not so sure of you."

Put one arm straight above your head to tell the cat you like it.

What do you think a *purr-snarl* sounds like? Can you make a purr-snarl?

What is a *purr session*?

Reading Strategy: Predicting
What would happen if a cat's whiskers were back and you stayed where you were?

What does the term *the silent communicator* mean?

restrain to hold down
depart to leave

alarmed very disturbed, as to send a warning

Reading Strategy: Predicting

Can you think of a situation that would cause a cat's fur to stand up while the cat arches its back?

When the fur at the base of the tail stands up, the word is "I am worried." This is usually about dogs or another cat in the vicinity.

The famous Halloween-cat pose—back arched high, fur standing up all over the body—is cat war talk. It is on the **defensive**, but it is also ready to attack. "I'm afraid, but watch out—I'm dangerous."

A lashing tail is anger.

The tail of a cat can say, "I'm humble." The legs are **flexed**; the tail is arched out from the body and curved upward at the tip like a dipping spoon.

This is rare talk. A cat is seldom humble.

The cat's face, like its tail, also talks to you in silence.

Read what it is saying. You can reply when you know what is being said.

How is cat talk similar to how humans talk to each other? How is it different?

When the ears are up and forward, the head tilted slightly downward, and the lower eyelids lifted, your cat is saying, "I like you." Its face is soft and loving.

Most people speak back to this face without knowing they're doing it. They pick up the cat and **caress** it. The "I like you" is hard to resist.

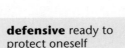

defensive ready to protect oneself	**flexed** bent	**caress** to touch lightly or gently

COMPARING LITERARY WORKS | Apply the Skills

How to Talk to Your Cat   by Jean Craighead George

Directions Choose the letter of the best answer or write the answer using complete sentences.

Comprehension: Identifying Facts

1. How did the Egyptians first encounter cats?
   - **A** The Egyptians hunted cats for their fur.
   - **B** Cats chased mice away from the Egyptians' granaries.
   - **C** Cats were brought by travelers to Egypt.
   - **D** An Egyptian goddess created the cat.

2. Which of the following is the scientific name of the first pet cat in Egypt?
   - **A** *Felis sylvestris*
   - **C** Goddess Bast
   - **B** Kaffir
   - **D** *Felis catus*

3. Why couldn't you easily start a conversation with a cat?

4. If you want two cats, why should you get them from the same litter?

5. How does the author suggest a cat will say "You've been gone a long time"?

6. Where are a cat's scent glands found?

7. Why doesn't a cat purr when it is alone?

8. Describe the whiskers of a cat that is ready to bite.

9. What does it mean when a cat's fur stands up at the base of the tail?

10. Describe the face of a cat that is saying "I love you."

Comprehension: Putting Ideas Together

11. Think about the two stories "Stray" and "How to Talk to Your Cat." How are the feelings you get while reading different?
    - **A** "Stray" is scary and "How to Talk to Your Cat" is funny.
    - **B** "Stray" is silly and "How to Talk to Your Cat" is exciting.
    - **C** "Stray" is confusing and "How to Talk to Your Cat" is surprising.
    - **D** "Stray" is serious and "How to Talk to Your Cat" is light.

12. Which word best describes the body parts of a happy cat?
    - **A** relaxed
    - **C** moving
    - **B** tight
    - **D** jerky

13. In "How to Talk to Your Cat," what is the contradiction that is discussed on the first page?

14. How did the Egyptians feel about wild cats?

Comparing continued on next page

15. In "Stray," how did the puppy show it was happy?

16. Describe three ways you would like your cat's tail to look. Explain your choices.

17. Give examples from "Stray" and "How to Talk to Your Cat" that show love of animals.

18. Based on "How to Talk to Your Cat," describe two ways that cats are loners.

19. In "Stray," do you think the puppy was a loner? Explain why or why not.

20. In "Stray," what is the contradiction about how Mr. Lacey feels about keeping the puppy?

Understanding Literature: Cause and Effect

Cause and effect is sometimes clearly shown in the writing. Other times, you have to look more closely to realize that one thing is caused by another.

21. How did the cat come to the attention of the Egyptians?

22. How did the puppy come to the attention of the Lacey family?

23. How might the location of a cat's scent glands affect how the cat smells things?

24. What do you think it was about the puppy that caused Doris to bring it home?

25. You are holding a cat. It purr-snarls, puts its claws out, throws its whiskers back, and starts moving its tail. What is likely to happen?

Critical Thinking

26. Explain what is meant by "A purr is an audible smile."

27. Do you think the information in the two selections is mostly fact or mostly opinion? Explain your answer.

28. Which of these selections do you think gives more convincing reasons to have a pet? Explain.

29. Can an author have more than one purpose for writing? Use examples from "Stray" and "How to Talk to Your Cat" to explain.

Thinking Creatively

30. "How to Talk to Your Cat" is very popular with children. List five things about a book that might make it popular with children.

Grammar Check

To show that something belongs to one person or another thing, you add –'s. This is called showing possession. For example:

- Food that belongs to a puppy is the puppy's food.
- A puppy that belongs to Doris is Doris's puppy.

Write four sentences about cats. In each, write about something that belongs to one person or thing and use –'s.

 Vocabulary Builder

Make two columns on a piece of paper. Title one column, "Things I Like About Cats." Title the other column, "Things I Don't Like About Cats." Write sentences in each column. Use at least 10 of the vocabulary words from "How to Talk to Your Cat."

 Writing on Your Own

Pretend you are a cat who is writing in a personal diary. Create a diary setup with space to write for seven days. Label the spaces Sunday through Saturday. Write what has gone on in your life for one week.

 Listening and Speaking

Imagine you have been invited to talk to a kindergarten class about talking to cats. What information would be important to tell them? Write these ideas down, listing the most important first, and so on. Practice your speech with your classmates.

 Research and Technology

Use the Internet or library to find another guide for talking to cats. Compare it to "How to Talk to Your Cat." Make a chart that compares the advice given in both.

Part 2

Reading Strategy:
Questioning

As you read the selections in this Part, ask yourself questions about what is happening. Also think about the facts and opinions that the author may use in the selections. Ask yourself:

- Can this information be proven? If so, it is a fact.
- Is this information someone's belief that cannot be proven? If so, it is likely an opinion.
- Clue words such as *best, worst, always,* and *never* often suggest opinions.

Literary Terms

biography a person's life story told by someone else

tone the attitude an author takes toward a subject

legend a story from folklore that features characters who actually lived, or real events or places

symbolism the larger meaning of a person, place, or object

symbol something that represents something else

My Papa, Mark Twain   by Susy Clemens

About the Author

Olivia Susan Clemens, called Susy, was the oldest daughter of American author Mark Twain. She was born in Elmira, New York, but grew up in Hartford, Connecticut. There, her parents had famous visitors and Susy had the chance to meet them.

It is said that Susy was her father's favorite daughter. After she died at age 24, Twain's writing turned darker and more serious.

In 1906, Mark Twain included parts of Susy's biography in his autobiography. Susy Clemens's complete biography of her father, *Papa: An Intimate Biography of Mark Twain*, was not published until 1985. It keeps her spelling and punctuation errors.

About the Selection

In "My Papa, Mark Twain," Susy Clemens describes her father in a loving, childlike way. She shares funny stories that show pieces of his personal life. For example, she talks about his ideas about cats, church, and school. She also shows how proud she is of her father for his writing successes.

Susy Clemens
1872–1896

Objectives

◆ To read and understand a biography

◆ To identify point of view in a work of literature

◆ To recognize the difference between fact and opinion

***Before Reading* continued on next page**

My Papa, Mark Twain   by Susy Clemens

biography
a person's life story told by someone else

Literary Terms A **biography** is a story of a person's life that is told by another person. In this case, Susy Clemens tells the story of her father's life. Susy tells the story from her own point of view. This means she writes about topics from her perspective—the way that she sees them. Her perspective is based on her beliefs and background. An author's perspective shows his or her own feelings or personal interest in a subject.

Reading on Your Own Nonfiction often includes an author's opinion as well as facts. A fact is information that can be proven. An opinion is a person's judgment or belief. To recognize clues that indicate an opinion, do this:

- Look for opinion clue words, such as *I believe* or *in my opinion*.
- Look for judgment clue words, such as *wonderful* or *terrible*.
- Look for sweeping statement clue words, such as *always, nobody, worst*, and *all*.

Writing on Your Own In "My Papa, Mark Twain," Susy Clemens writes her ideas about her father. Think about someone you admire. List three things you would include in a biography of that person.

Vocabulary Focus Susy Clemens was 13 years old when she wrote this story about her father. She made quite a few spelling and punctuation errors. Identify 10 spelling errors in this selection. Use a dictionary to help you. Write each word as it should be spelled.

Think Before You Read Talk with a partner. Discuss why you think the original publisher would not fix the spelling and punctuation errors.

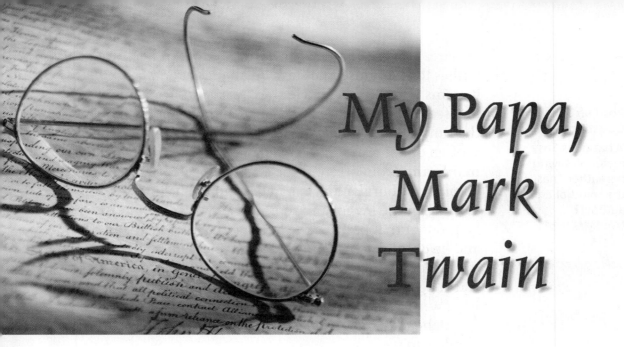

My Papa, Mark Twain

We are a very happy family. We consist of Papa, Mamma, Jean, Clara and me. It is papa I am writing about, and I shall have no trouble in not knowing what to say about him, as he is a *very* striking character.

Papa's appearance has been described many times, but very incorrectly. He has beautiful gray hair, not any too thick or any too long, but just right; a Roman nose which greatly improves the beauty of his features; kind blue eyes and a small mustache. He has a wonderfully shaped head and profile. He has a very good figure—in short, he is an **extrodinarily** fine looking man. All his features are perfect except that he hasn't extrodinary teeth. His **complexion** is very fair, and he doesn't ware a beard. He is a very good man and a very funny one. He has got a temper, but we all of us have in this family. He is the loveliest man I ever saw or ever hope to see—and oh, so **absentminded**.

As you read, think about the words the author uses to show her opinion.

Name one fact and one opinion here. What clue word helped you identify the opinion?

extraordinarily more than what is usual

complexion the feel and color of the skin

absentminded forgetful

Reading Strategy: Questioning

What does Susy mean by saying her father "has the mind of an author"?

Papa's favorite game is **billiards**, and when he is tired and wishes to rest himself he stays up all night and plays billiards, it seems to rest his head. He smokes a great deal almost **incessantly**. He has the mind of an author exactly, some of the simplest things he can't understand. Our burglar alarm is often out of order, and papa had been obliged to take the **mahogany** room off from the alarm altogether for a time, because the burglar alarm had been in the habit of ringing even when the mahogany-room window was closed. At length he thought that perhaps the burglar alarm might be in order, and he decided to try and see; accordingly he put it on and then went down and opened the window; **consequently** the alarm bell rang, it would even if the alarm had been in order. Papa went **despairingly** upstairs and said to mamma, "Livy the mahogany room won't go on. I have just opened the window to see."

"Why, Youth," mamma replied. "If you've opened the window, why of course the alarm will ring!"

Reading Strategy: Questioning

What is the meaning of the word "Youth" in this part of the story?

billiards a certain kind of game played on a pool table	**incessantly** without stopping	**consequently** as a result
	mahogany a type of reddish-brown wood	**despairingly** in a hopeless way

"That's what I've opened it for, why I just went down to see if it would ring!"

Mamma tried to explain to papa that when he wanted to go and see whether the alarm would ring while the window was closed he *mustn't go* and open the window—but in vain, papa couldn't understand, and got very impatient with mamma for trying to make him believe an impossible thing true.

Papa has a peculiar **gait** we like, it seems just to suit him, but most people do not; he always walks ups and down the room while thinking and between each coarse at meals.

Papa is very fond of animals particularly of cats, we had a dear little gray kitten once that he named "Lazy" (papa always wears gray to match his hair and eyes) and he would carry him around on his shoulder, it was a mighty pretty sight! the gray cat sound asleep against papa's gray coat and hair. The names that he has give our different cats are really remarkably funny, they are named Stray Kit, Abner, Motley, Fraeulein, Lazy, Buffalo Bill, Soapy Sall, Cleveland, Sour Mash, and **Pestilence** and **Famine**.

Papa uses very strong language, but I have an idea not nearly so strong as when he first married mamma. A lady acquaintance of his is rather **apt** to interrupt what one is saying, and papa told mamma he thought he should say to the lady's husband "I am glad your wife wasn't present when the **Deity** said Let there be light."

Papa said the other day, "I am a mugwump and a mugwump is pure from the **marrow** out." (Papa knows that I am writing this biography of him, and he said this for it.) He doesn't like to go to church at all, why I never understood, until just now, he told us the other day that he couldn't bear to hear anyone talk but himself, but that he could listen to himself talk for hours without getting tired, of course he said this in joke, but I've no dought it was founded on truth.

How might Papa's retelling of the burglar alarm incident be different from Susy's version?

Motley has two meanings: fool, or a collection of mismatched items. It can also refer to an old type of wool fabric. *Fräulein* is the German word for "young miss." *Buffalo Bill* (William Cody) was a well-known figure in the wild Old West.

Reading Strategy: Questioning

Why do you think the author finds the cat names to be funny?

A *mugwump* was a Republican who would not support Republican candidates in the 1884 election.

gait a way of walking	**famine** a great shortage of food	**deity** a god or goddess
pestilence a fast-spreading disease	**apt** likely to	**marrow** the tissue inside of bones

The Prince and the Pauper was first performed on stage in 1890. Mark Twain had no idea that it would also someday be made into several movies. The first, a 1915 silent film, starred a woman in both lead roles. The second film used identical twin boys.

Why does Susy Clemens believe that *The Prince and the Pauper* is her father's best book?

One of papa's latest books is "The Prince and the **Pauper**" and it is unquestionably the best book he has ever written, some people want him to keep to his old style, some gentleman wrote him, "I enjoyed Huckleberry Finn immensely and am glad to see that you have returned to your old style." That enoyed me, that enoyed me greatly, because it trobles me to have so few people know papa, I mean realy know him, they think of Mark Twain as a **humorist** joking at everything; "And with a mop of reddish brown hair which sorely needs the barbar brush, a roman nose, short stubby mustache, a sad care-worn face, with maney crows' feet" etc. That is the way people picture papa, I have wanted papa to write a book that would **reveal** something of his kind sympathetic nature, and "The Prince and the Pauper" partly does it. The book is full of lovely charming ideas, and oh the language! It is perfect. I think that one of the most touching scenes in it is where the pauper is riding on horseback with his nobles in the "**recognition** procession" and he sees his mother oh and then what followed! How she runs to his side, when she sees him throw up his hand palm outward, and is rudely pushed off by one of the King's officers, and then how the little pauper's conscience troubles him when he remembers the shameful words that were falling from his lips when she was turned from his side "I know you not woman" and how his **grandeurs** were **stricken** valueless and his pride **consumed** to ashes. It is a wonderfully beautiful and touching little scene, and papa has described it so wonderfully. I never saw a man with so much variety of feeling as papa has; now the "Prince and the Pauper" is full of touching places, but there is always a streak of humor in them somewhere. Papa very seldom writes a passage without some humor in it somewhere and I don't think he ever will.

pauper a very poor person	**reveal** to show	**stricken** knocked down
humorist one whose writing contains much humor	**recognition** special attention	**consumed** burned away
	grandeurs the state of being grand	

Clara and I are sure that papa played the trick on Grandma about the whipping that is related in "The Adventures of Tom Sawyer": "Hand me that **switch**." The switch hovered in the air, the peril was desperate—"My, look behind you Aunt!" The old lady whirled around and snatched her skirts out of danger. The lad fled on the instant, scrambling up the high board fence and disappeared over it.

We know papa played "Hookey" all the time. And how readily would papa pretend to be dying so as not to have to go to school! Grandma wouldn't make papa go to school, so she let him go into a printing office to learn the trade. He did so, and gradually picked up enough education to enable him to do about as well as those who were more **studious** in early life.

What details on this page show the author's feelings toward her subject?

The popularity of Twain's fiction did not make him wealthy. However, at his death in 1910, he left behind a rich collection of American literature.

What is Susy's opinion about true success? What facts about her father's life show this?

The Clemens family. Susy Clemens is pictured on the far right, next to her father.

switch a thin, flexible whip

studious having to do with studying

My Papa, Mark Twain   by Susy Clemens

Directions Choose the letter of the best answer or write the answer using complete sentences.

Comprehension: Identifying Facts

1. How many children were in the Clemens family?
A three boys
B two girls and one boy
C two boys and one girl
D three girls

2. Which of these characteristics would Susy say incorrectly describes her father?
A Roman nose
B short stubby mustache
C kind blue eyes
D full head of hair

3. Why doesn't the author think her father's temper is a problem?

4. According to Susy, what did her father do to relax?

5. Why was the author's father opening and shutting the windows in the mahogany room?

6. What kind of a pet did Mark Twain like best?

7. Did Mark Twain like being a mugwump? How do you know?

8. What does the author say Mark Twain always includes in his stories?

9. Which one of Mark Twain's childhood experiences did Susy think he used in a story?

10. In the story, what does it mean to play "Hookey"?

Comprehension: Putting Ideas Together

11. What do that cats' names suggest about Mark Twain?
A He does not like cats.
B He is a religious man.
C He speaks many languages.
D He is creative and funny.

12. What is the meaning of this quote: "I am glad your wife wasn't present when the Deity said Let there be light."
A No one would have wanted to look at his wife.
B His wife would have interrupted and we would have no light.
C The wife would have told the Deity what to do.
D His wife would have wanted to talk and talk about the light.

13. The author says that *The Prince and the Pauper* is the best book Mark Twain has ever written. Is she giving a fact or an opinion? Explain.

14. What opinion do you think Susy has about her father as a writer?

15. Why is Susy bothered by people thinking of Twain as someone who jokes at everything?

16. Do you think Susy actually read her father's books? Explain.

17. Susy says her father had gray hair. Why do you think she said other people thought he had reddish-brown hair?

18. What does Susy mean about her father's "variety of feeling"?

19. What facts does the author give about her father's education?

20. What can you tell about Mark Twain's family life—was it pleasant or difficult? Explain.

Understanding Literature: Author's Point of View

There are many ideas to write in a biography about a person like Mark Twain. Authors use their point of view to decide what to include and how to say it. These choices affect the mood of a book.

21. How did the author's childhood affect her point of view as an author?

22. Susy says her father has a temper and uses strong language. Why don't you think she gives any examples?

23. Identify two details of Susy Clemens's life that help you see her point of view.

24. How might the author's perspective be different if this biography were written by an outsider?

25. Imagine that an author who thinks Mark Twain was a rough, rude man decided to write about him. What might the author say?

Critical Thinking

26. Why might the author's mother call Mark Twain "Youth"?

27. Susy says that her father did "about as well as those who were more studious." Do you agree with her?

28. How does Susy's description of Twain compare to others' ideas of him? What does this comparison tell you about him?

29. In what ways is the author like her father? In what ways is she different?

Thinking Creatively

30. What questions do you have about Mark Twain after reading Susy Clemens's story?

After Reading **continued on next page**

My Papa, Mark Twain   by Susy Clemens

 Grammar Check

A pronoun is a word that takes the place of a noun or another pronoun. A personal pronoun refers to a specific noun in the sentence or paragraph. Possessive pronouns are adjectives that answer the question *Whose?* The chart below lists examples of the different types of pronouns.

Personal Pronouns	Possessive Pronouns
I, he, she, him, her, you, they, them, it	my, his, her, your, their

Complete each sentence with a pronoun that makes sense. Then, label each pronoun as *personal* or *possessive*.

1 Sharon lent me _____ pencil for the test.

2 "Where do _____ want to go?" Jen asked me.

3 An elephant uses _____ trunk like a hand.

 Vocabulary Builder

Describe each item by writing a sentence that uses a vocabulary word from the story.

1 a person who never stops talking

2 a cause and a result

3 someone with a bad memory

 Writing on Your Own

Write a paragraph comparing one of your parents to Mark Twain. To begin, create a three-column chart. In the first column, write three details that show what Susy thinks of her father. In the second, list three words you would use to describe Mark Twain. In the third, write three details to describe your parent. Identify one way your parent is like Twain by circling details that are alike. Identify one way your parent is different from him by underlining details that are different.

 Listening and Speaking

Imagine that you have been asked to present an award to Mark Twain. Use Susy Clemens's biography and your own research to prepare a short speech about Twain. Be sure to talk about Twain's books and why he was chosen for the award.

 Research and Technology

Work with a partner. Use the Internet and the library to research popular characters from Mark Twain's books. Then, make a poster showing some of Twain's best-known works and characters.

Names/Nombres   by Julia Alvarez

About the Author

Julia Alvarez was born in New York City. Soon after her birth, her family went back to their native Dominican Republic. The Dominican Republic is a small country located in the Caribbean Sea. Julia's father worked to overthrow the government leader there. Then he and his family fled the country. Julia was 10 years old when she came back to the United States.

Julia Alvarez
1950–

Alvarez realized in high school that she wanted to be a writer. The award-winning author says, "I write to find out what I'm thinking."

About the Selection

In "Names/Nombres," Julia Alvarez tells about her family's early years as immigrants in the United States. She describes her feelings about having family names spoken incorrectly. She wanted to fit in at school, so she let the mispronunciations go. She was proud of her native language and country, but struggled with being different.

Living in New York City, Julia felt she had to "translate her experiences into English." Sometimes, as she shows in "Names/Nombres," the English speakers did the translating.

Before Reading **continued on next page**

Objectives

◆ To read and understand nonfiction

◆ To recognize the difference between fact and opinion

◆ To identify tone in a selection

BEFORE READING THE SELECTION *(cont.)* | **Build Skills**

Names/Nombres   *by Julia Alvarez*

tone the attitude an author takes toward a subject

Literary Terms The **tone** of a piece of writing is the writer's attitude, or feelings, toward his or her subject. It can often be described in one word, such as *serious* or *humorous*. Tone can be created through word choice, sentence structure, and sentence length. For example, simpler, shorter sentences may help to create a light or funny piece. Often, tone gives a sense of the author's perspective.

Fact	Resource	True	False
Tigers live in only cold climates			✔

Reading on Your Own To understand nonfiction, you must understand the difference between fact and opinion. A fact can be proven. An opinion is a judgment that can be supported but not proven. Facts can be checked with resources like dictionaries, encyclopedias, and trusted Web sites. To help you keep track of facts found in a nonfiction work, use a chart like the one shown.

Writing on Your Own Julia Alvarez writes about the experiences of immigrants—people who move from one country to another. Think about your experiences in group settings, such as a sports team, class, or club. Write a paragraph about the benefits of being part of a group.

Vocabulary Focus Some Spanish words are spelled like English words, but sound very different. In "Names/Nombres," Alvarez writes some words as they sound, not as they are spelled. From these phonetic spellings, identify how the following letters are pronounced in Spanish: *a, j, r, v,* and *z*. Work with a partner to find words that use these letters, and practice your pronunciation.

Think Before You Read Think about an immigrant teenager. What problems might this person face in school? How can or should such a teenager deal with these problems?

Names/Nombres

As you read, look for details that give a feeling of a certain tone.

When we arrived in New York City, our names changed almost immediately. At **Immigration**, the officer asked my father, *Mister Elbures*, if he had anything to declare. My father shook his head, "No," and we were waved through. I was too afraid we wouldn't be let in if I corrected the man's pronunciation, but I said our name to myself, opening my mouth wide for the organ blast of the *a*, **trilling** my tongue for the drum-roll of the *r*, *All-vah-rrr-es*! How could anyone get *Elbures* out of that orchestra sound?

At the hotel my mother was *Missus Alburest*, and I was little girl, as in, "Hey, *little girl*, stop riding the elevator up and down. It's *not* a toy."

When we moved into our new apartment building, the super called my father *Mister Alberase*, and the neighbors who became mother's friends pronounced her name *Jew-lee-ah* instead of *Hoo-lee-ah*. I, her namesake, was known as *Hoo-lee-tah* at home. But at school, I was *Judy* or *Judith*, and once an English teacher mistook me for *Juliet*.

Immigration
a government agency
that checks people
in when they enter
a country

trilling rolling

Visitors and immigrants to a country must go through a government office called *Immigration*. Here they must show proof of who they are and why they have come. Immigration officials also make sure that no illegal items are brought into the country.

The word *super* is short for *superintendent*, the person in charge of an apartment building.

What does Julia experience when she arrives in New York City?

What attitude does the author have toward her different names?

Alcatraz is the name of a maximum security prison near San Francisco, California. The prison is now closed and is a tourist site.

Sancocho is a special spicy Dominican dish with meat, fruits, and vegetables.

Reading Strategy: Questioning

What opinion does the narrator give in the paragraph above?

At this point in the essay, what attitude do you think the author shows?

It took awhile to get used to my new names. I wondered if I shouldn't correct my teachers and new friends. But my mother argued that it didn't matter. "You know what your friend Shakespeare said, '*A rose by any other name would smell as sweet.*' " My father had gotten into the habit of calling any famous author "my friend" because I had begun to write poems and stories in English class.

By the time I was in high school, I was a popular kid, and it showed in my name. Friends called me *Jules* or *Hey Jude*, and once a group of troublemaking friends my mother forbade me to hang out with called me *Alcatraz*. I was *Hoo-lee-tah* only to Mami and Papi and uncles and aunts who came over to eat *sancocho* on Sunday afternoons—old world folk whom I would just as soon go back to where they came from and leave me to **pursue** whatever mischief I wanted to in America. JUDY ALCATRAZ: the name on the Wanted Poster would read. Who would ever trace her to me?

My older sister had the hardest time getting an American name for herself because *Mauricia* did not translate into English. **Ironically**, although she had the most foreign-sounding name, she and I were the Americans in the family. We had been born in New York City when our parents had first tried immigration and then gone back "home," too homesick to stay. My mother often told the story of how she had almost changed my sister's name in the hospital.

After the delivery, Mami and some other new mothers were cooing over their new baby sons and daughters and exchanging names and weights and delivery stories. My mother was embarrassed among the Sallys and Janes and Georges and Johns to **reveal** the rich, noisy name of *Mauricia*, so when her turn came to brag, she gave her baby's name as *Maureen*.

"Why'd ya give her an Irish name with so many pretty Spanish names to choose from?" one of the women asked.

pursue to look for, go after	**ironically** oddly enough; in a different way than expected	**reveal** to make known

My mother blushed and admitted her baby's real name to the group. Her mother-in-law had recently died, she apologized, and her husband had insisted that the first daughter be named after his mother, *Mauran*. My mother thought it was the ugliest name she had ever heard, and she talked my father into what she believed was an improvement, a combination of *Mauran* and her own mother's name, *Felicia*.

"Her name is *Mao-ree-shee-ah*," my mother said to the group of women.

"Why that's a beautiful name," the new mothers cried. "*Moor-ee-sha, Moor-ee-sha*," they cooed into the pink blanket. *Moor-ee-sha* it was when we returned to the States eleven years later. Sometimes, American tongues found even that mispronunciation tough to say and called her *Maria* or *Marsha* or *Maudy* from her nickname *Maury*. I pitied her. What an awful name to transport across borders!

My little sister, Ana, had the easiest time of all. She was plain *Anne*—that is, only her name was plain, for she turned out to be the pale, blond "American beauty" in the family. The only **Hispanic** thing about her was the **affectionate** nicknames her boyfriends sometimes gave her. *Anita*, or as one goofy guy used to sing to her to the tune of the banana advertisement, *Anita Banana*.

Later, during her college years in the late '60s, there was a push to pronounce Third World names correctly. I remember calling her long distance at her group house and a roommate answering.

"Can I speak to Ana?" I asked, pronouncing her name the American way.

"Ana?" The man's voice hesitated. "Oh! you must mean *Ah-nah*!"

Our first few years in the States, though, **ethnicity** was not yet "in." Those were the blond, blue-eyed, bobby sock years

Reading Strategy: Questioning

Why would the author's mother lie about her baby's name? Why does the author tell this story?

Based on what you have read, what would you say "transport across borders" means?

The banana ad had a character named "Chiquita Banana." *Anita Banana* is a play on this name.

Hispanic having Latin American ancestors	**affectionate** warm; loving	**ethnicity** belonging to a group with the same appearance and customs

Reading Strategy: Questioning

How could you check the fact that the narrator was born at Columbia Presbyterian Hospital?

of junior high and high school before the '60s **ushered** in peasant blouses, hoop earrings, serapes. My initial desire to be known by my correct Dominican name faded. I just wanted to be Judy and merge with the Sallys and Janes in my class. But **inevitably**, my accent and coloring gave me away. "So where are you from, Judy?"

"New York," I told my classmates. After all I had been born blocks away at Columbia Presbyterian Hospital.

"I mean, *originally*."

"From the Caribbean," I answered vaguely, for if I **specified**, no one was quite sure on what continent our island was located.

"Really? I've been to Bermuda. We went last April for spring vacation. I got the worst sunburn! So, are you from Portoriko?"

"No," I sighed. "From the Dominican Republic."

"Where's that?"

"Just south of Bermuda."

They were just being curious, I knew, but I burned with shame whenever they singled me out as a "foreigner," a rare, **exotic** friend.

"Say your name in Spanish, oh please say it!" I had made mouths drop one day by rattling off my full name, which according to Dominican custom, included my middle names, Mother's and Father's **surnames** for four generations back.

"Julia Altagracia María Teresa Álvarez Tavares Perello Espaillat Julia Pérez Rochet González," I pronounced it slowly, a name as **chaotic** with sounds as a Middle Eastern bazaar or market day in a South American village.

My Dominican **heritage** was never more apparent than when my extended family attended school occasions. For my graduation, they all came, the whole lot of aunts and uncles and the many little cousins who snuck in without tickets.

Reading Strategy: Questioning

Identify a fact and an opinion in the last paragraph on this page.

ushered directed	**specified** give exact detail	**chaotic** completely confused
inevitably not to be avoided	**exotic** unusual	**heritage** one's background, usually of family ties
	surnames last names	

They sat in the first row in order to better understand the Americans' fast-spoken English. But how could they listen when they were constantly speaking among themselves in **florid**-sounding phrases, rococo consonants, rich, rhyming vowels?

Introducing them to my friends was a further trial to me. These relatives had such **complicated** names and there were so many of them, and their relationships to myself were so **convoluted**. There was my Tía Josefina, who was not really an aunt but a much older cousin. And her daughter, Aida Margarita, who was adopted, *una hija de crianza*. My uncle of affection, Tío José, brought my *madrina* Tía Amelia and her *comadre* Tía Pilar. My friends rarely had more than a "Mom and Dad" to introduce.

After the **commencement** ceremony my family waited outside in the parking lot while my friends and I signed yearbooks with nicknames which recalled our high school good times: "Beans" and "Pepperoni" and "Alcatraz." We hugged and cried and promised to keep in touch.

Our goodbyes went on too long. I heard my father's voice calling out across the parking lot, "*Hoo-lee-tah! Vamonos!*"

Back home my *tíos* and *tías* and *primas*, Mami and Papi, and *mis hermanas* had a party for me with *sancocho* and a storebought *pudín*, **inscribed** with *Happy Graduation, Julie*. There were many gifts—that was a plus to a large family! I got several wallets and a suitcase with my initials and a graduation charm from my godmother and money from my uncles. The biggest gift was a portable typewriter from my parents for writing my stories and poems.

Someday, the family **predicted**, my name would be well-known throughout the United States. I laughed to myself, wondering which one I would go by.

Rococo is a highly decorated style of art from the early 18th century. Here it refers to the fancy, expressive style of the Spanish language.

Reading Strategy: Questioning
How could you check some of the meanings of the Spanish words?

Pudín is a tropical coconut dessert.

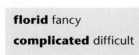

florid fancy	**convoluted** confusing	**inscribed** written on
complicated difficult	**commencement** graduation	**predicted** guessed about the future

Names/Nombres   *by Julia Alvarez*

Directions Choose the letter of the best answer or write the answer using complete sentences.

Comprehension: Identifying Facts

1. Which was not a name given to Julia's parents?
   A Elbures   **C** Alberase
   B Alburest   **D** Alcatraz

2. Why do many English speakers say Julia's name wrong?
   A The letter *J* has different sounds in English and Spanish.
   B They want her to sound more like an American.
   C They are confusing her with someone else.
   D They do not like her real name.

3. Why did Julia's father call Shakespeare her friend?

4. Why did Julia not want her aunts and uncles to visit her house?

5. Why did Julia's mother fib and say that her new baby's name was Maureen?

6. What were some popular things that Julia wore to school in the 1960s?

7. How does Julia respond when her classmates ask her where she is from?

8. How did Julia's Dominican background show when her family went to school events?

9. Why was it confusing for Julia to introduce her relatives to her friends?

10. What was the biggest gift Julia received for graduation?

Comprehension: Putting Ideas Together

11. How do Julia's feelings about how people say her family's names change over time?
   A She gets angrier and angrier at mispronunciations.
   B At first she does not care, but then it starts to bother her.
   C She thinks it is funnier and funnier as time goes on.
   D At first it bothers her, but then she stops worrying about it.

12. What do nicknames represent for Julia?
   A loss of heritage
   B disrespect from others
   C silly Americans
   D affection and acceptance

13. Who said that "Mauran" was the ugliest name ever? Is this statement a fact or opinion?

14. How much older is Mauricia than Julia? How do you know?

15. Where do you think Julia's sister Ana was born? Explain.

16. Why didn't Julia's classmates think she was born in New York?

17. Why did Julia feel shame when her friends singled her out as a foreigner?

18. Why does Julia not tell her classmates she is from the Dominican Republic?

19. How could you check on what American teenagers were wearing in the 1960s?

20. How does Julia's family feel about her graduating from high school? Explain.

Understanding Literature: Tone

Tone is a very personal thing between an author and a piece of writing. For example, someone who likes cats might describe something a cat did in a humorous tone. Someone who does not like cats might describe the same actions in an angry tone.

21. What words would you use to describe the tone of "Names/Nombres"?

22. From the tone, how do you think the author feels about being from the Dominican Republic?

23. What does the story about her graduation add to the overall tone?

24. How might the tone of the story change if the author was Julia's father?

25. Rewrite the following sentence to give it a different tone: "My mother blushed and admitted her baby's real name to the group."

Critical Thinking

26. How does the title capture the feeling of Alvarez's story?

27. How might you check the fact that Julia Alvarez was born in New York City?

28. What do you think is the main idea of this essay? Explain.

29. Which of Julia's names or nicknames do you think fit her the best?

Thinking Creatively

30. What would your name be if you had a "full Dominican name"?

After Reading continued on next page

Names/Nombres   by Julia Alvarez

 Grammar Check

A pronoun is a word that takes the place of a noun or another pronoun. Writers use pronouns so they do not have to use the same noun repeatedly. *Interrogative pronouns* are used in questions. *Indefinite pronouns* use the same spelling for both singular and plural.

Interrogative Pronouns	Indefinite Pronouns
who, whom, whose, what, which	some, other, none

Circle each pronoun and identify what type it is. Then use each pronoun in a new sentence.

1 None of the children had difficulty.

2 Which player needed a helmet?

3 Who will come with me to the store?

 Vocabulary Builder

In your notebook, explain why each statement is true or false. Use the vocabulary words as clues for your explanations.

1 A chaotic place is calm and relaxing.

2 A picture frame with initials carved onto it has been inscribed by someone.

3 If you do not study for a test, you will inevitably pass.

 Writing on Your Own

Review the first paragraph of "Names/Nombres." Write a brief description of the narrator's observations. Then, explain how you think the narrator feels about moving to the United States. Use details from the story to support your explanation.

 Listening and Speaking

Using the information in "Names/Nombres," write a descriptive speech. Present the thoughts of young Julia Alvarez as she first hears her name mispronounced. First, use the word *I* to express a personal point of view. Then include vocabulary that shows Alvarez's personality. Finally, give three reasons why it bothers you to have your name mispronounced.

  Media and Viewing

Work with a small group to create a presentation explaining why Alvarez's family immigrated. Research the history of the Dominican Republic in the early 1960s. Use the Internet and library resources to find your information. Create a computer-generated slideshow to share your findings with the class.

Atlas

In Part 2, you are learning the difference between fact and opinion. In an atlas, you can find many useful facts about specific places. These facts can help you understand what life is like in a different country.

About Atlases

An atlas is a book of maps showing cities, mountains, rivers, and roads. Some atlases include facts about the places. They might also have short articles on topics such as population and climate. Atlas maps usually contain the following:

- a *compass rose* that shows north, south, east, and west
- a *scale bar* that shows what real distance is represented by one inch on the map
- a *legend*, or *key*, that explains the map's symbols and colors
- *labels* that show the name and location of each place
- an *inset map* showing an area's location on the globe

Reading Skill

A generalization is a broad statement based on many examples. A generalization that is supported by facts is a valid, or true, generalization. A generalization that is not well supported is a faulty, or weak, generalization. The information in an atlas entry can help you make generalizations about a region. Use this checklist to make generalizations based on facts from an atlas:

Using an Atlas to Make Generalizations

- ❑ Use the compass rose to support generalizations about locations.
- ❑ Use the scale bar to support generalizations about distances.
- ❑ Use the key to support a number of different generalizations. Some of these might include city size, mountain height, and park location.

THE BRITISH ISLES

This opening section gives general information about the British Isles.

Great Britain and Ireland are the two largest islands that make up the more than 5,000 islands in the British Isles. Scotland, England, and Wales make up Great Britain. About 80% of the population of the islands lives in England. Great Britain and Northern Ireland together make up the country called the United Kingdom of Great Britain and Northern Ireland, which is commonly called the United Kingdom. The southern part of Ireland makes up the Republic of Ireland. Around the two large islands are many smaller ones, such as the Hebrides and Shetland Islands to the north, Anglesey and

This key shows different colors representing different land heights and different depths of the sea. The other key lists the symbols that show populations for cities and towns.

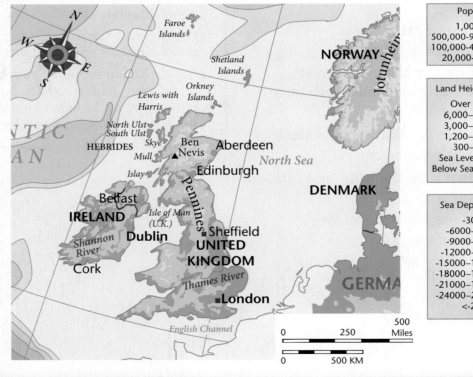

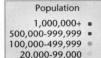

Population

1,000,000+	■
500,000-999,999	■
100,000-499,999	●
20,000-99,000	●

Land Height (in Feet)

Over 9,000
6,000–9,000
3,000–6,000
1,200–3,000
300–1,200
Sea Level–300
Below Sea Level

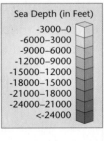

Sea Depth (in Feet)

-3000–0
-6000–3000
-9000–6000
-12000–9000
-15000–12000
-18000–15000
-21000–18000
-24000–21000
<-24000

0	250	500 Miles

0	500 KM

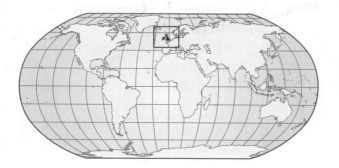

This inset map shows where the British Isles are located on the globe. A second inset shows them in relation to North America.

the Isle of Man in the center, and the Channel islands in the south.

THE LANDSCAPE

The British Isles were formed by a combination of mountains formed through volcanic eruptions and glacier movements that took place millions of years ago. The altitudes on the islands range greatly from very low lying areas, such as in the south of Great Britain, to mountainous areas, such as in the north of Great Britain. At 1,344 meters (4,409 feet), the Ben Nevis mountain in Scotland is the highest point in the British Isles. Many peninsulas jut out around the islands creating rugged coastlines.

A green plateau and gently rolling hills mark Central Ireland. A mountain chain runs near the coast. The result is a central plains area mostly surrounded by mountains. A few large lakes feed off Ireland's many rivers, with the largest lake being Lough Neagh. The tallest point in Ireland is Carrauntoohill, which is 1,039 meters (3,409 feet) above sea level.

Most of England is made up of rolling hills, but some mountains rise up in the north, with the tallest point in England being Scafell Pike at 977 meters. Some low, marshy land runs along the east side of England, but the people have drained much of it so it can be used for farming.

The 10 tallest mountains in the British Isles are all in Scotland. The northern part of Scotland is mountainous, wild, and picturesque. A narrow lowland strip runs between this mountainous area and the Southern Uplands, which is an area of hills that are usually less than 600 meters (2,000 feet) high. The Uplands meet up with the mountains in the north of England.

Monitor Your Progress

Directions Choose the letter of the best answer or write the answer using complete sentences.

1. Look at the "Population" key and the map on page 58. Which generalization makes sense?
   A Dublin is larger than Cork.
   B Cork has fewer people than Aberdeen does.
   C London is the largest city in England.
   D Edinburgh is the second-largest city in England.

2. Look at the information in "The Landscape." Which generalization makes sense?
   A There are no low areas in the British Isles.
   B The coastlines of the British Isles are straight and smooth.
   C The islands were formed by recent volcanic eruptions.
   D Mountains are spread out over most of the British Isles.

3. Look at the inset map on page 59. Which generalization makes sense?
   A The British Isles are larger than North America.
   B The British Isles are east of the United States.
   C The British Isles are surrounded by water on three sides.
   D The British Isles are south of Africa.

4. Would far northern Scotland be a good place for farming? Explain why or why not.

5. Ireland is often called one of the most beautiful places on Earth. What do you think makes it so beautiful?

Writing on Your Own

In which area of the British Isles would you most like to live? Explain your answer with facts from the atlas entry.

The Laughing Skull, A Dominican Legend, 1836   *by Lulu Delacre*

About the Author

Lulu Delacre was born in Rio Piedras, Puerto Rico. Today, she lives in Maryland, in the United States. She writes the stories and draws the pictures for the children's books she creates. Her first memories of drawing were on her grandmother's bedroom floor at age five. She had her first art training when she was 10. By the time she went to college, she knew she wanted to be an artist. She began by drawing pictures for children's books. She began both writing and drawing as a way to share stories she heard as a child. She wanted today's children to also know and love the stories.

Lulu Delacre
1957–

Many cultures have stories that people pass down from generation to generation. These stories are often spread by word of mouth and used as lessons about life. Often, people forget who first started telling the story. Such stories, or **legends,** are often thought of as historical, but they cannot be proven. In other words, people tend to believe they are true, but have no evidence. As the story is retold, details are often added to make it more exciting or meaningful.

About the Selection

The story of "The Laughing Skull" is a Dominican legend. It explains some issues about life and death. The tale is told through the actions of regular people going about their daily lives. Meaningful ideas are used throughout the tale. In the end, clear thought and strong leadership triumph over fear.

You will recall that Julia Alvarez, the author of "Names/ Nombres," is also from the Dominican Republic. As you read "The Laughing Skull," think about how legends may have influenced Alvarez and other members of her culture.

Comparing **continued on next page**

Objectives

◆ To read and understand a legend

◆ To recognize symbolism within a story

◆ To compare symbolism in fiction and nonfiction

The Laughing Skull, A Dominican Legend, 1836   *by Lulu Delacre*

legend a story from folklore that features characters who actually lived, or real events or places

symbol something that represents something else

symbolism the larger meaning of a person, place, or object

Literary Terms In literary works, **symbols** are often used to represent other things. The symbols might stand for feelings, ideas, or experiences that people have in common. The meaning of symbols can sometimes be understood by all people or only certain people. **Symbolism** is the larger meaning of the person, place, or object a symbol represents. This symbolism often stands for deep human experiences.

One way that symbolism is created is by connecting an idea to an object. These connections are not universal. In other words, one object can symbolize different things to different people. Some common symbols include the peace sign (symbolizing peace), and the heart (symbolizing love).

Reading on Your Own You may have read "Names/ Nombres" earlier in this unit. In that story, American names came to be symbols for Julia. They symbolized her identity as a Hispanic American. There are also symbols in the Dominican legend "The Laughing Skull." As you read the story, look for these symbols and their meanings.

Writing on Your Own Work with a partner to make a list of symbols in your lives. Think both about things you do and things you see.

Vocabulary Focus A suffix is a word ending that changes the meaning of the word. Use your knowledge of suffixes to figure out the meaning of words you might not recognize. For example, read this sentence: The wolves moved on noiseless feet. The suffix *–less* means "without." The wolves were moving without making noise.

Think Before You Read Why might a human skull be hung on a rock wall? With a partner, discuss how such a situation would be handled today.

The *Laughing* Skull

A DOMINICAN LEGEND, 1836

Long ago, next to the **Convent** of Santo Domingo, stood a stone wall. Nestled in that wall was an empty **niche**. But the niche had not always been empty. It is said that since the seventeenth century when the church was built, a human skull was displayed there. Perched on an iron stand, it was quite visible during the day. By nightfall, it was well-**illuminated** by the oil lamp above it. And hanging just beneath this niche was an ordinary wooden sign that read:

Oh, you passerby—
Look at me, please.
Like you I once was,
Like me, you will be!

As the years passed, people became so used to this sight that they walked right by the wall, ignoring the skull and the unusual **inscription**. That is, until one day, or rather one night, when a neighbor who lived near Hostos Street was on

convent the place where nuns live

niche a cut out or indented shelf in a wall

illuminated lighted

inscription carved writing, such as in stone

his way home. He heard some very strange noises coming from the skull, and he looked up. As his heart beat fast in sheer horror, he watched the skull nod once, then again, then shake its head as if it were at first approving—then disapproving of his thoughts. He raced home in shock, gasping and whimpering all the way.

The news of this strange event spread like wildfire. And those who feared the sight of the skull, or those who had something to hide, wisely did not go near the convent. However, the daring and curious would wander by the church at night to see the frightening scene for themselves. Then they would later boast of their courage in great detail, telling of how the skull appeared to read their minds.

Once, some young boys who stayed late to watch the skull were quite sure they heard it laugh at them in a loud, shrill tone. Soon after, fear grew and grew in the neighborhood, as did the stories and gossip. People went far out of their way to avoid passing the wall. Since most odd things happened after dark, the lamplighter was careful to light the lamp while the sun was out. Eventually, even the military police would not dare go near the wall.

One very dark night, however, two soldiers patrolling the area decided to defy their own fear, and cautiously approached the convent. As they looked inside the niche, they saw it with their own eyes. The skull was shaking, back and forth, clattering loudly against the stone wall. Without thinking twice, the men fled in panic, and did not stop until they reached their headquarters. There they pounded desperately on the gate. And it was this that triggered the events that later would break the spell of the skull.

At this particular time, it happened that Abad Alfau was second **lieutenant** of the **battalion** that patrolled the main square of Santo Domingo. He was nineteen years old, and was a very handsome and bright lad, whom everybody called

---

What does it mean that the news spread like wildfire?

In the days before electricity, street lights were lanterns that were hand-lit each night.

Years ago, it was common for police stations to be gated for protection. The protection, however, was for those within the gates, not those on the outside.

---

lieutenant a military officer	**battalion** a military unit

simply Abad. He was on duty the night the two soldiers fled from the horrifying sight. Abad was very upset at the **cowardice** of the soldiers and sternly **reprimanded** them. The next evening, when he found out that yet another patrol had detoured from the frightening corner to avoid the laughing skull, he flew into a rage. "This will stop immediately," he said to himself, "or these cowards will be dismissed from the force!"

The following night, Abad ordered two soldiers to bring him a ladder. Two hours before midnight he removed his uniform and dressed in dark pants and a long, dark cape. Then he bravely marched to the wall on Hostos Street, **brandishing** his sword in his right hand. The two soldiers carrying the ladder followed **sheepishly** behind him.

Reading Strategy:
Questioning

What could the lieutenant's changing into dark pants and a dark, long cape symbolize?

cowardice failure to show courage	**reprimanded** scolded **brandishing** holding and waving	**sheepishly** in an embarrassed way

Why do you think just one of the men turned to flee?

How high up do you think the skull in the niche was?

Why do you think people did not talk about the skull again?

They must have been about twenty feet from the niche in the wall when the skull began to shake, and laugh, and clatter, and moan. The noise was too much for one of Abad's companions, and he turned to flee.

"Stop!" cried Abad.

The soldier stopped as he was commanded.

"Now place the ladder in front of the niche," Abad ordered. The soldier did so.

Abad clung tightly to his sword and began to climb up. As he climbed higher, the noises became louder and louder. The skull shook once, twice, three times—until it began to spin violently. Chilling screeches emerged, screeches that would freeze the hearts of even the bravest of men. Oddly enough, Abad remained calm. He was determined to discover the mystery of the skull. As the soldiers held on firmly to the ladder, Abad reached the top. Slowly he lifted his weapon and, with the flat of his sword, he struck two heavy blows that sent the skull spinning and whirling and crashing to the ground.

It was this that **unveiled** the mystery. From beneath the skull, a **horde** of frightened mice scurried down the wall, onto the street, then into the darkness of the breezy island night.

People say that at dawn the broken skull was swept up by a street cleaner, and no one ever mentioned it again. Nearly seventy years later the ancient wall was **demolished**—and along with it, the empty niche.

---

unveiled made known   **horde** a large crowd   **demolished** torn down

COMPARING LITERARY WORKS | Apply the Skills

The Laughing Skull, A Dominican Legend, 1836   by Lulu Delacre

Directions Choose the letter of the best answer or write the answer using complete sentences.

Comprehension: Identifying Facts

1. Who was the first person to see the skull move?
  A a soldier
  B Abad Alfau
  C some young boys
  D a neighbor of the convent

2. At what time of day did most people visit the skull?
  A morning   C afternoon
  B noon   D nighttime

3. Describe the movements of the skull as the people of Santo Domingo saw them.

4. What event started the string of events that led to the discovery of the mice?

5. How did Abad feel about the soldiers who were frightened by the skull?

6. What did Abad carry with him when he went to check out the skull?

7. What happened to the skull as Abad got closer to it?

8. What was in the niche during the years after the skull was smashed?

9. Is "Names/Nombres" fiction or nonfiction? How do you know?

10. Is "The Laughing Skull" fiction or nonfiction? How do you know?

Comprehension: Putting Ideas Together

11. What does the title of "The Laughing Skull" have to do with the legend?
  A The mice were really laughing, not screeching.
  B The skull gave the people of the town many fun nights.
  C The skull had a smiling look about it that made people think it was laughing.
  D The skull laughs at people who confuse mice with a screaming skull.

12. How is the title "Names/Nombres" symbolic of Julia's teenage years?
  A It shows she does not prefer one language over the other.
  B It shows that she no longer knew if she was speaking English or Spanish.
  C It shows the confusion Julia felt over her heritage and her life.
  D This title made it clear that Julia was unhappy about living in the United States.

Comparing continued on next page

The Laughing Skull, A Dominican Legend, 1836   by Lulu Delacre

13. In "The Laughing Skull," when does the opening scene take place?

14. How would the skull be different if the lamplighter had not lit the light?

15. Describe the change in the skull's movement from the beginning to the end.

16. How would you explain the change in movements?

17. Did the sign under the skull have anything to do with its movements and noises? Explain.

18. After the skull was gone, what changes would you expect in the lamplighter's schedule?

19. How do you know that the soldiers hesitated to go visit the skull with Abad?

20. What clues does this legend give to Julia Alvarez's Dominican roots?

Understanding Literature: Symbolism

Symbolism lets authors and readers relate to a deeper meaning beyond the text. Sometimes writers use well-known symbols that readers can agree on. Other times, they use symbols that only have meaning in the one story they are writing. Different people may identify and understand symbols differently.

21. In "Names/Nombres," what do the American names symbolize for Julia?

22. In "The Laughing Skull," what could the mice symbolize before the mystery is solved?

23. In "The Laughing Skull," what might darkness be a symbol for?

24. What from "The Laughing Skull" could be a symbol for courage?

25. If the Dominican Republic were a symbol shared by these stories, what might it represent?

Critical Thinking

26. The neighbor who lived near Hostos Street was horrified when he saw the skull move. Why?

27. How would you explain the young boys' certainty that they heard the skull laugh at them?

28. Why do you think Abad changed his clothes before going to see the skull?

29. Why do you think Abad was not frightened by the noises coming from the skull?

Thinking Creatively

30. Make up a situation to explain who put the sign below the skull and why.

Grammar Check

An introductory phrase must be separated from the rest of the sentence with a comma. Look at these examples from the two selections:

"When we arrived in New York, our names changed almost immediately."

"From beneath the skull, a horde of frightened mice scurried down the wall."

Write four sentences of your own that begin with introductory phrases. Make sure to include commas.

 ## Vocabulary Builder

Work with a small group. Create a set of Bingo-type cards using vocabulary words from the two selections. Draw a 5 x 5-square grid on each card. Write the word BINGO across the top of each card. Write the vocabulary words randomly within the different columns. As a whole class, play BINGO. Have a caller call out a BINGO letter and a word definition. Mark squares that match both the BINGO letter and the definition.

 ## Writing on Your Own

Write two paragraphs about Julia telling the legend of "The Laughing Skull" to her friends. Make sure to explain why she chose to share this story. Also, tell what she had to say about the legend.

 ## Listening and Speaking

In a small group, discuss the symbols in the two selections. Choose three symbols that you think are meaningful. Explain your choices to the group. Listen and respond to other students' comments. Tell them if you agree or disagree and why.

 ## Research and Technology

Find another Caribbean legend in your library or on the Internet. Read the story. Then create a Venn diagram to compare and contrast the story to "The Laughing Skull." You can see a description of a Venn diagram in Appendix A.

Do You Know Now?

Like the words on the following list, *know* and *now* are easily confused. You most likely know the difference between words like these. However, when writing, you may forget and choose the wrong one. In addition, homonyms and homophones sound the same but are spelled differently. The spell-checker in a computer program will not find these errors, so proofread carefully.

Study the Word List. Make sure you know when to use each word.

Practice

Use words from the Word List to complete the sentences.

Word List
- our
- are
- than
- then
- know
- now
- lose
- loose
- accept
- except

1. I am afraid I will _____ this ring because it is _____.

2. I can _____ all your reasons _____ the last one.

3. Jen likes the idea more now _____ she did _____.

4. _____ books _____ in the classroom.

5. The class did not _____ the schedule until _____.

You are blocking our light!

In Unit 1, you read both fiction and nonfiction. "Stray" is a fiction story based on the author's childhood memories. "The Drive-In Movies" is a nonfiction story about a childhood experience of the author. "How to Talk to Your Cat," "My Papa, Mark Twain," and "Names/Nombres" are nonfiction. The "Laughing Skull" is fiction, although it could be based on something that really happened.

The author's purpose can be seen in each of the selections. For example, the purpose of both "Stray" and "The Drive-In Movies" is to entertain readers. "How to Talk to Your Cat" gives cat owners tips about living with their pets. In "My Papa, Mark Twain," Susy Clemens has one main purpose. She wants to tell what a wonderful man her father is. In both "Names/Nombres" and "The Laughing Skull" the authors want to share cultural experiences.

The authors' perspectives and attitudes affect the tone in all of the selections. For example, in "Names/Nombres," Julia Alvarez clearly liked her teenage years in New York. She had no problem with her friends using different names when they talked to her. The tone is friendly and warm. In "Stray," the family is very poor and loving. The author grew up understanding what this was like. This understanding shows in the warm, caring tone of the story.

Selections

- "Stray" by Cynthia Rylant is about a young girl who takes in a lost puppy.

- "The Drive-In Movies" by Gary Soto describes a special family outing.

- "How to Talk to Your Cat" by Jean Craighead George gives tips to help people understand cats.

- "My Papa, Mark Twain" by Susy Clemens is a biography about the famous author.

- "Names/Nombres" by Julia Alvarez shows how hard it is for an immigrant to fit in.

- "The Laughing Skull," by Lulu Delacre is a Dominican legend, dating back to 1836. It is a spooky tale with a not-so-scary ending.

Unit 1   REVIEW

Directions Choose the letter of the best answer or write the answer using complete sentences.

Comprehension: Identifying Facts

1. In "How to Talk to Your Cat," the author says that people must do four things: feel, look, _____, and _____.
   A think, talk   C sit, stand
   B smile, move   D listen, smell

2. In "Stray," what was Doris doing when she first saw the puppy?

3. In "The Drive-In Movies," what was the name of the theater where the family went?

4. What color clothing did Mark Twain wear and why?

5. How old was Abad in "The Laughing Skull"?

Comprehension: Putting Ideas Together

6. In "Names/Nombres," why did the immigration officer say their last name wrong?
   A He was not a nice man.
   B He was not a very bright man.
   C He gave the Spanish name an English pronunciation.
   D The only languages he could speak were French and German.

7. Would Doris's father be considered a crude man or a warm man? Use details from the story to explain your answer.

8. What problems did Gary have in "The Drive-In Movies" as he did the chores?

9. How do you "speak in scent" with a cat?

10. Would the mice have been in the wall if the skull had not been there? Explain.

Understanding Literature: Author's Perspective

Authors bring their perspective to everything they write. For example, an author who loves to swim may write positively about swimming. An author who is afraid of water may write fearfully about swimming. Understanding an author's perspective helps readers understand what they are reading.

11. What did Cynthia Rylant's childhood have to do with her perspective in "Stray"?

12. Pretend Gary Soto could have gone to the movies whenever he wanted to. How might his perspective in "The Drive-In Movies" change?

13. How do you think the author of "How to Talk to Your Cat" feels about cats?

14. From what perspective would you say Susy Clemens wrote "My Papa, Mark Twain"?

15. Julia's mother quoted Shakespeare when she said, "A rose by any other name would smell as sweet." What did she mean?

Critical Thinking

16. In "Stray," would the ending change if the puppy showed up on a sunny day?

17. What might the author of "The Drive-In Movies" have done differently to stay awake?

18. In "How to Talk to Your Cat," the author seems to know what cats think. How does she know this?

Thinking Creatively

19. Why did Susy Clemens and her father have different last names?

20. Choose the selection in the unit you liked best. Explain the reasons for your choice.

Speak and Listen

Review the stories "Stray" and "The Drive-In Movies." Make notes about things the two stories have in common and ways they are different. Use your notes to share your ideas with the class.

Writing on Your Own

Think of something you know how to do well. Write a one-page how-to piece telling others how to do the activity. Before you start, brainstorm ideas. Then, put your ideas in an order that makes sense. Use pictures if you think they will help readers understand.

Beyond Words

Work with a partner. Research the rules and health conditions at your local animal shelter. Role-play a conversation you would like to have with the people who work there. Your conversation can be about good things they do or things you think should change.

Test-Taking Tip

When studying for a test, use a marker to highlight key words and important concepts in your notes. For a final review, read what you highlighted.

Narration: Autobiographical Narrative

Some of the best stories are not made up. Instead, they are about real events in the writer's life. This type of story is called an autobiographical narrative. This means it is a story told in time order about the author's own experiences. Follow the steps outlined in this workshop to write an autobiographical narrative.

Assignment Write an autobiographical narrative about an event that taught you a lesson or helped you grow.

What to Include Your autobiographical narrative should include the following pieces:

- an attention-grabbing first sentence or opening paragraph
- a clear order of events, using chronological (time) order
- a central problem or conflict that you or someone else solves
- clear details that show the people, places, and events
- error-free writing, including correct use of pronouns

Prewriting
Choosing Your Topic

Work on finding the right topic for your autobiographical narrative. Think of events that were really special for you. Try one of these ideas to get started:

- **Freewriting** Write whatever thoughts come to mind about a general topic. Examples of general topics include holidays, adventures, or a problem solved. Focus more on getting your ideas down on paper than on writing correctly. After five minutes, read over your thoughts, and choose one for your topic.

- **Memory Quicklist** Make a three-column chart. In the first column, list special people, places, and memorable events. In the next column, describe each entry in the first column. In the last column, give an example to support each description. Choose one of these memories as your topic.

Using the Form
You may use parts of this form in these writing situations:
- letters
- journals
- persuasive essays
- anecdotes, or short stories about particular events

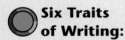 **Six Traits of Writing:**

Ideas message, details, and purpose

Narrowing Your Topic

Once you have chosen a topic, you will need to narrow it down. You can do this by focusing on one important part. For example, you could focus on a surprise or a problem. Choose some part of an experience that stands out in your mind.

Gathering Details

Make a timeline. Begin to gather the details that you will use to develop your story. List the events and supporting details in order on a timeline like the one shown.

Timeline

Event 1: I decided to take the canoe out after dark by myself.

Event 2: As I paddled to the far side of the lake, I heard thunder.

Event 3: The first bolt of lightning hit in the forest.

It was a calm night, so I thought my grandfather was wrong about a storm.

The thunder came in low rumbles at first, then louder and louder.

Suddenly, I was terrified! I had to seek shelter.

Writing Your Draft

Shaping Your Writing

Decide on the order of events. Review your timeline. Then, make a decision about the order for your events.

- **Chronological Order:** Many stories start with the first event. Then they add the others in the order in which they happened.

- **Chronological Order with Flashback:** Some stories begin at the end and flash back to the beginning. Then, through flashback, the writer tells the rest of the story in chronological order.

Six Traits of Writing:
Organization order, ideas tied together

Plan to present your conflict. Make a Plot Mountain similar to this one. List each event that builds toward the climax, the story's highest point of interest. Then, list events that follow the climax until the last scene, or resolution, takes place.

Use details from the Plot Mountain as you write.

Providing Elaboration

Choose vivid language. You can add interest to your autobiographical narrative with lively verbs, nouns, and adjectives.

Dull: As I went across the lake, I heard noises far away.

Vivid: As I paddled across the peaceful lake, I became aware of rumbles of thunder.

Use dialogue. Dialogue will help to bring life to your characters. Do not report everything a character says. Instead, choose the important conversations that show a character's thoughts and feelings.

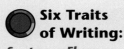

Six Traits of Writing:

Sentence Fluency smooth rhythm and flow

Revising

Revising Your Overall Structure

Identify and strengthen connections. Draw an arrow from each paragraph to the next. Explain the relationship between the paragraphs that each arrow links. Change a paragraph that is not clearly related to the ones before and after it. Rewrite it or think about moving it or even deleting it.

Revising Your Paragraphs

The first sentence of your autobiographical narrative should make readers want to keep reading on to find out what happens. These ideas might help you to pack more power into that all-important sentence:

- Start with an exciting action. *Crash! A bolt of lightning hit somewhere on the island, with ear-splitting, terrifying power.*
- Start with a hint about a possible problem. *The sky darkened unexpectedly with storm clouds.*
- Start with some lively character speech. *"Don't go out on that lake alone!" my grandfather warned.*

Editing and Proofreading

Check your essay for errors in grammar, spelling, and punctuation.

Focus on Punctuating Characters' Speech. If you include conversations in your writing, follow the proper formatting rules.

- Quotations in quotation marks: *"You were right," I said to Jim.*
- Comma after introduction of the speaker: *Jim replied, "Well, you learned a lesson today."*
- Commas and quotation marks before and after interrupting words: *"Next time," I said, "I guess I'll listen."*

Publishing and Presenting

Consider one of the following ways to share your writing:

- **Deliver a speech.** Use your autobiographical narrative as the basis for a public presentation.
- **Get it published.** Mail your narrative to a magazine that publishes student writing. Include a letter introducing your essay.

Reflecting on Your Writing

Writer's Journal Jot down your thoughts on writing an autobiographical narrative. Begin by answering these questions:

- How did gathering and using vivid details help you to tell your story?
- What new understanding did you gain in this experience?

Illustration for "Wynken, Blynken, & Nod"
Maxfield Parish

Unit 2 | Short Stories

S hort stories are works of fiction. Like novels, they have a theme, plot, setting, and characters. However, a short story is not simply a short novel. There are major differences between the two. Most short stories have only a few characters and one setting. The plot of a short story includes fewer details. Despite this, however, the language of a short story can be very rich. In this unit, you will find short stories with different themes, plots, and settings. Yet they all have rich language and interesting characters.

"A story to me means a plot where there is some surprise. . . . Because that is how life is— full of surprises."

—Isaac Bashevis Singer, **New York Times** interview, 1978

Unit 2 About Short Stories

Elements of Short Stories

The short story is a popular form of fiction. Like other types of fiction, a short story has a plot, characters, point of view, setting, and theme. Although all short stories are different, they all share the same basic elements.

Plot is the series of events in a story. Events that happen early in the story build the plot by bringing about later events. As the problem in the short story gets worse, the plot builds to the **climax.** A climax is the high point of interest or suspense in the story. Then there is a **resolution,** or solving of the problem, and the story ends.

Conflict is the struggle of the main character against himself or herself, another person, or nature.

- An **internal conflict** takes place in the mind of a character. The character struggles to make a decision or take an action.

- An **external conflict** is one in which a character struggles with an outside force such as another character or a force of nature.

Characters are the people or animals in a story, poem, or play.

- **Characterization** is the way a writer develops character qualities and personality traits.

- **Character traits** are a character's way of thinking, behaving, or speaking.

- A character's **motives** are the reasons for his or her actions.

Gentlemen, Regarding the recent rejection slip you sent me.

I think there might have been a misunderstanding.

What I really wanted was for you to publish my story, and send me fifty thousand dollars.

Didn't you realize that?

Setting is the time and place in a story. Different types of settings can be the year, time of day, or even the weather. The setting of a story can serve as the background for the plot.

- In a story that takes place in current times, the made-up world of the setting usually has real details.

- Stories based on events from history may have a mixture of fact and fiction.

Theme is the main idea of a story. The theme of the story may be stated or implied.

- A stated theme is expressed directly by the writer.

- An implied theme is suggested, or stated indirectly with what happens to the characters.

Part 1

Reading Strategy:
Inferencing

Sometimes the meaning of a text is not directly stated. You have to make an inference to figure out what the text means.

What You Know + What You Read = Inference

To make inferences, you have to think "beyond the text." Predicting what will happen next and explaining cause and effect are helpful strategies for making inferences.

Literary Terms

short story a brief work of prose fiction that includes plot, setting, characters, point of view, and theme

setting the time and place in a story

character a person or animal in a story, poem, or play

motive the reason a character does something

characterization the way a writer develops character qualities and personality traits

character trait a character's way of thinking, behaving, or speaking

exaggeration a use of words to make something seem more than it is; stretching the truth to a great extent

conflict the struggle of the main character against himself or herself, another person, or nature

plot the series of events in a story

rising action the buildup of excitement in a story

climax the high point of interest or suspense in a story or play

resolution the act of solving the conflict in a story

concrete image people and things that can be seen or touched

narrator one who tells a story

point of view the position from which the author or storyteller tells the story

third person a point of view where the narrator is not a character, and refers to characters as *he* or *she*

BEFORE READING THE SELECTION | Build Understanding

Cutthroat   *by Norma Fox Mazer*

About the Author

Norma Fox Mazer started writing when she was 12 years old. Sixteen years later, she and her husband Harry decided to write for one hour every day. Since then, Mazer has become one of the top writers of books for young people. She has published a large number of short stories and more than 25 novels. Some of her books have won awards. These books include a collection of short stories and a novel titled *After the Rain*.

Mazer has said that she writes not *for* teens but *about* them. Her goal is to write fiction that treats teens "with the respect and seriousness they deserve." She hopes that readers get two things from her work. One is an enjoyable reading experience. The other is something to think further about—perhaps a different way of looking at life.

About the Selection

Like many short stories, "Cutthroat" takes place during a brief time. The events occur within only a few hours. Yet during this brief time Jessie, the main character, has a big challenge. She has to rethink what friendship really means.

Much of "Cutthroat" takes place on a racquetball court in a clubhouse. Three characters named Jessie, Meadow, and Diane play racquetball. Racquetball is an indoor sport played on a special court. It has been popular since the 1970s. Cutthroat is a racquetball game in which two players play against a third player. Mazer played racquetball for the first time as an adult. Some of the details in the story are things she learned from playing the sport. She wrote "Cutthroat" in 1995.

Norma Fox Mazer
1931–

Objectives

- ◆ To read and understand a short story
- ◆ To understand how characters are developed in a short story
- ◆ To make inferences while reading

Before Reading continued on next page

Cutthroat   by Norma Fox Mazer

short story
a brief work of prose fiction that includes plot, setting, characters, point of view, and theme

setting the time and place in a story

character
a person or animal in a story, poem, or play

motive the reason a character does something

characterization the way a writer develops character qualities and personality traits

character trait
a character's way of thinking, behaving, or speaking

exaggeration
a use of words to make something seem more than it is; stretching the truth to a great extent

Literary Terms A **short story** is a brief work of prose fiction that includes plot, **setting, characters**, point of view, and theme. Setting is the time and place in a story. A character is a person or animal in a story, poem, or play. The characters in a story take part in the action. A character's **motive** is the reason a character does something. **Characterization** is the way a writer develops character qualities and personality traits. A **character trait** is a character's way of thinking, behaving, or speaking. In "Cutthroat," **exaggeration** is a trait of the main character. Exaggeration is the use of words to make something seem more than it is. In other words, it is stretching the truth to a great extent.

Reading on Your Own When you make an inference, you use what you already know to assume, or suppose, something. You also use details the author has included in his or her writing. These details serve as clues and help you make an inference. Pay close attention to details included in "Cutthroat" to make inferences about the characters.

Writing on Your Own Some friends may last your entire lifetime. In other cases, your feelings toward each other change. Think back to a time when your feelings toward a friend started to change. Write down notes that explain everything you remember about the experience.

Vocabulary Focus The story contains several words that are related to the sport of racquetball. They include *serve, forehand wall, looping the ball, serving box, ace, forehand,* and *backhand*. If any of them are unfamiliar, search for their meaning. Use a book about racquetball or an encyclopedia.

Think Before You Read As you read, think about the following question: How did a character you really liked change during the course of the story?

Cutthroat

As you read, think about the character traits that Jessie has.

"I took him home and fed him egg and milk," Jessie said. She looked out the window. Heaps of dirty snow everywhere, but it was cozy in the van. "Oh, man. You should have seen my mother's face when she walked in from work and saw that kitty sitting in my lap."

"Why doesn't she like cats?" Meadow said.

"Did I say that? He's a stray, he needs vet care, and Ma says that's like one of the most expensive things going. Anyway, she's in one of her poverty moods."

"What moods?"

"Poor. Poverty. Hello? She says we don't have any money to spare. Lots of bills and not enough bucks to go around."

There are many things more expensive than vet care. This is a case in which Jessie uses exaggeration. Look for other examples of exaggeration throughout the story.

Saying this, Jessie was **momentarily** furious, as if Meadow had forced the words out of her, as if it were a shameful thing that the Cowan family's brick house had three chimneys and four bathrooms, while Jessie, her mother, and Aunt Zis considered themselves lucky to be able to pay the heating bill on time and would think it pure heaven to have two bathrooms.

"The kitten's adorable," Jessie said, "although somewhat battered. I made him a box next to my bed. I'm soaking his injured paw. I think some jerk drove over it, or maybe it got hurt when whoever abandoned him tossed him away."

"Poor little thing," Meadow said **empathically**. The Cowans had three dogs and four cats, and they'd taken in strays, too. "What are you using on the paw?"

Epsom salts are salt crystals used for soaking sore muscles or making wounds heal.

"Hot water and Epsom salts."

Meadow tossed the little blue playing ball into the air and caught it. "Better get him to the vet," she advised.

momentarily for a short time	**empathically** done with the understanding of another person

How would you describe Jessie, based on what you have learned about her so far?

Jessie felt like pounding her best friend. Hard. Hadn't Meadow heard what she'd said about money?

"Everything okay back there, sweetie?" Mrs. Cowan called alertly from the front of the van, as if her motherly antennae had picked up Jessie's brief but sincere desire to do away with her daughter. Meadow's baby sister, Scout, was up front in the car seat, and her little brothers, Lance and Deaver, had taken over the middle. Jessie and Meadow had retreated to the back for **privacy**.

"Did you tell Diane what time we had the court?" Meadow put her feet up on the seat and relaced her sneakers.

"No, I didn't tell her the time. I said just come whenever you feel like it."

"So funny."

"So, do you think she's going to be on time?"

"I hope so, Meadow. We can go on and warm up if she's not."

"They get you off the court the instant your time is up. I want our full court time." She tapped her foot on the floor, as if the court time were already lost. "You said she was always late for things."

"Did I? I'm sure I didn't say that." Meeting Diane to play cutthroat had been Jessie's idea, which she was now starting to regret.

"You said it," Meadow said. "And you know her better than I do. She's your friend."

"Med, how late can she be? Relax!" Why did she keep trying to push Meadow and Diane together? It was that thing of wanting the friends you loved to love the friends you loved.

"You okay, Med?" her mother called again.

"Fine, Mommy."

"Fine, Mommy! Fine, Mommy!" Meadow's little brothers yelped.

"Shut up, you two," Meadow ordered.

"Shut up, you two," Lance and Deaver **mimicked**.

---

privacy a state of being away from others

mimicked imitated

"Disgusting brats," Meadow said.

Jessie unzipped Meadow's sports bag to make sure Meadow had brought a racket along for her. Because she was an only child herself, the way **siblings** got along was a mystery to her. Sometimes Meadow was all over her little brothers, hugging and kissing, as if she couldn't get enough of them. Other times, she sounded as if she were just waiting to drop them in the nearest garbage can.

Love-hate, Jessie thought. Like their friendship?

Their relationship had started back in the misty past, when they were a couple of kindergarten kids. Meadow, slight and skinny, with tight blond braids, could do the best cartwheels, somersaults, and leaps in the class. She was also the shyest person. Jessie, not only unafraid to speak up, but eager to do so, became Meadow's voice. "Mrs. Lesesne, Meadow wants to be blackboard monitor. . . . Mrs. Lesesne, Meadow wants to carry the milk for snacks. . . . Mrs. Lesesne, Meadow has to go to the bathroom. . . ."

At this point the author describes past events. What do these events tell you about the characters' personalities?

By now, they knew each other so well they could probably each predict what the other was going to eat for breakfast, a state that was both slightly annoying and terribly comforting to Jessie. A school **psychologist** had once told her she liked **routine** and repetition because her father had walked out on her and her mother years ago and upset the balance of her life. Okay. Maybe.

She knew people who changed their friends like they did their socks, and it was true she didn't understand that in the least. She had always assumed the Jessie-Meadow friendship would last forever. Now, though, a worm of doubt sometimes entered her mind and made her a little **nauseous**. She and Meadow were so far from a **harmonious** pair! They **bickered** and picked at each other like a grouchy married couple on the

siblings brothers and sisters	**routine** the normal order of activity	**harmonious** having similar feelings or ideas
psychologist a person who has studied behavior patterns	**nauseous** feeling sick to one's stomach	**bickered** argued

When something is on the *verge* of happening, it is just at the point of happening.

Jessie meets Diane at a YMCA or YWCA, called a "Y" for short. A YMCA or YWCA is a community organization where people play sports and take classes. *Improv* is short for *improvisation*. To do improv means to make up and perform a skit without previous planning.

The word *clones* refers to creatures that are exactly alike. The joke is that Diane and Jessie are similar but have skin of different colors. Therefore, they could not possibly be exactly alike.

verge of divorce. It had never seemed to matter before. What was different now? Well . . . Diane.

Jessie had met Diane McArdle last summer at an acting class down at the Y. They'd noticed each other right away, and when the purple-haired coach had called for teams to do improv, Diane had looked at Jessie and Jessie had looked at Diane, and they'd stood up at the same moment, as if it had all been planned. They'd put their heads together and then done a sketch about two friends who couldn't agree on anything— a real natural for Jessie! The class had loved it, and Jessie and Diane had loved themselves for being funny and loud and **spontaneous**.

After that, they were friends, so absurdly **compatible** they called themselves the B&W Clones. Private joke. Diane was black, Jessie white. It amused them when people noticed them on the street. They put their arms next to each other, looked at their skin—*that's* black? *that's* white?—and laughed their heads off. Everything amused them. They made jokes and **puns**, teased each other. Their minds were like a couple of runners, sprinting side by side along the same track.

Jessie and Meadow, on the other hand, were more like two goats butting heads. Sure, it was affectionate, but sometimes it got real heated and they'd have a big, slam-bang fight. Still, they always made up. They had something deep between them—all those years. Jessie knew it was unfair to put her friendships on a scale and weigh them against each other, but she found it hard to resist.

"Who is he?" Meadow breathed as they walked away from the check-in desk in the clubhouse. She tipped her head back toward the blond guy with muscles behind the counter, the one who was wearing a skintight T-shirt.

verge the edge or border	**spontaneous** happening naturally, without planning	**compatible** suited well for each other
		puns jokes made of plays on words

"Jack Kettle," Jessie said.

"How do you know his name?"

"The universe brought it to me on the wind, Med."

"What?" Meadow said in an **anguished** whisper.

Jessie took pity and pointed out that parading across the skimpy T-shirt that covered those amazing pecs were ten big red letters. "J-A-C-K!" she whispered into Meadow's ear. "K-E-T—"

"Shhh! He'll hear you!" Meadow glanced back. Her normally pale skin had gone even paler, and her eyes were round and **glazed**, as if she were under **hypnosis**.

Jessie recognized the look. Meadow had just been struck by a Fatal Crush—a silly thing, in Jessie's estimation, but a silly thing she and Meadow had been through together, and more than once.

The first time this **phenomenon** had been noticed—and named by Jessie—had been back in fifth grade when, midway through the term, their class got a new teacher: Mr. Rivera of the bright blue eyes and dazzling smile. Poor Meadow. She hadn't been able to get a word out for the rest of the term.

"Want me to introduce you to Jack?" Jessie said.

"You don't know him!"

"I can still introduce you."

"No! No, no." Meadow held Jessie's arm in an iron grip and rushed her down the stairs to the locker room.

Diane was waiting for them, doing sit-ups. "Hi guys." She was in powder blue sweats, her long black hair pulled up in a ponytail.

"How are you, sweetie pie baby doll?" Jessie scrubbed Diane's head.

"Just great, honey bunch piggy face."

Meadow yanked open a locker. "Jack Kettle," she mumbled.

"What's a Jack Kettle?" Diane asked.

> *Pecs* is short for pectoral muscles—the muscles across the chest.

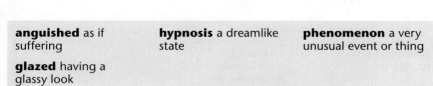

anguished as if suffering

glazed having a glassy look

hypnosis a dreamlike state

phenomenon a very unusual event or thing

"For most of us, Diane," Jessie said, "it's that blond bimbo with the overgrown muscles at the check-in desk. But for Meadow—"

"Shut up, Jessie," Meadow said.

"—he's a Fatal Crush."

"Is that like an Orange Crush?"

"Diane. Pu-leese! Fatal Crush, as in hopeless, impossible. As in the beloved is beyond your mortal reach."

"Beyond your *mere* mortal reach," Diane corrected.

"Meadow has had some very cool Fatal Crushes, Diane. Am I right, Med? But this time I don't think she's picked a winner." Jessie wound a bandanna around her head. "I'm afraid Jack Kettle hasn't got a single active brain cell to go with all those muscles."

"What are you talking about?" Meadow said. "How do you know anything about him, Jessie?"

"Med, guys who are **obsessed** with working out, guys who are always on the machines—"

"How do you know he works out? How do you know he goes on the machines? You never even saw him before today."

"Meadow, do I have to be dropped into the ocean to know it's wet? Do I have to burn my hand to know fire is hot?"

Shut up, Jessie, she told herself, as she often did. And as she often did—she didn't. "Do I have to see Jack Kettle, in the flesh, lifting weights, to know where he got those big puffy muscles?"

Meadow walked out of the locker room, slapping her racket against her leg.

"Well, let's get on the court so Meadow can beat us up," Jessie said. Now she felt bad for going on like that at Meadow's expense. Cheap shot. She'd done it to amuse Diane.

"Is Meadow a good player?" Diane asked.

Jessie laughed. "That's one way of putting it."

"She's very good?"

mere only; no more than	**obsessed** having all one's attention taken by one thing

"Let me just say I've seen her run *up* the wall after a ball and make the point."

Diane swung her racket a few times, whipping her wrist around.

They had Court Three, one of the glass-walled courts. The first thing Meadow did was inspect the floor. She picked up a curl of dust in the corner and threw it out the door. Then she scraped the soles of her sneakers against the wall to rough them up. "Who gets first serve?"

"You," Jessie said, knowing Meadow wanted it.

Meadow took the serving box, bounced the ball five or six times, then lifted her racket and drove it down for a serve that ran so tight against the forehand wall, it would have been a miracle if Diane had returned it.

"Ace," Diane said—a trifle tensely, Jessie noticed.

"One, nothing." Meadow said, bouncing the ball. This time she served into the backhand court, Jessie's side, looping the ball up so high and so soft it seemed to hover against the ceiling like a hummingbird.

"Got it, got it!" Jessie cried as the ball slid slowly down the wall and she tried to remember all the tips Meadow had given her. *Face the side wall. . . . Step into the ball. . . . Use your wrist, don't stiff-arm it. . . .* She barely got a piece of her racket on the ball. It was a weak return, and without even leaving the serving box, Meadow killed it against the front wall.

"Oh, shoot!" This was the first time Jessie had played racquetball with Diane. "Sorry, partner."

Reading Strategy: Inferencing

What do Meadow's actions on the court tell you about her?

BFF
Jessie,
Meadow + Diane

Reading Strategy: Inferencing

What has changed in Jessie's thinking about the differences between Meadow and Diane?

Jennifer Capriati is a former world-champion tennis player.

What do you think Jessie is serious about here—perhaps without realizing it? What is her motive?

Tonya Harding is a former Olympic ice skater from the United States. She was involved in an attack on Nancy Kerrigan, another skater, at the 1994 Olympics.

"We'll get her this time," Diane said.

"Come on, team," Jessie added, but she was a little taken aback to see the same nearly grim, I-play-to-win look on Diane's round face that she was used to seeing on Meadow's leaner features.

"Two, nothing," Meadow said briskly.

"Let's get her, Jessie!"

"Yeah, let's get tough." Jessie **smirked** at Meadow and crouched, swinging her racket like Jennifer Capriati.

On the seventh point, Diane looped the ball up into the air, forcing Meadow back, and she and Jessie made their first point. "Finally!" Diane yelled, punching her fist into the air.

"Yaaay, Diane! Yaaay, us! Yaaay for the good guys!" Jessie was determined not to be too serious about the game.

On the next point Meadow's serve came **caroming** off the back wall. Jessie picked it up low, something she rarely managed, and heard that thrilling sound of the racket connecting perfectly with the ball.

"Nice return," Meadow complimented her, and lofted the ball high and soft down the middle, driving Diane and Jessie to the back wall, where they **collided** as they both tried to take the return shot.

"Oh, now I'm mad, partner," Jessie said.

"Mad, mad, mad," Diane agreed.

"Breathing hard," Jessie said.

"Snorting fire! Watch out, Meadow!"

Meadow gave them a Tonya Harding smile, but they made the next two points. After that, though, it was Meadow's game all the way. She won, no surprise, 21–7.

smirked smiled in a self-satisfied way	**caroming** to strike something so that it returns, hitting something else	**collided** ran into each other

In the second game, with different partners, the score was reversed. Diane, playing hard, managed to make seven points. "I should have done better," she said when they went off court for a drink of water.

"You were playing against the Jessie-Meadow team," Jessie said. "What did you expect? Oh, excuse me, I mean, it was *supposed* to be the Jessie-Meadow team. Maybe you thought you were just playing Meadow."

Meadow had been an **irritating dynamo**, picking up every shot Jessie was slow getting to, playing the back wall, both sides of the court, the ceiling, and up front.

"I could have brought my blankey and taken a nap," Jessie said. Meadow only smiled.

The last game, it was Jessie against Diane and Meadow. She started with some confidence—after all, she wasn't a bad, *bad* player. Besides, she had some of that I-wanna-win energy going for her right now, if only to show Meadow she could do it.

On her first serve, she stepped into the ball, used her wrist, and slammed it out of the serving box. "Ace!" she screamed. Too soon. Meadow killed it neatly against the front wall.

Unfortunately, that play was a prediction of things to come. Jessie served, Meadow killed. "This is getting **monotonous**," Jessie complained halfway through the game.

"Come on, Jess, go for it," Diane urged. "Get that killer instinct going."

"I have it, I have it!" Jessie cried, but the final score was a **humiliating** 21–3.

"Your forehand is improving, Jess," Meadow said kindly as they stepped into the showers. "Your big weakness is your backhand. You should really practice your swing at home."

Was there anything worse than being given advice you hadn't asked for? Yes. Being given advice you hadn't asked for by the person who'd just beaten you thoroughly.

irritating annoying or bothersome

dynamo a forceful person with a lot of energy

monotonous with little or no change; boring

humiliating causing one to feel embarrassed

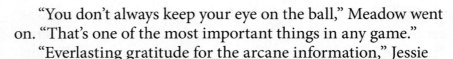

"You don't always keep your eye on the ball," Meadow went on. "That's one of the most important things in any game."

"Everlasting gratitude for the arcane information," Jessie said, grabbing her towel.

"Oh, she's mad," Meadow said. "She's mad about losing."

"Hey, I am not. I love losing. It's so much fun."

"Whenever Jessie's mad, Diane," Meadow said, "she uses words no one understands. *Arcane*. Sounds dirty."

Jessie turned on the hair dryer. "Relax, sweetie, it only means 'secret.' "

"Oh, I know that," Meadow said.

"Oh, sure you do."

They were sneering at each other, but suddenly Meadow grabbed Jessie and mashed their noses together so hard Jessie grunted. "Pig! Pig! Pig!" Meadow said.

Now Jessie was supposed to say "Oink oink oink." In grade school this had been their make-up-the-fight routine.

"Pig! Pig! Pig!" Meadow repeated forcefully.

Tying her sneakers, Diane gave a snorting laugh that sounded almost as piglike as the reply Jessie was supposed to have made. "Oink oink oink," Jessie said finally, **mortified** that Diane was watching this.

But the truth was that, as soon as she said it, she felt much better and loved Meadow again and knew she always would. How could she not love her—they had been friends now for seven years, half her lifetime.

Yes, she would love Meadow and keep her for a friend, no matter what. Even if, she thought, she was beaten at cutthroat every week of her life, she would still love Meadow.

mortified feeling a great sense of shame

Cutthroat   *by Norma Fox Mazer*

Directions Choose the letter of the best answer or write the answer using complete sentences.

Comprehension: Identifying Facts

1. What subject does Jessie feel as if Meadow has forced her to talk about?
   A the high cost of vet care for the kitten
   B Jessie's mother's dislike of the kitten
   C the lack of money in Jessie's family
   D the small size of Jessie's house

2. Where did Jessie and Meadow first meet?
   A at the Y
   B at a vet's office
   C in kindergarten
   D on a racquetball court

3. According to a school psychologist, why does Jessie like routine in a friendship?

4. What causes Jessie to doubt the strength of her friendship with Meadow?

5. What had Jessie and Diane done well together when they first met?

6. What does Jessie exaggerate about Jack Kettle?

7. What does Jessie see on Diane's face that surprises her?

8. What does Meadow say that Jessie does whenever she is mad?

9. Why does Jessie not want to add "Oink oink oink" to Meadow's "Pig! Pig! Pig!"?

10. How does Jessie feel after she says "Oink oink oink"?

Comprehension: Putting Ideas Together

11. In which of the following do Jessie and Meadow differ?
   A family members
   B number of pets
   C size of house
   D all of the above

12. About which of the following does Jessie exaggerate?
   A being furious with Meadow
   B wanting to hit Meadow
   C feeling cozy in Meadow's van
   D telling Meadow about the kitten

13. Why else might Meadow be asking if Diane will be on time?

14. What similarity does Jessie see between her relationship with Meadow and Meadow's relationship with her siblings?

After Reading **continued on next page**

15. How do you think Meadow feels when Jessie tells Diane about Meadow's "fatal crushes"?

16. Why does Jessie wonder if Diane thought she was "just playing Meadow"?

17. What does Jessie's exaggeration that she could have "taken a nap" say about the game?

18. What might be Jessie's motive for using difficult words when she is angry?

19. Describe two of Meadow's character traits.

20. How is Jessie's friendship with Meadow different from her friendship with Diane?

Understanding Literature: Characterization

Characterization is the way a writer develops characters and shows their traits. There are two types of characterization: direct and indirect. With direct characterization, writers make direct statements about the character. With indirect characterization, writers present a character's thoughts, words, and actions. They also present other characters' thoughts about, reactions to, and words said to the character.

21. What direct characterizations does the author make about Meadow and Jessie when first describing their friendship?

22. What do you indirectly learn about Jessie from the story of how she met Diane?

23. Name one thing Meadow does that shows her feelings for Jessie.

24. Is Jessie's frequent exaggerating direct or indirect characterization?

25. What does the end of their conflict tell you about Jessie and Meadow?

Critical Thinking

26. What can you infer about the differences between Jessie and Meadow?

27. Do you think Jessie has the "killer instinct" Diane wants her to show?

28. What do you think is Meadow's motive for giving Jessie advice after the game ends?

29. Were you surprised by how the story ended? Why or why not?

Thinking Creatively

30. Would you change the title of this story? If so, what would you call it and why? If not, why not?

Grammar Check

A sentence fragment is a group of words that does not express a complete thought. Sentence fragments should be avoided in formal writing. However, they are often used in fiction. Writers usually want their characters to seem real and natural. One way to do this is to have characters talk and think in sentence fragments. Here are two fragments from "Cutthroat": "Love-hate, Jessie thought. Like their friendship?"

Find at least five other fragments in the selection. What do they tell you about the characters?

 ## Vocabulary Builder

An idiom is a phrase that has a different meaning than its words really mean. Here is an example from "Cutthroat": *put their heads together*. The idiom means "to share ideas," even though none of the words directly mean this.

The story is full of idioms. Find four others and explain them in your own words.

 ## Writing on Your Own

Write a description of Jessie that shows how she develops as a character. Take into account any words the author uses to describe her. Consider Jessie's own words, thoughts, and actions. Also consider what Meadow and Diane say to her and about her. Before you begin to write, complete a Character Analysis Guide. (See Appendix A for a description of this graphic organizer.)

 ## Listening and Speaking

Dialogue is the conversation among characters in a story. "Cutthroat" contains a lot of dialogue. With one or two classmates, choose a scene to act out. Write the scene, using only the words the characters speak. Add lines of dialogue that will help viewers get the idea of what is not said. After practicing the dialogue, present it to the class. Ask for feedback after the presentation.

  ## Media and Viewing

Watch a movie scene in which two or three young people have a dialogue. Observe how they say their lines. How do they make their lines seem natural? Note their voice and body language. Use what you have observed to improve your presentation of the dialogue you wrote.

Zlateh the Goat   *by Isaac Bashevis Singer*

Isaac Bashevis Singer
1904–1991

Objectives

◆ To read and understand a short story

◆ To identify parts of a story's plot, including rising action, climax, and resolution

◆ To identify and interpret conflict in a short story

About the Author

Isaac Bashevis Singer was born in 1904 in a village in Poland. When he was four, his family moved to Warsaw, the capital city. His father was a rabbi, a Jewish religious leader, who received many visitors at home. Some people came to study and pray, while others came to tell stories. Young Isaac would listen to those stories. He would remember some of them years later when he started writing fiction.

Protests against Jews made Singer leave Poland for New York in 1935. World War II began soon after that. During the war, Jewish neighborhoods of Eastern Europe were destroyed. Singer's mother and a brother were killed as a result. Sorrow stopped Singer from writing for seven years. When he finally started writing again, he wrote about the vanished world he remembered. In many of his stories and novels, he brought Polish neighborhoods and villages to life.

Throughout his life, Singer wrote in his first language of Yiddish. He rewrote many of his stories in English. He strongly believed that a writer had to write in his own language. In 1978 he won the Nobel Prize for Literature. He was the first Yiddish-language author to receive this honor.

About the Selection

Singer wrote many novels, short stories, and works of nonfiction. He was best known for his short stories and collections for children. "Zlateh the Goat" was part of a children's collection first published in 1966. In this story, a boy named Aaron becomes lost in a blizzard. He and his goat must help each other stay alive. Singer thought that serious writers should write about current problems. Yet he also believed that the most important role of fiction is to entertain. "Zlateh the Goat" is proof of this belief.

Literary Terms In most short stories, a main character experiences a **conflict.** A conflict is the main character's struggle against himself or herself, another person, or nature. A story may have several related conflicts. In a short story, the conflict drives the series of events, or **plot.** Most plots follow a similar format. In the beginning, the setting, characters, and basic situation are introduced. Usually an event follows to introduce the main conflict. The conflict increases and the excitement builds during the **rising action.** The plot finally reaches a high point of interest or suspense, called the **climax.** The story moves toward a **resolution,** in which the main conflict is solved. Throughout the action of "Zlateh the Goat," readers come across many **concrete images.** These are images that refer to people and things that can be seen or touched.

Reading on Your Own Using what you already know or have experienced often helps you when making inferences as you read. Think about a situation where you felt unsure of your safety. It may have occurred recently or many years ago. How did you feel before, during, and after the situation? Remember this as you read the story.

Writing on Your Own In this story, a blizzard becomes a deadly enemy for a boy and a goat. A blizzard is one of many problems or dangerous situations that weather can cause. Write a paragraph about the problems natural disasters can cause.

Vocabulary Focus Many words in English are spelled the same but have more than one meaning. There are three in this story: *bound, bored,* and *trace.* As you read, use context clues to figure out their meanings.

Think Before You Read If you were lost in a storm, how do you think you would react?

conflict the struggle of the main character against himself or herself, another person, or nature

plot the series of events in a story

rising action the buildup of excitement in a story

climax the high point of interest or suspense in a story or play

resolution the act of solving the conflict in a story

concrete image people and things that can be seen or touched

Zlateh the Goat

Text copyright © 1966 by Isaac Bashevis Singer, copyright renewed 1994 by Alma Singer. Printed with permission from HarperCollins Publishers.

As you read, think about the types of conflicts that occur in the story.

Hanukkah is a Jewish festival celebrated for eight days in early winter. It is also called the "festival of lights." This is because a candle is lit on each of the eight days.

A *furrier* is a person who makes items of clothing from fur. A *gulden* is a unit of money.

At Hanukkah time the road from the village to the town is usually covered with snow, but this year the winter had been a mild one. Hanukkah had almost come, yet little snow had fallen. The sun shone most of the time. The peasants complained that because of the dry weather there would be a poor harvest of winter grain. New grass sprouted, and the peasants sent their cattle out to pasture.

For Reuven the furrier it was a bad year, and after long hesitation he decided to sell Zlateh the goat. She was old and gave little milk. Feivel the town butcher had offered eight gulden for her. Such a sum would buy Hanukkah candles, potatoes and oil for pancakes, gifts for the children, and other holiday necessaries for the house. Reuven told his oldest boy Aaron to take the goat to town.

Aaron understood what taking the goat to Feivel meant, but had to obey his father. Leah, his mother, wiped the tears from her eyes when she heard the news. Aaron's younger sisters, Anna and Miriam, cried loudly. Aaron put on his quilted jacket and a cap with earmuffs, bound a rope around Zlateh's neck, and took along two slices of bread with cheese to eat on the road. Aaron was supposed to deliver the goat by evening, spend the night at the butcher's, and return the next day with the money.

While the family said goodbye to the goat, and Aaron placed the rope around her neck, Zlateh stood as patiently and good-naturedly as ever. She licked Reuven's hand. She shook her small white beard. Zlateh trusted human beings. She knew that they always fed her and never did her any harm.

When Aaron brought her out on the road to town, she seemed somewhat astonished. She'd never been led in that direction before. She looked back at him questioningly, as if to say, "Where are you taking me?" But after a while she seemed to come to the conclusion that a goat shouldn't ask questions. Still, the road was different. They passed new fields, pastures, and huts with thatched roofs. Here and there a dog barked and came running after them, but Aaron chased it away with his stick.

The sun was shining when Aaron left the village. Suddenly the weather changed. A large black cloud with a bluish center appeared in the east and spread itself rapidly over the sky. A cold wind blew in with it. The crows flew low, croaking. At first it looked as if it would rain, but instead it began to hail as in summer. It was early in the day, but it became dark as dusk. After a while the hail turned to snow.

In his twelve years Aaron had seen all kinds of weather, but he had never experienced a snow like this one. It was so dense it shut out the light of the day. In a short time their path was completely covered. The wind became as cold as ice. The road to town was narrow and winding. Aaron no longer knew

What conflict is resolved when Reuven decides to sell Zlateh?

Reading Strategy: Inferencing

Using what you know already, what can you tell about the family's feelings toward Zlateh?

Summarize the beginning of the story. Describe the setting, characters, and basic situation.

Note the rising action of the story. The excitement is beginning to build.

In what ways are the snow and wind in conflict with Aaron?

where he was. He could not see through the snow. The cold soon **penetrated** his quilted jacket.

At first Zlateh didn't seem to mind the change in weather. She, too, was twelve years old and knew what winter meant. But when her legs sank deeper and deeper into the snow, she began to turn her head and look at Aaron in wonderment. Her mild eyes seemed to ask, "Why are we out in such a storm?" Aaron hoped that a peasant would come along with his cart, but no one passed by.

The snow grew thicker, falling to the ground in large, whirling flakes. Beneath it Aaron's boots touched the softness of a plowed field. He realized that he was no longer on the road. He had gone astray. He could no longer figure out which was east or west, which way was the village, the town. The wind whistled, howled, whirled the snow about in **eddies**. It looked as if white imps were playing tag on the fields. A white dust rose above the ground. Zlateh stopped. She could walk no longer. Stubbornly she anchored her **cleft** hooves in the earth and bleated as if pleading to be taken home. Icicles hung from her white beard, and her horns were **glazed** with frost.

Aaron did not want to admit the danger, but he knew just the same that if they did not find shelter they would freeze to death. This was no ordinary storm. It was a mighty blizzard. The snowfall had reached his knees. His hands were numb, and he could no longer feel his toes. He choked when he breathed. His nose felt like wood, and he rubbed it with snow. Zlateh's bleating began to sound like crying. Those humans in whom she had so much confidence had dragged her into a trap. Aaron began to pray to God for himself and for the innocent animal.

Suddenly he made out the shape of a hill. He wondered what it could be. Who had piled snow into such a huge heap? He moved toward it, dragging Zlateh after him. When he

Think about the writing style in this paragraph. What feeling does it help to present?

Describe the climate in the story.

penetrated passed into	**eddies** currents of air moving in circular motions like little whirlwinds	**cleft** split into two parts
		glazed having a glassy look

came near it, he realized that it was a large haystack which the snow had blanketed.

Aaron realized immediately that they were saved. With great effort he dug his way through the snow. He was a village boy and knew what to do. When he reached the hay, he hollowed out a nest for himself and the goat. No matter how cold it may be outside, in the hay it is always warm. And hay was food for Zlateh. The moment she smelled it she became contented and began to eat. Outside, the snow continued to fall. It quickly covered the passageway Aaron had dug. But a boy and an animal need to breathe, and there was hardly any air in their hideout. Aaron bored a kind of a window through the hay and snow and carefully kept the passage clear.

Zlateh, having eaten her fill, sat down on her hind legs and seemed to have regained her confidence in man. Aaron ate his two slices of bread and cheese, but after the difficult journey he was still hungry. He looked at Zlateh and noticed her udders were full. He lay down next to her, placing himself so that when he milked her he could squirt the milk into his mouth. It was rich and sweet. Zlateh was not accustomed to being milked that way, but she did not resist. On the contrary, she seemed eager to reward Aaron for bringing her to a shelter whose very walls, floor, and ceiling were made of food.

Through the window Aaron could catch a glimpse of the chaos outside. The wind carried before it whole drifts of snow. It was completely dark, and he did not know whether night had already come or whether it was the darkness of the storm. Thank God that in the hay it was not cold. The dried hay, grass, and field flowers **exuded** the warmth of the summer sun. Zlateh ate frequently; she nibbled from above, below, from the left and right. Her body gave forth an animal warmth, and Aaron cuddled up to her. He had always loved Zlateh, but now she was like a sister. He was alone, cut off from his family, and

> How has Aaron's discovery of the haystack resolved his problem for the time being?

> The *udders* of a goat or cow are the parts from which milk comes.

> Zlateh presents a concrete image. Notice how the author describes Aaron's experiences through how Zlateh looks, smells, sounds, and feels.

exuded gave off

wanted to talk. He began to talk to Zlateh. "Zlateh, what do you think about what has happened to us?" he asked.

"Maaaa," Zlateh answered.

"If we hadn't found this stack of hay, we would both be frozen stiff by now," Aaron said.

"Maaaa," was the goat's reply.

"If the snow keeps on falling like this, we may have to stay here for days," Aaron explained.

"Maaaa," Zlateh bleated.

"What does 'maaaa' mean?" Aaron asked. "You'd better speak up clearly."

"Maaaa, maaaa," Zlateh tried.

"Well, let it be 'maaaa' then," Aaron said patiently. "You can't speak, but I know you understand. I need you and you need me. Isn't that right?"

"Maaaa."

Aaron became sleepy. He made a pillow out of some hay, leaned his head on it, and dozed off. Zlateh, too, fell asleep.

When Aaron opened his eyes, he didn't know whether it was morning or night. The snow had blocked up his window. He tried to clear it, but when he had bored through to the length of his arm, he still hadn't reached the outside. Luckily he had his stick with him and was able to break through to the open air. It was still dark outside. The snow continued to fall and the wind wailed, first with one voice and then with many. Sometimes it had the sound of devilish laughter. Zlateh, too, awoke, and when Aaron greeted her, she answered, "Maaaa." Yes, Zlateh's language consisted of only one word, but it meant many things. Now she was saying, "We must accept all that God gives us—heat, cold, hunger, satisfaction, light, and darkness."

Aaron had awakened hungry. He had eaten up his food, but Zlateh had plenty of milk.

For three days Aaron and Zlateh stayed in the haystack. Aaron had always loved Zlateh, but in these three days he loved her more and more. She fed him with her milk and helped him keep warm. She comforted him with her patience. He told her many stories, and she always cocked her ears and

In what way are Aaron and Zlateh still in danger from the storm?

listened. When he patted her, she licked his hand and his face. Then she said, "Maaaa," and he knew it meant, I love you, too.

The snow fell for three days, though after the first day it was not as thick and the wind quieted down. Sometimes Aaron felt that there could never have been a summer, that the snow had always fallen, ever since he could remember. He, Aaron, never had a father or mother or sisters. He was a snow child, born of the snow, and so was Zlateh. It was so quiet in the hay that his ears rang in the stillness. Aaron and Zlateh slept all night and a good part of the day. As for Aaron's dreams, they were all about warm weather. He dreamed of green fields, trees covered with blossoms, clear brooks, and singing birds. By the third night the snow had stopped, but Aaron did not dare to find his way home in the darkness. The sky became clear and the moon shone, casting silvery nets on the snow. Aaron dug his way out and looked at the world. It was all white, quiet, dreaming dreams of heavenly splendor. The stars were large and close. The moon swam in the sky as in a sea.

On the morning of the fourth day Aaron heard the ringing of sleigh bells. The haystack was not far from the road. The peasant who drove the sleigh pointed out the way to him—not to the town and Feivel the butcher, but home to the village. Aaron had decided in the haystack that he would never part with Zlateh.

Aaron's family and their neighbors had searched for the boy and the goat but had found no trace of them during the storm. They feared they were lost. Aaron's mother and sisters cried for him; his father remained silent and gloomy. Suddenly one of the neighbors came running to their house with the news that Aaron and Zlateh were coming up the road.

There was great joy in the family. Aaron told them how he had found the stack of hay and how Zlateh had fed him with her milk. Aaron's sisters kissed and hugged Zlateh and gave her a special treat of chopped carrots and potato peels, which Zlateh gobbled up hungrily.

Reading Strategy:
Inferencing
Think about Aaron's experience in the haystack. Using your own experience, what can you infer about how he feels?

Predict what Aaron will do when he is able to leave the haystack.

How is the family's conflict over selling Zlateh resolved?

A *dreidel* is a small top with Hebrew letters on each of four sides. It is spun in a game played by children.

Nobody ever again thought of selling Zlateh, and now that the cold weather had finally set in, the villagers needed the services of Reuven the furrier once more. When Hanukkah came, Aaron's mother was able to fry pancakes every evening, and Zlateh got her portion, too. Even though Zlateh had her own pen, she often came to the kitchen, knocking on the door with her horns to indicate that she was ready to visit, and she was always admitted. In the evening Aaron, Miriam, and Anna played dreidel. Zlateh sat near the stove watching the children and the flickering of the Hanukkah candles.

Once in a while Aaron would ask her, "Zlateh, do you remember the three days we spent together?"

And Zlateh would scratch her neck with a horn, shake her white bearded head, and come out with the single sound which expressed all her thoughts, and all her love.

AFTER READING THE SELECTION | Apply the Skills

Zlateh the Goat   by Isaac Bashevis Singer

Directions Choose the letter of the best answer or write the answer using complete sentences.

Comprehension: Identifying Facts

1. During what time of year does the story take place?
   - **A** summer
   - **B** fall
   - **C** winter
   - **D** spring

2. What difficult decision does Reuven make?
   - **A** to move his family to the town
   - **B** to stop working as a furrier
   - **C** to not celebrate Hanukkah
   - **D** to sell the family goat

3. Why does Aaron leave with Zlateh for town, even though he does not want to?

4. At what point does Aaron realize he is lost?

5. What shelter does Aaron find?

6. Why is Zlateh happy about the shelter that Aaron finds?

7. Why does Aaron make a hole in the haystack?

8. After Aaron finishes the bread and cheese he has, what is the food that keeps him alive?

9. Why does Aaron not leave the haystack right after the snow stops falling?

10. At the end, how does Reuven's money situation change?

Comprehension: Putting Ideas Together

11. Why is the Hanukkah festival important to the story?
    - **A** Zlateh likes to watch the flickering Hanukkah candles.
    - **B** Reuven decides to sell Zlateh to buy things for Hanukkah.
    - **C** Aaron and his family celebrate Hanukkah every year.
    - **D** Hanukkah is the time of year when an animal is killed.

12. Which of the following is not part of the rising action of the story?
    - **A** Aaron put a rope around Zlateh's neck.
    - **B** The snow grew thicker.
    - **C** A large black cloud appeared in the sky.
    - **D** Aaron's sisters kissed and hugged Zlateh.

13. At what point does Aaron's situation become similar to Zlateh's?

14. Name two details that support the inference that Aaron is quick-thinking and brave.

15. How do Aaron and Zlateh help each other during the storm?

16. Why does Aaron begin to think of Zlateh like a family member?

17. What is the most likely reason that Aaron thinks Zlateh's "Maaaa" means many different things?

18. Why does Aaron probably dream about warm weather?

19. What is the most important effect of the blizzard in this story?

20. Why does the family start allowing Zlateh to enter the house whenever she "knocks"?

Understanding Literature: Conflict

The conflict in a short story is the main character's struggle against something or someone. The conflict can be of three types. It may be between the character and another person. It may be between the character and nature or other conditions in his or her life. It may be between the character and himself or herself. These first two types of conflict are called external, which means "outside." The third type is called internal, which means "inside." A short story may have more than one conflict.

21. What is Reuven's conflict at the beginning of the story?

22. Is Reuven's conflict internal or external? Explain your answer.

23. What conflict does the family experience because of Reuven's struggles?

24. Aaron and Zlateh need food and shelter, yet they are caught in a blizzard. Is this conflict external or internal? Why?

25. How does Aaron resolve this conflict?

Critical Thinking

26. Why would the author use Zlateh's name but not Aaron's in the title?

27. Describe how Zlateh's feelings toward humans change during the course of the story.

28. Was Aaron right not to obey his father's order to take Zlateh to the butcher? Why or why not?

29. What do you think is a main message of this story? Support your answer with details.

Thinking Creatively

30. How would the story be different if Zlateh were a different animal than a goat?

After Reading continued on next page

Grammar Check

Every verb has four main forms, or principal parts. These parts are used to form verb tenses that show time. They include present, present participle, past, and past participle. Regular verbs form their past tense and past participles by adding *-ed* or *-d*. Irregular verbs form these tenses in different ways.

	Regular	**Irregular**
Present	talk	drive
Present Participle	(am) talking	(am) driving
Past	talked	drove
Past Participle	(have) talked	(have) driven

Reread the first two paragraphs of the story. Find at least two examples of the following: a regular past tense, an irregular past tense, and an irregular past participle. Find one example of a regular past participle.

 ### Vocabulary Builder

Make the vocabulary words from the story become part of your working vocabulary. Work with a partner to pronounce the words and use them in at least one sentence. Check a dictionary if you are unsure about their pronunciations.

 ### Writing on Your Own

Imagine that Aaron was trying to persuade his father not to sell Zlateh. Write a short speech that Aaron might use to do this. In the first paragraph, state a position in favor of keeping the goat. Then support this position with reasons Reuven would most likely agree with. Revise your speech to remove one or two of the weaker reasons you included.

 ### Listening and Speaking

A monologue is a speech given by one person. Speaking as Zlateh, deliver a monologue. In the monologue say what you think about the humans' behavior. Change the tone and volume of your voice to show your feelings. Use facial expressions to show the meanings of your words.

 ### Research and Technology

A *shtetl* was a Jewish village in Eastern Europe. With a small group, find out about shtetls on the Internet. Ask questions like, What were the homes in a shtetl like? How did most people make a living? What responsibilities might a 12-year-old boy have had? Prepare a chart that shows what Aaron's day-to-day life might have been like.

Textbooks

In Part 1, you are learning about making inferences in literature. Inferences are also helpful when reading textbooks. Knowing that "Zlateh the Goat" takes place in Poland helps you make inferences about Polish customs. Other reading materials help you make inferences about the population and land of modern Poland. You can use the textbook article, maps, and charts that follow to do this.

About Textbooks

A textbook gives factual information about a subject, such as math or world history. The purpose of a textbook is to help students learn new information. The information is usually divided into units, chapters, and sections. Questions and activities throughout the textbook help students review what they have read. Textbooks also include aids and text features to help readers understand and use the information. Some examples follow.

Text Aids	Text Features
• chapter titles • main headings and subheadings • highlighted vocabulary	• maps, graphs, and charts • photographs, drawings, and diagrams with captions

Reading Skill

Text aids and text features organize details in a textbook and highlight important information. Here are some tips for using text aids and text features effectively.

Tips for Using Text Aids and Text Features

❑ Headings and subheadings tell you the main ideas of the chapters.
❑ Maps, graphs, and charts help you understand the main ideas of the chapters.
❑ Pictures and diagrams with captions give examples or explain the main ideas of the chapters.

POLAND

Tradition in Poland

> Notice the title "Poland" and the subhead "Tradition in Poland." These give you the main ideas of the chapter.

Since Poland's communist government fell, the country has moved away from a communist economy in which the government owned and ran all the businesses.

> *Free enterprise* is a vocabulary term and an important idea. It is boldfaced to stand out.

Instead, Poland has adopted the **free enterprise** system, or capitalism. In it, people can run their own businesses. But not all of life in Poland has changed. As you travel in the countryside, you see signs of a way of life that existed long before communist rule.

The Polish Countryside For a look at tradition in Poland, you might visit the northeast corner of the country. Here, the Polish border has shifted many times. Again and again, other countries have seized this area. Sometimes, it belonged to Russia. At other times, it was controlled by Lithuania (lith oo ay nee uh) or Germany. There were even times when other countries took over all of Poland. But no matter what happened, the traditions of Polish life stayed the same. This is true even today.

Farms dot the countryside on the way to the Tatra Mountains in Poland.

After World War II, Poland became a communist nation. At public festivals, Poles had to pledge loyalty to communism. When crops did not grow, Poles relied on money from the communist government. When Poles were sick, they went to doctors who were paid by the government. When they were too old to farm, they knew they would receive a government pension.

Now all that has changed. It is up to the farmer to save money for old age. If the crops fail, the farmer must try to borrow money to start again. Learning this new way of life has been hard for some Poles.

The Polish Language Like Roman Catholicism, the language of the Poles has also stood the test of time. Some foreign rulers banned the use of Polish in schools and in the government. The communists did not ban Polish but did force Polish schoolchildren to learn Russian, the main language of the Soviet Union.

Today, the Polish language is alive and well. It ties the people of the nation together and it gives them the strong feeling that being Polish is something different and special. As a Slavic language, it also links the nation to other Slavic nations in Eastern Europe.

These two graphics help readers understand information in the chapter. One is a pie chart about the labor force. The other is a line graph showing how much money is received from exports.

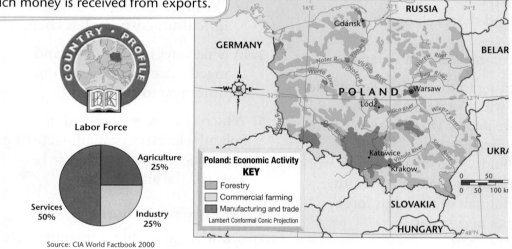

COUNTRY · PROFILE

Labor Force

Agriculture 25%

Services 50%

Industry 25%

Source: CIA World Factbook 2000

Poland: Economic Activity
KEY
- Forestry
- Commercial farming
- Manufacturing and trade

Lambert Conformal Conic Projection

GERMANY, Gdánsk, RUSSIA, BELAR, Notec R., Vistula R., Narew River, Bug River, Warta River, Notec R., Vistula River, POLAND, Warsaw, 52°N, Łódź, Pilica River, Wieprz River, UKRA, Katowice, Vistula River, San River, Krakow, SLOVAKIA, HUNGARY, 48°N, 52°N, 16°E, 20°E, 24°E

0 50
0 50 100 km

Income From Agricultural Exports

Millions of Dollars: 3,000 / 2,500 / 2,000 / 1,500 / 1,000 / 500 / 0

Year: 1965, 1970, 1975, 1980, 1985, 1990, 1995, 1999

Source: Food and agriculture Organization of the United Nations

Visuals such as maps, graphs, and charts give readers additional information at a glance.

Economics The map and charts show the importance of agriculture in Poland. **Map and Chart Study** (a) Look at the information on this page and list three pieces of evidence that show that agriculture is important to Poland.

(b) How much money did Poland make from agricultural exports in 1999?

Monitor Your Progress

Directions Choose the letter of the best answer or write the answer using complete sentences.

1. According to the map of Poland, which statement is true?
   A Most of the land is used for commercial farming.
   B Most of the land is used for forestry.
   C Poland shares a border with Hungary.
   D Germany is east of Poland.

2. According to the "Labor Force" pie chart, which statement is true?
   A More people work in agriculture than in industry.
   B About twice as many people work in industry than in agriculture.
   C About half of the labor force works in services.
   D Today, there are only 25 agricultural workers in Poland.

3. Which statement can be proven by making inferences from this chapter's headings and subheadings?
   A Two important parts of Polish tradition come from its countryside and its language.
   B Poland's economy has switched to capitalism.
   C The communists forced Polish students to learn Russian.
   D The income from Poland's agricultural exports has risen.

4. In what ways has life in Poland changed since it switched from communism to capitalism?

5. Which is more widespread in Poland—forestry or manufacturing and trade? What text feature helped you find the answer?

Writing on Your Own

Explain why agriculture (or commercial farming) is important to the people and the economy of Poland. Support your answer with details from the text aids and features.

COMPARING LITERARY WORKS | Build Understanding

Lillian and Grand-père   by Sharon Hart Addy

About the Author

Sharon Hart Addy has been a writer for more than 20 years. She has written stories, picture books, poetry, and articles. Many of her stories have appeared in magazines for children and young adults. Addy has covered many topics in her writing, but her main interest is historical stories. In *A Visit with Great-Grandma*, a girl and her great-grandmother speak different languages. This award-winning book explores how they are still able to communicate. Addy's interest in the Old West appears in her picture book *When Wishes Were Horses*.

One of her more recent books, *Lucky Jake*, was inspired by her mother. Her mother grew up in difficult times during the Great Depression. She believed that "luck is a combination of using what you have and working hard." This idea can be seen in *Lucky Jake*, which takes place during the Gold Rush. Among her nonfiction is a book entitled *Kidding Around Milwaukee*. Addy lives in Wisconsin; this book tells about interesting things in her state's largest city.

About the Selection

"Lillian and Grand-père" appeared in the magazine *Cricket* in 2005. Lillian is a girl who changes the way she thinks about her grandfather. She calls him Grand-père, which is French for "grandfather." Only six months earlier, he and Grand-mère, Lillian's grandmother, left France. They have settled in a small town in North America near Lake Ontario. Lillian speaks both French and English, but Grand-père still speaks only French.

As you read "Lillian and Grand-père," compare Lillian's experience to Jessie's in "Cutthroat." Pay attention to what is similar or different in how each meets her needs.

Sharon Hart Addy
1943–

Objectives

- ◆ To read and understand a short story
- ◆ To identify features of third-person point of view
- ◆ To compare character development in two short stories

Comparing **continued on next page**

Lillian and Grand-père   *by Sharon Hart Addy*

narrator one who tells a story

point of view the position from which the author or storyteller tells the story

third person a point of view where the narrator is not a character, and refers to characters as *he* or *she*

Literary Terms The **narrator** of a story is the one who tells it. The author usually creates a character, or "voice," to be the narrator. The **point of view** is the position from which the author or storyteller tells the story. **Third person** is a point of view in which the narrator is not a character. In third person, the narrator refers to characters as *he* or *she*. "Lillian and Grand-père" and "Cutthroat" are both told from the third-person point of view.

Reading on Your Own Think about ways that point of view might change how a story's events are told. How would "Cutthroat" be different if the author had used first-person point of view? Think about this as you read "Lillian and Grand-père."

Writing on Your Own Write a paragraph about an interesting experience you had with another person. However, do not tell about it using *I, me, my,* and *mine*. Instead, as the narrator, tell about the experience from a third-person point of view.

Vocabulary Focus "Lillian and Grand-père" contains many words and phrases in French. They appear in italics. Look for words, phrases, and sentences near each French word or phrase to find its meaning.

Think Before Your Read Has the way you once thought about someone changed over time? Did it change for the better—or for the worse? Compare your experience with what happens to Lillian.

Lillian and Grand-père

Lillian held her long skirt and stepped from the farm wagon's high seat to the dusty road. She lifted her **valise** from the wagon bed and carried it to the wooden walk in front of Grand-père's clock shop.

She looked back at her brother Pierre. The horses' reins lay in his hands as he watched smoke puff across the clear sky from a locomotive on the new railroad line.

Lillian asked, "Aren't you coming in?"

Pierre looked at her and laughed. "And face Grand-père?"

"It's not yet noon. He will be working." She pleaded with her eyes. "Grand-mère may have lemonade."

Pierre laughed again. "Not even for lemonade with a great ice chip on this hot day. It is you they want. You with your fine English. I will be back next week, when the apples are to be shipped." He signaled to the horses and rode off.

Lillian turned to the clock shop. She wondered why she had been summoned. Perhaps Grand-mère wanted her to help with customers. That would be pleasant. If she stayed in the shop, she would not **encounter** Grand-père.

The shop's door opened. Grand-mère called, "*Bonjour, ma petite!*" She held out her arms, and Lillian hugged her. Grand-mère said, "Come," and **ushered** Lillian inside.

Lillian stepped into the cool, dim shop. It looked just as it had six months earlier when Grand-mère and Grand-père had come from France and set it up. Clocks sat on shelves along one wall. On the opposite wall, hanging clocks swung their **pendulum** tails in measured arcs. Ticking filled the room. Lillian smiled as she imagined the wheels and **cogs** inside the clocks clinking off bits of time.

As you read, notice how the point of view affects how you "see" Grand-père.

In the days before refrigerators readily provided ice cubes, ice was an uncommon treat.

Reading Strategy: Inferencing

What can you infer about Grand-père so far?

The word *petite* means "small" in French. You can tell from the surrounding text that *Bonjour, ma petite!* is a greeting. It means "Good morning, my little one!"

valise a traveling bag	**pendulum** the part of a clock that hangs down and swings	**cogs** the teeth around a wheel or gear
encounter to run into		
ushered directed to a place		

Anglais is French for "English." *Le français* refers to the language of French.

Reading Strategy:
Inferencing
Explaining cause and effect can help you make inferences. Explain why Lillian has been sent for.

Lake Ontario is the smallest of the five Great Lakes. It is located between the state of New York and the Canadian province of Ontario.

When Grand-père wants something, he pulls a cord that makes a bell ring in the kitchen. The author could have used *rang* instead of *jangled*. What is the effect of using *jangled*?

Grand-mère pointed to several old clocks in a glass cabinet behind the counter. "Not all people want the new machine-made clocks of Seth Thomas. Gentlemen ask if the old, handmade clocks they carried from Europe can be repaired. That is why we need you with your *anglais*. *Le français* is not much spoken here."

"You speak well," Lillian answered.

"I was lucky to learn as a child. I also can practice with customers and neighbors. Grand-père learns little, alone in his workshop. This would not be a problem if Grand-père and I had settled in New York City. Many speak French there. But we followed your family farther west. The land gives many grapes and apples near Lake Ontario, but few French come to grow them. Grand-père must learn the language of our new country. You will help him." She smiled.

Lillian smiled in return, but her heart thumped as she thought of Grand-père, who never smiled.

Grand-mère led the way to the living quarters. Lillian took off her straw hat as she followed.

In the kitchen, Grand-mère said, "We will have lemonade." She nodded toward the icebox. "You will have some?"

Lillian chipped a **sliver** of ice from the block, pleased to be offered this treat. She dropped the slippery bit into the glass of lemonade Grand-mère held out to her.

A bell on the kitchen wall jangled. Grand-mère explained, "Grand-père wants coffee. The heat does not bother him. You will take it to him."

While the coffee boiled, Lillian searched for courage. If she was very quiet when she entered the room, Grand-père might not know she was there. She would put the coffee near him and leave quickly. He would have no reason to unleash his sharp tongue as he had when Pierre dropped a parcel during the last visit.

sliver a thin, sometimes sharp piece of a material

Grand-mère handed Lillian the steaming cup on a saucer. "Do not knock," Grand-mère advised her. "Open the door and go in."

Balancing the cup on the saucer, Lillian walked the hall to Grand-père's workroom.

She turned the knob and pushed. The door swung easily and banged against the wall. Lillian stood as still as the ladder-back chair Grand-père sat in at his worktable. Grand-père's gray head jerked, creasing the collar of his blue work **smock**, but the tool in his hand remained perfectly still.

> **smock** a loose piece of clothing worn to protect the clothes underneath it

At this point the rising action of the story begins.

Reading Strategy: **Inferencing**

When Lillian enters, Grand-père moves suddenly without upsetting his tools. What does this tell you about him?

Lillian tiptoed to him, her eyes caught by the clockwork before Grand-père. She slid the coffee onto a corner of the table.

Grand-père's sharp "Bah!" broke her stare. "Clumsy, thoughtless girl," he growled in French. His finger **jabbed** at the pile of clock parts around the saucer. "Look what you have done! These pieces are plowed into a heap as if they were **clods** of dirt. It will take hours to sort them and check for damage. These are not machine-made parts! They are old! They must be handled carefully. What were you thinking? Do you think at all?"

Covering her face, Lillian fled. In the kitchen, she cried on Grand-mère's shoulder.

"His anger is sharp," Grand-mère whispered, "but it is short. Learn from it. What sent him into a rage?"

"I slid the coffee onto the table and moved pieces."

Grand-mère sighed. "That you must never do. Everything must be left where he puts it."

At noon, Lillian asked to eat in the kitchen while Grand-mère and Grand-père ate in the dining room. She had no courage to face Grand-père again.

After lunch, Lillian gathered the dishes and prepared to wash them.

Grand-mère nodded her approval. "I will take the pickle **crock** to the cellar." She picked up the crock and moved toward the cellar door. "We did not have pickles until we came to *Amérique*. They are good. I am glad your *maman* shared them with us." Grand-mère opened the door to the stairs, lifted her long skirt, and took the first step.

A cat yowled, and Grand-mère gave a startled "Oh!" Thumping sounds followed. Grand-père's bell jangled. Lillian ignored it and ran down the steps to Grand-mère.

Grand-mère sat in a puddle of pickles and **brine**.

"Grand-mère! Are you hurt?"

Amérique means "America." Notice how similar the spellings of these words are. From this clue, what would you guess *maman* means?

jabbed poked quickly or suddenly	**crock** a clay pot used to store food items	**brine** very salty water
clods lumps		

"*Non*," Grand-mère answered, laughing. "But the pickles are."

Lillian took the crock from Grand-mère. "Let me help you up."

"I will do that!" Grand-père's French boomed from the kitchen doorway. He thundered down the stairs.

Lillian backed away as Grand-père kicked pickles aside and lifted Grand-mère to her feet.

Grand-mère **winced** as she stood. Lillian rushed to her side.

Grand-père waved Lillian away like a bothersome fly. He wrapped his arm around Grand-mère. She leaned against him. They went up the stairs together.

Lillian **salved** her hurt feelings by cleaning up the pickle mess.

When Lillian returned to the kitchen, Grand-mère sat in a wooden chair on a pillow. Her foot rested on a low stool from the sitting room. "My ankle hurts," she explained with a twinkle in her eye, "and my bottom is sore from bouncing."

When their laughter **subsided**, hoofbeats drew Lillian to the window. Peeking around the window shade, she watched a boy jump from a delivery wagon and lift a wooden box from the wagon bed.

Lillian said, "Someone is bringing a crate."

"Go," Grand-mère said. "Bring him here."

Lillian led the boy to the kitchen. He set the crate on the table, took an envelope off the top, and handed it to Grand-mère.

She opened the envelope and scanned the paper inside. "It is in *français*. Grand-père must see this."

Lillian glanced at the delivery boy.

"No, *ma chère*," Grand-mère told her. "You must take it."

Lillian trembled as she carried the envelope. She opened the workroom door carefully and held the knob so the door would not hit the wall.

Ma chère means "my dear." Why does Grand-mère tell Lillian that she must take the paper to Grand-père? What does Lillian think will happen?

winced drew back, as in pain **salved** calmed **subsided** became less

Grand-père was bent over the toothed wheels, tiny screws, and other clock bits that covered his table. His smock stretched across his shoulders as he reached for something she could not see.

Lillian tiptoed to the worktable. She stood beside it, hoping Grand-père would see her so she wouldn't need to speak.

Grand-père slid his eyeglasses to the top of his head and picked up his **loupe**. He set the eyepiece against his right eye and **probed** the clockwork before him.

Lillian thought longingly of the kitchen. Grand-mère would be laughing as she talked with the delivery boy. He would be enjoying the coolness of the kitchen, where a breeze fluttered the window shades. But he could not **dally** long. His wagon was full of packages to be delivered. Grand-père must read the message. "Grand-père," she whispered.

He did not reply.

She kept her eyes from the clockwork that pulled at her attention. "*Excusez-moi*, Grand-père."

Excusez-moi means "excuse me." Why is Grand-père so upset with what Lillian says?

Although the tweezers in Grand-père's hand remained perfectly still, his head jerked up. "*Anglais!*" he demanded.

Lillian stepped back. "Delivery boy—" She held out the letter and pointed toward the door.

With a scowl, Grand-père took the loupe from his eye and snatched the letter from her. He patted his smock pockets and scanned the table. In French he commanded, "Find my spectacles!"

Lillian stared at the glasses perched on his head. How could he not know they were there? She reached to her own head. Wouldn't he feel them?

Why does the author include this part about Grand-père's spectacles? What does it tell you about Grand-père?

Grand-père looked toward the shelves behind her as she touched her head. He said, "Ah," and dropped the glasses into place. He read the letter quickly, then stood up.

His fingers **prodded** her shoulder. "*Va-t'en!*" He ordered her to go.

---

loupe a type of magnifying glass worn close to the eye

probed searched into

dally to waste time

prodded poked

Laughter floated from the kitchen. Lillian ran to the sound. "Grand-père," she gasped to Grand-mère and the delivery boy, "is coming."

Grand-père's heavy steps took him to the crate on the table. "*C'est l'horloge de Monsieur LaRouix*," Grand-père explained to Grand-mère.

Lillian **translated** to herself as Grand-père continued in French. The clock is old, very special to the family. If it cannot be repaired, it is to go back.

Grand-père **pried** open the wooden crate and removed a cloth-wrapped bundle. He opened the fabric and **revealed** a pendulum shelf clock decorated with tiny, painted flowers.

Grand-père paid no heed to the clock's beauty. He turned it over, examined the workings, and muttered something in French.

"It stays," Grand-mère explained to the delivery boy.

Grand-père looked at Lillian. "*Viens*." He gestured toward the empty crate.

Lillian glanced at Grand-mère, who nodded encouragement. Lillian picked up the crate and followed Grand-père.

In the workroom, Grand-père pointed to the floor under a small table. Lillian set the box in place, then stepped away, ready to flee to the safety of the kitchen.

Grand-père stared at her over the rim of his glasses.

Lillian swallowed to quiet the jitters within her. She would be brave. She would not let him frighten her.

C'est l'horloge de Monsieur LaRouix means "This is Mr. LaRouix's clock."

Reading Strategy: Inferencing

Predicting is a helpful strategy for making inferences. Predict what is going to happen to Lillian in Grand-père's workroom.

---

translated changed to or from another language

pried used force to draw out

revealed showed; made known

"*Toi.*" He pointed to a spot beside the table.

She stepped to her place. Grand-père spread a cloth on the table and positioned the clock on it.

He folded his glasses and dropped them into a pocket. In French he said, "This is a handmade clock. If a part falls, you must search for it." Grand-père pointed to several long, flat basins on a shelf across the room. "*Apporte-les.*"

Lillian collected the basins and brought them to Grand-père. He positioned them on the table and filled them with a clear liquid.

Lillian watched, entranced, as he removed tiny screws, toothed wheels, and other special parts, then arranged them in the basins. "*Nettoie-les.*" He glanced at Lillian.

She supplied the English. "To clean them."

Grand-père repeated the phrase.

Lillian stood, waiting for him to remove the pieces from their bath. She was eager to watch him put each piece in place so the clock would click and clack with the rhythm of time, but Grand-père grunted his satisfaction and got up from his stool.

Lillian moved toward the door and freedom. Grand-père's voice caught her.

"Tomorrow," he said in French, "we reassemble the clock. Tell Grand-mère dinner at seven today." To himself he mumbled, "I trust we will not have pickles."

Reading Strategy: Inferencing

Why does Lillian bite her lip "to hold in her smile"? What does this tell you about her feelings for Grand-père?

What do you think is Lillian's "good news"?

Lillian pictured Grand-mère in the puddle of pickles. She bit her lip to hold in her smile. Grand-père did not make jokes. Or did he? She peeked at him. The **glint** in his eye made her wonder.

Her glance fell on the clock parts. Tomorrow she would watch the miracle as they became a ticking whole! She smiled and whispered, "Thank you, Grand-père."

She turned the door handle carefully, stepped into the hall, and closed the door slowly, silently. Then she raced to tell Grand-mère the good news.

glint sparkle

COMPARING LITERARY WORKS | Apply the Skills

Lillian and Grand-père   by Sharon Hart Addy

Directions Choose the letter of the best answer or write the answer using complete sentences.

Comprehension: Identifying Facts

1. What does Lillian say to persuade her brother to go inside their grandparents' house?
   A that the house will be cool
   B that it is his duty to greet them
   C that he may get to drink lemonade
   D that he must rest before going home

2. What does Lillian hope is the reason for which she has been sent?
   A to teach her grandparents English
   B to wait on customers in the shop
   C to learn how to repair clocks
   D to help her grandmother with housework

3. Why did Pierre not want to go inside his grandparents' house?

4. Why does Grand-père get angry when Lillian slides the coffee onto his work table?

5. What is Lillian's reaction to the jangling bell after Grand-mère falls on the stairs?

6. Why does Lillian prefer being in the kitchen rather than delivering a message to Grand-père?

7. When does Grand-père first seem to value Lillian's help with English?

8. What does Jessie in "Cutthroat" hope will happen between Meadow and Diane? What does Lillian hope will happen when she arrives at her grandparents' house? Does either one get her wish?

9. Name one thing that upsets Lillian and one thing that upsets Jessie.

10. What is humorous at the end of each story?

Comprehension: Putting Ideas Together

11. Which character in "Lillian and Grand-père," tries to help Lillian understand Grand-père?
    A Lillian's brother
    B Pierre
    C the delivery boy
    D Grand-mère

12. Why does Jessie plan for Meadow to meet Diane?
    A She wants her closest friends to like each other.
    B She thinks Meadow could learn more about racquetball.
    C She hopes Diane can introduce Meadow to Jack Kettle.
    D She wants to play a really good game of cutthroat.

Comparing continued on next page

Lillian and Grand-père   by Sharon Hart Addy

13. Which words or phrases work well to describe Jessie and Lillian?

14. What purpose does a character like Diane serve in "Cutthroat"?

15. Compare the setting of both "Cutthroat" and "Lillian and Grand-père."

16. What do Jessie and Meadow have in common?

17. Do Lillian and Grand-père have anything in common? Explain.

18. What is the climax of each story?

19. Why are Jessie and Lillian happy at the end of each story?

20. What has Jessie learned by the end of the story? What has Lillian learned?

Understanding Literature: Characterization

Characterization is the way a writer develops character qualities and personality traits. Writers may describe or tell about a character. They may develop a character by letting other characters tell about that character. They can also let a character indirectly show readers things about himself or herself.

21. Name at least one direct way and one indirect way the author develops Meadow's personality.

22. Name at least one direct way and one indirect way the author develops Grand-père's personality.

23. What is different in the way the authors developed Meadow and Grand-père? What is similar?

24. Jessie and Lillian each begin to "see" another character differently. Where does this happen in each story?

25. Choose a character from each story. How did the author make that character "real" to you?

Critical Thinking

26. How does the style of writing in "Cutthroat" differ from that of "Lillian and Grand-père"?

27. Think about Meadow and Grand-père. What was unexpected about each of their personalities?

28. With which character do you identify more—Jessie or Lillian?

29. Do the two stories have a similar important message? Explain.

Thinking Creatively

30. Imagine each story took place in the other story's setting. How would each be the same or different?

Grammar Check

An indirect quotation is not the exact words that a person says, thinks, or writes. An example is *Lillian wondered why she had been summoned*. A direct quotation is the exact words and is usually set off in quotation marks. The author of "Lillian and Grand-père" might have used the following direct quotation: *"Why have I been summoned?" Lillian wondered*. Which are used more in "Cutthroat" and "Lillian and Grand-père"—direct or indirect quotations? Scan the stories to find the answer.

 Vocabulary Builder

The Latin root -*spec*- means "look or see." *Spectacles* is a word that comes from this Latin root. It is a word for glasses that are used to see better. Look up the meaning of each of the following words in a dictionary: *inspector, spectacle, spectator, speculate*. Explain how each meaning relates to the idea of "look or see." Then use each word in a sentence.

 Writing on Your Own

Jessie and Lillian live in very different situations and historical times. However, there are similarities between them. Write a response to literature in which you compare the two characters. Use a thesaurus to find interesting words to use in your response. Before you begin writing, use a Venn Diagram to record helpful details. (See Appendix A for a description of this graphic organizer.)

 Listening and Speaking

In a small group, hold a casual discussion to consider this question: Should you make a judgment about people based on their words and actions?

Each group member should offer his or her opinion backed up with personal experiences. Events from "Cutthroat" and "Lillian and Grand-père" may also be used as support.

 Research and Technology

Explore the history of objects used to tell time. Discover the differences between the clocks Grand-père works on and the "new machine-made clocks of Seth Thomas." Use *clocks* and *history* as the search keywords.

Part 2

Reading Strategy:
Inferencing

Readers use inferences to find meaning in a text when the meaning is not directly stated. Another way to describe an inference is "drawing conclusions." This is connecting details to make decisions or form opinions about a text—to make meaning of a text. Drawing conclusions is just another term for inferencing.

**What You Know + What You Read =
Inference (Draw Conclusions)**

Literary Terms

theme the main idea of a literary work

first person a point of view where the narrator is also a character, using the pronouns *I* and *we*

figurative language writing or speech not meant to be understood exactly as it is written

suspense a quality in a story that makes the reader uncertain or nervous about what will happen next

dialogue the conversation among characters in a story

BEFORE READING THE SELECTION | Build Understanding

The Circuit   by Francisco Jiménez

About the Author

Francisco Jiménez was born in Mexico. When he was four, his family left their small village and moved to California. They were hoping to find work in the United States. In California, the family became migrant workers. Like the narrator in "The Circuit," Jiménez could not go to school until the harvest had ended. However, when he was not in school, he still learned. He once said, "I came to realize that learning and knowledge were the only stable things in my life. Whatever I learned in school, that knowledge would stay with me no matter how many times we moved."

Francisco Jiménez

Soon after he started high school, the family's situation changed. His father could no longer do migrant work because of back pains. The family stayed in one place, and Jiménez was able to be a full-time student. His excellent grades won him three college scholarships. He went on to become an outstanding teacher, as well as an award-winning writer.

Objectives

- ◆ To read and understand a short story
- ◆ To identify the theme of a short story
- ◆ To identify first-person point of view

About the Selection

"The Circuit" is about a family of migrant workers. Migrant workers pick crops when they are ready to be harvested. Most migrant workers in the United States move often, as crops ripen. In some places migrant workers live in labor camps near the fields where they work. The whole family usually travels together, with children helping adults in the fields. In some cases children start school late in the fall to help with the harvest. In other cases they leave early in the spring. In "The Circuit," Panchito is the narrator. He starts school the first week in November after the grape harvest is over.

Before Reading continued on next page

The Circuit — by Francisco Jiménez

theme the main idea of a literary work

first person a point of view where the narrator is also a character, using the pronouns *I* and *we*

figurative language writing or speech not meant to be understood exactly as it is written

Literary Terms A **theme** is the main idea of a literary work. In many works, including "The Circuit," the author does not directly state the theme. The narrator of a story is the one who tells it. The author usually creates a character, or "voice," to be the narrator. "The Circuit" is told in **first person**. First person is a point of view where the narrator is also a character. The narrator uses the pronouns *I* and *we*. Authors often use **figurative language** to express ideas in vivid or imaginative ways. Figurative language is writing or speech not meant to be understood exactly as it is written. You will find examples of figurative language in "The Circuit."

Reading on Your Own Think back to "Cutthroat" and "Lillian and Grand-père." Both stories were told in third-person point of view. As you read "The Circuit," think about how the first-person point of view affects you. What if it had been told in the third-person point of view?

Writing on Your Own Imagine regularly having to be the "new kid" at school. This is what would happen if your family moved a lot because of work. At first, you would probably feel like an outsider in each new school. Write either a poem or a few paragraphs describing your experiences as the "new kid." Include many details and use first-person point of view.

Vocabulary Focus This story contains several words, phrases, and sentences in Spanish. As you read, keep a list of Spanish words and their meanings. Look for clues to their meaning in the text. If you do not speak Spanish, ask others to help you with pronunciation.

Think Before You Read A *circuit* is a circular line or path that goes around an object or an area. As you read, think about how this idea applies to the story.

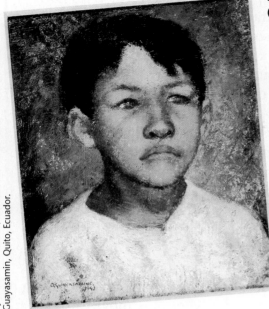

Oil on wood, 15-7/8 x 12-3/4". The Museum of Modern Art/Licensed by Scala-Art Resource, NY. Inter-American Fund. Museo Fundacion Guayasamin, Quito, Ecuador.

My Brother, 1942, Guayasamin
(Oswaldo Guayasamin Calero)

THE CIRCUIT

As you read, pay special attention to how the main character thinks about events. This will help you discover the story's theme.

It was that time of year again. Ito, the strawberry sharecropper, did not smile. It was natural. The peak of the strawberry season was over and the last few days the workers, most of them *braceros*, were not picking as many boxes as they had during the months of June and July.

A *sharecropper* works to own part of the harvested crops. *Braceros* are migrant Mexican farm laborers who harvest crops.

As the last days of August disappeared, so did the number of *braceros*. Sunday, only one—the best picker—came to work. I liked him. Sometimes we talked during our half-hour lunch break. That is how I found out he was from Jalisco, the same state in Mexico my family was from. That Sunday was the last time I saw him.

Jalisco is located in the west-central part of Mexico.

When the sun had tired and sunk behind the mountains, Ito signaled us that it was time to go home. "*Ya esora,*" he yelled in his broken Spanish. Those were the words I waited for twelve hours a day, every day, seven days a week, week after week. And the thought of not hearing them again saddened me.

Notice that the narrator uses *I, we,* and *my* instead of *he, they,* and *his.*

Ya esora means "It's time." In other words, it is time to quit working and go home.

What clues do this event and the narrator's actions give you about the theme?

Fresno is a city in central California. Predict what is waiting for Panchito and his family there.

As we drove home Papá did not say a word. With both hands on the wheel, he stared at the dirt road. My older brother, Roberto, was also silent. He leaned his head back and closed his eyes. Once in a while he cleared from his throat the dust that blew in from outside.

Yes, it was that time of year. When I opened the front door to the shack, I stopped. Everything we owned was neatly packed in cardboard boxes. Suddenly I felt even more the weight of hours, days, weeks, and months of work. I sat down on a box. The thought of having to move to Fresno and knowing what was in store for me there brought tears to my eyes.

That night I could not sleep. I lay in bed thinking about how much I hated this move.

A little before five o'clock in the morning, Papá woke everyone up. A few minutes later, the yelling and screaming of my little brothers and sisters, for whom the move was a great adventure, broke the silence of dawn. Shortly, the barking of the dogs accompanied them.

While we packed the breakfast dishes, Papá went outside to start the "Carcanchita." That was the name Papá gave his old '38 black Plymouth. He bought it in a used-car lot in Santa Rosa in the winter of 1949. Papá was very proud of his little **jalopy**. He had a right to be proud of it. He spent a lot of time looking at other cars before buying this one. When he finally chose the "Carcanchita," he checked it thoroughly before driving it out of the car lot. He examined every inch of the car. He listened to the motor, tilting his head from side to side like a parrot, trying to **detect** any noises that spelled car trouble. After being satisfied with the looks and sounds of the car, Papá then insisted on knowing who the **original** owner was. He never did find out from the car salesman, but he bought the car anyway. Papá figured the original owner must have been an important man because behind the rear seat of the car he found a blue necktie.

Think about the phrase "tilting his head from side to side like a parrot." How does this figurative language help you understand Papá's actions?

jalopy an old car in bad condition   **detect** to discover   **original** first

Papá parked the car out in front and left the motor running. "*Listo*," he yelled. Without saying a word, Roberto and I began to carry the boxes out to the car. Roberto carried the two big boxes and I carried the two smaller ones. Papá then threw the mattress on top of the car roof and tied it with ropes to the front and rear bumpers.

Listo means "ready" in Spanish.

Everything was packed except Mamá's pot. It was an old large **galvanized** pot she had picked up at an army **surplus** store in Santa María the year I was born. The pot had many dents and nicks, and the more dents and nicks it acquired the more Mamá liked it. "*Mi olla*," she used to say proudly.

I held the front door open as Mamá carefully carried out her pot by both handles, making sure not to spill the cooked beans. When she got to the car, Papá reached out to help her with it. Roberto opened the rear car door and Papá gently placed it on the floor behind the front seat. All of us then climbed in. Papá sighed, wiped the sweat off his forehead with his sleeve, and said wearily: "*Es todo*."

Mi olla means "my pot" in Spanish. What do you think makes it so special to Mamá?

As we drove away, I felt a lump in my throat. I turned around and looked at our little shack for the last time.

Es todo means "That's everything" in Spanish.

At sunset we drove into a labor camp near Fresno. Since Papá did not speak English, Mamá asked the camp foreman if he needed any more workers. "We don't need no more," said the foreman, scratching his head. "Check with Sullivan down the road. Can't miss him. He lives in a big white house with a fence around it."

Reading Strategy:
Inferencing

What can you infer about how the family feels about moving again? How do you know?

When we got there, Mamá walked up to the house. She went through a white gate, past a row of rose bushes, up the stairs to the front door. She rang the doorbell. The porch light went on and a tall husky man came out. They exchanged a few words. After the man went in, Mamá **clasped** her hands and hurried back to the car. "We have work! Mr. Sullivan said we can stay there the whole season," she said, gasping and pointing to an old garage near the stables.

---

galvanized coated with the metal zinc to prevent rusting

surplus the amount that remains after needs are met

clasped held together tightly

The garage was worn out by the years. It had no windows. The walls, eaten by **termites**, strained to support the roof full of holes. The dirt floor, **populated** by earthworms, looked like a gray road map.

That night, by the light of a kerosene lamp, we unpacked and cleaned our new home. Roberto swept away the loose dirt, leaving the hard ground. Papá plugged the holes in the walls with old newspapers and tin can tops. Mamá fed my little brothers and sisters. Papá and Roberto then brought in the mattress and placed it on the far corner of the garage. "Mamá, you and the little ones sleep on the mattress. Roberto, Panchito, and I will sleep outside under the trees," Papá said.

Early next morning Mr. Sullivan showed us where his crop was, and after breakfast, Papá, Roberto, and I headed for the vineyard to pick.

termites winged insects that eat the wood in trees and buildings

populated inhabited

Around nine o'clock the temperature had risen to almost one hundred degrees. I was completely soaked in sweat and my mouth felt as if I had been chewing on a handkerchief. I walked over to the end of the row, picked up the jug of water we had brought, and began drinking. "Don't drink too much; you'll get sick," Roberto shouted. No sooner had he said that than I felt sick to my stomach. I dropped to my knees and let the jug roll off my hands. I remained motionless with my eyes glued on the hot sandy ground. All I could hear was the **drone** of insects. Slowly I began to recover. I poured water over my face and neck and watched the dirty water run down my arms to the ground.

I still felt a little dizzy when we took a break to eat lunch. It was past two o'clock and we sat underneath a large walnut tree that was on the side of the road. While we ate, Papá **jotted** down the number of boxes we had picked. Roberto drew designs on the ground with a stick. Suddenly I noticed Papá's face turn pale as he looked down the road. "Here comes the school bus," he whispered loudly in alarm. **Instinctively**, Roberto and I ran and hid in the vineyards. We did not want to get in trouble for not going to school. The neatly dressed boys about my age got off. They carried books under their arms. After they crossed the street, the bus drove away. Roberto and I came out from hiding and joined Papá. "*Tienen que tener cuidado,*" he warned us.

After lunch we went back to work. The sun kept beating down. The buzzing insects, the wet sweat, and the hot dry dust made the afternoon seem to last forever. Finally the mountains around the valley reached out and swallowed the sun. Within an hour it was too dark to continue picking. The vines blanketed the grapes, making it difficult to see the bunches. "*Vámonos,*" said Papá, signaling to us that it was time to quit work. Papá then took out a pencil and began to figure out how much we had earned our first day. He wrote down numbers, crossed some out, wrote down some more. "*Quince,*" he murmured.

Tienen que tener cuidado is Spanish for "You have to be careful." What does Papá want the boys to be careful about?

Vámonos means "Let's go" in Spanish. *Quince* means "fifteen."

---

drone a continuous humming sound

jotted took a quick, short note

instinctively done without thinking

Carne con chile is a dish of ground meat, hot peppers, beans, and tomatoes.

What makes work in the vineyard hard for Panchito?

How does the first-person point of view affect your understanding of the story?

Grade is a word with more than one meaning. Here, a less familiar meaning is used: a sloping surface.

When we arrived home, we took a cold shower underneath a waterhose. We then sat down to eat dinner around some wooden crates that served as a table. Mamá had cooked a special meal for us. We had rice and tortillas with "*carne con chile,*" my favorite dish.

The next morning I could hardly move. My body ached all over. I felt little control over my arms and legs. This feeling went on every morning for days until my muscles finally got used to the work.

It was Monday, the first week of November. The grape season was over and I could now go to school. I woke up early that morning and lay in bed, looking at the stars and **savoring** the thought of not going to work and of starting sixth grade for the first time that year. Since I could not sleep, I decided to get up and join Papá and Roberto at breakfast. I sat at the table across from Roberto, but I kept my head down. I did not want to look up and face him. I knew he was sad. He was not going to school today. He was not going tomorrow, or next week, or next month. He would not go until the cotton season was over, and that was sometime in February. I rubbed my hands together and watched the dry, acid stained skin fall to the floor in little rolls.

When Papá and Roberto left for work, I felt relief. I walked to the top of a small grade next to the shack and watched the "Carcanchita" disappear in the distance in a cloud of dust.

Two hours later, around eight o'clock, I stood by the side of the road waiting for school bus number twenty. When it arrived I climbed in. Everyone was busy either talking or yelling. I sat in an empty seat in the back.

When the bus stopped in front of the school, I felt very nervous. I looked out the bus window and saw boys and girls carrying books under their arms. I put my hands in my pant pockets and walked to the principal's office. When I entered

savoring enjoying

Reading Strategy: Inferencing

Why do you think the narrator is startled when he first hears English spoken?

Reading Strategy: Inferencing

Based on the details in this paragraph, what can you infer about Mr. Lema?

I heard a woman's voice say: "May I help you?" I was startled. I had not heard English for months. For a few seconds I remained speechless. I looked at the lady who waited for my answer. My first instinct was to answer her in Spanish, but I held back. Finally, after struggling for English words, I managed to tell her that I wanted to **enroll** in the sixth grade. After answering many questions, I was led to the classroom.

Mr. Lema, the sixth-grade teacher, greeted me and assigned me a desk. He then introduced me to the class. I was so nervous and scared at that moment when everyone's eyes were on me that I wished I were with Papá and Roberto picking cotton. After taking roll, Mr. Lema gave the class the assignment for the first hour. "The first thing we have to do this morning is finish reading the story we began yesterday," he said enthusiastically. He walked up to me, handed me an English book, and asked me to read. "We are on page 125," he said politely. When I heard this, I felt my blood rush to my head; I felt dizzy. "Would you like to read?" he asked hesitantly. I opened the book to page 125. My mouth was dry. My eyes began to water. I could not begin. "You can read later," Mr. Lema said understandingly.

For the rest of the reading period I kept getting angrier and angrier at myself. I should have read, I thought to myself.

During recess I went into the restroom and opened my English book to page 125. I began to read in a low voice, pretending I was in class. There were many words I did not know. I closed the book and headed back to the classroom.

Mr. Lema was sitting at his desk correcting papers. When I entered he looked up at me and smiled. I felt better. I walked up to him and asked if he could help me with the new words. "Gladly," he said.

The rest of the month I spent my lunch hours working on English with Mr. Lema, my best friend at school.

---

enroll to sign up for

One Friday during lunch hour Mr. Lema asked me to take a walk with him to the music room. "Do you like music?" he asked me as we entered the building.

"Yes, I like *corridos*," I answered. He then picked up a trumpet, blew on it and handed it to me. The sound gave me goose bumps. I knew that sound. I had heard it in many corridos. "How would you like to learn how to play it?" he asked. He must have read my face because before I could answer, he added: "I'll teach you how to play it during our lunch hours."

That day I could hardly wait to get home to tell Papá and Mamá the great news. As I got off the bus, my little brothers and sisters ran up to meet me. They were yelling and screaming. I thought they were happy to see me, but when I opened the door to our shack, I saw that everything we owned was neatly packed in cardboard boxes.

Corridos means "ballads." A ballad is a song or poem that tells a story. A corrido or ballad usually has simple words and short verses.

The Circuit   by Francisco Jiménez

Directions Choose the letter of the best answer or write the answer using complete sentences.

Comprehension: Identifying Facts

1. At the beginning of the story, why have most of the *braceros* left?
   A They are tired of not getting paid.
   B They have started their journey back to Mexico.
   C The season for the crop they have been picking is over.
   D They have found better work in a different area of the state.

2. Why does Panchito have a hard time sleeping the night after they finish picking strawberries for Ito?
   A He cannot get warm.
   B His bed is too uncomfortable.
   C He is too tired and sore from working.
   D He is angry that he has to move.

3. How does the way Panchito feels about moving differ from the way his younger brothers and sisters feel?

4. What do Roberto and Panchito help Papá and Mamá pack into the car?

5. Who talks to the foreman of the labor camp? Why?

6. What makes Panchito feel sick on the first day he picks grapes?

7. Why do Roberto and Panchito hide when the school bus comes?

8. What has to happen before Panchito can start sixth grade?

9. What does Panchito do during his lunch hour at school?

10. What does Mr. Lema offer to teach Panchito?

Comprehension: Putting Ideas Together

11. What two things make Panchito sad about having to move to Fresno?
    A no longer hearing "It's time"; seeing packed cardboard boxes
    B saying good-bye to the man from Jalisco; watching his brother during the drive home
    C picking fewer strawberries; seeing the sun sink behind the mountains
    D seeing Papá stare at the dirt road while driving; going inside his family's shack

12. Why is Papá proud of the "Carcanchita"?
    A He thinks he has made a good choice for his family.
    B He thinks an important man owned it before him.
    C He had spent a lot of time looking at cars before buying it.
    D all of the above

13. Why was the blue necktie Papá found in the "Carcanchita" so important to him?

14. Why is Mamá so proud about her cooking pot? Why is this important?

15. Compare Mr. Sullivan's house to the garage where Panchito's family stays while working for him.

16. Why is Panchito nervous when the bus stops in front of the school?

17. Why does Panchito not read aloud on his first day at school?

18. Why do you think Panchito calls Mr. Lema his "best friend at school"?

19. What is the best thing that happens to Panchito on his last day of school? What is the worst thing?

20. At the end of the story, why are the family's belongings packed in boxes?

Understanding Literature: Theme

The theme of a story is not a summary of the plot. It is the "big" idea that the author wants to share with readers. Some stories may have more than one theme. Sometimes it is stated directly; sometimes readers must figure out what the theme is. They do this by finding out what the story says about life and people.

21. How does Panchito feel about the *bracero* from Jalisco? Why is this important?

22. Why does Panchito feel relief when his brother and father leave for work?

23. Why is Roberto sad about not going to school?

24. What does Panchito think about trumpet lessons? Why is this important?

25. What do you think is the theme of "The Circuit"?

Critical Thinking

26. What do you predict will happen to Panchito and his family?

27. Would this story be as interesting if told from the third-person point of view? Explain.

28. What conclusion can you make about how Panchito's family members feel about each other?

29. Explain how figurative language is used in this story.

Thinking Creatively

30. What do you think is more important—having close friends or having many belongings? Explain.

After Reading continued on next page

The Circuit   *by Francisco Jiménez*

 ## Grammar Check

A verb is a word that expresses an action or a state of being. A verb tense shows the time of the action or state of being the verb expresses. Form the past tense of regular verbs with *-ed* or *-d*. Memorize the past tense of irregular verbs. All future tenses use the helping verb *will*.

Tenses	Regular Verb: Cheer	Irregular Verb: Sit	Irregular Verb: Be
Present	I cheer.	I sit.	I am.
Past	I cheered.	I sat.	I was.
Future	I will cheer.	I will sit.	I will be.

In "The Circuit," find the past tense of four regular verbs and four irregular verbs. Write these verbs on a sheet of paper.

 ## Vocabulary Builder

The suffix *-ly* means "in a way." Almost any adjective becomes an adverb when you add the suffix *-ly*.

Add the suffix *-ly* to form adverbs from the following adjectives: *polite, hesitant, understanding, glad*. Find these adverbs in the last eight paragraphs of "The Circuit." Then use each word in a sentence. Use a dictionary if necessary.

 ## Writing on Your Own

Choose your favorite scene in "The Circuit." Rewrite this part from a third-person point of view. Use Panchito's name where you find the words *I, my,* and *mine*. Add words to describe how Panchito feels. Notice how the story changes with a different point of view.

  ## Listening and Speaking

Working with a partner, prepare and role-play an interview about life as a migrant worker. Decide who will play the worker and the reporter. Search the Internet for articles about migrant workers. Prepare a list of questions and answers. After you practice going through the interview, conduct it in front of the class.

 ## Media and Viewing

On the Internet, locate at least three news articles and broadcasts on migrant workers. Watch each broadcast and read each article. Then determine the main message of the article or broadcast. Ask yourself what is being said and how. Think about how the messages are different and similar.

BEFORE READING THE SELECTION | Build Understanding

About the Author

Jack London's life was brief, but it was full of adventure. Before he turned 20, he had traveled through Canada and the United States. He had been a sailor on a ship to Japan. He had even been the captain of a pirate ship! When he was 21, London traveled to northwestern Canada to search for gold in the Klondike. Dawson was the second largest town in the Klondike at that time. Like most people, he did not find any gold. However, he did have amazing experiences on the way to Dawson. For instance, he made a boat from trees and ran the dangerous rapids on the Whitehorse River.

Jack London
1876–1916

London's experiences and adventures inspired him to start writing. His stories quickly became popular, and many have stayed popular. His novel *The Call of the Wild* is among the most widely read American novels. Altogether, London wrote more than 50 books, including another well-known novel titled *White Fang*.

About the Selection

In 1896, gold was found in the Klondike region of northwestern Canada. Thousands of people rushed there to claim land and "strike it rich." In "The King of Mazy May," the main character, Walt Masters, and his father arrived in the region before gold was discovered. Since that discovery they have been working hard to find gold. Some of the many newcomers, however, have come to steal other people's claims. Fourteen-year-old Walt has to outsmart some of these criminals. Like Jack London in real life, the boy has a thrilling trip to Dawson.

Objectives

◆ To read and understand a short story

◆ To recognize details of the setting in a short story

◆ To identify suspense in a short story

Before Reading **continued on next page**

The King of Mazy May   *by Jack London*

suspense
a quality in a story that makes the reader uncertain or nervous about what will happen next

Literary Terms Setting is the time and place in a story. In some stories, the setting may be almost as important as a character. This is the case in "The King of Mazy May." Walt Masters, the main character, is in conflict against some parts of the setting. As Walt struggles toward a goal, the **suspense** builds more and more. Suspense is a quality in a story that makes the reader uncertain or nervous about what will happen next. Finally, the action of the story reaches a climax, the highest point of suspense or interest.

Reading on Your Own Many of the sentences in "The King of Mazy May" are quite long. London included many compound, complex, and compound-complex sentences. Breaking down such a sentence into parts will help you understand its meaning. Identify the clauses, and pay attention to commas, semicolons, and dashes. Then read the sentence several times.

Writing on Your Own What do you already know about a gold rush? You may not be familiar with the one that took place in the Klondike in 1896. However, certain things about any gold rush are the same. Write short phrases about what you already know. After finishing the story, look at the phrases to see how much more you have learned.

Vocabulary Focus You will probably find that the story contains several words that are new to you. Some of these words were more common during London's life than they are now. Examples are *haste,* which means "hurry," and *comrade,* which means "friend." Other words such as *amongst*, or "among," however, are commonly used today in a different form.

Think Before You Read In what type of situation would you defend someone who is being treated unfairly?

The King of Mazy May

Walt Masters is not a very large boy, but there is manliness in his make-up, and he himself, although he does not know a great deal that most boys know, knows much that other boys do not know. He has never seen a train of cars nor an elevator in his life, and for that matter he has never once looked upon a cornfield, a plow, a cow, or even a chicken. He has never had a pair of shoes on his feet, nor gone to a picnic or a party, nor talked to a girl. But he has seen the sun at midnight, watched the ice jams on one of the mightiest of rivers, and played beneath the northern lights, the one white child in thousands of square miles of frozen wilderness.

Walt has walked all the fourteen years of his life in sun-tanned, moose-hide moccasins, and he can go to the Indian camps and "talk big" with the men, and trade **calico** and beads with them for their precious furs. He can make bread without baking powder, yeast, or **hops**, shoot a moose at three hundred yards, and drive the wild wolf dogs fifty miles a day on the packed trail.

Last of all, he has a good heart, and is not afraid of the darkness and loneliness, of man or beast or thing. His father is a good man, strong and brave, and Walt is growing up like him.

As you read, think about how the setting is important to this story.

In far northern regions, the sun does not set during part of the summer. Here, glowing bands of light—called the northern lights—sometimes appear in the night sky.

What does the setting of frozen wilderness tell you about Walt's life?

calico a type of simple cotton fabric

hops a type of grain with a bitter flavor

The *Yukon* is a river flowing through the Yukon Territory of northwest Canada.

Walt was born a thousand miles or so down the Yukon, in a trading post below the Ramparts. After his mother died, his father and he came up on the river, step by step, from camp to camp, till now they are settled down on the Mazy May Creek in the Klondike country. Last year they and several others had spent much toil and time on the Mazy May, and endured great hardships; the creek, in turn, was just beginning to show up its richness and to reward them for their heavy labor. But with the news of their discoveries, strange men began to come and go through the short days and long nights, and many unjust things they did to the men who had worked so long upon the creek.

A claim that is "jumped" is stolen by someone else. Why would someone jump another person's claim?

Si Hartman had gone away on a moose hunt, to return and find new stakes driven and his claim jumped. George Lukens and his brother had lost their claims in a like manner, having delayed too long on the way to Dawson to record them. In short, it was the old story, and quite a number of the earnest, **industrious** prospectors had suffered similar losses.

But Walt Masters's father had recorded his claim at the start, so Walt had nothing to fear now that his father had gone on a short trip up the White River prospecting for **quartz**. Walt was well able to stay by himself in the cabin, cook his three meals a day, and look after things. Not only did he look after his father's claim, but he had agreed to keep an eye on the **adjoining** one of Loren Hall, who had started for Dawson to record it.

How does the time of the story affect travel and communication?

Loren Hall was an old man, and he had no dogs, so he had to travel very slowly. After he had been gone some time, word came up the river that he had broken through the ice at Rosebud Creek and frozen his feet so badly that he would not be able to travel for a couple of weeks. Then Walt Masters received the news that old Loren was nearly all right again, and about to move on afoot for Dawson as fast as a weakened man could.

industrious hard-working	**quartz** a crystal-like mineral	**adjoining** next to

Walt was worried, however; the claim was **liable** to be jumped at any moment because of this delay, and a fresh stampede had started in on the Mazy May. He did not like the looks of the newcomers, and one day, when five of them came by with crack dog teams and the lightest of camping outfits, he could see that they were prepared to make speed, and **resolved** to keep an eye on them. So he locked up the cabin and followed them, being at the same time careful to remain hidden.

He had not watched them long before he was sure that they were professional stampeders, bent on jumping all the claims in sight. Walt crept along the snow at the rim of the creek and saw them change many stakes, destroy old ones, and set up new ones.

In the afternoon, with Walt always trailing on their heels, they came back down the creek, unharnessed their dogs, and went into camp within two claims of his cabin. When he saw them make preparations to cook, he hurried home to get something to eat himself, and then hurried back. He crept so close that he could hear them talking quite plainly, and by pushing the underbrush aside he could catch occasional glimpses of them. They had finished eating and were smoking around the fire.

"The creek is all right, boys," a large, black-bearded man, evidently the leader, said, "and I think the best thing we can do is to pull out tonight. The dogs can follow the trail; besides, it's going to be moonlight. What say you?"

"But it's going to be beastly cold," objected one of the party. "It's forty below zero now."

"An' sure, can't ye keep warm by jumpin' off the sleds an' runnin' after the dogs?" cried an Irishman. "An' who wouldn't? The creek's as rich as a United States mint! Faith, it's an ilegant chanst to be gettin' a run fer yer money! An' if ye don't run, it's mebbe you'll not get the money at all, at all."

The word *crack*, when used to describe a dog team, means "having excellent skill."

Reading Strategy: Inferencing
What do Walt's actions tell you about his opinion of the men?

What does the Irishman say that a sled driver can do to keep warm?

A *mint* is a place where money is produced, or made into coins.

---

liable likely to do something; likely to happen

resolved made the decision

"That's it," said the leader. "If we can get to Dawson and record, we're rich men; and there's no telling who's been sneaking along in our tracks, watching us, and perhaps now off to give the alarm. The thing for us to do is to rest the dogs a bit, and then hit the trail as hard as we can. What do you say?"

Evidently the men had agreed with their leader, for Walt Masters could hear nothing but the rattle of the tin dishes which were being washed. Peering out cautiously, he could see the leader studying a piece of paper. Walt knew what it was at a glance—a list of all the unrecorded claims on Mazy May. Any man could get these lists by applying to the gold **commissioner** at Dawson.

"Thirty-two," the leader said, lifting his face to the men. "Thirty-two isn't recorded, and this is thirty-three. Come on; let's take a look at it. I saw somebody had been working on it when we came up this morning."

Why is the leader interested in the unrecorded claim?

commissioner an official in charge of something

Three of the men went with him, leaving one to remain in camp. Walt crept carefully after them till they came to Loren Hall's shaft. One of the men went down and built a fire on the bottom to thaw out the frozen gravel, while the others built another fire on the dump and melted water in a couple of gold pans. This they poured into a piece of canvas stretched between two logs, used by Loren Hall in which to wash his gold.

In a short time a couple of buckets of dirt were sent up by the man in the shaft, and Walt could see the others grouped anxiously about their leader as he proceeded to wash it. When this was finished, they stared at the broad streak of black sand and yellow gold grains on the bottom of the pan, and one of them called excitedly for the man who had remained in camp to come. Loren Hall had struck it rich and his claim was not yet recorded. It was plain that they were going to jump it.

Walt lay in the snow, thinking rapidly. He was only a boy, but in the face of the threatened injustice to old lame Loren Hall he felt that he must do something. He waited and watched, with his mind made up, till he saw the men begin to square up new stakes. Then he crawled away till out of hearing, and broke into a run for the camp of the stampeders. Walt's father had taken their own dogs with him prospecting, and the boy knew how impossible it was for him to undertake the seventy miles to Dawson without the aid of dogs.

Gaining the camp, he picked out, with an experienced eye, the easiest running sled and started to harness up the stampeders' dogs. There were three teams of six each, and from these he chose ten of the best. Realizing how necessary it was to have a good head dog, he **strove** to discover a leader amongst them; but he had little time in which to do it, for he could hear the voices of the returning men. By the time the team was in shape and everything ready, the claim-jumpers came into sight in an open place not more than a hundred yards from the trail, which ran down the bed of the creek.

Gaining the camp means "reaching the camp." *Giving heed* means "paying attention."

strove tried very hard

They cried out to Walt, but instead of giving heed to them he grabbed up one of their fur sleeping robes, which lay loosely in the snow, and leaped upon the sled.

"Mush! Hi! Mush on!" he cried to the animals, snapping the **keen**-lashed whip among them.

The dogs sprang against the yoke straps, and the sled jerked under way so suddenly as to almost throw him off. Then it curved into the creek, **poising perilously** on the runner. He was almost breathless with suspense, when it finally righted with a bound and sprang ahead again. The creek bank was high and he could not see the men, although he could hear their cries and knew they were running to cut him off. He did not dare to think what would happen if they caught him; he just clung to the sled, his heart beating wildly, and watched the snow rim of the bank above him.

Suddenly, over this snow rim came the flying body of the Irishman, who had leaped straight for the sled in a desperate attempt to capture it; but he was an instant too late. Striking on the very rear of it, he was thrown from his feet, backward, into the snow. Yet, with the quickness of a cat, he had clutched the end of the sled with one hand, turned over, and was dragging behind on his breast, swearing at the boy and threatening all kinds of terrible things if he did not stop the dogs; but Walt cracked him sharply across the knuckles with the butt of the dog whip till he let go.

It was eight miles from Walt's claim to the Yukon—eight very crooked miles, for the creek wound back and forth like a snake, "tying knots in itself," as George Lukens said. And because it was so crooked the dogs could not get up their best speed, while the sled ground heavily on its side against the curves, now to the right, now to the left.

Travelers who had come up and down the Mazy May on foot, with packs on their backs, had declined to go round all the bends, and instead had made shortcuts across the narrow

What conditions make it difficult for Walt to get to Dawson? Why is this important to know?

What does the author say in this paragraph to increase the feeling of suspense?

keen sharp	**poising** balancing	**perilously** dangerously

necks of creek bottom. Two of his **pursuers** had gone back to harness the remaining dogs, but the others took advantage of these shortcuts, running on foot, and before he knew it they had almost overtaken him.

"Halt!" they cried after him. "Stop, or we'll shoot!"

But Walt only yelled the harder at the dogs, and dashed around the bend with a couple of revolver bullets singing after him. At the next bend they had drawn up closer still, and the bullets struck uncomfortably near him but at this point the Mazy May straightened out and ran for half a mile as the crow flies. Here the dogs stretched out in their long wolf swing, and the stampeders, quickly winded, slowed down and waited for their own sled to come up.

As the crow flies means "in a direct line" or "the shortest distance between two points."

Looking over his shoulder, Walt reasoned that they had not given up the chase for good, and that they would soon be after him again. So he wrapped the fur robe about him to shut out the stinging air, and lay flat on the empty sled, encouraging the dogs, as he well knew how.

At last, twisting **abruptly** between two river islands, he came upon the mighty Yukon sweeping grandly to the north. He could not see from bank to bank, and in the quick-falling twilight it loomed a great white sea of frozen stillness. There was not a sound, save the breathing of the dogs, and the churn of the steel-shod sled.

Why is it good for Walt that it has not snowed recently?

No snow had fallen for several weeks, and the traffic had packed the main river trail till it was hard and glassy as glare ice. Over this the sled flew along, and the dogs kept the trail fairly well, although Walt quickly discovered he had made a mistake in choosing the leader. As they were driven in single file, without reins, he had to guide them by his voice, and it was evident the head dog had never learned the meaning of "gee" and "haw." He hugged the inside of the curves too closely, often forcing his comrades behind him into the soft snow, while several times he thus **capsized** the sled.

Gee and haw are commands used to tell an animal to turn to the right or the left.

---

pursuers persons chasing someone   **abruptly** quickly or suddenly   **capsized** overturned

There was no wind, but the speed at which he traveled created a bitter blast, and with the thermometer down to forty below, this bit through fur and flesh to the very bones. Aware that if he remained constantly upon the sled he would freeze to death, and knowing the practice of Arctic travelers, Walt shortened up one of the lashing thongs, and whenever he felt chilled, seized hold of it, jumped off, and ran behind till warmth was restored. Then he would climb on and rest till the process had to be repeated.

Looking back he could see the sled of his pursuers, drawn by eight dogs, rising and falling over the ice **hummocks** like a boat in a seaway. The Irishman and the black-bearded leader were with it, taking turns in running and riding.

Night fell, and in the blackness of the first hour or so Walt toiled desperately with his dogs. On account of the poor lead dog, they were continually **floundering** off the beaten track into the soft snow, and the sled was as often riding on its side or top as it was in the proper way. This work and strain tried his strength sorely. Had he not been in such **haste** he could have avoided much of it, but he feared the stampeders would creep up in the darkness and overtake him. However, he could hear them yelling to their dogs, and knew from the sounds they were coming up very slowly.

When the moon rose he was off Sixty Mile, and Dawson was only fifty miles away. He was almost exhausted, and breathed a sigh of relief as he climbed on the sled again. Looking back, he saw his enemies had crawled up within four hundred yards. At this space they remained, a black speck of motion on the white river breast. Strive as they would, they could not shorten this distance, and strive as he would, he could not increase it.

Reading Strategy:
Inferencing
What do Walt's actions to stay warm tell you about his determination?

What advantage do the men chasing Walt have over him?

hummocks rises or ridges in a field of ice	**floundering** struggling to move in an awkward way	**haste** a hurry

Walt had now discovered the proper lead dog, and he knew he could easily run away from them if he could only change the bad leader for the good one. But this was impossible, for a moment's delay, at the speed they were running, would bring the men behind upon him.

When he was off the mouth of Rosebud Creek, just as he was topping a rise, the report of a gun and the ping of a bullet on the ice beside him told him that they were this time shooting at him with a rifle. And from then on, as he cleared the **summit** of each ice jam, he stretched flat on the leaping sled till the rifle shot from the rear warned him that he was safe till the next ice jam was reached.

How would having the proper lead dog help Walt?

summit the highest
part

To what does the author compare the sled?

Now it is very hard to lie on a moving sled, jumping and plunging and **yawing** like a boat before the wind, and to shoot through the deceiving moonlight at an object four hundred yards away on another moving sled performing equally wild **antics**. So it is not to be wondered at that the black-bearded leader did not hit him.

After several hours of this, during which, perhaps, a score of bullets had struck about him, their ammunition began to give out and their fire slackened. They took greater care, and shot at him at the most favorable opportunities. He was also leaving them behind, the distance slowly increasing to six hundred yards.

Lifting clear on the crest of a great jam off Indian River, Walt Masters met with his first accident. A bullet sang past his ears, and struck the bad lead dog.

The poor **brute** plunged in a heap, with the rest of the team on top of him.

The *traces* here are straps that connect the dogs' harness to the sled.

Like a flash Walt was by the leader. Cutting the traces with his hunting knife, he dragged the dying animal to one side and straightened out the team.

He glanced back. The other sled was coming up like an express train. With half the dogs still over their traces, he cried "Mush on!" and leaped upon the sled just as the pursuers dashed **abreast** of him.

Reading Strategy:
Inferencing

Based on your own experiences, what do you think gives Walt the strength to continue?

The Irishman was preparing to spring for him—they were so sure they had him that they did not shoot—when Walt turned fiercely upon them with his whip.

He struck at their faces, and men must save their faces with their hands. So there was no shooting just then. Before they could recover from the hot rain of blows, Walt reached out from his sled, catching their wheel dog by the forelegs in midspring, and throwing him heavily. This snarled the team, capsizing the sled and tangling his enemies up beautifully.

The *wheel dog* is the dog harnessed closest to the sled. Walt has caught this dog as it is off the ground.

yawing swinging from side to side	**antics** wild actions	**abreast** alongside
	brute an animal	

Away Walt flew, the runners of his sled fairly screaming as they bounded over the frozen surface. And what had seemed an accident proved to be a blessing in disguise. The proper lead dog was now to the fore, and he stretched low and whined with joy as he jerked his comrades along.

To the fore means in front. To what accident is the narrator referring? How has it become a blessing?

By the time he reached Ainslie's Creek, seventeen miles from Dawson, Walt had left his pursuers, a tiny speck, far behind. At Monte Cristo Island he could no longer see them. And at Swede Creek, just as daylight was silvering the pines, he ran plump into the camp of old Loren Hall.

Almost as quick as it takes to tell it, Loren had his sleeping furs rolled up, and had joined Walt on the sled. They permitted the dogs to travel more slowly, as there was no sign of the chase in the rear, and just as they pulled up at the gold commissioner's office in Dawson, Walt, who had kept his eyes open to the last, fell asleep.

And because of what Walt Masters did on this night, the men of the Yukon have become proud of him, and speak of him now as the King of Mazy May.

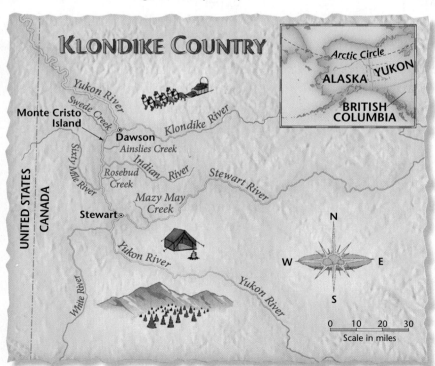

The King of Mazy May   *by Jack London*

Directions Choose the letter of the best answer or write the answer using complete sentences.

Comprehension: Identifying Facts

1. What is something Walt has done that most boys his age have not done?
  A gone to a picnic
  B seen the sun at midnight
  C talked to a girl
  D looked across a cornfield

2. Where was Walt born?
  A at a mining camp
  B on the bank of Mazy May Creek
  C at a trading post
  D in the town of Dawson

3. What are Walt's responsibilities while his father is away?

4. Why is Loren Hall not looking after his own claim?

5. What makes Walt suspicious of the five stampeders?

6. How does Walt get a sled to travel to Dawson?

7. Why does Walt lie down on the sled?

8. What does Walt do to keep from freezing to death?

9. At what point does Walt exchange the bad lead dog for a better one?

10. Why does Walt become known as the King of Mazy May?

Comprehension: Putting Ideas Together

11. Which of these phrases best describes Walt?
  A experienced at driving a team of dogs
  B lonely living so far from other people
  C wishing to have more normal experiences
  D comfortable living in a wilderness

12. What causes Walt to worry about Loren Hall's claim?
  A Stampeders come, looking like professional claim-jumpers.
  B Loren has been gone so long that Walt thinks he moved away.
  C Walt's father leaves him alone without dogs to protect him.
  D Walt fears it is too cold for Loren to stake his claim.

13. What are the stampeders so excited about?

14. Why does Walt need to get to Dawson?

15. What about the setting makes it impossible for Walt to travel 70 miles without dogs?

16. After Walt starts traveling on the frozen Yukon, what mistake does he realize he made?

17. What is the result of Walt's mistake?

18. Why are shots fired at Walt?

19. Why does Walt fall asleep when the sled pulls into Dawson?

20. Name two events that take place during the resolution of the story.

Understanding Literature: Setting

The setting of a literary work is the time and place of the action. The time may be a time period like the present or the future. It may be the season of the year or even the hour of the day. The place can be as general as outer space or as specific as a particular street or room. In some stories, the setting is not important. However, in others, such as "The King of Mazy May," it greatly affects characters' actions.

21. What is so important about the time of the story?

22. What does the setting of the story tell you about the characters?

23. In what ways is climate an important part of the setting?

24. How does the coming of night add to the suspense in the story?

25. How might the setting of this story be considered almost like a character?

Critical Thinking

26. What concrete images best describe Walt's journey over the frozen river?

27. If Walt had determined the lead dog sooner, would his situation have been different?

28. Name two external conflicts in the story. Why are these important for creating suspense?

29. Do you think the author gave Walt the last name of "Masters" on purpose? Explain your answer.

Thinking Creatively

30. Many of Jack London's stories, including "The King of Mazy May," have remained popular for many years. Why do you think this has happened?

After Reading **continued on next page**

The King of Mazy May   *by Jack London*

 Grammar Check

A verb tense shows the time of the action or state of being the verb expresses. The perfect tenses of verbs combine a form of *have* with the past participle.

- *Present perfect tense:* shows an action that began in the past and continues into the present. For example, They have voted.

- *Past perfect tense:* shows a past action or condition that ended before another past action began. For example, They had voted when we arrived.

- *Future perfect tense:* shows a future action or condition that will have ended before another begins. For example, The council will have voted by summer.

In "The King of Mazy May," find at least three uses of the present perfect tense. Find at least two uses of the past perfect tense. Write these on a sheet of paper.

 Vocabulary Builder

The suffixes *-able* and *-ible* often mean "able to be." The word *identifiable* contains the suffix *-able*. When an animal is identifiable, it is able to be identified. Use a dictionary to help you explain the meanings of *favorable, comfortable, collectible, breakable,* and *noticeable.* Include the word *able* in your definition.

 Writing on Your Own

Like Walt, you have probably had to struggle to meet a goal. Use this experience to write a brief personal narrative. A personal narrative is a story that captures the details of an experience. It also captures your thoughts and feelings about it. Before you start writing, make a timeline of events. Then add details that describe the events. Refer to your timeline as you write. Be sure to tell how you felt at each stage.

 Listening and Speaking

Imagine that you are Walt and are being rewarded for your courage. Prepare your acceptance speech. Write an outline and brief notes of what you will say. Do not write a speech with complete sentences. When you give the speech in front of the class, talk from the outline and notes.

 Research and Technology

In a small group, prepare a presentation on gold mining. Use the Internet and nonfiction books to research the life of a miner. Do a keyword search for "gold mining in Canada." Use maps to show where gold was mined. Share your findings with the class.

Classified Ads

In Part 2, you are learning about making inferences in literature. Making inferences is also helpful when looking for something in classified ads. You make inferences when examining the list of groups, or sections, of classified ads. You infer in which section you will most likely find a certain type of classified ad.

About Classified Ads

Classified advertisements, or ads, are short public notices. One part, or section, of most newspapers is made up only of classified ads. Businesses and other people pay money to place ads in newspapers. Some businesses announce jobs in ads; others announce the services they offer. Some people use ads to rent houses or to sell things they no longer want.

People look at classified ads for several reasons. Some people want to find a job. Others want to locate a service. Still others want to buy or rent an object or a house.

Reading Skill

When you look through classified ads, you are reading to locate information. The information is classified, or divided into groups or sections. Here are some tips for locating particular classified ads and reading them.

Tips for Locating and Reading Classified Ads

❑ Usually an index is at the beginning of the classified ads in a newspaper. The index lists each section, or type, of ad. Examples are *Pets and Animals* and *Home Repairs and Services.*

❑ The classified ads are in columns. Usually there are several columns on each page. Each section or type of ad begins after the heading that names it.

Courier Classifieds

CLARKESVILLECOURIER.COM/CLASSIFIEDS • FRIDAY, JANUARY 12, 2007 • SECTION C

CLASSIFIED INDEX

GOODS FOR SALE

500 APPLIANCES

STOVE, electric, in good condition. Black. Asking $350. Call 555-8989.

TV, 60", 2 yrs old. $500. 555-9177

VACUUM CLEANER, never used. With attachments. $75 or best offer. 555-0862.

> Classified ads in each section are arranged in alphabetical order.

530 FURNITURE

COUCH AND CHAIR, dark brown leather. A few scratches. $95. 555-0845.

DINING RM TABLE and 6 matching chairs. All made of dark walnut wood. Like new. $375. 555-1100.

ROCKING CHAIR, over 100 yrs old. Needs refinishing. $200 or best offer. 555-9761.

TWIN BED, perfect for a young child. Made of solid oak. Only 1 yr old. $175. Call 555-7655.

> Abbreviations are sometimes used in classified ads. In these ads the following abbreviations are used: yr for "year" and yrs for "years," rm for "room," co for "company," hrs for "hours," wk for "week," and exp for "experience."

Courier Classifieds

EMPLOYMENT

710 PART-TIME

> *Employment* means "work" or "jobs." Employment ads include ads for part-time and full-time jobs.

BABY-SITTER. Take care of 2 children while I work. Monday through Friday 8 a.m.– 12 noon. 555-8120.

BOOKKEEPER, 20 hrs/wk. Small office. Must have 2 yrs exp. Call Tim at 555-9066.

COOK needed for busy restaurant. Weekend work, day and night shifts. $7/hour. 555-9367.

720 FULL-TIME

COMPUTER OPERATOR. Must be able to use several types computer software. New company. 4 positions open. 555-7342.

720 FULL-TIME

SALESPERSON at auto parts store. Must have 1 yr exp. Will also deliver parts; must have own car and good driving record. Call John at 555-9090.

SECRETARY for bank president. Must have excellent office skills. Call Ms. Ohlen at 555-8109.

Monitor Your Progress

Directions Choose the letter of the best answer or write the answer using complete sentences.

1. Which of the following is in alphabetical order in the classified ads section of a newspaper?
   A the items in the Classified Index
   B the classified ads in each section
   C both A and B
   D neither A nor B

2. For which of the following might someone read classified ads?
   A to meet new people
   B to give away kittens
   C to learn a new language
   D to find the best prices of vegetables

3. What is the purpose of the index found at the beginning of classified ads?

4. What do you have to infer when you are using classified ads?

5. What have you or someone you know looked for in classified ads?

Writing on Your Own

Review what you have learned about using classified ads. Then write a summary of what you have learned. Imagine that you are going to give your summary to someone new to the United States.

COMPARING LITERARY WORKS | Build Understanding

Business at Eleven   by Toshio Mori

About the Author

Toshio Mori was born in Oakland, California. When he was young, his dream was not to become a writer. He wanted to be a baseball player, an artist, or a Buddhist missionary. Instead, he started working in a flower nursery. His great love for reading led him to start writing.

His writing career, however, was interrupted by a major event: World War II. After Japan attacked the United States at Pearl Harbor, Mori was forced to move. The forced move was called "relocation." He and around 100,000 other Japanese Americans had to live in relocation camps from 1941 to 1944. Mori lived at a camp in Topaz, Utah. There, he helped start a newspaper and kept a history of the camp. He finished his first book, a collection of stories titled *Yokohama, California,* in 1942. However, it was not published until 1949. Along with many of his other works, this book tells about ordinary Japanese Americans' lives. The setting for many of the works is California during the 1930s and 1940s.

About the Selection

"Business at Eleven" takes place in northern California. Yet apart from this fact it is unlike many of Toshio Mori's other stories. The two characters could possibly be Japanese Americans, but nothing in the story points to this. The setting is unimportant. It is the characters themselves and their conversations that drive the story.

Through those conversations, the narrator discovers more and more about the main character, Johnny. He becomes impressed with the boy's business sense. However, an unexpected event interrupts their friendship. As you read, compare this selection to "The Circuit." Pay attention to how the point of view affects your understanding of the story.

Toshio Mori
1910–1980

Objectives

◆ To read and understand a short story containing dialogue

◆ To compare theme in two short stories

◆ To compare first-person point of view in two short stories

Comparing continued on next page

dialogue
the conversation among characters in a story

Literary Terms As you have learned, the theme is the main idea of a literary work. Different writers can use different characters and events to develop a similar theme. "The Circuit" and "Business at Eleven" have one theme in common. Yet the events and many traits of the characters are very different. One way a writer develops characters is through **dialogue.** Dialogue is the conversation among characters in a story. "Business at Eleven" contains much more dialogue than "The Circuit" does.

Reading on Your Own Like "The Circuit," "Business at Eleven" is written in first-person point of view. However, there is a difference. Panchito is the narrator of "The Circuit" and is also the main character. The narrator of "Business at Eleven" is not the main character. How do you think this difference in point of view will make the stories different?

Writing on Your Own Work with a partner. Choose an important trait that a main character might have. Give this character a name and a friend. Then write a short dialogue between the main character and the friend. Use the dialogue to help readers understand the trait you chose.

Vocabulary Focus A *denotation* is a word's dictionary meaning. A word's *connotation* is the images or emotions that are connected to it. For example, the word *ambition* has different connotations. People with ambition can be admired for their goals. They can also be disliked for hurting others to achieve their goals. As you read, notice the denotation and connotations of vocabulary words.

Think Before You Read Why do you think the author might have chosen the title "Business at Eleven"? What do you think the title means?

BUSINESS AT ELEVEN

When he came to our house one day and knocked on the door and immediately sold me a copy of *The Saturday Evening Post*, it was the beginning of our friendship and also the beginning of our business relationship.

His name is John. I call him Johnny and he is eleven. It is the age when he should be crazy about baseball or football or fishing. But he isn't. Instead he came again to our door and made a business **proposition**.

"I think you have many old magazines here," he said.

"Yes," I said, "I have magazines of all kinds in the basement."

"Will you let me see them?" he said.

"Sure," I said.

I took him down to the basement where the stacks of magazines stood in the corner. Immediately this little boy went over to the piles and lifted a number of magazines and examined the dates of each number and the names.

"Do you want to keep these?" he said.

"No. You can have them," I said.

As you read, think about the main character's actions. How do those actions help you to identify a possible theme?

The Saturday Evening Post was a popular weekly magazine, published from 1821 to 1969. Like other magazines in this story, it contained nonfiction articles, short stories by famous writers, and cartoons.

Predict why Johnny wants the old magazines.

proposition an offer

"No. I don't want them for nothing," he said. "How much do you want for them?"

"You can have them for nothing," I said.

"No, I want to buy them," he said. "How much do you want for them?"

This was a boy of eleven, all seriousness and purpose.

"What are you going to do with the old magazines?"

"I am going to sell them to people," he said.

We arranged the **financial** matters **satisfactorily**. We agreed he was to pay three cents for each copy he took home. On the first day he took home an *Esquire*, a couple of old *Saturday Evening Posts*, a *Scribner's*, an *Atlantic Monthly*, and a *Collier's*. He said he would be back soon to buy more magazines.

What character traits does Johnny demonstrate?

When he came back several days later, I learned his name was John so I began calling him Johnny.

"How did you make out, Johnny?" I said.

"I sold them all," he said. "I made seventy cents altogether."

"Good for you," I said. "How do you manage to get seventy cents for old magazines?"

Johnny said as he made the rounds selling *The Saturday Evening Post*, he also asked the folks if there were any back numbers they particularly wanted. Sometimes, he said, people will pay unbelievable prices for copies they had missed and wanted very much to see some particular articles or pictures, or their favorite writers' stories.

Reading Strategy: Inferencing

Back numbers of a magazine are issues published in the past. Why would people pay money for back numbers of *The Saturday Evening Post*?

"You are a smart boy," I said.

"Papa says, if I want to be a salesman, be a good salesman," Johnny said. "I'm going to be a good salesman."

"That's the way to talk," I said. "And what does your father do?"

"Dad doesn't do anything. He stays at home," Johnny said.

"Is he sick or something?" I said.

"No, he isn't sick," he said. "He's all right. There's nothing wrong with him."

financial having to do with money	**satisfactorily** in a way that fulfills a need or a goal

"How long have you been selling *The Saturday Evening Post*?" I asked.

"Five years," he said. "I began at six."

"Your father is lucky to have a smart boy like you for a son," I said.

That day he took home a dozen or so of the old magazines. He said he had five standing orders, an *Esquire* issue of June 1937, *Atlantic Monthly* February 1938 number, a copy of December 11, 1937 issue of *The New Yorker*, *Story Magazine* of February 1934, and a *Collier's* of April 2, 1938. The others, he said, he was taking a chance at.

"I can sell them," Johnny said.

Several days later I saw Johnny again at the door.

"Hello, Johnny," I said. "Did you sell them already?"

"Not all," he said. "I have two left. But I want some more."

"All right," I said. "You must have good business."

"Yes," he said, "I am doing pretty good these days. I broke my own record selling *The Saturday Evening Post* this week."

"How much is that?" I said.

A *standing order* is a demand for something that has not yet been delivered. What chance is Johnny taking by having standing orders?

"I sold 167 copies this week," he said. "Most boys feel lucky if they sell seventy-five or one hundred copies. But not for me."

"How many are there in your family, Johnny?" I said.

"Six counting myself," he said. "There is my father, three smaller brothers, and two small sisters."

"Where's your mother?" I said.

"Mother died a year ago," Johnny said.

How many people are in Johnny's family, and who are they?

He stayed in the basement a good one hour sorting out the magazines he wished. I stood by and talked to him as he lifted each copy and inspected it thoroughly. When I asked him if he had made a good sale with the old magazines recently, he said yes. He sold the *Scribner's* Fiftieth Anniversary Issue for sixty cents. Then he said he made several good sales with *Esquire* and a *Vanity Fair* this week.

"You have a smart head, Johnny," I said. "You have found a new way to make money."

Johnny smiled and said nothing. Then he gathered up the fourteen copies he picked out and said he must be going now.

"Johnny," I said, "hereafter you pay two cents a copy. That will be enough."

Johnny looked at me.

"No," he said. "Three cents is all right. You must make a profit, too."

An eleven-year-old boy—I watched him go out with his short business-like stride.

Next day he was back early in the morning. "Back so soon?" I said.

"Yesterday's were all orders," he said. "I want some more today."

"You certainly have a good trade," I said.

"The people know me pretty good. And I know them pretty good," he said. And about ten minutes later he picked out seven copies and said that was all he was taking today.

"I am taking Dad shopping," he said. "I am going to buy a new hat and shoes for him today."

Reading Strategy: **Inferencing**

Why would Johnny turn down a chance for more money? What does this tell you about him?

"He must be **tickled**," I said.

"You bet he is," Johnny said. "He told me to be sure and come home early."

So he said he was taking these seven copies to the customers who ordered them and then run home to get Dad.

Two days later Johnny wanted some more magazines. He said a Mr. Whitman who lived up a block wanted all the magazines with Theodore Dreiser's stories inside. Then he went on talking about other customers of his. Miss White, the schoolteacher, read Hemingway, and he said she would buy back copies with Hemingway stories anytime he brought them in. Some liked Sinclair Lewis, others Saroyan, Faulkner, Steinbeck, Mann, Faith Baldwin, Fannie Hurst, Thomas Wolfe. So it went. It was amazing how an eleven-year-old boy could remember the customers' **preferences** and not get mixed up.

One day I asked him what he wanted to do when he grew up. He said he wanted a book shop all his own. He said he would handle old books and old magazines as well as the new ones and own the biggest bookstore around the Bay Region.

"That is a good **ambition**," I said. "You can do it. Just keep up the good work and hold your customers."

On the same day, in the afternoon, he came around to the house holding several packages.

"This is for you," he said, handing over a package.

"What is this?" I said.

Johnny laughed. "Open up and see for yourself," he said.

I opened it. It was a book rest, a simple affair but handy.

"I am giving these to all my customers," Johnny said.

"This is too expensive to give away, Johnny," I said. "You will lose all your profits."

"I picked them up cheap," he said. "I'm giving these away so the customers will remember me."

"That is right, too," I said. "You have good sense."

After that he came in about half a dozen times, each time taking with him ten or twelve copies of various magazines.

Reading Strategy: Inferencing

Based on what you have read so far, why do you think Johnny works so hard?

The people mentioned here were all writers of the early 20th century.

The *Bay Region* is the area that surrounds San Francisco Bay in California. It includes the cities of San Francisco, Oakland, San Jose, and Sausalito.

| **tickled** greatly pleased or delighted | **preferences** things that are wanted most | **ambition** an important goal for the future |

He said he was doing swell. Also, he said he was now selling *Liberty* along with the *The Saturday Evening Posts*.

Then for two straight weeks I did not see him once. I could not understand this. He had never missed coming to the house in two or three days. Something must be wrong, I thought. He must be sick, I thought.

One day I saw Johnny at the door. "Hello, Johnny," I said. "Where were you? Were you sick?"

"No. I wasn't sick," Johnny said.

"What's the matter? What happened?" I said.

"I'm moving away," Johnny said. "My father is moving to Los Angeles."

"Sit down, Johnny," I said. "Tell me all about it."

He sat down. He told me what had happened in two weeks. He said his dad went and got married to a woman he, Johnny, did not know. And now, his dad and this woman say they are moving to Los Angeles. And about all there was for him to do was to go along with them.

"I don't know what to say, Johnny," I said.

Johnny said nothing. We sat quietly and watched the time move.

"Too bad you will lose your good trade," I finally said.

"Yes. I know," he said. "But I can sell magazines in Los Angeles."

"Yes, that is true," I said.

Then he said he must be going. I wished him good luck. We shook hands. "I will come and see you again," he said.

"And when I visit Los Angeles some day," I said, "I will see you in the largest bookstore in the city."

Johnny smiled. As he walked away, up the street and out of sight, I saw the last of him walking like a good businessman, walking briskly, **energetically**, purposefully.

What do Johnny's smile, and the narrator's description in the last sentence, suggest about Johnny?

energetically with a lot of energy

COMPARING LITERARY WORKS | Apply the Skills

Business at Eleven   by Toshio Mori

Directions Choose the letter of the best answer or write the answer using complete sentences.

Comprehension: Identifying Facts

1. When do the narrator and Johnny first meet?
   A when Johnny asks to buy the narrator's magazines
   B when Johnny sells the narrator a magazine
   C when Johnny comes to talk about baseball with the narrator
   D when Johnny asks the narrator what he likes to read

2. What is the first thing the narrator finds surprising about Johnny?
   A He is more interested in making money than in sports.
   B He talks to the narrator as if they were old friends.
   C He knows what his customers will want to buy.
   D He works hard to find particular old magazines.

3. What is Johnny's "new way to make money"?

4. What does Johnny remember that impresses the narrator?

5. Considering Johnny's age, what is surprising about what he is going to do with his father?

6. What does Johnny do to make his customers remember him?

7. Why does Johnny not go to the narrator's house for two weeks?

8. How are Panchito's family and Johnny's family similar?

9. What is Johnny's work? What is Panchito's work?

10. What is the change that each boy experiences at the end of each story?

Comprehension: Putting Ideas Together

11. Which of the following words describes both Johnny and Panchito throughout the stories?
    A friendly   C hard-working
    B hopeful   D disappointed

12. Why must both Johnny and Panchito work so hard?
    A to save money for their future
    B to help support their family
    C to save money to go to college
    D to learn a skill quickly

13. Compare Panchito's and Johnny's feelings about their work.

14. How does each main character's job affect the way he feels about himself?

Comparing **continued on next page**

Business at Eleven   *by Toshio Mori*

15. What is unusual about the relationships between Johnny and the narrator, and Panchito and Mr. Lema?

16. What clues does Panchito's first day of school give about his personality?

17. What does Johnny's statement "I can sell magazines in Los Angeles" tell about his personality?

18. What can you infer about how Panchito and Johnny each feel about moving?

19. How does their work affect how Panchito and Johnny feel about moving?

20. Name one thing from each story that gives a clue about the main characters' personalities.

Understanding Literature: Characters' Motives

Real people say and do things for certain reasons, or motives. Characters in short stories also have motives for saying and doing things. Writers make their characters have motives so they will be more believable. Knowing a character's motives helps the reader better understand those characters.

21. What would you infer is Johnny's motive for selling magazines?

22. What motive besides learning might explain why Panchito wants Mr. Lema's help reading English?

23. Are the motives of Johnny and Panchito based on their character traits or their situations? Explain.

24. Does Panchito or Johnny seem more believable to you? Explain.

25. To which character's motives can you better relate? Explain.

Critical Thinking

26. Compare Johnny's father to Panchito's father. What traits, if any, do they have in common?

27. In which story are readers more aware of the thoughts of the main character? Explain.

28. Why do you think one author used dialogue more than the other?

29. "Business at Eleven" and "The Circuit" are told from a first-person point of view. However, only in "The Circuit" is the narrator also the main character. Did you react differently to the two stories because of this?

Thinking Creatively

30. Imagine Johnny and Panchito were friends. What might they teach each other?

Grammar Check

"Business at Eleven" contains a lot of dialogue. Dialogue is written using certain rules of punctuation and capitalization. You should enclose a character's exact words in quotation marks. The first word of the quotation is always capitalized. Commas and periods should be placed inside the final quotation mark. Place a question mark or an exclamation point outside the final quotation mark. If the question mark or exclamation point is part of the quotation, place it inside the final quotation mark.

Find four examples of dialogue in the story and examine the use of punctuation and capitalization.

 Vocabulary Builder

Review the story's vocabulary words and their meanings. Group the words by part of speech. Write a sentence for each vocabulary word, leaving a blank where the word goes. Have another student complete the sentences.

 Writing on Your Own

Both stories deal with the topic of work. In a short essay, compare the themes of the stories. Consider these questions:

- In each story, is the group or the individual more important?
- In what ways does each main character depend on others?
- What challenge does each main character face?

Carefully proofread your first draft. If the writing seems choppy, try to combine sentences.

 Listening and Speaking

With a partner, select and practice one of the conversations between the narrator and Johnny. Perform it for the class. Then ask listeners for feedback. Listeners should name one thing they liked about the performance and one way to improve it.

 Media and Viewing

Which would make a better short movie, "Business at Eleven" or "The Circuit"? Work with other students to decide the answer to this question. Take notes on the reasons for your decision. Then make a written plan of the music that would go best with the movie. You can name either the types of music or actual songs. In your plan, include reasons for your choices.

Adding a suffix to a word can change its spelling. Knowing the rules can help you spell words with suffixes correctly.

Rules for Adding Suffixes

- Change the *y* to *i* and add the suffix if the *y* follows a consonant. (*happy + ly = happily*)

- When the word ends in *y*, do not change the *y* before adding the suffix *-ing*. (*copy + ing = copying*)

- Double the last letter when the word is one syllable and ends in a consonant. (*sun + y = sunny*)

- Double the last letter if the final syllable is stressed and ends in a single consonant. (*begin + ing = beginning*)

- If the final syllable is unstressed, do not double the last letter. (*remember + ed = remembered*)

- Never double the last letter when a word ends in more than one consonant. (*work + able = workable*)

Practice

For each word on the Word List, state which rule to use when adding the suffix. If a word does not follow any of the rules, explain that it is an exception. Then group together the words that follow the same rule. Add one word to each list to show another example of a word that follows the rule.

Word List
calmly
quietly
traveling
canceling
appealing
admirable
notable
workable
responsibly
typically

By day he was a mild-mannered teacher of adjectives, by night he was Adverb Man!

The short story has been a popular form of fiction since the 1800s. Short stories have some things in common with other forms of fiction. They have a plot, or a sequence of events. The plot is usually driven by a conflict.

Like novels, short stories also have a setting, which tells the time and place of the story. Usually, because of a story's shorter length, there is only one setting. In some short stories the setting is unimportant. In others, the setting is almost as important as a character. The writer places one or more characters in the setting. The writer presents a character's thoughts, words, and actions, and also tells what other characters think by using dialogue. Finally, short stories have a theme. A theme is the main message that the writer would like to share with readers.

This unit has presented stories that are very different from each other. From these differences you can see how varied this form of fiction is.

Selections

- "Cutthroat," by Norma Fox Mazer, explores a girl's feelings toward an old friendship. Those feelings are influenced by a newer friendship.

- "Zlateh the Goat," by Isaac Bashevis Singer, tells how a boy and a goat help each other survive an unexpected blizzard. The experience changes the fate of the goat.

- "Lillian and Grand-père," by Sharon Hart Addy, is the story of a young girl. She goes to her grandparents' house to help her grandfather learn English. She soon discovers that he is not the man she thought he was.

- "The Circuit," by Francisco Jiménez, tells about a young migrant worker who is never able to settle in one place. His family must always go where crops are ready for harvesting.

- "The King of Mazy May," by Jack London, is about a 14-year-old boy who protects his neighbor's gold-prospecting claim. He must struggle against a difficult landscape and weather cold conditions to do so.

- "Business at Eleven," by Toshio Mori, is the story of an ambitious boy who, at 11 years old, has several businesses. One of them is selling magazines.

Directions Choose the letter of the best answer or write the answer using complete sentences.

Comprehension: Identifying Facts

1. Which word describes how Zlateh feels about her owners at the beginning of the story?

A suspicious **C** trusting

B angry **D** confused

2. In "Lillian and Grand-père," when does Grand-père first show that he is not always gruff?

3. What does Panchito realize when he goes home after the trumpet lesson?

4. In "The King of Mazy May," what first slows down Walt's travel pace?

5. Who is the narrator in "Business at Eleven"?

Comprehension: Putting Ideas Together

6. In "Cutthroat," when do Jessie's feelings toward Meadow change back to what they used to be?

A after Meadow gets interested in Jack Kettle

B after Meadow starts their routine to make up

C after Meadow takes out the racket she has brought for Jessie

D after Meadow gives her advice about playing racquetball

7. In "Zlateh the Goat," what does Aaron realize from his experience in the haystack?

8. What is Lillian so excited about at the end of "Lillian and Grand-père"?

9. In "The Circuit," why is Mamá's *olla*—her cooking pot—important to her?

10. In "Business at Eleven," what do Johnny's business skills suggest about him?

Understanding Literature: Point of View

The point of view is the position from which the author or storyteller tells the story. A story told in first person is narrated by one of the characters. A story told in third person is narrated by someone outside the story.

11. Which stories in this unit are told from a first-person point of view?

12. Which stories in this unit are told from the third-person point of view?

13. Which point of view do you think creates a more powerful type of story? Explain your answer.

14. Could one of these stories be told in a different point of view and still be effective? Explain your answer.

15. Choose your favorite story from this unit and identify the point of view. Why do you think the author chose to tell the story from this point of view?

Critical Thinking

16. In what ways are Aaron and Zlateh alike? How do they become more alike?

17. How does the title of "The Circuit" relate to the story's theme?

18. In your opinion, which story in the unit has the most interesting climax? Why?

19. Which story do you think uses the strongest figurative language? Explain your answer.

Thinking Creatively

20. Which story in Unit 2 do you think would make the best movie? Explain.

Speak and Listen

Choose an excerpt, or part, of a story in Unit 2 that you think is well written. (The excerpt should take at least two minutes to read out loud.) Imagine what the narrator and characters are thinking and feeling. Use this information to help you read this excerpt with as much expression as possible. Practice reading the excerpt several times. Then read it to a small group of students.

Writing on Your Own

Which character in Unit 2 did you like best? Write at least six journal entries that this character might have written. Be sure to express your feelings and opinions as that character. Include details that give support for those feelings and opinions. Ask a partner to review your finished work and suggest ways to improve your writing.

Beyond Words

Choose two main characters from the stories in Unit 2. What do they experience or learn? For each character, think about a song whose words would best apply. In other words, what is a song to which each character could relate? Be ready to explain your choice of songs.

Test-Taking Tip

It is easier to learn new vocabulary words if you make them part of your speaking and writing in other discussions and subject areas.

Narration: Short Story

Short stories are brief works of fiction. They are meant to entertain, explore ideas, or tell truths about life. They often feature a conflict, or problem, faced by one or more characters. Follow the steps outlined in the workshop to write your own short story.

Assignment Write a short story about a person who faces a difficult challenge.

What to Include Your short story should contain the following:

- one or more well-developed characters
- an interesting conflict, or problem
- a plot that moves toward resolving the conflict
- one clear point of view
- concrete details used to establish the setting
- dialogue, or conversations among characters
- error-free grammar, including the use of verb tenses

Using the Form
You may use elements of this form in these types of writing:
- letters
- scripts and screenplays

Six Traits of Writing:

Ideas message, details, and purpose

Prewriting
Choosing Your Topic

Use one of these writing plans to help choose a topic for your short story:

Freewriting Set a timer and write whatever comes to mind for five minutes. Maybe start with an image—for example, a person in a boat in the middle of the ocean. Or start with a feeling—such as curiosity, fear, or loneliness. During freewriting, focus more on the flow of ideas than on spelling or grammar. After five minutes, review your freewriting. Circle ideas to use in your story.

Art and Photo Review Study several photos or pieces of fine art. Look in textbooks or other sources. For each image, imagine a story based on what the image shows. Base your story on one of these ideas.

Narrowing Your Topic

Once you have a general idea of the story you will tell, determine its conflict. The conflict is the struggle between two opposing forces. To identify the conflict, ask yourself these questions:

- What does my main character want?
- Who or what is getting in the way?
- What will the character do to overcome whomever or whatever is getting in the way?

Gathering Details

Create your main character. Fill in a chart like the one shown. This will help you get to know your main character.

Title your story. With a clear idea of your topic and main character, list possible titles for your story. Then look through your list. Choose the title that best captures the important message of your story.

Physical Traits: tall, blonde, braces

Personality Quirks: lots of energy, has trouble sleeping

Name: Kate

Likes: being the center of attention, ice cream

Dislikes: noise, crowds

Writing Your Draft
Shaping Your Writing

Develop your plot. Next, you want to organize the sequence of events in your short story. To do this, use a Plot Mountain like the one shown. Follow the five stages of plot as you write: exposition, rising action, climax, falling action, and resolution.

Climax

Rising Action

Falling Action

Exposition

Resolution

Conflict Introduced

Providing Elaboration

Use details that appeal to the senses. As you write your story, make your characters and setting come alive. One way to do this is to include details that appeal to the senses. That is, use language that describes how things look, sound, feel, taste, and smell.

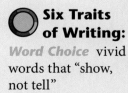

Six Traits of Writing:

Word Choice vivid words that "show, not tell"

Write from a single point of view. Make sure the point of view is clear. Also, make sure that you use only one point of view. If you want to be a participant in your story, use first-person point of view. If you want to be an observer, use third-person point of view.

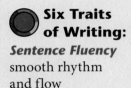

Six Traits of Writing:

Sentence Fluency
smooth rhythm and flow

Revising
Revising Your Overall Structure

Create connections between events that make sense. The first step in revising your story is to make sure that your plot makes sense. Use a bead chart to make sure that events are logically connected.

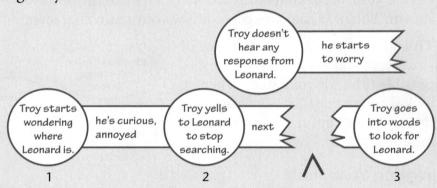

- Underline each major event in your story.

- Summarize each event in a "bead" on a chart like the one shown. Show the connections between events by writing a word or phrase in the connector string. Look at the chart for examples.

- Review the chart. Add events if most of your connectors say *next*. If you cannot think of a good connection between two events, get rid of one.

- Try to add variety to your "string" of events. You can do this by using suspense, foreshadowing, or flashback.

Revising Your Paragraphs

Using dialogue to "show" rather than "tell." Bring your story to life with dialogue. Dialogue is words you have written as though the characters have said them. Dialogue that seems real and natural can include slang and interrupted speech. Review your draft for places to add dialogue.

Editing and Proofreading

Check your paper to correct errors in spelling, punctuation, and grammar.

Focus on Punctuating Dialogue: Pay particular attention to proofreading your story's dialogue. Note these examples of different ways of showing—and punctuating—the words that characters say.

- "You can have three wishes," the genie said.
- Victor announced, "I will not go one step farther!"
- "May I have a word with you?" asked Sylvia.
- "Everyone is here," noted Trenell, "except Keisha."

Six Traits of Writing:
Conventions correct grammar, spelling, and mechanics

Publishing and Presenting

Consider one of the following ways to share your writing:

Submit your story. Submit your story to your school's literary magazine, a national magazine, or an e-zine. You could also enter it into a contest that publishes student writing. Ask your teacher for suggestions.

Give a reading. With other classmates, present a literary reading for an audience at your school.

Reflecting on Your Writing

Writer's Journal Jot down your thoughts on writing a short story. Begin by answering these questions:

- What part of the process did you like most? Why?
- The next time you write a story, what do you think you might do differently?

People Reading Newspaper
Thomas Ustick Walter

Nonfiction writing is about real people, places, ideas, and experiences. A magazine article about a sports team is nonfiction. A how-to article, a movie review, and a person's diary are also examples of nonfiction. The purpose of nonfiction is to describe, explain, persuade, entertain, or tell. Many works of nonfiction have more than one of these purposes.

Nonfiction writing can take many forms. In this unit you will read essays, a biography, part of an autobiography, and a letter. You will discover how nonfiction writers use some of the tools of fiction writing to present facts.

"Books are the carriers of civilization. Without books, history is silent, literature dumb, science crippled, thought and speculation at a standstill."

—Henry David Thoreau, U.S. Transcendentalist author (1817–1862)

Unit 3 About Types of Nonfiction

Elements of Nonfiction Writing

Nonfiction writing is about real people and events.

Most nonfiction is organized in a way that shows information clearly.

- **Chronological organization** is a plot that moves forward in order of time.

- **Cause-and-effect organization** shows the link between events.

- **Comparison-and-contrast organization** shows the ways in which two or more things are the same and different.

The experience of the writer is a very important part of nonfiction writing.

- An **author's influences** are the writer's customs, culture, and feelings.

- The **author's style** is the way he or she puts ideas into words.

The writer's style might be formal, friendly, or fun.

- Influences and style can have a strong effect on the **mood**, or feeling, of the essay or article.

- The **author's purpose** is the reason for which the author writes. The purpose can be to entertain, to inform, to express opinions, or to persuade.

Types of Nonfiction Writing

Some examples of nonfiction writing are the following:

Letters, journals, and **diaries** express an author's feelings or first impressions about a subject.

Biographies and **autobiographies** tell life stories. A **biography** is a person's life story told by someone else. An **autobiography** is a person's life story, written by that person.

Media accounts are nonfiction stories written for newspapers, magazines, television, or radio.

Essays and **articles** show a writer's opinions on some basic or current issues. Essays and articles can be the following:

- **Historical writing** gives facts and explanations about events in history.

- **Persuasive writing** is meant to influence the reader.

- **Descriptive writing** uses the five senses.

- **Expository writing** shows facts, talks about ideas, or explains something.

- **Narrative writing** tells the story of real-life experiences.

- **Visual writing** joins words and images together to share information.

- **Reflective writing** talks about an event in the writer's life and why it is important.

Part 1

Reading Strategy:
Text Structure

Understanding how text is organized helps readers decide which information is most important. Before you begin reading this unit, look at how it is organized.

■ Look at the title, headings, boldfaced words, and photographs.

■ Ask yourself: Is the text a problem and solution, description, or sequence? Is it compare and contrast or cause and effect?

■ Summarize the text by thinking about its structure.

Literary Terms

nonfiction writing about real people and events

autobiography a person's life story, written by that person

narrative a story, usually told in chronological order

chronological order a plot that moves forward in order of time

essay a written work that shows a writer's opinions on some basic or current issue

biography a person's life story told by someone else

conflict the struggle of the main character against himself or herself, another person, or nature

author's purpose the reason(s) for which the author writes: to entertain, to inform, to express opinions, or to persuade

point of view the position from which the author or storyteller tells the story

About the Author

Before Helen Keller was two years old, her mother learned a sad truth. A serious illness had left the young child blind and deaf. There was no hope for a cure. So she would never again be able to hear or see. When Keller was seven years old, her mother decided to find a teacher for her. She contacted the director of a school for the blind called the Perkins Institute. The director talked to Anne Sullivan, a woman who had been at the school. Sullivan agreed to work with Keller. With Sullivan's help, Keller made great progress. She achieved what had once seemed impossible. She learned to read using Braille, a system of raised dots forming letters and words. She also learned how to type and to speak.

Helen Keller was the first deaf and blind person to graduate from college. Doing this brought her fame and the respect of people around the world. She wrote several books, articles, and essays. They told about her experiences of learning to connect with people. Years later, the story of Keller and her amazing teacher was made into a movie. It was called "The Miracle Worker."

Helen Keller
1880–1968

Objectives

- ◆ To read and understand nonfiction
- ◆ To understand an autobiographical narrative essay
- ◆ To identify the text structure of a narrative essay

About the Selection

"Water" describes a life-changing event. Helen Keller tells about one of her early lessons with her teacher, Anne Sullivan. Keller had been an angry and poorly behaved child. In her dark and silent world, she felt lost and scared. When Sullivan entered her life, Keller did not even know what words were. Over time, this patient teacher helped Keller understand that every object has a name. This was a magical step for the young girl. From that point on, she was eager and excited to learn. Keller's life would never again be the same.

Before Reading continued on next page

nonfiction
writing about real
people and events

autobiography
a person's life story,
written by that
person

narrative a story,
usually told in
chronological order

**chronological
order** a plot that
moves forward in
order of time

essay a written
work that shows a
writer's opinions
on some basic or
current issue

Literary Terms **Nonfiction** is writing about real people
and events. One kind of nonfiction is **autobiography.** An
autobiography is a person's life story, written by that person.
It often includes the writer's own thoughts and feelings. An
autobiography can be written as a **narrative** essay. A narrative
is a story, usually told in **chronological order.** That means
that it has a plot that moves forward in order of time. An
essay is a written work that shows a writer's opinions on
some basic or current issue.

Reading on Your Own An author can have more than one
reason for writing. As you read, look for details that are clues
to the reasons for Helen Keller's essay. For example, facts or
numbers may be used to inform or persuade. Stories about
experiences may be used to entertain. Thoughts and opinions
may be used to talk about an experience.

Writing on Your Own Helen Keller tells about an
important moment in her life: her teacher found a way to help
her understand language. Write a journal entry about a time
when a teacher really helped you. Use a thesaurus to find
words that make your writing come alive.

Vocabulary Focus In this essay, the author uses many
words to describe her emotions. These include *impatient,
sorrow,* and *delighted.* If you are unsure of their meanings,
use a dictionary. Make a list of these feelings. Next to each
one, note when you have also felt this way. Also note what
caused the feelings.

Think Before You Read "Water" was written by a blind
and deaf person who really lived. It presents some of the
challenges she faced. Think about other people you have met
or seen in movies or TV shows. What similar challenges did
they face? What would it be like to live their life?

Water

As you read, look for details showing that this is an autobiographical narrative essay.

The morning after my teacher came she led me into her room and gave me a doll. The little blind children at the Perkins Institution had sent it and Laura Bridgman had dressed it; but I did not know this until afterward. When I had played with it a little while, Miss Sullivan slowly spelled into my hand the word "d-o-l-l." I was at once interested in this finger play and tried to imitate it. When I finally succeeded in making the letters correctly I was flushed with childish pleasure and pride. Running downstairs to my mother I held up my hand and made the letters for doll. I did not know that I was spelling a word or even that words existed; I was simply making my fingers go in monkey-like imitation. In the days that followed I learned to spell in this **uncomprehending** way a great many words, among them *pin, hat, cup* and a few verbs like *sit, stand* and *walk*. But my teacher had been with me several weeks before I understood that everything has a name.

Laura Bridgman was a deaf-blind student at the school called the Perkins Institute. (Keller mistakenly called it the Perkins Institution.) She became famous for learning finger spelling there. Thousands of people visited her at the school.

uncomprehending
not understanding the real meaning of

A *tussle* is a disagreement or argument. The word is not used very often nowadays.

Reading Strategy: Text Structure

What do you think is the text structure of this essay? Is it a problem and solution, description, or sequence? What did you base your answer on?

Honeysuckle is a colorful shrub or vine that has a strong, sweet-smelling *fragrance*, or scent.

Think about the details in this paragraph. What do you think is Helen Keller's purpose for writing?

One day, while I was playing with my new doll, Miss Sullivan put my big rag doll into my lap also, spelled "d-o-l-l" and tried to make me understand that "d-o-1-1" applied to both. Earlier in the day we had had a tussle over the words "m-u-g" and "w-a-t-e-r." Miss Sullivan had tried to impress it upon me that "m-u-g" is *mug* and that "w-a-t-e-r" is *water* but I **persisted** in **confounding** the two. In despair she had dropped the subject for the time, only to **renew** it at the first opportunity. I became impatient at her repeated attempts and, seizing the new doll, I dashed it upon the floor. I was keenly delighted when I felt the **fragments** of the broken doll at my feet. Neither sorrow nor regret followed my **passionate** outburst. I had not loved the doll. In the still, dark world in which I lived there was no strong **sentiment** or tenderness. I felt my teacher sweep the fragments to one side of the hearth, and I had a sense of satisfaction that the cause of my **discomfort** was removed. She brought me my hat, and I knew I was going out into the warm sunshine. This thought, if a wordless sensation may be called a thought, made me hop and skip with pleasure.

We walked down the path to the well-house, attracted by the fragrance of the honeysuckle with which it was covered. Some one was drawing water and my teacher placed my hand under the spout. As the cool stream gushed over one hand she spelled into the other the word *water*, first slowly, then rapidly. I stood still, my whole attention fixed upon the motions of her fingers. Suddenly I felt a misty consciousness of something forgotten—a thrill of returning thought; and somehow the mystery of language was revealed to me. I knew then that "w-a-t-e-r" meant the wonderful cool something that was flowing over my hand. That living word awakened my soul,

persisted refused to give up	**renew** start again	**sentiment** a gentle feeling
confounding confusing or mixing things up	**fragments** pieces broken off	**discomfort** not at ease
	passionate showing strong feeling	

gave it light, hope, joy, set it free! There were **barriers** still, it is true, but barriers that could in time be swept away.

I left the well-house eager to learn. Everything had a name, and each name gave birth to a new thought. As we returned to the house every object which I touched seemed to quiver with life. That was because I saw everything with the strange, new sight that had come to me. On entering the door I remembered the doll I had broken. I felt my way to the hearth and picked up the pieces. I tried vainly to put them together. Then my eyes filled with tears; for I realized what I had done, and for the first time I felt **repentance** and sorrow.

I learned a great many new words that day. I do not remember what they all were; but I do know that *mother, father, sister, teacher* were among them—words that were to make the world blossom for me, "like Aaron's rod, with flowers." It would have been difficult to find a happier child than I was as I lay in my crib at the close of that eventful day and lived over the joys it had brought me, and for the first time longed for a new day to come.

What do you think causes Helen to, all of a sudden, connect words to objects?

The phrase "like Aaron's rod, with flowers" refers to a story in the Bible.

What purpose for writing do the details in this paragraph best support?

Reading Strategy:
Text Structure

Notice the chronological order of the story. What time of day does the story begin? What time of day does it end?

barriers things that block the way

repentance changing one's ways after doing something wrong

Water   *by Helen Keller*

Directions Choose the letter of the best answer or write the answer using complete sentences.

Comprehension: Identifying Facts

1. Which object's name does Keller first learn to spell?
   A pin   **C** hat
   B doll   **D** cap

2. What causes Keller to "hop and skip with pleasure"?

3. What is Keller doing when she begins to understand the mystery of language?

Comprehension: Putting Ideas Together

4. How does Keller react when the doll breaks?
   A with delight
   B with disappointment
   C with relief
   D with tenderness

5. Keller changes between arriving at the well-house and leaving it. Describe this change.

6. Describe three times when Keller feels happy.

Understanding Literature: Nonfiction

Since "Water" is a true story, it is a work of nonfiction. It is also a good example of other kinds of writing. First, it is an autobiography because Helen Keller wrote it about her own life. Next, it is a narrative, a story told in chronological order. Finally, it is an essay, since the author includes her own opinions and ideas.

7. Think about why Keller includes certain events in her autobiography. Choose an event from the narrative, for example, when she breaks her doll. Consider Keller's thoughts and feelings about the event. Also think about why she chose to include it in her essay.

8. Imagine that "Water" had been a biographical narrative essay written by Anne Sullivan. Which details would not have been included?

Critical Thinking

9. Which clues in the essay show that the events did not take place in modern times?

Thinking Creatively

10. Why do you think Helen Keller became famous around the world for telling her life story?

Grammar Check

An adjective is a word that describes a person, place, or thing. An adjective answers: *What kind?*, *Which one?*, *How many?*, or *How much? A*, *an*, and *the* are articles, a special kind of adjective.

Copy each sentence. Underline each adjective and circle each article. Draw an arrow to the word that each adjective or article describes. Which of the four questions above is answered by each adjective?

1 Helen smashed the second doll to pieces.

2 Fragrant honeysuckle covered the well-house.

3 Helen received two toys from nearby neighbors.

 Vocabulary Builder

The suffix -*ment* means "the state, act, or result of." Adding -*ment* creates a new noun meaning "the state or result" of the original verb. For example, a *disagreement* is what comes when people *disagree*. Which new words are formed by adding -*ment* to *excite*, *govern*, *disappoint*, and *enjoy*? Explain what each new word means.

 Writing on Your Own

Imagine that you are Anne Sullivan. It is the evening of the day Keller learned the real meaning of *w-a-t-e-r*. As a former student of the Perkins Institute, write a letter to the school director. Describe the amazing finger-spelling lesson that occurred at the well-house. Explain why you either want to stay on the job or quit.

 Listening and Speaking

With a partner, prepare a lesson to present to young children. Share what Keller learned in "Water" and why her experiences were important. Include details about her history and life. Explain how her disabilities created enormous challenges. Use simple language that young children will understand.

 Media and Viewing

Do some research on careers in educating blind or deaf people. Explore the subject in newspapers, encyclopedias, Web sites, and online news groups. Work in a small group, and have each member gather information from a different source. As a group, prepare a project, such as a brochure, poster, or radio news story.

BEFORE READING THE SELECTION | Build Understanding

Objectives

- ◆ To read and understand a biography
- ◆ To analyze conflict in a biography

About the Author

Kathy Ishizuka has built a successful career in the field of nonfiction. Working as a writer, editor, and journalist, her pieces have been widely published. Magazines and journals have printed many of her articles on a wide variety of subjects. As a mother of two, the themes of her work are home, health, family, and children.

Ishizuka has also written several books, including two biographies for young readers. One of them, *Asian American Authors*, is a collection of brief essays about 10 authors. The authors share an Asian heritage. However, their backgrounds are quite different. Each author has had a major influence on American literature. Ishizuka tells stories and gives ideas about how they became writers. She discusses their lives and careers from childhood to adulthood. The biography of one of those authors, Amy Tan, is the next selection.

About the Selection

This selection is about an award-winning writer named Amy Tan. She became famous after her book *The Joy Luck Club* was made into a popular movie. In her books for all ages, she explores the ideas of love and humanity. Tan is the daughter of Chinese parents living in the United States. When she was young, she refused to accept Asian culture—its language and customs. She experienced several sad events and much conflict on her journey to becoming an author. One of the sad events was her mother's serious illness. After that, Tan learned the importance of family and culture.

Literary Terms A **biography** is a person's life story told by someone else. What do a biography and an autobiography have in common? They both are a type of nonfiction writing, and are usually in narrative form. Also, they both are a person's life story. However, an autobiography is written by the same person. Like fiction, a biography or autobiography can have **conflict**. Conflict is a struggle against oneself, another person, or nature. A character in a story experiences a conflict, as does a real person in a biography or autobiography.

Reading on Your Own Text structure refers to the way a piece of writing is organized. Being aware of the structure can help you, the reader, to better understand the writing. As you read, pay attention to how the author presents information. Answering these questions can help you identify text structure:

- What is the time sequence of the story?
- Are two or more things being compared?
- How are people, places, and objects being described?
- What is the cause and effect of things that happen?

Writing on Your Own Imagine that someone was writing your biography. Take notes on what you would like included in it. Also note the text structure that would best fit your biography, and explain why.

Vocabulary Focus Amy Tan is a well-educated person. The following terms from the biography are related to her education. Write the meaning of each one.

- pre-med student
- master's degree
- fellowship
- bachelor's degree
- doctoral program
- English major

Think Before You Read Almost everyone has had some form of conflict in their lives. As you read, think about the conflict in Amy Tan's life. Does it make you like her more, less, or about the same?

---

biography
a person's life story told by someone else

conflict the struggle of the main character against himself or herself, another person, or nature

AMY TAN

**Reading Strategy:
Text Structure**

As you read,
notice how the
story progresses
from childhood to
adulthood.

When she was a child, Amy Tan slept with a clothespin on her nose, hoping to change its Asian shape. She also thought it might make her more American if she ate less Chinese food.

By **rejecting** anything Chinese, Amy **clashed** with her mother. With her broken English, **traditional** dress, and other Chinese customs—such as serving fish with the heads still on—everything about Daisy Tan embarrassed young Amy. Mother and daughter shared a difficult relationship. During one of their many arguments, Daisy told her daughter, "You don't know little percent of me."

What do you
think Daisy meant
by "You don't
know little
percent of me"?

Years later, when Amy Tan came to better understand Daisy, she dedicated her first book to her mother. An **emotional** story about mothers and daughters, *The Joy Luck Club* spoke to millions of readers, and became a much-loved best-seller.

Amy Tan was born in Oakland, California, on February 19, 1952. Her father, John Tan, had **emigrated** from China to the United States in 1947. He became both an engineer and a Baptist minister. Amy's mother, Daisy, the daughter of an upper-class Chinese family, arrived from Shanghai in 1942. In the United States, she met and married John Tan, and they had three children.

A *minister* is
a leader of a
particular church.
Baptists are part
of the Christian
religion.

rejecting not accepting

clashed had a conflict

traditional based on long-held customs

emotional producing strong feelings

emigrated left one's own country to move to another

Like many immigrant parents, the Tans had high hopes for their children. "From the age of six," remembered Amy, "I was led to believe that I would grow up to be a neurosurgeon by trade and a concert pianist by hobby."

Amy grew up thinking she could never please her parents. If she came home with a B they asked why it was not an A. Later, as an adult, Amy understood that her parents wanted only the best for her. But in her childhood, she felt enormous pressure, particularly from her mother.

When Amy was fourteen, the Tan family was struck by **tragedy.** Amy's sixteen-year-old brother, Peter, died suddenly of a brain **tumor.** Just seven months later their father also died of brain cancer.

It was then that their mother made a shocking announcement. Back in China, she had left three daughters from a previous marriage. She had planned to bring them to the United States, but Chinese law forced her to give up **custody** to the children's father, who had abused Daisy. After the Communists took over China in 1949, she had lost contact with the children.

Still grieving for her father and brother, Amy was **devastated** by the news. Who were these other daughters? she wondered. Amy began to view herself as the "bad" daughter and directed her anger at her mother. "We got into terrible battles by the time I reached my teens," remembered Tan. "It wasn't until my twenties that we began to get along."

A *neurosurgeon* is a doctor who performs operations on the brain or the nervous system. A neurosurgeon is very skilled, and the work is highly paid. Why might Tan's parents want her to be a neurosurgeon?

Communists are supporters or members of the Communist Party. This political system holds that property should be owned by the state and shared by everyone.

---

tragedy a very sad event; a disaster

tumor a clump of growing tissue

custody care or protection over another

devastated very upset; destroyed

Believing their California home was cursed, Daisy took fifteen-year-old Amy and her younger brother, John Jr., to live in Europe. They eventually settled in Montreux, Switzerland, where Amy attended high school. She fell in with the drug crowd and was arrested when she was sixteen. Despite her teenage **rebellion,** Amy managed to graduate from high school.

After a year the Tans returned to the United States. In 1969, Amy enrolled at Linfield College in Oregon as a pre-med student. But Amy decided that medical school was not for her and switched her major to English. Her mother was so disappointed that she did not speak to Amy for six months.

In Oregon, Amy fell in love with Lou DeMattei. She followed Lou to California and eventually joined him at San Jose State University. There she earned her bachelor's degree in English and **linguistics** in 1973. A master's degree followed in 1974, the same year she married Lou, who became a tax **attorney.** As she began a doctoral fellowship in linguistics at the University of California at Berkeley, tragedy struck again.

During a robbery, one of Tan and her husband's close friends was **brutally murdered.** "For me, something broke inside," says Tan. That same day she turned twenty-four. Tan took a hard look at what she was doing with her life.

Tan dropped out of the doctoral program and began working with **disabled** children. Of the jobs she held, working in special education was especially meaningful. "That experience was a crash course about **humanity,** what hope means and things that matter most," said Tan. It was rewarding and sad and it helped me identify with many different kinds of people." But the work was draining, and she left the field.

In the U.S., there are three main levels of higher education. The first is a *bachelor's degree,* followed by the *master's degree.* A *doctoral degree,* or Ph.D., is the highest level of study in a particular subject. Each level includes at least two years of schooling, if not more. A fellowship allows a master's or doctoral student to gain work experience also while studying.

What do you think "broke" inside Tan? How does this relate to the conflict presented in the biography?

rebellion a great struggle against power

linguistics the science of speech and language

attorney lawyer

brutally in a very cruel manner

murdered killed by another

disabled not having certain abilities

humanity human beings as a group

Amy Tan with her mother, Daisy.

By 1983, Tan was working as a business writer, crafting speeches and reports for big **corporations,** including IBM and AT&T. Tan was earning a good living. At last her mother considered her a success. But working ninety hours a week took its toll. Exhausted and unhappy, Tan sought help from **psychological** counseling. But when her therapist kept falling asleep, Tan turned to other **outlets**: jazz piano lessons and writing stories.

The year 1986 marked another **fateful** event: Daisy Tan was rushed to the hospital. It was a turning point for both mother and daughter. Believing she was near death, Daisy wondered about her **legacy,** what Amy would remember. "I decided that if my mother was okay," said Amy, "I'd get to know her. I'd take her to China and I'd write a book." Daisy recovered, and Amy, who had been encouraged by an agent, began an outline for a book.

The following year, Tan, her husband, and her mother went to China. Meeting her long-lost sisters for the first time, Tan said, "There was an instant bond." The trip also helped Tan take pride in her Chinese **heritage.** She was finally able to say, "I'm both Chinese and American."

A *therapist* is a person who treats a physical or mental problem or illness. Tan went to a type of therapist who helps people work out problems in their lives.

Think of your own heritage. Where were you born? Where do your parents and earlier generations come from?

Reading Strategy:
Text Structure

Think about the author's purpose for writing this biography. Then think about the text structure. How do these two things go together?

corporations large companies

psychological having to do with the mind

outlets ways of expressing oneself

fateful bringing some significant event

legacy that which is handed down from previous generations

heritage what is inherited from one's ancestors

Amy Tan   by Kathy Ishizuka

Directions Choose the letter of the best answer or write the answer using complete sentences.

Comprehension: Identifying Facts

1. What was an expectation Amy Tan's parents had of her that she did not meet?

  A becoming a lawyer

  B becoming a writer

  C becoming a teacher

  D becoming a doctor

2. What two sad events happened to Tan in less than a year?

3. What life change did Tan make when she was 24 years old?

Comprehension: Putting Ideas Together

4. Why did Tan not meet her three older sisters until she was grown?

  A Tan was in her teens before she found out the sisters existed.

  B Communists kidnapped her sisters when they were born.

  C They all had had terrible battles and did not want to meet.

  D Daisy's first husband did not approve of a visit from Tan.

5. What did Tan do while in Switzerland that most likely disappointed her mother? What did she do that probably made her mother proud?

6. Tan worked in special education and as a business writer. What did these two jobs have in common?

Understanding Literature: Conflict

Conflict is a necessary part of any story, whether fiction or nonfiction. Conflict may be internal, that is, within a person. Conflict may be external, that is, between a person and something or someone else. Conflict makes a story more interesting to readers.

7. Name an external conflict that Tan experienced.

8. What are two examples of internal conflict in the biography of Amy Tan?

Critical Thinking

9. Why would Tan feel like the "bad daughter" compared to her long-lost sisters?

Thinking Creatively

10. The name of Amy Tan's best-selling book is *The Joy Luck Club*. What do you think the title means? Use your imagination and information from the biography.

Grammar Check

Compound words contain two separate words that have meaning and can stand alone. When put together, their meanings are combined. Usually, compound words are nouns. In some cases they are verbs or adjectives. The word *teenage* is in "Amy Tan." Which two words make up *teenage*? Find at least two other examples of compound words in the biography.

 Vocabulary Builder

The suffix *-ful* means "full of," "tending to," or "having the nature of." Adding *-ful* to a word makes the new word a noun that means "full of" something. Apply this to *powerful* and *painful*. Find two words in "Amy Tan" that have the suffix *-ful*. Explain what each word means.

 Writing on Your Own

Imagine learning that you have a brother or sister you never knew about before. Since this person lives far away, you have to wait to meet him or her. In the meantime, write a card or letter to introduce yourself. Share your feelings about the situation. Write in a way that this person gets an idea of who you are.

 Listening and Speaking

Tan worked as a business writer for corporations. She wrote speeches and reports. Think of an invention, product, or service that you would enjoy selling. Write a pitch, a speech used to try to sell something. Describe the history, quality, and purpose of what you are selling. Use speaking tips in Appendix E to prepare your speech. Then present your speech to the class.

  Media and Viewing

A collage is a work of art made by using pictures, photos, materials, and found objects. Make a collage with the theme of China. You might use pictures from magazines, newspapers, or travel brochures. Arrange them into a pattern and glue them onto a large piece of paper. Share your art collage with other students.

Dictionary Entry

In Part 1, you are learning about text structure in order to better understand information. This skill is useful in learning how to use a dictionary quickly and easily. A dictionary is a book that defines and describes every word in a language. The words, or entries, are listed in alphabetical order, from A to Z. Each entry has specific parts and is structured—or arranged and organized—in a certain way.

About Dictionary Entries

If you visit a library, you will see that there are many different dictionaries available. There is a separate one for each language, like English or Spanish or French. Most of them arrange the material they contain in a similar manner. Within one dictionary, all the pages and entries will follow the same layout, or structure. In the first pages, there is usually a chart explaining what each page and entry contains.

The following elements, or parts, are standard features on a dictionary page:

- **Entries** are short or long paragraphs listing a word and providing facts about it.

An entry shows how to spell, define, pronounce, and use that word.

- **Guide words** are placed at the upper left and right corners of the page. They tell you the first and last words to be defined on that page.

- **Keys** explain symbols and abbreviations that appear in each entry. A pronunciation key is located at the bottom of most pages. This is a list of every vowel sound used in words. For example, there are four ways to pronounce the vowel *a*. Using the key helps you understand which *a* sound to use.

guide words

mouth 314 **music**

mouth (mouth), *n., pl.,* **mouths** (mouthz). **1.** an opening through which a human or animal takes in food. **2.** a part of a river where its water empties into a larger body: *the mouth of the Nile.* [German *mund*] **mouth´less,** *adj.*

mov•ie (mōō´vē), *n.* **1.** See **motion picture. 2.** a motion-picture theater: *The movie is next to the drugstore.* **3. movies,** motion pictures: *The people go to the movies.*

Mu•si•al (myoo´ zē l) *n.* Stanley Frank ("Stan the Man") Born 1920, U.S. baseball player.

mu•sic (myoo´ zik), *n.* **1.** a sound which expresses ideas and feelings using rhythm, melody, and harmony. **2.** a musical work for singing or playing. [Greek *mousikē* (the art) of the Muse]

entries listed in alphabetical order

a - act, ā - āble, â - dâre, ä - ärm, e - ebb, ē - ēven, i - it, ī - īce, o - hot, ō - ōver, ô - ôrder, oi - oil, o͝o - bo͝ok, ōō - lōōt, ou - out, u - up, û - ûrge, ch - chief, ng - sing, sh - shoe, th - thin, t͟h - t͟his, zh - vision, ə = *a* as in *ago.*

pronunciation key

Reading Skill

In any written piece, you may come across words that are unfamiliar or difficult. As you read, it is wise to keep a dictionary nearby to look up words. This will increase your enjoyment of a book, story, article, or poem.

Parts of a Dictionary Entry

The following elements are usually contained in a dictionary entry:

- the **main word** entry at the beginning, in bold type
- a **phonetic spelling** telling you what sounds to use to pronounce, or say, the word
- the **part of speech** of the word, such as noun, verb, or adjective
- its **plural** form, if the word is a noun, when there is more than one

- numbered **definitions**, explaining each meaning of the word
- sample sentences or phrases showing how the word can be used
- **synonyms**, which are other words that have similar meanings
- different forms of the main word, such as its past tense
- **cross-references**, or directions telling you where in the dictionary to look for more information

> The abbreviation *pl* tells you that this is the plural form of the noun. In some cases a spelling change is needed first.

i•vo•ry (ī´ və rē, ī´ vrē), *n.*, *pl.* **-ies** [ME < OF *ivurie*] **1.** the hard creamy-white dentine that composes the tusks of the elephant, walrus, etc. **2.** the substance used to make carvings, billiard balls, etc. **3.** a yellowish- white color. **4.** something made of ivory (as dice or piano keys) or of a similar substance. **–ivory** *adj.*

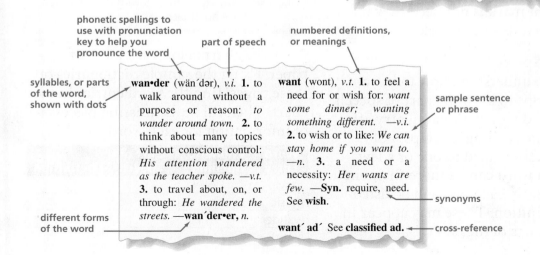

phonetic spellings to use with pronunciation key to help you pronounce the word

part of speech

numbered definitions, or meanings

syllables, or parts of the word, shown with dots

wan•der (wän´dər), *v.i.* **1.** to walk around without a purpose or reason: *to wander around town.* **2.** to think about many topics without conscious control: *His attention wandered as the teacher spoke.* —*v.t.* **3.** to travel about, on, or through: *He wandered the streets.* —**wan´der•er,** *n.*

want (wont), *v.t.* **1.** to feel a need for or wish for: *want some dinner; wanting something different.* —*v.i.* **2.** to wish or to like: *We can stay home if you want to.* —*n.* **3.** a need or a necessity: *Her wants are few.* —**Syn.** require, need. See **wish.**

want´ ad´ See **classified ad.**

sample sentence or phrase

synonyms

cross-reference

different forms of the word

Pronouncing a Word

A dictionary entry has three features to help you pronounce a word.

- The main word appears in **syllables**, or word parts, at the beginning of the entry. Syllables each contain one vowel sound. Each syllable can be spoken as a separate unit. A syllable may be only one letter long (such as the vowel *a*) or a group of letters. Sometimes, dots are placed between the syllables.

- A **phonetic spelling** is given for each entry. This appears in parentheses after the main word in bold. Special symbols are often used to show how a vowel is pronounced. Match the vowel sounds in the entry word with those listed in the pronunciation key.

- An **accent mark** is a symbol placed at the end of one of the syllables. The accent shows which syllable gets the most stress, or is spoken the loudest. An accent mark is not necessary if a word has only one syllable.

Parts of Speech

In order to understand how to use a word, it helps to know its part of speech. This is listed in a dictionary entry after the phonetic spelling. Each part of speech is abbreviated to one or a few letters. If a word can be more than one part of speech, each one will be listed with a definition. These may appear in different parts of the entry.

Here is a list of **abbreviations** for parts of speech, followed by their meanings:

> An *abbreviation* is a shorter version of a written word, so that the part stands for the whole

n.	=	noun: names a person, place, thing, or idea
pron.	=	pronoun: replaces a noun (he, she, me, that, everyone)
adj.	=	adjective: describes a noun or pronoun
v.	=	verb: expresses action or a state of being (run, sing, look, become)
adv.	=	adverb: tells how, when, where, or how much (very, slowly, quickly)
prep.	=	preposition: shows a relationship between a noun or pronoun and another part of the sentence (in, above, near)
conj.	=	conjunction: connects sentences or parts of a sentence (and, because, or)
interj.	=	interjection: a word that expresses feelings (Oh! Wow!)
v.t.	=	verb, transitive: a verb that needs an object to complete its meaning. An object is a noun or a pronoun.
v.i.	=	verb, intransitive: a verb that does not have an object.

Copy the chart below on a piece of paper. Using the sample dictionaries on these pages, find the word entries in the chart. Then fill in the missing pieces of information for each word.

Word Entry	Phonetic Spelling	Part of Speech	Definition
movie			
music			
wander			
ivory			
want			

Monitor Your Progress

Directions Choose the letter of the best answer or write the answer using complete sentences.

1. Where would you find the guide words in a dictionary?
   A at the bottom of the page, in the center
   B underneath the pronunciation key
   C at the top of each page, to the left and right
   D on the first page of the dictionary

2. Which abbreviation means "a word that describes a noun or pronoun"?
   A adv.   **C** prep.
   B adj.   **D** pron.

3. According to the dictionary entry below, how many syllables does the word entry "encyclopedia" contain?
   en•cy•clo•pe•dia
   A three   **C** five
   B four   **D** six

4. What are three definitions for the word *want*? What is the part of speech for each definition?

5. What are three synonyms for the word *want*?

Writing on Your Own

Make up a brand-new word. Be creative! Decide how your word is pronounced and what it means. It should have at least two syllables, two synonyms, and three definitions. Write a complete dictionary entry for your new word using the above information. Include at least one sentence in which the word is used.

COMPARING LITERARY WORKS | Build Understanding

from *Rosa Parks: My Story*   by Rosa Parks with Jim Haskins

Rosa Parks
1913–2005

Objectives

- To identify author's purpose in an autobiography
- To identify point of view in an autobiography
- To compare a biography with an autobiography

About the Author

Rosa Parks is known as the "mother of the civil rights movement." This means her actions helped others recognize the equal dignity of all in society.

Parks was a seamstress living in Montgomery, Alabama, during a time when African Americans had few rights. There was segregation in many public places, including on city buses. Segregation is the forced separation of people based on race—the physical qualities people share. On December 1, 1955, Parks refused to give up her bus seat to a white rider. The bus driver had her arrested for this brave action.

This led to a boycott of the city-owned bus company for over a year. In a boycott, people refuse to buy something or use a service. They hope to bring about change with their actions. A young Baptist minister, Dr. King, brought the Montgomery boycott to the attention of the world. Later, members of the U.S. Supreme Court made an important decision. They decided that separating people on public transportation because of their race was illegal. Parks's example has inspired people around the world to seek freedom and equality.

About the Selection

This selection is from Rosa Parks's 1992 autobiography. Not all people who write autobiographies are writers. Sometimes they allow others to help them write their story in a clear way. Parks wrote her autobiography with the help of Jim Haskins. Haskins is a writer known for his stories about African Americans who overcame their struggles.

Parks describes her experiences of being unfairly treated as an African American. One theme of the selection is being a minority in a mostly white American culture. This idea is also found in the biography on Amy Tan. As you read, compare the point of view of these two stories.

Literary Terms The **author's purpose** is the reason for which the author writes. The two types of nonfiction, biography and autobiography, share a similar author's purpose. This purpose is to teach information about real people. The difference is in the **point of view**, or position from which the author tells the story. A biography is written in the third-person point of view about someone else. An autobiography is written in the first-person point of view about the author's own life.

Reading on Your Own The author of a biography uses pronouns like *he* and *she* when writing about the subject. The author of an autobiography uses pronouns like *I*, *me*, and *my* when writing about the subject. That subject, of course, is herself or himself. Read the titles of the selections about Amy Tan and Rosa Parks. Then read the first two paragraphs from each selection. What pronouns are used? What other clues can you find that the selection is a biography or autobiography?

Writing on Your Own Think of a time in your life when you were treated unfairly. Write down as many details as you can remember. Describe your thoughts and feelings about what happened. Then write the story from two different points of view. Tell it first as an autobiography, then as a biography. As an author, notice which form of nonfiction you find more enjoyable to write.

Vocabulary Focus In this selection, Rosa Parks uses three words that look similar: *registered, registration, registrars*. Using a dictionary or other reference material, compare these words. How are their meanings similar or different? In what way are they related? What part of speech is each word?

Think Before You Read Have you ever seen someone treated meanly? Do you know how it feels to be given a hard time? Use these reflections to help you understand the author's point of view.

---

author's purpose the reason(s) for which the author writes: to entertain, to inform, to express opinions, or to persuade

point of view the position from which the author or storyteller tells the story

from

Rosa Parks: My Story

Rosa Parks stands with another civil rights leader, Reverend Thomas Kilgore Jr.

As you read, notice the number of details the author gives. These include names, places, and dates. What was her purpose for doing this?

The *National Association for the Advancement of Colored People* is often called the NAACP. It is a famous civil rights group in the United States. Its goal is to end the unfair treatment of African Americans and other minority groups.

Mr. Edgar Daniel Nixon was one of the most active African Americans in Montgomery. He was a railroad porter and president of the local branch of the Brotherhood of Sleeping Car Porters, which was a black railroad workers' union founded by Mr. A. Philip Randolph. Mr. Nixon had founded the Montgomery branch of the Brotherhood of Sleeping Car Porters back in the 1920s. When I first met him in 1943, he was president of the Montgomery Branch of the National Association for the **Advancement** of Colored People. He was a proud, dignified man who carried himself straight as an arrow. In getting black people registered to vote, he had the help of a black lawyer named Arthur A. Madison, a native of Alabama who was practicing in New York City. Mr. Madison came down for a while and worked with quite a few of us, giving us instructions on getting registered. He said there was no need for us to have to wait until some white person approved of us and took us down to the **registration** office to **vouch** for us. He also told us about the test we would

advancement forward movement	**registration** the act of signing up on a list or record	**vouch** to give proof of a fact

have to take, which was called a **literacy** test, to see if we could read and write and understand the U.S. Constitution. He was arrested and jailed for trying to help us, and later returned to New York.

I decided to get registered. The first year I tried was 1943. They would open the registration books only at a certain time. If you didn't know when that was, you missed your chance. They didn't make any public announcements. You had to call and find out. And then they might decide to have registration on a Wednesday morning from ten o'clock until noon, when they knew most black working people couldn't get there. Even if you took off from work to be there, it didn't mean you would get to register. If noontime came, they would close the doors, no matter how many people were still standing in line. All this was to keep African Americans from being able to register.

Even if you got inside, you couldn't necessarily be registered. It used to be that you needed to own property, but by the time I tried to register, they said, "You should have property, but if you can pass the test by answering the questions correctly, you don't have to own property." So you either had to own property or pass the test.

The first day in 1943 that was selected for registration was a working day for me, so I couldn't go. Mr. Nixon and, I'm sure, **Attorney** Madison were able to pass the word to the black community, so a long line of black people formed around the **courthouse** waiting to register. My mother and my cousin were a part of that group. They, along with many others, received their voter's certificates in the mail. Certificates were mailed to African Americans, while **Caucasians** received them immediately after completing the test.

> To what does the author compare the way Mr. Nixon carries himself? Why do you think she did this?

> Today, it is easy for any United States citizen to register to vote. One can simply fill out a form at the post office.

> **Reading Strategy: Text Structure**
>
> How does the author compare and contrast the treatment of African Americans and *Caucasians*, or white people? What is her proof that these two racial groups were treated differently?

---

literacy the ability to read and write

attorney lawyer

courthouse a building in which courts of law are held

Caucasians white people

The following day, which was my day off, I went down to register and take my test, but I did not receive a certificate in the mail.

The second time I tried, I was denied. They just told me, "You didn't pass." They didn't have to give you a reason. I thought I had passed the test, but I had no way of knowing. They could say you didn't pass the test and there would be nothing you could do about it. The **registrars** could do whatever they wanted to do.

I was pretty sure I had passed the test. So, the third time I took the test, in 1945, I made a copy of my answers to those twenty-one questions. They didn't have copy machines in those days. I copied them out by hand. I was going to keep that copy and use it to bring suit against the voter-registration board. But I received my certificate in the mail. I was finally a registered voter. The next thing I had to do was to pay my **accumulated poll** tax.

The poll tax was $1.50 a year, and every registered voter had to pay it. But it was mostly black people who had to pay it **retroactive.** They didn't deny the right to vote to whites; so the white person, when he was twenty-one years old (you couldn't vote at eighteen at that time), could go in and get registered and just pay the $1.50 a year from then on. If you were older and registered, you had to pay the poll tax back to the time you were twenty-one. I got registered in 1945 when I was thirty-two years old, so I had to pay $1.50 for each of the eleven years between the time I was twenty-one and the time I was thirty-two. At that time $16.50 was a considerable amount of money.

If I had brought suit against the voter-registration people, I would have had to get someone to represent me. And in the beginning there was no black lawyer in Montgomery I could

To *bring suit* means to take a case to a court of law. The purpose is to ask for something from the person or group being sued.

A *poll tax* is no longer charged for the right to vote in the United States. Who might these taxes have prevented from voting?

registrars officials who keep records or lists

accumulated built up little by little

poll an expression of opinion in voting

retroactive influencing what has already happened

call on. In fact, there were very few black lawyers practicing in Alabama at that time. The only lawyer we could call on when we needed to was Arthur D. Shores of Birmingham. He would occasionally come down. I knew he had represented William P. Mitchell and some others who wanted to get registered in Macon County. But by this time we had the help of Arthur A. Madison. I remember going down to the polling place with Mr. Nixon and Attorney Madison. But that time I did get registered, so I didn't have to bring a **lawsuit**.

A *polling place* is a building where people go to vote.

I remember the first election for governor that I voted in. I voted for Jim Folsom, who was running against a very **reactionary** and very **racist** man named Handy Ellis. There were no unpleasant incidents, and I felt that I had gone through an awful lot of trouble to do something so simple and uneventful.

The second time I tried to register to vote, I was put off a Montgomery city bus for the first time. I didn't follow the rules.

Black people had special rules to follow. Some drivers made black passengers step in the front door and pay their fare, and then we had to get off and go around to the back door and get on. Often, before the black passengers got around to the back door, the bus would take off without them. There were thirty-six seats on a Montgomery bus. The first ten were reserved for whites, even if there were no white passengers on the bus. There was no law about the ten seats in the back of the bus, but it was sort of understood that they

Whites and blacks remain segregated on this Texas bus in 1956.

lawsuit a case in a law court between two people

reactionary a person who favors a return to a past state of affairs

racist one who shows hatred toward a particular group of people

were for black people. Blacks were required to sit in the back of the bus, and even if there were empty seats in the front, we couldn't sit in them. Once the seats in the back were filled, then all the other black passengers had to stand. If whites filled up the front section, some drivers would demand that blacks give up their seats in the back section.

It was up to the bus drivers, if they chose, to adjust the seating in the middle sixteen seats. They carried guns and had what they called police power to rearrange the seating and **enforce** all the other rules of **segregation** on the buses. Some bus drivers were meaner than others. Not all of them were hateful, but segregation itself is vicious, and to my mind there was no way you could make segregation decent or nice or acceptable.

The driver who put me off was a mean one. He was tall and **thickset** with an **intimidating** posture. His skin was rough-looking, and he had a mole near his mouth. He just treated everybody black badly. I had been on his bus as a passenger before, and I remember when a young woman got on the bus at the front and started to the back and he made her get off the bus and go around to the back door. One day in the winter of 1943 the bus came along, and the back was crowded with black people. They were even standing on the steps leading up from the back door. But up front there were vacant seats right up to the very front seats. So I got on at the front and went through this little bunch of folks standing in the back, and I looked toward the front and saw the driver standing there and looking at me. He told me to get off the bus and go to the back door and get on. I told him I was already on the bus and didn't see the need of getting off and getting back on when people were standing in the **stepwell**,

Parks uses the term *police power*. This means the power to act like a police officer without really being one.

Imagine you found out that the driver of your public or school bus carried a gun. Would it change the way you acted?

enforce to cause something to be carried out	**segregation** forced separation from others	**intimidating** to cause others to be frightened
	thickset thick in form or build	**stepwell** an opening for stairs

212   *Unit 3 Part 1 Types of Nonfiction*

and how was I going to squeeze on anyway? So he told me if I couldn't go through the back door that I would have to get off the bus—"my bus," he called it. I stood where I was. He came back and he took my coat sleeve; not my arm, just my coat sleeve.

He didn't take his gun out. I was hardly worth the effort because I wasn't resisting. I just didn't get off and go around like he told me. So after he took my coat sleeve, I went up to the front, and I dropped my purse. Rather than stoop or bend over to get it, I sat right down in the front seat and from a sitting position I picked up my purse.

He was standing over me and he said, "Get off my bus." I said, "I will get off." He looked like he was ready to hit me. I said, "I know one thing. You better not hit me." He didn't strike me. I got off, and I heard someone mumble from the back, "How come she don't go around and get in the back?"

The bus driver calls it "my bus" instead of "the bus." How does his use of the pronoun *my* change the meaning? Why does he say this?

Rosa chooses to sit down in a white person's seat before picking up her purse. What message is Rosa sending to the bus driver by doing this?

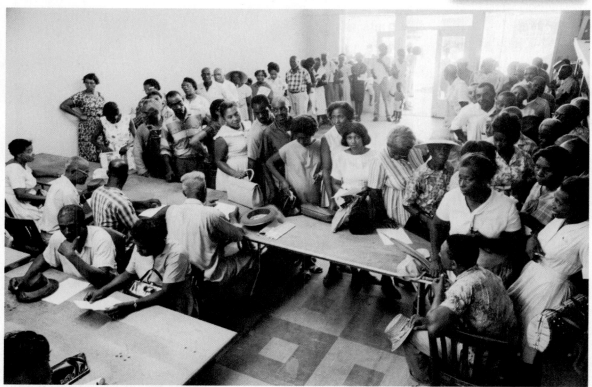

African Americans wait in line to vote.

**Reading Strategy:
Text Structure**

Summarize the selection. Let the text structure of the selection guide you in making your summary.

A *transfer slip* is a piece of paper used by some bus riders. It lets a rider change from one bus to another without paying again.

I guess the black people were getting tired because they wanted to get home and they were standing in the back and were tired of standing up. I do know they were mumbling and grumbling as I went up there to get myself off the bus. "She ought to go around the back and get on." They always wondered why you didn't want to be like the rest of the black people. That was the 1940s, when people took a lot without fighting back.

I did not get back on the bus through the rear door. I was coming from work, and so I had already gotten a transfer slip to give the next driver. I never wanted to be on that man's bus again. After that, I made a point of looking at who was driving the bus before I got on. I didn't want any more **run-ins** with that mean one.

run-ins unpleasant meetings or discussions with someone

from *Rosa Parks: My Story*   by Rosa Parks with Jim Haskins

Directions Choose the letter of the best answer or write the answer using complete sentences.

Comprehension: Identifying Facts

1. Which of the following did Edgar Daniel Nixon do?
   A founded the NAACP
   B founded a black railroad workers' union
   C helped African Americans register to vote
   D taught African Americans how to pass a literacy test

2. What did white officials in Montgomery do to prevent African Americans from voting?
   A They did not announce when African Americans could register.
   B They opened the registration office only at night.
   C Both A and B
   D Neither A nor B

3. What was the purpose of the literacy test at the registration office?

4. What type of office machine did not yet exist in the mid-1940s?

5. Why did Parks not bring suit against voter-registration officials?

6. What was one rule African Americans had to follow in Montgomery's buses?

7. What did Parks do to be able to sit down at the front of the bus?

8. What did Tan's husband Lou DeMattei, Arthur D. Shores, and Arthur A. Madison have in common?

9. In what states did the events in each selection mainly take place?

10. Name one thing that Amy Tan and Rosa Parks each felt strongly about.

Comprehension: Putting Ideas Together

11. What do Rosa Parks and Amy Tan have in common?
    A fought for civil rights
    B born during the 1900s
    C came to the United States from another country
    D wrote an autobiography

12. Which of the following people in the two selections were arrested?
    A Arthur A. Madison
    B Rosa Parks
    C Amy Tan
    D All of the above

13. Parks discusses people in Montgomery registering to vote in the 1940s. According to her, how was this different for African Americans and whites?

Comparing **continued on next page**

from *Rosa Parks: My Story* by Rosa Parks with Jim Haskins

14. How did other African Americans on the bus react when Parks did not follow the rules?

15. Compare the types of jobs held by Amy Tan and Rosa Parks.

16. What word describes both Parks and Tan? What word describes Parks but not Tan? What word describes Tan but not Parks?

17. Discuss how Parks and Tan felt they were not fully a part of their culture.

18. Which selection focuses on some conflicts that are internal, or within, the main character?

19. Which of the two selections contains more information about the main character's family?

20. In both selections, something violent happens or almost happens. Describe these events.

Understanding Literature: Biography and Autobiography

There are many ways to write a story based on true events. An author can choose to leave out certain facts and details. A biography often tells more general events from another person's life. It can be made more personal by including quotes from the main character. An autobiography sounds more personal because it was written by the person who lived it.

21. Which of the two selections includes quotes to tell the story? Name three quotes from that selection.

22. What is a phrase that describes the author's purpose in both selections?

23. Name a detail that gives a good idea about the kind of person Tan is.

24. Name a detail that gives a good idea about the kind of person Parks was.

25. How much do readers learn about Parks's feelings in *Rosa Parks: My Story*? How much do you learn about Tan's feelings in "Amy Tan"? Explain.

Critical Thinking

26. Which of the two selections did you enjoy more? Why?

27. Do you identify more with Rosa Parks or with Amy Tan? Why?

28. How is writing important for both Parks and Tan?

29. Compare and contrast the main conflict in Parks's and Tan's lives.

Thinking Creatively

30. Rosa Parks was born before Amy Tan. What advice do you think Parks might give Tan if they had a conversation?

Grammar Check

Hyphens are marks placed between words that modify another word. Hyphens are also used to connect the parts of a compound word. Look at the following phrases from the two selections. Add hyphens in the correct place or places in each phrase.

1 voter registration board

2 twenty one questions

3 sixteen year old brother

4 much loved best seller

5 upper class Chinese family

 ## Vocabulary Builder

A synonym of a word has the same or almost the same meaning as that word. For example, a synonym of *great* is "excellent." In some cases, by using synonyms you can avoid repeating a word in your writing.

Find a synonym for the underlined words in the following sentences. Then replace each word with its synonym and read the new sentence.

1 Tan was <u>devastated</u> by the news.

2 Tan married Lou, who became a tax <u>attorney</u>.

3 Tan took pride in her Chinese <u>heritage</u>.

4 Segregation itself is <u>vicious</u>.

 ## Writing on Your Own

Write a short essay to compare Amy Tan and Rosa Parks. Before you start writing, organize your ideas using a Venn Diagram. (See Appendix A for a description of this graphic organizer.) You might want to compare and contrast their character traits, careers, talents, relationships, and what they considered important. If these two women met, do you think they would be friends?

 ## Listening and Speaking

Imagine that, like Parks, you are working for civil rights for all people. You want to write a speech about freedom and equality. Think about your own personal experiences and what you consider important. Write a short speech sharing your ideas. Present the speech to classmates.

 ## Research and Technology

Create a bibliography of Rosa Parks's and Amy Tan's books. A bibliography is a list of books and other materials used as sources of information. List them in order of when they were published. Include the titles, publishers, dates, and number of pages. Refer to the information on bibliographies in Appendix C.

Part 2

Reading Strategy:
Summarizing

When readers summarize, they ask questions about what they are reading. As you read the text in this chapter, ask yourself the following questions:

- Who or what is this about?
- What is the main thing being said about this topic?
- What details are important to the main idea?

Literary Terms

genre a specific type, or kind, of literature

memoir writing based on a personal experience

anecdote a short account of an interesting event in someone's life

mood the feeling that writing creates

image a word or phrase that appeals to the senses and allows the reader to picture events

style an author's way of writing

tone the attitude an author takes toward a subject

letter impressions and feelings written to a specific person

Turkeys   by Bailey White

Bailey White
1950–

About the Author

Bailey White is a talented writer who has published both
nonfiction and fiction. She was born and raised in a small
Georgia town. Her father was a writer, and from him she
might have come to love words. She started writing in her
teen years. Her mother Rosalie, a farmer, taught her to
admire nature.

After graduating from college, White began a career as a
first-grade teacher. Several years later, though, she decided
to write full time. She never expected to become famous.
However, fate took her in that direction. In 1990, she became
a commentator on a national radio program. White shared
stories about life in rural Georgia with thousands of listeners.
This theme led her to write two successful books, each starring
her unusual mother. Both books became very popular.

About the Selection

"Turkeys" is a narrative essay in which White recalls an
amazing event from her childhood. Sick with measles and
a high fever, she becomes part of an unusual experiment.
Her mother enjoys regular visits by a group of scientists who
study birds. These scientists are making efforts to save a kind
of wild turkey from dying out. After accidentally scaring the
mother turkey away from her nest, they have a brilliant idea.
The surprise ending is both funny and informative.

This selection shows how people connect to nature and
wildlife. It also shows how animals and humans depend
on each other for different things.

Before Reading **continued on next page**

Objectives

◆ To read and
   understand a
   nonfiction memoir
◆ To identify key
   details that point
   to a main idea
◆ To summarize a
   literary work

genre a specific type, or kind, of literature

memoir writing based on a personal experience

anecdote a short account of an interesting event in someone's life

Literary Terms As a literary work, "Turkeys" fits into more than one **genre.** A genre is a specific type, or kind, of literature. The writer, Bailey White, recalls true events from her childhood, making the selection nonfiction and autobiographical. It is also a narrative essay, since she is telling a story in chronological order. Finally, it is a **memoir,** or a piece of writing based on personal experiences. Memoirs, autobiographies, biographies, and narrative essays often contain **anecdotes.** An anecdote is a short account of an interesting event in someone's life.

Reading on Your Own The main idea is the most important point in a literary work. Sometimes it is stated directly. Other times, you must figure it out by looking for key details in the text. These details often reveal what a literary work is about. The details may be repeated two or more times in the text. They are related to other details in a work. As you read "Turkeys," identify key details and write them in a graphic organizer. (See Appendix A for different types of graphic organizers.) Use these details to determine the main idea of this essay.

Writing on Your Own Authors tell anecdotes about people or events to make stories more interesting. Think about a funny, serious, or strange thing that has happened to you. Tell this anecdote in a brief paragraph. Include details and feelings.

Vocabulary Focus The word *ornithologists* appears in the first two paragraphs of "Turkeys." It is probably a new word for you. If you did not have a dictionary to look it up, what would you do? Clues to a word's meaning can sometimes be found in the text. The clues may be in the same sentence or the one just before or after. What do you think *ornithologists* means?

Think Before You Read Why might scientists be interested in saving the wild turkey—or any other species? Think of at least two answers. Then see if either one relates to the essay you are about to read.

Turkeys

Something about my mother attracts **ornithologists.** It all started years ago when a couple of them discovered she had a rare species of woodpecker coming to her bird feeder. They came in the house and sat around the window, exclaiming and taking pictures with big fancy cameras. But long after the red cockaded woodpeckers had gone to **roost,** the ornithologists were still there. There always seemed to be three or four of them wandering around our place and staying for supper.

In those days, during the 1950's, the big concern of ornithologists in our area was the wild turkey. They were rare, and the pure-strain wild turkeys had begun to interbreed with farmers' domestic stock. The species was being **degraded.** It was **extinction** by **dilution,** and to the ornithologists it was just as tragic as the more dramatic **demise** of the passenger pigeon or the Carolina parakeet.

One ornithologist had devised a formula to **compute** the ratio of domestic to pure-strain wild turkey in an individual bird by comparing the angle of flight at takeoff and the rate of acceleration. And in those sad days, the turkeys were flying low and slow.

It was during that time, the spring when I was six years old, that I caught the measles. I had a high fever, and my mother was worried about me. She kept the house quiet and

Reading Strategy:
Summarizing

As you read, think about how you will explain this essay in two or three sentences.

Pure-strain animals breed with like animals—in this case, wild turkeys with wild turkeys. *Domestic stock* means animals that are bred and raised by farmers or ranchers.

What is the main idea of this paragraph? What details tell you this?

With this paragraph the author begins an anecdote. Where does the anecdote end?

ornithologists people who study birds

roost a perch where birds rest

degraded lowered in quality

extinction not living anymore

dilution process of weakening by mixing with something else

demise death

compute to figure out using math

dark and crept around silently, trying different **methods** of cooling me down.

Even the ornithologists stayed away—but not out of fear of the measles or respect for a household with sickness. The fact was, they had discovered a wild turkey nest. According to the formula, the hen was pure-strain wild—not a **taint** of the **sluggish** domestic bird in her blood—and the ornithologists were camping in the woods, protecting her nest from **predators** and taking pictures.

Predict why the ornithologist is going to the White family's house right away.

One night our phone rang. It was one of the ornithologists. "Does your little girl still have measles?" he asked.

"Yes," said my mother. "She's very sick. Her temperature is 102."

"I'll be right over," said the ornithologist.

In five minutes a whole carload of them arrived. They marched solemnly into the house, carrying a cardboard box. "A hundred and two, did you say? Where is she?" they asked my mother.

This paragraph contains a good example of a simile. Name the simile. What objects are being compared?

They crept into my room and set the box down on the bed. I was barely conscious, and when I opened my eyes, their worried faces hovering over me seemed to float out of the darkness like giant, glowing eggs. They snatched the covers off me and felt me all over. They consulted in whispers.

"Feels just right, I'd say."

"A hundred two—can't miss if we tuck them up close and she lies still."

Reading Strategy: Summarizing

What key detail do you learn here that is important to the ornithologists' plan?

I closed my eyes then, and after a while the ornithologists drifted away, their pale faces bobbing up and down on the black wave of fever.

The next morning I was better. For the first time in days I could think. The memory of the ornithologists with their whispered voices was like a dream from another life. But when I pulled down the covers, there staring up at me with googly eyes and wide mouths were sixteen fuzzy baby turkeys, and the cracked chips and caps of sixteen brown speckled eggs.

Black wave of fever is a metaphor. What is being compared?

methods ways of doing something	**taint** a small amount	**predators** animals or people that feed upon others
	sluggish slow-moving	

I was a sensible child. I gently stretched myself out. The eggshells crackled, and the turkey babies fluttered and cheeped and snuggled against me. I laid my aching head back on the pillow and closed my eyes. "The ornithologists," I whispered. "The ornithologists have been here."

It seems the turkey hen had been so disturbed by the elaborate protective measures that had been undertaken on her behalf that she had abandoned her nest on the night the eggs were due to hatch. It was a cold night. The ornithologists, not having an incubator on hand, used their heads and came up with the next best thing.

An *incubator* is a box or chamber for keeping eggs warm so they will hatch.

The baby turkeys and I gained our strength together. When I was finally able to get out of bed and feebly creep around the house, the turkeys peeped and cheeped around my ankles, scrambling to keep up with me and tripping over their own big **spraddle**-toed feet. When I went outside for the first time, the turkeys tumbled after me down the steps and scratched around in the yard while I sat in the sun.

Finally, in late summer, the day came when they were ready to fly for the first time as adult birds. The ornithologists gathered. I ran down the hill, and the turkeys ran too. Then, one by one, they took off. They flew high and fast. The ornithologists made Vs with their thumbs and forefingers, measuring angles. They consulted their stopwatches and paced off distances. They scribbled in their tiny notebooks. Finally they looked at each other. They sighed. They smiled. They jumped up and down and hugged each other. "One hundred percent pure wild turkey!" they said.

Reading Strategy:
Summarizing
The final paragraph gives a brief summary of what happened over the past 40 years. What two main events does the author focus on?

Nearly forty years have passed since then. Now there's a vaccine for measles. And the woods where I live are full of pure wild turkeys. I like to think they are all descendants of those sixteen birds I saved from the **vigilance** of the ornithologists.

---

spraddle spread out or stretched wide apart **vigilance** watchfulness

Turkeys   by Bailey White

Directions Choose the letter of the best answer or write the answer using complete sentences.

Comprehension: Identifying Facts

1. Which kind of bird do the ornithologists first come to study?
   A passenger pigeon
   B wild turkey
   C red cockaded woodpecker
   D Carolina parakeet

2. Why do the ornithologists need to think up a formula?

3. Describe the appearance and tell the number of the wild turkey eggs that hatch.

Comprehension: Putting Ideas Together

4. Why could the mother turkey not hatch the eggs by herself?
   A It was too cold.
   B She had abandoned the nest.
   C There were too many eggs to cover with her body.
   D Other birds started to attack the nest.

5. What types of activities do the ornithologists do in order to study birds?

6. How did placing the eggs in the bed with the narrator protect the wild turkey population?

Understanding Literature: Memoir

A memoir is influenced by many factors from the author's past life. On a personal scale, these factors include family life, culture, and the place and time of birth. On a larger scale, these factors include world history and global events during the author's lifetime. As you read, look for details that indicate an author's influences.

7. List factors that may have influenced White's writing of "Turkeys." Group them under the following headings: "Time and Place," "Cultural Background," "World Events." Which factors do you think had the greatest influence on her?

8. How would this essay have been different if White had grown up in the city?

Critical Thinking

9. Do you think the ornithologists care more about the turkey's welfare than the girl's? Explain you answer.

Thinking Creatively

10. If you could watch wild animal babies being born, what animal species would you choose? Would you want to keep them, or allow them to go back into nature?

Grammar Check

An adverb is a word that modifies, or describes, a verb, adjective, or another adverb. An adverb answers *where, when, how,* and *to what extent.* Here is a sentence from "Turkeys": *And in those sad days, the turkeys were flying low and slow. Low* tells where the turkeys flew, and *slow* tells how they flew. Find at least three other sentences that have adverbs. Tell which word the adverb modifies and the question it answers.

 ## Vocabulary Builder

Some words have more than one meaning. The meanings may be close or very different. To identify which meaning is intended for a word, look closely at the surrounding text. *Strain, spring, rate,* and *hatch* are words found in "Turkeys." Give two meanings of each word and name their parts of speech.

 ## Writing on Your Own

Write a journal entry as if you were a young Bailey White. Choose a single event that you liked from her essay "Turkeys." Write notes about White's reaction to the event as she lived it. Then write a paragraph from her point of view. Describe what happened in detail. Acting as White, include your thoughts and feelings, rather than just details about the event.

 ## Listening and Speaking

With a partner, perform a dramatic reading from "Turkeys." Imagine you are a young Bailey White waking to find baby turkeys in your bed. Use your voice and gestures to communicate meaning and feelings. Pause or speak slowly to show wonder. Ask your partner to give you feedback on your presentation. Then revise it to include his or her comments.

 ## Research and Technology

Conservation is the effort to keep rare plant and animal groups alive. With a group, prepare a report on conservation to present to the class. Choose a topic to focus on, such as land or animal conservation. Use the Internet and library resources to research your topic. Take notes about the history, problems, and solutions connected to it. Then create a poster to use when you present your report.

Dewey Decimal System

In Part 2, you are learning how to summarize works of literature. It is also a helpful skill to have for finding and reading informational materials. In libraries you can find an enormous amount of informational materials. These include books, periodicals (magazines, newspapers, and newsletters), and electronic media.

The method used for locating most nonfiction items is called the Dewey Decimal System. A **decimal** is a number that contains a point between a whole number and a fraction. The Dewey Decimal System is based on summarizing basic information down to a series of letters and numbers. Magazines, newspapers, and fiction books are not covered under the Dewey system.

About the Dewey Decimal System

The Dewey Decimal System is used by libraries to arrange, classify, and organize informational materials. It not only helps visitors find materials, it also helps library workers put them away. A librarian named Melvil Dewey

Melvil Dewey, the librarian who invented the Dewey Decimal System.

invented this book-filing system in 1876. He started the first school for training librarians, at which he taught this system.

The Dewey Decimal System uses decimals based on the number 10. Each book or other item is assigned its own special code. This Dewey Decimal number, or **call number**, includes a series of numbers and letters. They indicate both the subject matter and its location on the shelf. Every library book has this call number printed on its spine, or flat edge. The call number faces out from the shelf so that people can easily see it.

Reading Skill

Before visiting the library, it helps to make notes on a slip of paper. List the book titles, authors, or subjects you are interested in looking up. Summarize key details to make your task easier. In this way, you will save time at the library.

Categories of the Dewey Decimal System

Since decimals are based on the number 10, Dewey's system divides things up into tens. There are 10 subject groups and 10 number groups. These cover all the fields of general knowledge. This method makes it simple to locate almost any library book quickly and easily.

All nonfiction books are divided into 10 main subject categories, as shown in the box. Each category is assigned its own range of call numbers. The left column lists the 10 groups of call numbers. They start at 0 (000) and go up to 999. The right column lists all the subjects that correspond to the call numbers on the left.

Each subject is divided into one or more smaller groups, called **subtopics**. These are listed in italics under the main subject heading. The subtopics are more specific areas of learning. Books belonging to the same subtopic are all placed together on a library shelf.

Arts and Recreation 700–799	700–799 General Arts
	710–719 Landscape Art
	720–729 Architecture

Numbers	Subjects and Subtopics
000–099	General Works *Encyclopedias, periodicals, library facts*
100–199	Philosophy and Psychology *Logic, mental health*
200–299	Religion *Mythology*
300–399	Social Sciences *Government, education, economics*
400–499	Language *Dictionaries, foreign languages, grammar*
500–599	Pure Sciences *Biology, mathematics, botany, chemistry*
600–699	Technology (Applied Sciences) *Engineering, aviation, home economics*
700–799	Arts and Recreation *Fine art, music, sports, architecture*
800–899	Literature *Poetry, plays, speeches, humor*
900–999	History and Geography *Travel, biography*

Example

Arts and Recreation is one of the 10 major subjects. This group is divided into smaller subtopics that are all related to arts and recreation: fine art, music, sports, and architecture.

Sculpture and painting are both fine arts. So they also would be part of that subtopic. Rock and roll is a type of music. So it would be part of that subtopic.

Ice hockey is a kind of sport. So it would be part of that subtopic.

Call Numbers in the Dewey Decimal System

Each call number has three numbers before and after the decimal point, and letters below.

- The numbers before the decimal point stand for the main subject and subtopic.

- The numbers after the decimal point stand for even more specific groupings. This means that even the subtopics have more subtopics below them.

- The author's last name determines which letters will go under the call number.

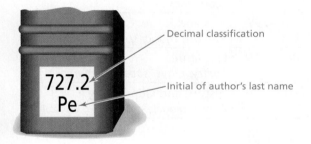

Decimal classification

Initial of author's last name

In the example above, the call number is 727.2/Pe. According to the chart on the previous page, 700 is the subject code for Arts and Recreation. The example shows that 727 falls in the subtopic of architecture. The first letters of the author's last name are "Pe," such as in Peterson.

How to Find a Book on the Library Shelf

To locate a book on the shelf, first look up its call number. Today's libraries have computers with listings, or catalogs, of every item on the shelves. Get the listing you want by typing in one of three pieces of information:

- the title
- the author's name
- the subject

The record in the catalog will then provide the Dewey Decimal call number.

After you write the call number down, look for the book on the shelves. If it is missing, someone else probably checked it out. In that case, you are still looking in the right place. Other books on the same subject and with a similar call number will be nearby.

Examine the chart at the bottom of page 229, which shows five sample call numbers.

- Libraries arrange books first by the number.

- Call numbers go from left to right on the shelf. This means that books with smaller numbers start on the left.

- Next, books are put in alphabetical order by the author's last name.

Monitor Your Progress

Directions Choose the letter of the best answer or write the answer using complete sentences.

1. Which of the following purposes would not be served by the Dewey Decimal System?
   A finding a magazine article about the rainforest
   B reading a collection of poetry from the 1700s
   C locating a Spanish-language dictionary
   D checking out a DVD about how to play the guitar

2. Which of the following subjects is listed with the wrong subtopic or call number?
   A 400–499 Language: Grammar
   B 800–899 Literature: Humor
   C 100–199 Religion: Philosophy
   D 600–699 Technology: Home Economics

3. What does the letter or letters under the call number stand for?
   A the main subject
   B the subtopic
   C the initials of the library
   D the author's last name

4. What did Melvil Dewey achieve?

5. What is another word for the Applied Sciences category?

Writing on Your Own

Take another look at the chart of numbers and subjects for the Dewey Decimal System.

Each subject has several subtopics. Each subtopic could itself be broken down into smaller groups. Write down the names of five subtopics. Think of two more subject groups that could fit under each of these. For example, *biography* could contain the subtopics *men* and *women*. Explain the reasons for your choices.

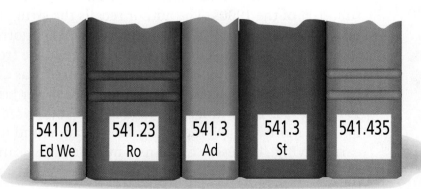

541.01 Ed We   541.23 Ro   541.3 Ad   541.3 St   541.435

La Leña Buena   by John Phillip Santos

John Phillip Santos
1957–

Objectives

◆ To read and understand a narrative essay

◆ To analyze mood in a narrative essay

◆ To separate important from unimportant details

About the Author

John Phillip Santos is a writer with strong ties to his culture. His work honors the values and points of view of the Latino culture and community. In his first book, Santos told the story of his family's history. His grandparents moved from Mexico to Texas, where he was born and raised.

Santos started writing poetry when he was young and developed a love for words. Education was important to him, and he earned four college degrees. He is the first Mexican American to win a Rhodes scholarship—an honor for college students.

Santos went on to become a writer, journalist, filmmaker, and producer. He has written and produced over 40 television documentaries, which are nonfiction films. Their themes focus mostly on culture, religion, and politics. Today, Santos often speaks to groups of students. He reminds them that people of many different cultures live in the United States. He encourages young people to find their own stories by studying their past.

About the Selection

"La Leña Buena" is a narrative essay. The time period is the first part of the 1900s. The author recalls the struggles of his great-uncle, Tío Abrán. This proud man supported his family in Mexico by selling the charcoal he made from wood. Abrán's ability to support his family, however, was affected by the Mexican Revolution. This violent civil war lasted from 1910 to 1920. The war left the land in bad condition, stripped of trees. Many people, including Tío Abrán, found it hard to earn a living. The essay explains why many Mexicans crossed the border into the United States. They were eager for better opportunities.

Literary Terms **Mood** is the feeling that writing creates. Nonfiction works can present a mood, just as works of fiction can. For example, the mood of a narrative essay may be happy, sad, scary, or hopeful. In some literary works, there is a single mood throughout. In others, the mood changes. To create a certain mood, writers choose words carefully. They hope that these words will affect the reader in a certain way. Writers also create **images**. An image is a word or phrase that appeals to the senses and allows the reader to picture events.

Reading on Your Own Asking what the main idea of a literary work is helps you to summarize the work. To determine the main idea, separate important details from unimportant details. Important details are small pieces of information that tell more about the main idea. As you read the essay, look for important details.

Writing on Your Own In this essay, the author recalls stories passed down by members of his family. The brother of his great-grandfather shared what life was like in Mexico before he left. Write a paragraph about such stories. Explain how young people can benefit from stories told by older family members. What words of wisdom do older relatives have to share?

Vocabulary Focus As you read the essay, write down the Spanish words. Try saying each one aloud. Notice which ones start with a capital letter and are proper nouns. Guess which words are the names of persons or places.

Think Before You Read Read the first paragraph of "La Leña Buena." Identify the main character and the main idea of the paragraph. The author gives detailed information about a single subject at the beginning of the essay. Predict the theme of the essay from these details.

> **mood** the feeling that writing creates
>
> **image** a word or phrase that appeals to the senses and allows the reader to picture events

La Leña Buena

Reading Strategy:
Summarizing

As you read, notice how the word choice sets the mood for the main idea.

Tío means "uncle" in Spanish. *Sierra* means a range of hills or mountains that look like the teeth of a saw. The origin of the word is the Latin *serra,* which means "saw."

Notice that the same sentence opens both the first and third paragraphs. What effect is the author trying to achieve?

Notice how the mood of the essay has changed starting with this paragraph. How would you describe the mood now?

Good wood is like a jewel, Tío Abrán, my great-grandfather Jacobo's twin brother, used to say. Huisache burns fast, in twisting yellow flames, **engulfing** the log in a cocoon of fire. It burns brightly, so it is sought after for Easter bonfires. But it does not burn hot, so it's poor wood for home fires. On a cold morning in the sierra, you can burn a whole tree by noon. Mesquite, and even better, cedar—these are noble, hard woods. They burn hot and long. Their smoke is fragrant. And if you know how to do it, they make **exquisite** charcoal.

"La leña buena es como una joya"

Good wood is like a jewel. And old Tío Abrán knew wood the way a jeweler knows stones, and in northern Coahuila, from Múzquiz to Rosita, his charcoal was highly regarded for its sweet, long-burning fire.

Abrán was one of the last of the Garcias to come north. Somewhere around 1920, he finally had to come across the border with his family. He was weary of the **treacheries** along the roads that had become a part of life in the sierra towns since the beginning of the revolution ten years earlier. Most of the land near town had been **deforested** and the only wood he could find around Palaú was huisache. To find any of the few pastures left with **arbors** of mesquite trees, he had to take the unpaved mountain road west from Múzquiz, along a

engulfing surrounding completely	**exquisite** of the highest quality	**deforested** cleared of trees or forests
	treacheries harmful acts against another	**arbors** groups of trees

route where many of the militantes had their camps. Out by the old **Villa** las Rusias, in a valley far off the road, there were mesquite trees in every direction as far as you could see. He made an arrangement with the owner of the villa to give him a cut from the sale of charcoal he made from the mesquite. But many times, the revolucionarios **confiscated** his day's load of wood, leaving him to return home, **humiliated,** with an empty wagon.

Aside from Tía Pepa and Tío Anacleto, who had returned to Mexico by then, he had been the last of the Garcias left in Mexico, and he had left **reluctantly.** On the day he arrived in San Antonio with his family, he had told his brother Abuelo Jacobo, "If there was still any mesquite that was easy to get to, we would've stayed."

What are the most important details in this paragraph? What details are less important?

Militantes means "militants" in Spanish. Militants are people who fight or are willing to fight. *Revolucionarios* is Spanish for "revolutionaries." Revolutionaries want to bring about a sudden change in government or society.

Reading Strategy: **Summarizing**

What is the main thing being said about this topic? Answering this question will help you summarize the essay.

villa a country home

confiscated took by force

humiliated shamed; disgraced

reluctantly unwillingly

La Leña Buena   by John Phillip Santos

Directions Choose the letter of the best answer or write the answer using complete sentences.

Comprehension: Identifying Facts

1. Which types of wood does the author say are noble, hard woods?
   A oak and huisache
   B cedar and mesquite
   C charcoal and mesquite
   D huisache and elm

2. What was the last name of the author's family back in Mexico?

3. To which U.S. city did Tío Abrán go when he left Mexico?

Comprehension: Putting Ideas Together

4. Why was collecting wood so important to Tío Abrán?
   A He could exchange the wood for jewels.
   B He was a master at wood carving.
   C His family burned the wood to keep warm.
   D He earned his living selling the charcoal.

5. What problems did Abrán have in trying to collect mesquite?

6. What caused Abrán to make a special deal with the owner of Villa las Rusias?

Understanding Literature: Mood

Mood is the overall feeling or state of mind that writing creates in a reader. To identify the mood of a piece of writing, think about the author's choice of words. Also, think about the images, or word pictures, that the author has used. Images often include details, such as sound and color, that appeal to the reader's senses. Remember that some literary works present a single mood. In other works, the mood changes.

7. What are two moods created in this essay? Explain your answer.

8. Choose one of these moods. What words and images created this mood?

Critical Thinking

9. Imagine that the purpose of the essay was only to tell about Tío Abrán. In this case, which details in the essay would be considered less important?

Thinking Creatively

10. Imagine you lived in a place where natural resources, such as trees, were being destroyed. How would it affect your life? What would you do about it?

Grammar Check

Conjunctions are parts of speech that connect the parts of a sentence. They help show how different pieces of information are related to each other. The words *and, or, but, nor, for, yet,* and *so* are all conjunctions. They connect words, groups of words, and whole sentences. Find at least three sentences in the selection that contain conjunctions.

 Vocabulary Builder

Gain more practice with the vocabulary words from the selection. First, find a synonym for each word. Write a set of original sentences. In each sentence use one of the synonyms you found. Exchange your sentences with a partner. Your partner should cross through the synonym and write the vocabulary word above it.

 Writing on Your Own

When someone moves to a different country, it is usually hard to adjust to the new culture. When Tío Abrán arrived in the United States, family members were already there to help him adjust. Write a problem-and-solution essay to help immigrants adjust to some part of their new life. In your essay, begin by clearly stating a particular problem that immigrants might face. Then, provide a step-by-step solution. Give details and information that support your suggested solution.

 Research and Technology

In this story you may have discovered a new use for wood—making charcoal. Find out how charcoal is made by searching the Internet or your library. Try using Tío Abrán's favorite woods as keywords: huisache, cedar, mesquite. Prepare a report that explains the process and where the best charcoal is made.

  Media and Viewing

Explore how a movie, as well as a literary work, can present one or more moods. Watch all or part of one of your favorite movies. Take notes on mood. At which points does the mood change? What visual images did the filmmaker use to create each mood? Which words used by the characters help to create each mood?

Letter to Scottie   by F. Scott Fitzgerald

F. Scott Fitzgerald
1896–1940

About the Author

F. Scott Fitzgerald was a writer of short stories, screenplays,
and novels. He was a distant relative of Francis Scott Key,
author of the national anthem. Born in Minnesota, Fitzgerald
published his first novel in 1920 when he was 23. Titled
This Side of Paradise, its instant success brought him fame
and wealth. After serving in the army, Fitzgerald married
Zelda Sayre. This glamorous couple lived during the Roaring
Twenties, a famous time in American history. During this
time, many people started to give importance only to money
and what it could buy. The Fitzgeralds joined this crowd and
began to live a wild lifestyle.

Then the Great Depression hit the United States. The 1929
stock market crash changed the couple's lives for the worse.
Fitzgerald's writing career was affected, and Zelda suffered
nervous illnesses. Despite all this, Fitzgerald produced
dozens of written works. He also worked in Hollywood as
a screenwriter. Over time, he developed a distrust of the very
society he had enjoyed so much. His writing examined the
sense of joy and hopelessness of his time. Fitzgerald's best-
known novel, *The Great Gatsby,* explored this theme. He died
in 1940 of a heart attack.

About the Selection

In 1921, the Fitzgeralds had a daughter, Frances Scott,
whose nicknames were "Scottie" and "Pie." Because of her
parents' travels, Scottie spent her youth in boarding schools
and summer camps. She was at a camp when she received
the letter that is this selection. By this date, the author was
worried about money, his ill wife, and his work. Just like Tío
Abrán in "La Leña Buena," Fitzgerald was sad when he wrote
this letter. The cause of each person's sadness, however, was
very different.

Literary Terms **Style** is how an author writes. Each author has a personal style of writing. To identify an author's style, you should think about his or her use of language. What type of words has the author chosen? How are they arranged? What images or word pictures are created, if any? You should also examine the **tone** of the work. Tone is the attitude an author takes toward a subject. The author's attitude toward a subject expresses his or her feelings and ideas. The following selection is a **letter**. A letter is impressions and feelings written to a specific person.

Reading on Your Own The way an author begins a literary piece is very important. The tone is usually set early on. The first sentence or paragraph usually either attracts or pushes away a reader. You might compare this to getting a first impression of someone you have just met. Read the first paragraph of "Letter to Scottie" and of "La Leña Buena." Which one interests you more, and why?

Writing on Your Own Fitzgerald includes a list of things to worry about and not to worry about in life. Before reading his list, make your own. Imagine that you are writing the list for a good friend. Include at least five things to worry about and five things not to worry about. Compare your list to Fitzgerald's.

Vocabulary Focus Fitzgerald uses a number of phrases whose meaning is different from what the words mean. For example, a "bad egg" refers to someone who spoils life for others. In other words, that person does what a rotten egg does to good food. Try to figure out the meaning of these other phrases as they are used: *fertile mind, shake it off,* and *borrow trouble.*

Think Before You Read Consider that "Letter to Scottie" is written by a father to his daughter. He is giving her advice on the best way to live her life. How does this advice compare to what a parent or other relative would give you?

> **style** an author's way of writing
>
> **tone** the attitude an author takes toward a subject
>
> **letter** impressions and feelings written to a specific person

Letter to Scottie

As you read the letter, ask yourself whether the language is formal or informal.

La Paix, Rodgers' Forge
Towson, Maryland
August 8, 1933

Dear Pie:

I feel very strongly about you doing [your] duty. Would you give me a little more **documentation** about your reading in French? I am glad you are happy—but I never believe much in happiness. I never believe in **misery** either. Those are things you see on the stage or the screen or the printed page, they never really happen to you in life.

All I believe in in life is the rewards for **virtue** (according to your talents) and the *punishments* for not fulfilling your duties, which are doubly costly. If there is such a volume in the camp library, will you ask Mrs. Tyson to let you look up a sonnet of Shakespeare's in which the line occurs *"Lilies that **fester** smell far worse than weeds."*

Have had no thoughts today, life seems **composed** of getting up a *Saturday Evening Post* story. I think of you, and always pleasantly; but if you call me "Pappy" again I am going to take the White Cat out and beat his bottom hard, *six times for every time you are **impertinent**.* Do you react to that?

The *stage* is a synonym for live theater. The *screen* is a synonym for film, or the movies. The *printed page* means the written word, usually published works such as books or newspapers.

A *sonnet* is a fourteen-line poem divided into four sections. It has a formal rhyme scheme.

The Saturday Evening Post was a weekly magazine for which Fitzgerald wrote. He uses *getting up* to mean "getting together" or "writing."

documentation supporting evidence

misery a great sorrow

virtue goodness

fester to decay or rot

composed made up

impertinent showing a lack of proper respect

I will arrange the camp bill.
Halfwit, I will conclude.
Things to worry about:
Worry about courage
Worry about cleanliness
Worry about **efficiency**
Worry about **horsemanship**
Worry about . . .
Things not to worry about:
Don't worry about popular opinion
Don't worry about dolls
Don't worry about the past
Don't worry about the future
Don't worry about growing up
Don't worry about anybody getting ahead of you
Don't worry about triumph
Don't worry about failure unless it comes through your
    own fault
Don't worry about mosquitoes
Don't worry about flies
Don't worry about insects in general
Don't worry about parents
Don't worry about boys
Don't worry about disappointments
Don't worry about pleasures
Don't worry about satisfactions
Things to think about:
What am I really aiming at?
How good am I really in comparison to my
contemporaries in regard to:
(a) **Scholarship**
(b) Do I really understand about people and am I able to
    get along with them?

Reading Strategy:
Summarizing
Why does the
author say "I will
conclude" just
before starting
a long list of
thoughts? What is
the main idea or
theme of this list?

What makes this
section of the letter
straightforward and
uncomplicated?

halfwit a foolish
person

efficiency doing
things without wasting
time or energy

horsemanship the
art or skill of riding on
horseback

contemporaries
peers

scholarship quality
of knowledge and
learning

Is the author's style here humorous, serious, or both? Explain.

P.S. stands for *postscript*, which means "after writing." It is used at the end of a letter when the author adds another comment.

(c) Am I trying to make my body a useful instrument or am I neglecting it?

With dearest love,
[Daddy]

P.S. My come-back to your calling me Pappy is **christening** you by the word Egg, which **implies** that you belong to a very **rudimentary** state of life and that I could break you up and crack you open at my will and I think it would be a word that would hang on if I ever told it to your contemporaries. "Egg Fitzgerald." How would you like that to go through life with—"Eggie Fitzgerald" or "Bad Egg Fitzgerald" or any form that might occur to fertile minds? Try it once more and I swear I will hang it on you and it will be up to you to shake it off. Why borrow trouble?

Love anyhow.

christening giving a name to	**implies** quietly suggests	**rudimentary** basic or undeveloped

COMPARING LITERARY WORKS | Apply the Skills

Letter to Scottie   by F. Scott Fitzgerald

Directions Choose the letter of the best answer or write the answer using complete sentences.

Comprehension: Identifying Facts

1. What two things does Fitzgerald believe never happen in real life?
   A courage and cleanliness
   B rewards and punishments
   C happiness and misery
   D triumph and failure

2. What does Fitzgerald ask his daughter to find at the camp library?
   A a story he has written
   B a work by Shakespeare
   C a book on good advice
   D a copy of *The Saturday Evening Post*

3. Who is Mrs. Tyson?

4. What does Fitzgerald say that he is mainly concerned with at the present time?

5. What has Scottie called her father that he does not like?

6. Which items in Fitzgerald's "Don't worry" list have to do with doing better than others?

7. What nickname does Fitzgerald threaten to call Scottie?

8. Why has Fitzgerald chosen this type of name to call Scottie?

9. In which selection is a famous playwright quoted?

10. Which selection begins with a simile about nature?

Comprehension: Putting Ideas Together

11. Which of the following does Fitzgerald mention twice in the letter to his daughter?
    A doing one's duty
    B not worrying about failure
    C worrying about courage
    D understanding people

12. What theme do the two selections have in common?
    A people who are at risk of danger
    B authors who are close to family members
    C parents who love their children
    D immigrants who move to another country

13. How does Fitzgerald seem to feel about Scottie's nickname for him? What details support your answer?

14. Find a sentence in each selection that discusses or mentions nature.

15. In which selection does the author discuss mostly his own thoughts and opinions?

Comparing continued on next page

Letter to Scottie   by F. Scott Fitzgerald

16. Which selection shows admiration, and to whom or for what?

17. What is a character trait that Fitzgerald and Tío Abrán have in common?

18. In which selection does some type of conflict play a part? What is the conflict?

19. Which selection contains the most information about the author's family?

20. Compare the mood of the two selections.

Understanding Literature: Author's Style

The way an author writes is called style. Tone, word choice, and use of images affect an author's style. These things help an author to create a certain feeling in readers. An author's style can give you a clue about how he or she thinks. It can also tell you what is important to the author.

21. Which author uses humor as a writing style?

22. Compare the tone of the *postscript* in Fitzgerald's letter with the tone of the rest of the letter.

23. What is different about the sentence styles in "Letter to Scottie" and "La Leña Buena"?

24. For which selection does the author's style better fit his purpose for writing the work? Explain your answer.

25. Think about the word choice in each selection. Which author's word choice surprised you more? Why?

Critical Thinking

26. Consider Fitzgerald's advice not to "worry about failure unless it comes through your own fault." How might this apply to Tío Abrán?

27. In your opinion, which sentence in each selection contains the best image?

28. Which selection connects more with the cultural heritage of the author? Explain your answer.

29. Based on the selections, do you think Santos and Fitzgerald have similar attitudes toward family? Explain your answer.

Thinking Creatively

30. If you wrote a letter to either Tío Abrán or Fitzgerald, what advice would you give?

Grammar Check

A stringy sentence contains too many ideas connected with conjunctions such as *and, or, but,* and *so.* In such a sentence, you cannot easily tell how the ideas relate to each other. This makes it hard to understand what the writer is saying. Read the first sentence of the *postscript* in Fitzgerald's letter. How would you write it so that it is not a stringy sentence?

 Vocabulary Builder

The suffix *-ship* can mean "having the art or skill of." It can also mean "showing or having the quality, state, condition, or character of." Which of these meanings applies to *scholarship* and *horsemanship?* Form new words by adding *-ship* to *fellow, friend, relation, partner,* and *hard.* Explain what each new word means.

 Writing on Your Own

Compare the overall tone of "La Leña Buena" to "Letter to Scottie."

Write an essay discussing the ways each author reveals his style. Use these questions to get started:

- What kind of words does the author use?

- What images does the author include?
- What feelings do these words and images express?

 Listening and Speaking

With a partner, create a skit to present to the class. Choose one of the following to role-play:

- Tío Abrán and a *militante* trying to steal his wood

- Tío Abrán talking to his brother Jacobo when he arrives in San Antonio

- F. Scott Fitzgerald giving Scottie advice in person

Write a dialogue, or conversation between two people, based on the selection. Choose believable words for the characters to say. Practice the skit several times before performing it.

 Research and Technology

Find out more about the time period in which F. Scott Fitzgerald rose to fame. Use the Internet to do research on the "Roaring Twenties." What music and dances became popular during that time? Which other authors were writing then? What well-known events took place?

Some words require spelling changes when endings like *-ed* and *-ing* are added. Other words do not. Some words also have irregular plural forms. There are several rules that can help you form words like these.

Review the Rules

Nearly all base words follow specific rules for adding *-ed* and *-ing*. Some plural words have irregular spellings, but there are rules for these words, too.

Rules for Adding *-ed* and *-ing*

- For most verbs, do not double the final consonant.
- For most one-syllable verbs ending in one vowel and one consonant, double the final consonant.

- For verbs that end in a vowel + *y*, generally keep the *y*.
- For verbs that end in a consonant + *y*, keep the *y* when adding *-ing*. Change *y* to *i* when adding *-ed*.

Spelling Irregular Plurals

- For many words ending in *f*, change *f* to *v* and add *-es*.
- For some plurals, use the same spelling as the singular.
- For some irregular plurals, add a special ending to the word.

Practice

Add *-ed* and *-ing* to each of the following words.

1. hurry
2. leak
3. occur
4. delay

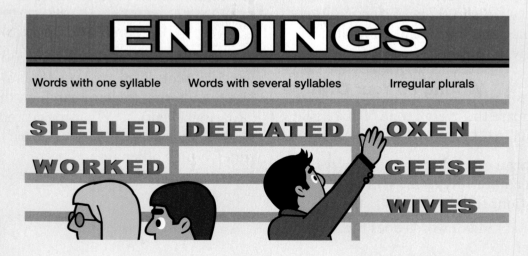

ENDINGS

Words with one syllable	Words with several syllables	Irregular plurals
SPELLED	DEFEATED	OXEN
WORKED		GEESE
		WIVES

Nonfiction writing is about real people and their experiences. It presents facts and information, as well as a writer's ideas. Nonfiction works do not need a plot or setting, as fiction works do. Unlike fiction, nonfiction may not have a theme or character development. However, some forms of nonfiction do contain some of these elements. For example, essays often have a theme. A biography or autobiography may have character development and a setting.

Other elements that fiction writers use are also used by nonfiction writers. These include mood, tone, images, and conflict. Also, a nonfiction writer, like a fiction writer, has a certain writing style.

A nonfiction work can have the purpose of explaining, persuading, describing, or entertaining. Many nonfiction works have multiple purposes. A humorous biography may tell readers about a person's life while also entertaining them. An essay may describe recycling while also trying to persuade readers to recycle.

This unit has presented several literary forms: narrative essay, autobiography, biography, memoir, and letter. This group gives you a sense of the wide range of nonfiction literary works.

Selections

- "Water," by Helen Keller, is an autobiographical narrative essay that describes a deaf-blind girl's experience. She finds meaning and purpose in a dark, silent world with the help of her teacher, Anne Sullivan.

- "Amy Tan," by Kathy Ishizuka, is a biography of the popular author. It describes Tan's conflict with her Chinese heritage, her difficult childhood, and her desire to rebel against tradition.

- *Rosa Parks: My Story*, by Rosa Parks with Jim Haskins, is the autobiography of a civil rights leader. Parks tells her experience of racism during a time when African Americans were second-class citizens.

- "Turkeys," by Bailey White, is an autobiographical narrative essay about a childhood event. A group of strange ornithologists use her fevered body as an incubator for turkey eggs.

- "La Leña Buena," by John Phillip Santos, is also a narrative essay. The essay shows the author's pride in his family heritage. It details how his great-uncle, a wood collector, struggled to survive after the Mexican Revolution.

- "Letter to Scottie," by F. Scott Fitzgerald, shows the private side of a public figure. He shares thoughts about life with his daughter, who is at camp.

Directions Choose the letter of the best answer or write the answer using complete sentences.

Comprehension: Identifying Facts

1. Why does Helen Keller break her doll?
   - **A** to make her teacher angry
   - **B** to express the idea that she is growing up
   - **C** to show her teacher how strong she is
   - **D** to get rid of something that makes her uncomfortable

2. What effect does the serious illness of her mother have on Amy Tan?

3. What do officials repeatedly prevent Rosa Parks from doing?

4. Why do the ornithologists first start spending time at Bailey White's house?

5. In what two ways does Fitzgerald threaten to get back at Scottie because she called him "Pappy"?

Comprehension: Putting Ideas Together

6. In which situation does Rosa Parks have to face racism?
   - **A** when riding a bus
   - **B** when arriving at her job
   - **C** when going to get her mail
   - **D** when joining a workers' union

7. How does Helen Keller's attitude change from the beginning of the essay to the end?

8. What behaviors by the ornithologists suggest they are more interested in birds than in humans?

9. What keeps Tío Abrán from continuing his work as a woodcutter in Mexico?

10. What does F. Scott Fitzgerald tell Scottie is important in life?

Understanding Literature: Mood

A movie can create an overall feeling in viewers. So can a written work. This overall feeling is called mood. The mood of a nonfiction work may be joyful or hopeless, practical or dreamlike. A work may have a single mood or several of them.

11. Which author's writing contains the greatest number of images? Give a few examples.

12. Describe the changing moods of "La Leña Buena" and of "Water."

13. Name something Rosa Parks does to create an anxious mood in *Rosa Parks: My Story*.

14. Which selection do you think has the most light-hearted mood? Why?

15. Which selection do you think has the most unexpected mood? Explain your choice.

Critical Thinking

16. Explain why the text structure of *Rosa Parks: My Story* could be called both sequence and description.

17. Summarize the selection you liked best. Think about the selection's text structure as you write the summary.

18. Of all the people you read about in this unit, choose two. Compare their character traits, as well as important events they experienced.

19. What purpose other than informing might Ishizuka have had for writing Tan's biography? Explain your answer.

Thinking Creatively

20. If you could change places with one of the characters for one week, who would it be? Whose life would you most like to experience? How would you be changed when you returned to your own life?

Speak and Listen

Choose a character from one of the selections. Perform a short monologue, or one-person speech, based on that person. Pick a scene or event that the character actually went through. As the character, explain what happened to you. Then share your thoughts and feelings about the experience. As you perform in front of the class, use your best acting skills to be more believable.

Writing on Your Own

Imagine that it is 1925. You are working for an organization that wants to plant trees in Mexico. You will be writing a letter to ask people to donate money to this cause. Do research on the Mexican Revolution. Learn details about how that war destroyed natural resources. In the letter, explain what happened and how it hurt the people living there. Explain the benefits of planting trees in these areas.

Beyond Words

Imagine that one of the selections is being made into a movie. You and another student have been asked to write the theme song for the movie. With your partner, choose the selection and write the song. It should reflect an important theme in the selection. Be sure to give your song a title.

Test-Taking Tip

Before you start a test, look it over so you can plan how to use your time.

Exposition: Persuasive Essay

A persuasive essay argues for or against a particular position, or opinion. It urges a specific course of action. Follow the steps outlined in this workshop to write your own persuasive essay.

Assignment Write a persuasive essay to convince readers to improve their lives in a specific way.

What to Include A good persuasive essay features the following elements:

- a clear thesis or statement that presents a position on an issue having at least two sides
- facts, examples, and reasons that support the position
- powerful language to appeal to a specific audience
- evidence and arguments to address readers' concerns
- a clear structure, including an introduction, a body, and a strong conclusion
- error-free writing, including correct spelling, grammar, and punctuation

Using the Form
You may use elements of persuasion in these types of writing:
- speeches
- advertisements
- problem-solution essays

Six Traits of Writing:

Ideas message, details, and purpose

Prewriting
Choosing Your Topic

The best topic is one that is important to you. The topic should have one point of view you can support and one you can oppose. Use the following strategies to help you find a suitable topic:

- **Conduct a media review.** Think about the local issues in the news now. Look through newspapers for stories. Read the letters to the editor in newspapers. Watch and listen to local television and radio news programs. List all the topics that appeal to you, and then choose one for your essay.

- **Organize a round table.** Gather classmates for a discussion of places and groups that are important to you. Think of issues that affect the locations and people you have listed. Jot down any ideas that interest you, and choose a topic.

Narrowing Your Topic

Once you choose a topic, make sure it is not too big for a short persuasive essay. Use a graphic organizer like the one shown to narrow your topic.

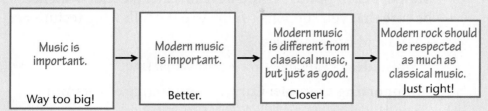

Music is important.	Modern music is important.	Modern music is different from classical music, but just as good.	Modern rock should be respected as much as classical music.
Way too big!	Better.	Closer!	Just right!

Gathering Details

Collect support for your position. Identify facts, examples, numbers, quotations, and personal observations that support your position. Take notes on the sources of your information. You will use these notes to credit any ideas or words that are not your own.

Plan ahead for arguments against your position. Look ahead to identify readers' questions. Predict points of view that might differ from your position. Be prepared to include facts that you think will overcome these objections.

Writing Your Draft

Shaping Your Writing

Write a thesis statement. The evidence, or support, you have gathered will help you argue your position. Prepare a thesis statement—one sentence that names your issue and expresses your position.

Sample Thesis Statements

1. Our school should have recycling bins.

2. Young people should exercise 20 minutes every day.

Create a clear organization. Review the chart shown here to clearly organize your thoughts. Include your thesis statement in your introduction. Support your thesis statement in the body. Organize supporting information

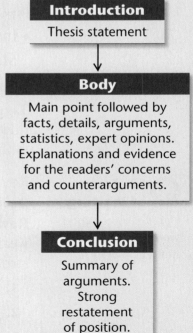

Introduction
Thesis statement

Body
Main point followed by facts, details, arguments, statistics, expert opinions. Explanations and evidence for the readers' concerns and counterarguments.

Conclusion
Summary of arguments. Strong restatement of position.

Six Traits of Writing:
Organization order, ideas tied together

into paragraphs. Each paragraph should focus on one reason you give for your position. Conclude by repeating your thesis.

Providing Elaboration

Support each point. As you develop each piece of evidence, be sure that you support it fully. Use the following techniques:

- Find and use examples.

  Main idea: Vegetables are healthy snacks.

  Supporting example: Carrots are a source of Vitamin A.

- Use facts or statistics.

  Main idea: Rock music is often loud, but it is still music.

  Supporting fact: Rock music follows patterns of rhythm.

- Include quotations and expert opinions.

  Main idea: Our nation depends on volunteers.

  Supporting quotation: "Ask not what your country can do for you; ask what you can do for your country." —President John F. Kennedy

- Include personal observations to appeal to emotions.

  Main idea: Doctors agree that daily exercise is important.

  Supporting observation: I always feel better after jogging.

Target your audience. Consider the ages of your readers and their knowledge about your topic. Then develop your draft with this information in mind.

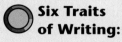

Six Traits of Writing:
Word Choice vivid words that "show, not tell"

Revising

Revising Your Paragraphs

Revise to improve support. Review your draft and look for weak arguments. Follow these steps to make your arguments stronger and to better support your thesis:

1. Underline your thesis statement.

2. Put a star next to each supporting point. Add more support if you have only one star.

3. Draw attention to a well-supported point by adding interesting language or a colorful comparison.

4. If you find a paragraph without support, review your prewriting notes and add support. If necessary, do extra research to find the support you need.

Revising Your Sentences

Revise to strengthen images and observations. Look for places where you need to make your point stronger. Then, add or improve an image or personal observation. Use words that call specific pictures or sensory details to mind. Vivid language will appeal to your readers' emotions, or feelings. It will also help persuade them to agree with you.

Editing and Proofreading

Review your draft to fix errors in grammar, spelling, and punctuation.

Focus on Sentence Fragments: Correct any incomplete sentences that are missing a subject or a predicate. Change any sentences that do not express a complete thought.

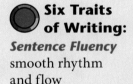

Six Traits of Writing:
Sentence Fluency smooth rhythm and flow

Publishing and Presenting

Consider one of the following ways to share your writing:

Deliver a speech. Use your persuasive essay to create a speech that you can give to your classmates.

Post your essay. Post your persuasive essay on a class or school bulletin board. Encourage others to read and discuss it.

Reflecting on Your Writing

Writer's Journal Jot down your thoughts on writing a persuasive essay. Begin by answering these questions:

• How did gathering details to support your position change your feelings about the issue?

• While writing your essay, what did you learn about building a strong and fair argument?

The Princess Who Lived In a Tree
Lou Wall

Unit | 4 Poetry

This unit explores poetry. Having existed since ancient times, it was once used to tell long stories aloud. Today, it is often used to express feelings or to tell about memories. Poetry looks different from other forms of literature. It is set up in lines. It uses a few words to express a lot. It uses language in a rich and meaningful way.

In this unit, you will read poems from different times and places.

"Poetry . . . is man's natural form of expression. There are no peoples without poetry, there are some without prose."

—Octavio Paz, *The Bow and the Lyre*, 1967, tr. 1973

Unit 4 About Poetry

Elements of Poetry

Poetry writers use language to make pictures, tell stories, explore feelings, and explain experiences. Writers use many different methods to do this.

Sound devices add a quality of music to poetry. Writers use these devices to add to a poem's mood and meaning.

- **Rhyme** is words that end with the same or similar sound.

- **Rhythm** is a pattern created by the ending sounds of the lines of a poem.

- **Repetition** is using a word, phrase, or image more than once, for emphasis.

- **Onomatopoeia** is using words that sound like their meaning.

- **Alliteration** is repeating sounds by using words whose beginning sounds are the same.

Figurative language is writing or speech not meant to be understood exactly as it is written. Writers use figurative language to express ideas in vivid or imaginative ways. The many types of figurative language are called **figures of speech.** A figure of speech is a word or phrase that has meaning different from the actual meaning. Different figures of speech are metaphors, similes, and personification.

- A **metaphor** is a figure of speech that makes a comparison but does not use *like* or *as.* Metaphors often point to a likeness between two unlike things:

  The snow was a white blanket over the town.

- A **simile** is a figure of speech in which two things are compared using a phrase that includes the words *like* or *as.*

  She is as slow as a turtle.

- **Personification** is giving characters such as animals or objects the characteristics or qualities of humans.

  The ocean crashed angrily during the storm.

Sensory language is writing or speech that uses one or more of the five senses—sight, sound, smell, taste, and touch. This language makes word pictures, or **images.** Poetry writers use these word pictures to help the reader enjoy the poem.

Forms of Poetry

Narrative poetry is a poem that tells a story. Narrative poems are like short stories because they often both have characters and a plot.

Lyric poetry is a short poem that expresses a person's emotions or feelings.

Concrete poetry is a poem made to look like the writer's subject. The writer makes the lines of the poem into a picture on the page.

Haiku poetry is a form of Japanese poetry. It has three lines with five syllables in the first line, seven in the second, and five in the third.

A **limerick** is a humorous five-line poem in which the first, second, and fifth lines, and third and fourth lines, rhyme.

Part 1

Reading Strategy:
Text Structure

Looking at the boldfaced words is one way to understand how a text is organized. As you preview a text, you will likely notice some words that are unfamiliar to you. You can use context clues to help figure out the meanings of these difficult words. Context clues are the text around an unfamiliar word that helps you figure out the meaning. Use context clues to help you better understand what you are reading.

Literary Terms

rhythm a pattern created by the stressed and unstressed syllables in a line of poetry

rhyme words that end with the same or similar sounds

figurative language writing or speech not meant to be understood exactly as it is written

simile a figure of speech that makes a comparison using the words *like* or *as*

metaphor a figure of speech that makes a comparison but does not use *like* or *as*

personification giving characters such as animals or objects the characteristics or qualities of humans

image a word or phrase that appeals to the senses and allows the reader to picture events

imagery pictures created by words; the use of words that appeal to the five senses

mood the feeling that writing creates

About the Authors and Selections

Ogden Nash, one of America's best-loved poets and humor writers, threw away his first poetry attempt. Luckily, he pulled it out of the trash. He then sent it to the *New Yorker* magazine—which published it immediately! During his 40-year career, Nash wrote more than 30 poetry books. In "Adventures of Isabel," Isabel meets a lot of troublesome characters. She manages to get rid of them all.

Ogden Nash
1902–1971

Jack Prelutsky
1940–

As a child, Jack Prelutsky was not a fan of poetry. As an adult, he made drawings of imaginary creatures. He decided to write some poems to accompany his drawings. Prelutsky soon published his first book of poems. He went on to write many more books of humorous verse. "Ankylosaurus" uses humor to give the reader a look into the past.

Frances E. W. Harper was born in Baltimore, Maryland. Her parents were free, but many African Americans around her were still slaves. Unlike the woman in "Learning to Read," Harper received a good education. She worked hard for the rights of African Americans and women. She traveled, giving lectures and reading her poetry. The speaker in "Learning to Read" has a different life story. Like many women Harper knew, she is coming to education late in life.

Frances E. W. Harper
1825–1911

Objectives

- To read and understand poetry
- To identify rhythm and rhyme in poetry

Before Reading **continued on next page**

rhythm a pattern created by the stressed and unstressed syllables in a line of poetry

rhyme words that end with the same or similar sounds

Literary Terms **Rhythm** and **rhyme** add a musical quality to poems. Rhythm is the sound pattern created by stressed and unstressed syllables.

Example: JACK and JILL went UP the HILL (4 stressed/ 3 unstressed)

Rhyme is the repetition of sounds at the ends of words.

Example: Jack fell <u>down</u>/And broke his <u>crown</u>.

Reading on Your Own Context clues are found in the text surrounding an unfamiliar word. They may be words with the same meaning. They may be descriptions or explanations. To use context clues, ask these questions:

• What kind of word is it?

• What word can I use in place of the unfamiliar word?

• Does the new sentence make sense?

Example: He lengthened his <u>stride</u> to catch up with us.
Question: What kind of word is it?
Answer: It is a noun. It names a way you move to catch up.

Writing on Your Own Two of the poems in this collection use humor. One uses amusing images to tell about something serious. Write three sentences about what makes something funny. Why do people sometimes disagree on what is funny?

Vocabulary Focus Suffixes can be a useful clue to the meaning of unfamiliar words. Suffixes can tell you the part of speech of the word. For example, the suffix *-ous* usually turns a noun into an adjective, as in *courageous*. The suffix *-er* usually turns a verb into a noun, as in *farmer*. As you read, use these suffixes to get clues about the meanings of new words.

Think Before You Read How do poets choose their subjects? What would you write about if you were writing a poem?

Adventures of Isabel

Isabel met an enormous bear,
Isabel, Isabel, didn't care;
The bear was hungry, the bear was **ravenous**,
The bear's big mouth was cruel and **cavernous**.
5 The bear said, Isabel, glad to meet you,
How do, Isabel, now I'll eat you!
Isabel, Isabel, didn't worry,
Isabel didn't scream or scurry.
She washed her hands and she straightened her hair up,
10 Then Isabel quietly ate the bear up.

Once in a night as black as **pitch**
Isabel met a wicked old witch.
The witch's face was cross and wrinkled,
The witch's gums with teeth were sprinkled.
15 Ho ho, Isabel! the old witch crowed,
I'll turn you into an ugly toad!
Isabel, Isabel, didn't worry,
Isabel didn't scream or scurry,
She showed no rage and she showed no **rancor**,
20 But she turned the witch into milk and drank her.

Isabel met a hideous giant,
Isabel continued **self-reliant.**
The giant was hairy, the giant was horrid,
He had one eye in the middle of his forehead.
25 Good morning Isabel, the giant said,
I'll grind your bones to make my bread.
Isabel, Isabel, didn't worry,
Isabel didn't scream or scurry.

> As you read, think about the pattern of rhyme in each stanza.

ravenous greedily hungry

cavernous vast and deep

pitch tar

rancor bitter hate or ill will

self-reliant able to take care of oneself

What two-word rhymes are used in lines 29 and 30?

She nibbled the **zwieback** that she always fed off,
30 And when it was gone, she cut the giant's head off.

Isabel met a troublesome doctor,
He punched and he poked till he really shocked her.
The doctor's talk was of coughs and chills
And the doctor's satchel bulged with pills.
35 The doctor said unto Isabel,
Swallow this, it will make you well.
Isabel, Isabel, didn't worry,
Isabel didn't scream or scurry.
She took those pills from the pill **concocter,**
40 And Isabel calmly cured the doctor.
— *Ogden Nash*

Reading Strategy:
Text Structure

What clues help you understand that a satchel is something that holds things?

zwieback a dry, toastlike cracker

concocter one who creates something by mixing things together

Ankylosaurus

Clankity Clankity Clankity Clank!
Ankylosaurus was built like a tank,
its hide was a fortress as sturdy as steel,
it tended to be an **inedible** meal.

5 It was armored in front, it was armored behind,
there wasn't a thing on its **minuscule** mind,
it waddled about on its four **stubby** legs,
nibbling on plants with a mouthful of pegs.

Ankylosaurus was best left alone,
10 its tail was a **cudgel** of **gristle** and bone,
Clankity Clankity Clankity Clank!
Ankylosaurus was built like a tank.
— *Jack Prelutsky*

Ankylosaurus was a very large dinosaur with heavy armor and a large bony tail. Its skeletons have been found in Wyoming and Montana.

inedible not fit to be eaten

minuscule very small

stubby short and thick

cudgel a club

gristle a tough, stringy tissue found in meat

What is the pattern of rhymes at the ends of the lines in each stanza?

Learning to Read

Very soon the Yankee teachers
    Came down and set up school;
But, oh! how the Rebs did hate it,—
    It was **agin'** their rule.

5 Our masters always tried to hide
    Book learning from our eyes;
Knowledge didn't agree with slavery—
    'Twould make us all too wise.

But some of us would try to steal
10   A little from the book,
And put the words together,
    And learn by hook or crook.

I remember Uncle Caldwell,
    Who took **pot-liquor** fat
15 And greased the pages of his book,
    And hid it in his hat.

And had his master ever seen
    The **leaves** upon his head,
He'd have thought them greasy papers,
20   But nothing to be read.

And there was Mr. Turner's Ben,
    Who heard the children spell,
And picked the words right up by heart,
    And learned to read 'em well.

Reading Strategy: Text Structure
How can you tell that *agin'* here is not short for *aging*? What clues can you use?

The word *'twould* is a contraction for "it would."

The phrase *by hook or crook* means "one way or another."

agin' against   **pot-liquor** the liquid in which meat has been cooked   **leaves** pages

The *Yankees*
were the Union
supporters from
the North in the
Civil War. The *Rebs,*
or Rebels, were
the Confederate
supporters from
the South. The
Civil War lasted
from 1861–1865.

Rising sixty means
"coming close to
60 years of age."

25 Well, the Northern folks kept sending
    The Yankee teachers down;
And they stood right up and helped us,
    Though Rebs did sneer and frown.

And, I longed to read my Bible,
30   For precious words it said;
But when I begun to learn it,
    Folks just shook their heads,

And said there is no use trying,
    Oh! Chloe, you're too late;
35 But as I was rising sixty,
    I had no time to wait.

So I got a pair of glasses,
    And straight to work I went,
And never stopped till I could read
40 The hymns and Testament.

Then I got a little cabin—
    A place to call my own—
And I felt as independent
    As the queen upon her throne.
— *Frances E. W. Harper*

Adventures of Isabel | Ankylosaurus | Learning to Read

Directions Choose the letter of the best answer or write the answer using complete sentences.

Comprehension: Identifying Facts

1. In "Adventures of Isabel," what did Isabel do to the giant?
   A She ate him all up.
   B She turned him into milk.
   C She cut his head off.
   D She washed his hair.

2. What was the dinosaur built like in "Ankylosaurus"?

3. In "Learning to Read," where did Uncle Caldwell hide his book?

Comprehension: Putting Ideas Together

4. What word might you use to describe Isabel in "Adventures of Isabel"?
   A confident   C artistic
   B fearful   D peaceful

5. What does "Ankylosaurus was built like a tank" mean?

6. In "Learning to Read," who is Chloe?

Understanding Literature: Rhythm and Rhyme

A careful poet arranges words so that they fall into a pattern, or rhythm.

Rhythm adds meaning to the poem by giving more weight to important words and ideas. Sometimes the rhythm is a singsong beat. Sometimes it is harder to hear.

When words end with the same sound, we call that rhyme. Poets may use rhyme for many reasons. Rhyme may call attention to certain words. It may help structure a poem by connecting one stanza to another. Usually, rhyme appears at the ends of lines. Sometimes it appears within lines.

7. How many stressed syllables are in these lines of poetry?

   Isabel met an enormous bear,/
   Isabel, Isabel, didn't care.

8. Name two pairs of rhyming words in lines 1–8 of "Learning to Read."

Critical Thinking

9. Why do you think Prelutsky began "Ankylosaurus" with the sound words "Clankity Clankity Clankity Clank"?

Thinking Creatively

10. Which poem in this collection would make a good song? Why do you think so?

After Reading **continued on next page**

Grammar Check

A simple sentence can contain a simple subject or a compound subject. A simple subject is the person, place, or thing about which the sentence is written. A compound subject is two or more simple subjects, usually joined by *and*.

Example: <u>Uncle Caldwell</u> learned to read. <u>Ben</u> learned to read. <u>Uncle Caldwell and Ben</u> learned to read.

Write four sentences about Isabel in "Adventures of Isabel." Use simple subjects in two sentences. Use compound subjects in the other two.

 Vocabulary Builder

The prefix *in-* has more than one meaning. In the word *inedible,* it means "not." In the word *indent,* it means "in." Copy the words below. Circle the ones in which *in-* means "not." Underline the ones in which *in-* means "in."

independent	infect	infinite
inhabitant	injection	inoffensive
insert	intolerant	

 Writing on Your Own

One way to respond to literature is to write a letter to an author. You do not need to send the letter; it is just for your own use. Choose one of the poets in this collection. Write a letter to him or her. Tell the poet whether you like the poem and if so, what you like about it. Begin with a sentence that states your overall opinion. Follow with examples and reasons.

 Listening and Speaking

With a partner, plan an interview with Chloe of "Learning to Read." One person can be the interviewer, and the other can be Chloe. The interviewer should first develop a list of questions to ask. Next, he or she should organize the questions in order. The person playing Chloe should do some research on slavery. Then, act out the interview together.

 Research and Technology

Use library resources to find several poems and stories about dinosaurs. Copy them and organize them into a mini-book. Include illustrations. Write a one-sentence comment about each poem and story. In your comment, compare the work with "Ankylosaurus."

Recipes

In Part 1, you have seen how text structure helps you define unfamiliar words. Context clues can also help you define special terms in informational materials such as recipes.

About Recipes

Recipes are instructions for preparing food or drinks. Most recipes have some common parts. Once you learn to recognize these features, you will find recipes easier to follow. These common parts include:

- a title that names the dish
- a list of ingredients, the food items you need to make the dish
- directions that explain the steps to follow to make the dish
- the number of people the dish will serve

Many recipes include additional information:

- the amount of time it takes to prepare the dish
- information about amounts of fat or sugar
- serving suggestions

The recipes here are for three simple dishes. You will also see a list of common recipe abbreviations.

Reading Skill

As you follow a recipe, you may come across unfamiliar words. You may see familiar words used in unfamiliar ways. When this happens, use context clues. The words surrounding an unfamiliar word or phrase can help you understand its meaning. Pictures can also provide context clues.

As you read the recipe, use a diagram like this one. List the context clues that help you figure out the meanings of unfamiliar words or phrases.

Unfamiliar Word	simmer
Sentence in Which It Appears	Bring to a boil, reduce heat, and simmer for 5 minutes.
Context Clue	reduce heat
Possible Meaning	cook at a temperature that is not as hot as a boil

Recipe for: Avocado Dip   Recipe from: Mitch

1 avocado, chopped
2 large tomatoes, chopped
1/4 cup chopped green onion
1 garlic clove, peeled and diced
   fine with a sharp knife
1/2 tablespoon lemon juice

(optional for spice-lovers:
1 hot pepper, diced fine)
1 tablespoon chopped
   fresh parsley
1 tablespoon olive oil

In a large bowl, mix all the above together.
Serve with corn chips.

Time to make: 30 minutes
Serves: 6

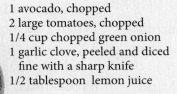

Recipe for: Fruit Dump Cake   Recipe from: Mrs. Banning

1 20-oz. can crushed pineapple
1 20-oz. can cherry or apple pie
   filling
1 package yellow cake mix

1 stick of butter, chopped
   into small pieces
1/2 cup chopped nuts

Dump the pineapple into the bottom of a 9" x 13" cake pan. Top with
the pie filling. Toss the yellow cake mix on top and press lightly. Top
the cake mix with the butter pieces. Toss nuts on top. Bake 70 minutes
at 350° or until golden brown.

Time to make: 30 minutes + baking time
Serves: 6

> Directions
> appear in
> step-by-step
> order.

Recipe for: Tacos

Recipe from: Ann

The ingredients are listed in the order in which you will need them.

1 lb. ground beef
1 pkg. taco mix
8 soft taco shells
1 medium onion, chopped

2 tomatoes
4 c. lettuce, chopped
2 c. cheese, shredded
1 c. sour cream

Follow taco mix directions to prepare ground beef and taco mix. Microwave taco shells on high for 30 seconds. Fill each taco shell with taco meat, onions, tomatoes, lettuce, cheese, and sour cream. Eat right away.

Time to make: 25 minutes
Serves: 4

1 Cup
3/4 Cup
1/2 Cup
1/4 Cup

Abbreviations Used in Recipes

lb. = pound
oz. = ounce
doz. = dozen
pkg. = package
tsp. = teaspoon
t. = teaspoon
tbsp. = tablespoon
T.= tablespoon

min. = minute
hr. = hour
pt. = pint
qt. = quart
F. = Fahrenheit
g = gram
c. = cup
sq. = square

Recipes may use abbreviations to save space.

Monitor Your Progress

Directions Choose the letter of the best answer or write the answer using complete sentences.

1. Which ingredient could you leave out of Avocado Dip?
   A garlic   **C** avocado
   B pepper   **D** tomatoes

2. Which step comes first in the making of Fruit Dump Cake?
   A Putting pineapple in the pan.
   B Mixing the cake mix together.
   C Layering on the pie filling.
   D Sprinkling the nuts on top.

3. Which recipe(s) requires no heating or cooking?
   I. Avocado Dip
   II. Fruit Dump Cake
   III. Tacos

   A I only   **C** I and II
   B II only   **D** II and III

4. What context clues help you understand the meaning of *diced* in the recipe for Avocado Dip? What does the word mean?

5. To make the recipe for Tacos, how much ground beef should you buy? How big a package of shredded cheese should you buy?

Writing on Your Own

Think of a food you know how to make. Briefly explain simple directions for making that food. Include all needed tools and ingredients. List the steps in order.

About the Authors and Selections

Eve Merriam fell in love very early with the music of language. She wrote award-winning poetry for adults and children. She also wrote and directed musical theater productions. Among her many books for young readers are *There Is No Rhyme for Silver* and *Rainbow Writing*. In "Simile: Willow and Ginkgo," she compares two unlike trees.

Eve Merriam
1916–1992

Emily Dickinson
1830–1886

After one year of college, Emily Dickinson was homesick. She returned to her parents' house in Amherst, Massachusetts. For the rest of her life, she seldom traveled or received guests. Dickinson read many books and wrote more than 1,700 poems. The poems form a kind of lifelong diary of her deepest thoughts. She is considered one of the leading voices of American poetry. "Fame Is a Bee" is typical of her work. In few words, she uses a comparison to describe the appeal and pain of fame.

Langston Hughes traveled to Africa and Europe as a young man. Later he settled in Harlem in New York City. In the 1920s, he was one of the leaders of the Harlem Renaissance. This was a period in which African American writers, artists, and musicians produced brilliant works. Hughes won awards for his poetry, drama, and novels. "April Rain Song" paints a vivid picture of a gentle rain.

Langston Hughes
1902–1967

Objectives

◆ To read and understand poetry
◆ To recognize figurative language in poetry

Before Reading continued on next page

figurative language
writing or speech not meant to be understood exactly as it is written

simile a figure of speech that makes a comparison using the words *like* or *as*

metaphor a figure of speech that makes a comparison but does not use *like* or *as*

personification giving characters such as animals or objects the characteristics or qualities of humans

Literary Terms **Figurative language** is speech that is not meant to be understood exactly as it is expressed. Authors use figurative language to state ideas in fresh ways. For example:

- **Similes** compare two unlike things using the words *like* or *as*. *Example:* The wind was as gentle as a lamb.

- **Metaphors** compare two unlike things by stating that one thing is another. *Example:* The wind was a wild beast.

- **Personification** compares an animal or object to a human by giving the animal or object human qualities. *Example:* The wind caressed my cheek.

Reading on Your Own Context is the situation in which a word or expression is used. Details in the surrounding text give you clues to the word's meaning. Some words have more than one meaning. Look for context clues that help you understand which meaning is being used. These examples show how context makes the meaning of *hide* clear.

Example: The children tried to <u>hide</u> the broken vase.
The elephant's gray <u>hide</u> was tough and leathery.

Writing on Your Own Poets paint unexpected pictures of people, places, and things, often by using comparisons. Complete this sentence with an unusual comparison.

A puppy is like a _____ because they both _____.

Vocabulary Focus In English, we often use a hyphen to join words together. Sometimes this makes a compound word, as in *merry-go-round* or *mother-in-law*. The hyphen helps the reader connect the words. Skim the three poems in this collection. Find three pairs of words that are joined by hyphens. Think about how the hyphens change the meaning of the connected words.

Think Before You Read Why do you think so many poets choose to write about nature?

Simile: Willow and Ginkgo

The willow is like an **etching**,
Fine-lined against the sky.
The ginkgo is like a **crude** sketch,
Hardly worthy to be signed.

5   The willow's music is like a **soprano,**
Delicate and thin.
The ginkgo's tune is like a chorus
With everyone joining in.

The willow is sleek as a velvet-nosed calf;
10 The ginkgo is leathery as an old bull.
The willow's branches are like silken thread;
The ginkgo's like stubby rough wool.

The willow is like a **nymph** with streaming hair;
Wherever it grows, there is green and gold and fair.
15 The willow dips to the water,
Protected and precious, like the king's favorite daughter.

The ginkgo forces its way through gray concrete;
Like a city child, it grows up in the street.
Thrust against the metal sky,
20 Somehow it **survives** and even thrives.

My eyes feast upon the willow,
But my heart goes to the ginkgo.
— Eve Merriam

Reading Strategy:
Text Structure
Crude has more than one meaning. What does it mean here? How do you know?

Ginkgo trees have large, upright branches and fan-shaped leaves. Willow trees have long, drooping branches and long, delicate leaves. As you read, look for other differences between the two.

What kind of figurative language tells how the ginkgo grows?

etching a print of a drawing made on metal, glass, or wood

crude simple and rough

soprano one who uses the highest singing voice of women or boys

nymph a goddess of nature, thought of as a beautiful maiden

survives carries on; continues to live

FAME IS A BEE

Based on the
figurative language
of the poem,
what are the
characteristics
of fame?

Fame is a bee.
It has a song—
It has a sting—
Ah, too, it has a wing.
— *Emily Dickinson*

April Rain Song

Reading Strategy:
Text Structure

How does this
poem's repetition
add to the
experience of
the poem?

Let the rain kiss you.
Let the rain beat upon your head with silver liquid drops.
Let the rain sing you a lullaby.

5   The rain makes still pools on the sidewalk.
The rain makes running pools in the gutter.
The rain plays a little sleep-song on our roof at night—

And I love the rain.
— *Langston Hughes*

AFTER READING THE SELECTIONS | Apply the Skills

Simile: Willow and Ginkgo | Fame Is a Bee | April Rain Song

Directions Choose the letter of the best answer or write the answer using complete sentences.

Comprehension: Identifying Facts

1. Which stanza in "Simile: Willow and Ginkgo" deals <u>only</u> with the willow?
   A stanza 1 C stanza 3
   B stanza 2 D stanza 4

2. According to Dickinson, what three things does fame have that a bee also has?

3. In "April Rain Song," what kind of song does the rain sing?

Comprehension: Putting Ideas Together

4. In stanza 1, Merriam first compares the willow and gingko to drawings. What types of comparison does she use in stanza 3?
   A singers and songs
   B storybook characters
   C languages and music
   D animals and fabrics

5. What does Dickinson mean when she says that fame "has a wing"?

6. What are the speaker's feelings about rain in "April Rain Song"?

Understanding Literature: Figurative Language

Poets use figurative language to help readers see things in new ways. Most figurative language gives us ways to compare things that are not really alike. Similes and metaphors are comparisons. In similes, one thing is said to be like another. In metaphors, one thing is said to be the other. Personification is another kind of comparison that gives an object or animal human traits. When Langston Hughes says "Let the rain kiss you," he is using personification. Unlike humans, the rain cannot kiss, but its gentle touch can feel like a kiss.

7. In "Simile: Willow and Ginkgo," how is the willow "like a nymph with streaming hair"?

8. Name two other examples of personification in "April Rain Song."

Critical Thinking

9. What overall impression do you get of the two trees in "Simile: Willow and Ginkgo"? Think about how they look and grow.

Thinking Creatively

10. In your opinion, which poem would make the best painting? Why?

After Reading **continued on next page**

Simile: Willow and Ginkgo | *Fame Is a Bee* | *April Rain Song*

 Grammar Check

Sentences may be labeled according to what they do. A *declarative* sentence states an idea. An *interrogative* sentence asks a question. An *imperative* sentence gives an order or direction. An *exclamatory* sentence expresses strong emotion.

Look back at "April Rain Song." Find two kinds of sentences in the poem. Tell what kind of sentences they are.

 Vocabulary Builder

Compound words are made up of two or more smaller words. The small words help you understand the meaning of the compound word. For example, *sidewalk* is *side + walk*. It names a path by the side of the road on which you can walk.

Separate these compound words into their smaller words. Tell the meaning of the compound word.

thumbprint   newsstand   fundraising
empty-handed   passer-by   self-service

 Writing on Your Own

Write a poem using figurative language. Pick a subject that you have positive feelings about. For example, you might pick sunshine, a summer breeze, stars, or moonlight. Use a Concept Map (see Appendix A) to record the qualities of your subject. Think of other things with those qualities that could be used in a comparison. Using your notes, draft a poem. Include at least one example of figurative language.

 Listening and Speaking

Prepare a poetry reading. Select one of the poems in this group or one that you have read elsewhere. Practice reading the poem aloud, using expression and pauses. Pay attention to the periods that mark the ends of thoughts or ideas. Memorize and present your selected poem to the class. Speak slowly.

 Research and Technology

With a small group, research and prepare a report. Your report will tell about the characteristics of a tree that grows in your community. Find art or pictures to go with the oral report. Prepare an outline for your presentation. Make each member of the group responsible for one section of the report. Present your report to the class. Then display the artwork on a bulletin board.

COMPARING LITERARY WORKS | Build Understanding

Dust of Snow   by Robert Frost

About the Author

Although Robert Frost was born in California, he spent most of his life in New England. His love for this region is reflected in much of his poetry and writing.

Frost began writing poetry in high school. He kept writing while he worked as a farmer, mill worker, newspaper reporter, and teacher. Frost became one of America's most loved poets by finding poetry in the language of everyday speech. His writing often explores the way humans connect with the natural world. His book *North of Boston* became a bestseller in 1914. He went on to win four Pulitzer Prizes.

Robert Frost
1874–1963

Objectives

◆ To read and understand a poem
◆ To compare imagery in poetry
◆ To recognize mood in poetry

About the Selection

New England winters are long, cold, and snowy, and the landscape has plentiful forests. Evergreens do not lose their needles, so during the winter, snow-covered pine trees are a familiar sight to New Englanders.

In "Dust of Snow," Frost describes a small incident in nature. More important is his description of how the incident makes him feel. As you read, compare the feelings of this speaker to the narrator of "April Rain Song."

Comparing continued on next page

image a word or phrase that appeals to the senses and allows the reader to picture events

imagery pictures created by words; the use of words that appeal to the five senses

mood the feeling that writing creates

Literary Terms An **image** is a word or phrase that appeals to one of the five senses. Those senses include sight, hearing, touch, taste, and smell. Writers use this kind of language—**imagery**—to create word pictures.

- Images can create a feeling of movement. For example, "the autumn leaves floated to the ground" shows the reader *how* the leaves fell.

- Imagery helps a writer express a **mood** or emotion. A mood is the feeling created by the writing—the way it makes you feel.

- An image can appeal to more than one sense. "Soft carpet of yellow prairie flowers" appeals to both touch and sight.

Reading on Your Own Look at the title of the poem. What does a "Dust of Snow" mean to you? What might happen to cause a "dust of snow"?

Writing on Your Own This poem uses imagery to describe an important change. Jot down a change you have experienced that has affected you. Then, describe a sight, sound, smell, touch, or taste that you connect with the change.

Vocabulary Focus Homophones are words that sound alike. They have different meanings and often different spellings. Use a dictionary. Look up these three homophones. Then try to use each one in a sentence.

rude   rued   rood

Think Before You Read Robert Frost served as poet laureate of the United States from 1958 to 1959. A poet laureate's job is to help people in the nation better appreciate poetry. What kind of qualities would you look for if you were hiring a poet laureate?

Dust of Snow

The way a crow
Shook down on me
The dust of snow
From a **hemlock** tree

5 Has given my heart
A change of mood
And saved some part
Of a day I had **rued**.

As you read, think about which senses the image of a dust of snow appeals to.

What clues help you guess the meaning of *rued*?

hemlock an evergreen tree in the pine family

rued regretted

Directions Choose the letter of the best answer or write the answer using complete sentences.

Comprehension: Identifying Facts

1. According to the poem, what is in the tree above the speaker?

   A pine cones   **C** tree frogs

   B an owl   **D** a crow

2. What is the action that changes the speaker's mood?

3. What is the change that the action brings about in the speaker?

Comprehension: Putting Ideas Together

4. How did the speaker feel before the action began?

   A carefree   **C** depressed

   B humble   **D** amused

5. Why did the action affect the speaker the way it did?

6. When the speaker mentions his "heart," what does he mean?

Understanding Literature: Imagery and Mood

Poets use imagery to paint pictures for their readers. The poet uses words that appeal to the senses. In this way, the poet allows a reader to imagine what is being described. Poets choose words carefully to construct images. Vivid adjectives and exact nouns and verbs are part of good imagery.

Imagery can affect the mood of a poem. The poet creates an image that makes the reader feel calm, or sad, or amused. A simple change in words can change the mood from positive to negative or back again.

7. Look back at "April Rain Song." How is the mood of that poem similar to that in "Dust of Snow"?

8. Compare one image that makes rain seem appealing to the image of a "dust of snow."

Critical Thinking

9. What lesson about nature do both "Dust of Snow" and "April Rain Song" teach us?

Thinking Creatively

10. What images from nature improve your mood? What natural events do you "love"?

Grammar Check

A prepositional phrase is a group of words. It begins with a preposition and ends with a noun or pronoun. The preposition connects the noun or pronoun to other words in the sentence.

Example: Shook down <u>on me</u>/The dust <u>of snow</u>

On me is a prepositional phrase. The preposition *on* connects *me* to *down*. The phrase answers the question "down where?" *Of snow* is another prepositional phrase. The preposition *of* connects *snow* to *dust*. The phrase answers the question "what kind of dust?"

Find three more prepositional phrases in "Dust of Snow." Explain what words are connected and what question is answered.

 Vocabulary Builder

Answer each question and explain your answer.

1 If you rued an action, would you feel good about it?

2 Do the leaves of a hemlock turn color in autumn?

 Writing on Your Own

Write a short essay. Compare the role nature plays in "Dust of Snow" to "April Rain Song." Consider the time of year and setting for each poem. Ask yourself:

- In each poem, is the image of nature positive or negative? What words or phrases help you know this?
- Does nature play a central role, or is it part of the background for the action?
- What words or phrases add to the image of nature?

 Listening and Speaking

Choose your favorite poem from Part 1. Think about its imagery, figurative language, mood, rhythm, and rhyme. Explain to a partner why you like the poem, using at least four of these words:

image   rhythm   simile
metaphor   personification   mood

 Media and Viewing

Listen to a recording of Robert Frost reading his poems. One recording is the CD *Robert Frost* from *The Voice of the Poet* series. Think about whether Frost sounds the way you thought he would. How does hearing him read his poetry help you understand his mood and meaning?

Part 2

Reading Strategy:
Visualizing

Visualizing is another strategy that helps readers understand what they are reading. It is like creating a movie in your mind. Use the following ways to visualize a text:

■ Look at the photographs, illustrations, and descriptive words.

■ Think about experiences in your own life that may add to the images.

■ Notice the order in which things are happening and what you think might happen next.

Literary Terms

haiku a form of Japanese poetry having three lines with five syllables in the first, seven in the second, and five in the third

limerick a humorous five-line poem in which the first, second, and fifth lines, and the third and fourth lines, rhyme

concrete poem a poem shaped to look like its subject

sound devices words that create musical sounds in poetry

repetition using a word, phrase, or image more than once, for emphasis

alliteration repeating sounds by using words whose beginning sounds are the same

onomatopoeia using words that sound like their meaning

sensory language writing or speech that appeals to the five senses

About the Authors and Selections

Bashō was born into a family of Japanese landowners. When Bashō was 12, his father died. Bashō then entered the service of a local landowner and began to write poetry. He was an important developer of the haiku form and one of its greatest masters. Bashō wrote "An old silent pond" in the spring of 1686. He revised the poem several times until he felt that it was right. He even changed the tense of the poem from past to present. The Japanese have built a monument near the place where Bashō probably wrote this haiku.

Matsuo Bashō
1644–1694

Most limericks are passed from person to person until no author is remembered. The limerick here features words that sound alike. These words make it into a tongue twister and give it a light-hearted tone.

As a child growing up in New Jersey, Lillian Morrison played street games and sports. The rhymes and chants she heard on the playground inspired her love of poetry. As an adult, Morrison spent nearly 40 years working in the New York Public Library. She has written several books of poetry. They include *The Sidewalk Racer and Other Poems of Sports and Motion.* Many of her poems, such as "The Sidewalk Racer," celebrate the human body in motion. This poem uses a unique structure that helps the reader "see" the action more clearly.

Lillian Morrison
1917–

***Before Reading* continued on next page**

Objectives

◆ To read and understand a haiku

◆ To read and understand a limerick

◆ To read and understand a concrete poem

BEFORE READING THE SELECTIONS *(cont.)* | **Build Skills**

Haiku | *Limerick* | *The Sidewalk Racer*

haiku a form of Japanese poetry having three lines with five syllables in the first, seven in the second, and five in the third

limerick a humorous five-line poem in which the first, second, and fifth lines, and the third and fourth lines, rhyme

concrete poem a poem shaped to look like its subject

Literary Terms Poets use different forms of poetry suited to the ideas, images, and feelings they want to express. A **haiku** is a Japanese verse form with three lines. Line 1 has five syllables, line 2 has seven, and line 3 has five. A **limerick** is a funny poem of five lines. Lines 1, 2, and 5 rhyme and have three beats, or stressed syllables. Lines 3 and 4 rhyme and have two beats. In a **concrete poem**, words are arranged in a shape that reflects the poem's subject.

Reading on Your Own Visualizing is using your imagination to "see" what an author describes. To visualize, you use the author's words plus your own experience. You picture the scene in your mind. Poets often use vivid adjectives and exact nouns and verbs to help you visualize.

Writing on Your Own In poetry, everyday actions, scenes, and words are presented in a fresh, new way. Bashō's haiku brings one moment in nature into sharp focus. A limerick twists simple words into hilarious knots. "The Sidewalk Racer" captures the joy of skateboarding. Make a list of everyday actions you think you could describe in new ways.

Vocabulary Focus The suffix *-er* and the suffix *-or* mean the same thing. They are added to a verb to make a noun. The new noun means "someone who [performs the verb]." Here are three such words from the poems. What is the verb in each? What does the new noun mean?

racer   driver   sailor

Think Before You Read How many words are needed to describe a scene so a reader can "see" it? Can it be done in a paragraph? A sentence? Read these poems to find out.

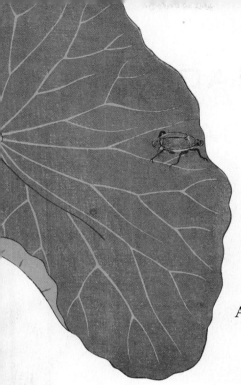

Haiku

An old silent pond . . .
A frog jumps into the pond,
splash! Silence again.
— *Bashō*

Reading Strategy:
Visualizing

What do you see
when you read
this? What do
you hear?

A flea and a fly in a **flue**
Were caught, so what could they do?
    Said the fly, "Let us flee."
    "Let us fly," said the flea.
5 So they flew through a **flaw** in the flue.
— *Anonymous*

As you read,
compare the poem
to the definition of
a limerick on page
282. Does this
poem follow the
rules?

flue a passage for
smoke or hot air, as
in a chimney

flaw a break or crack

THE SIDEWALK RACER OR ON THE SKATEBOARD

What does the shape of this poem have to do with its subject?

Reading Strategy:
Visualizing

What words might describe the spirit of both this skateboarder and the poem?

Skimming
an asphalt sea
I **swerve,** I curve, I
sway; I speed to **whirring**
5   sound an inch above the
ground; I'm the sailor
and the sail, I'm the
driver and the wheel
I'm the one and only
10   single engine
human auto
mobile.
— *Lillian Morrison*

swerve to turn sharply   **whirring** moving with a buzzing sound

Haiku | Limerick | The Sidewalk Racer

Directions Choose the letter of the best answer or write the answer using complete sentences.

Comprehension: Identifying Facts

1. What is the setting of the haiku?
   A a riverbed   **C** a creek
   B a pond   **D** an aquarium

2. What consonant sound is repeated in the limerick?

3. To what does the speaker in "The Sidewalk Racer" compare herself?

Comprehension: Putting Ideas Together

4. As the haiku ends, what does the speaker hear?
   A frogs chirping
   B a large splash
   C nothing at all
   D a waterfall

5. What happens in lines 3–5 of the limerick?

6. How does the speaker in "The Sidewalk Racer" feel about skateboarding?

Understanding Literature: Haiku, Limerick, and Concrete Poem

Poetry comes in many forms. A haiku is usually a poem about nature. It is arranged in three lines. The first and third lines have five syllables each. The second line has seven syllables. Haiku have a single speaker and a single subject.

A limerick always has five lines. Unlike haiku, limericks must rhyme. Their first, second, and fifth lines rhyme. Their third and fourth lines rhyme, too. Limericks are meant to be funny. Like jokes and riddles, many limericks are passed down over time.

Concrete poetry is a modern form. Concrete poems look like their subject matter. Their lines are shaped to remind the reader of an object or image.

7. What image or word picture is presented in each line of the haiku?

8. Suppose "The Sidewalk Racer" were written in a different shape. Would it have a different effect? Explain.

Critical Thinking

9. How does sound add to the humor in the limerick?

Thinking Creatively

10. Which of these three forms of poetry do you think might be easiest to write? Which would be most difficult? Why do you think so?

After Reading **continued on next page**

Grammar Check

A contraction is a shortened form of a word. It is usually used in conversation or informal writing. Contractions use apostrophes to show where letters are left out. Most contractions are formed from a pronoun plus a verb, or from a verb plus *not*.

> let + us = let's   I + am = I'm
> do + not = don't   can + not = can't

Write the contractions that can be made by joining these words. Then use each contraction in a sentence.

1 is + not

2 did + not

3 who + is

4 should + not

5 you + are

6 they + had

 Vocabulary Builder

Idioms are expressions that mean something different than the actual meaning of the words. For example, "I ran into Mike at the mall," does not mean that you crashed into Mike. It means that you saw him but did not expect to do so. Think of some other idioms you hear in everyday life. Restate them in your own words to understand their meanings.

 Writing on Your Own

You have read examples of a haiku, a limerick, and a concrete poem. Now, choose one of these forms of poetry and write your own poem.

Brainstorm for topics. If you are writing a limerick, for example, think of rhyming words you might use. Follow the patterns of the poem form you chose. Read your poem to a small group of classmates.

 Listening and Speaking

Prepare and deliver an oral response to one of the poems in this collection. First, give a clear oral reading of the poem. Next, provide your own explanation of the poem's meaning. Support your explanation with examples. Then, tell your opinion of the poem. Finally, ask your classmates for feedback.

 Research and Technology

Choose one of the poems from this collection. Use a computer to design a display of the poem. Remember that the lines of the poem must appear as they are written. Choose a style of type that will be easy to read. Use tabs to set off indented lines. Put the title in large type. When the poem is set the way you want it, insert pictures to illustrate it.

BEFORE READING THE SELECTIONS | Build Understanding

Camping Out | Wind and water and stone | The Sun

About the Authors and Selections

Antonio Vallone went to school in New
York State. He now teaches English,
creative writing, and film studies at
Penn State in Dubois, Pennsylvania.
He is also a publisher of books of poetry.
His poetry for children and adults has
appeared in several collections and many
journals. He often writes about childhood
memories, as he does in "Camping Out in
the Backyard."

Antonio Vallone
1957–

Octavio Paz
1914–1998

Although Octavio Paz lived in many places, he remained
tied to his native Mexico. He began his career as a writer at
the age of 17. He wrote in Spanish, but many of his works
were translated into other languages. Paz won a Nobel Prize
in Literature in 1990. In "Wind and water and stone," he
describes a Mexican landscape. He uses it to suggest how
a culture changes and yet stays the same.

William Wordsworth
1770–1850

William Wordsworth was born in the Lake District of
England. He published his first poems in 1793. Two years
later, he met Samuel Coleridge, another poet. Their friendship
would last for years. In 1798, they produced a work called
Lyrical Ballads. They argued in favor of a new form of poetry.
This poetry would be emotional and romantic. It would
show a love of nature and an interest in the common man.
Wordsworth's other important friendship was with his sister,
Dorothy. "The Sun Has Long Been Set" is one of Wordsworth's
shorter poems. It shows his fondness for nature over society.

Objectives

◆ To read and
understand poetry

◆ To recognize
sound devices in
poetry

Before Reading continued on next page

sound devices
words that create
musical sounds in
poetry

repetition using
a word, phrase, or
image more than
once, for emphasis

alliteration
repeating sounds
by using words
whose beginning
sounds are the
same

onomatopoeia
using words that
sound like their
meaning

Literary Terms **Sound devices** are tools for a writer. They bring out the music in words, and they express feelings. Sound devices commonly used in poetry include the following:

- **Repetition**: the use, more than once, of any element of language.
  Example: "of the people, by the people, and for the People."

- **Alliteration**: the repeating of beginning consonant sounds.
  Example: "big bad wolf."

- **Onomatopoeia**: the use of a word that sounds like what it means.
  Examples: roar, buzz, ring.

Reading on Your Own Use descriptive words to help you visualize a scene. Think: "What words did the poet use to show me how this looks?" Then picture the scene in your mind. Remember that a poet may compare two things to help you imagine what is being described.

Writing on Your Own These poems contain vivid descriptions of ordinary things. One describes a backyard at night. One describes a landscape. One describes a summer night. Why might a poet choose such common topics? Write your ideas.

Vocabulary Focus Some vocabulary words are names of kinds of plants or animals. Knowing the plant or animal can help you understand why the poet chose those words. Look up these words in the dictionary before you read the poems in this collection.

willow   lilac   cuckoo   thrush

Think Before You Read What does each poem's title tell you about the setting of the poem?

Camping Out in the Backyard

To hold off sleep, my cousin Mike and I swore
and punched each other on the arms.

Twilight crept out from under roots and rocks,
hoarding shadows and sneaking up on us.

5 The twelve pines my uncle planted lined up
like **mute** angels.
                    The willow became a man,
black suit and overcoat blowing in the wind.

The powdery odor of lilacs was perfume
10 worn by old women at funerals.

I squinted through my glasses into the dark.
Even my cousin's better eyes went blind.

Like a black skeleton, the clothes pole reached
out, rapped me on the head with its bony arm.

15 I stumbled, and an owl called *who, who, who,*
the sound of breath over an open grave.

We talked about stars that looked like bullet holes,
the bloody moon hidden by shreds of clouds.

Something scraped against the tent. Leaves scampered
20 across the opening like thin, brown rats.

Flashlights in front of us like swords, we **hacked**
a path into the house to save our mothers.
— *Antonio Vallone*

hoarding storing up   **mute** silent   **hacked** chopped;
and hiding from others   slashed

As you read, look
for groups of words
that add alliteration
to the poem.

Reading Strategy:
Visualizing
What does the
willow look like?
Can you imagine it?

How does the poet
use onomatopoeia
to create a scary
mood?

Reading Strategy:
Visualizing
Are these images
positive or
negative? What is
the speaker trying
to get you to see?

Wind and water and stone

The water hollowed the stone,
the wind **dispersed** the water,
the stone stopped the wind.
Water and wind and stone.

5 The wind **sculpted** the stone,
the stone is a cup of water,
the water runs off and is wind.
Stone and wind and water.

The wind sings in its turnings,
10 the water murmurs as it goes,
the motionless stone is quiet.
Wind and water and stone.

One is the other, and is neither:
among their empty names
15 they pass and disappear,
water and stone and wind.
— *Octavio Paz*

Reading Strategy: Visualizing

What does the stone look like? Why does it look that way?

What effect is created by repeating the words in the fourth line of each stanza?

dispersed sent off in many directions   **sculpted** carved

The Sun Has Long Been Set

The sun has long been set,
    The stars are out by twos and threes,
The little birds are piping yet
    Among the bushes and trees;
5 There's a **cuckoo,** and one or two **thrushes,**
And a far-off wind that rushes,
And a sound of water that gushes,
And the cuckoo's **sovereign** cry
Fills all the hollow of the sky.

10   Who would go "parading"
In London, and "**masquerading**,"
On such a night of June
With that beautiful soft half-moon,
And all these innocent **blisses?**
15 On such a night as this is!
    — *William Wordsworth*

> Find an example of alliteration in the first line of the poem.

> Why does the speaker repeat "on such a night"?

cuckoo a long-tailed bird with a two-note call

thrushes robin-sized, brown birds

sovereign above all others; superior

masquerading dressing up, especially in costume

blisses delights

Directions Choose the letter of the best answer or write the answer using complete sentences.

Comprehension: Identifying Facts

1. In "Camping Out in the Backyard," what is sneaking up on the boys?
A an owl
B a skeleton
C twilight
D mute angels

2 According to "Wind and water and stone," what does each of the three natural elements do?

3. In what month does "The Sun Has Long Been Set" take place?

Comprehension: Putting Ideas Together

4. What are the boys most afraid of in "Camping Out in the Backyard"?
A the dark
B wild animals
C grown-ups
D strangers

5. How do the three elements in "Wind and water and stone" depend on each other?

6. In "The Sun Has Long Been Set," what does the speaker prefer to "parading" in London?

Understanding Literature: Sound Devices

Poetry is different from other written works. In poetry, writers use sound devices to express feeling and give language a musical sound. Repetition, such as alliteration, may give a poem a sing-song sound. In alliteration, the first letter sounds in stressed syllables are the same. Another sound device is onomatopoeia. Words such as *crash* or *whir* sound like their meanings. They add sound to poems and appeal to a reader's sense of hearing.

7. Find one example of alliteration in each of the three poems.

8. A cuckoo makes a loud, two-note cry that is often written "Cuckoo! Cuckoo!" Which sound device is this?

Critical Thinking

9. Why is a poet's choice of words so important to the sound of the poem?

Thinking Creatively

10. Which poem is easiest for you to "see" in your mind? Why do you think that is so?

Grammar Check

A predicate noun renames or identifies the subject of a sentence. A predicate adjective describes the subject of a sentence.

Predicate noun: The stone is a <u>cup</u> of water.

Predicate adjective: The sun has long been <u>set</u>.

Identify the predicate noun or the predicate adjective in each sentence.

1 The sculpture is beautiful.
2 Glacier National Park is a huge area.
3 A brisk walk is good exercise.
4 The laundry was quite clean.
5 Tran is a trained musician.

 Vocabulary Builder

Answer each question based on the meaning of the underlined word.

1 What might people be <u>hoarding</u> in a storm?

2 Why might a crowd have suddenly <u>dispersed</u>?

3 What are some of the <u>blisses</u> of your life?

 Writing on Your Own

Select one poem from this collection to further explore. Write a description of the scene suggested by the poem. Make a list of words that capture the details and emotion in the scene. Make sure the words you use appeal to the senses. Write a paragraph using your list. Try to re-create the picture that the poet painted.

 Listening and Speaking

Give a formal reading of one of the poems in this collection. Rehearse your reading of the poem. Pay close attention to end marks and pauses. Change the loudness and tone of your voice to show strong feelings. Look up from the page. After your reading, ask your classmates to rate your performance.

 Research and Technology

A résumé is a summary of important information about a person's career and education. It also lists important achievements. Prepare a résumé for a poet from this collection. First, search online for information about the poet. Look for the schools he or she attended, titles of books, and awards. Then, ask your teacher for examples of common résumé formats. Choose one. Then, write a résumé to show what you have learned about the poet.

Applications

Would you rather read poetry than write it? If so, a library card application can open the door to a world of poetry. Filling out applications is an important skill. It can help you in many situations, such as applying for colleges or finding a job.

About Applications

Applications contain information that helps an individual or group decide something based on that information. Here are some reasons that people fill out applications:

- to get a library card
- to get a job
- to be admitted to a school
- to open a savings account
- to join a club
- to get a driver's license

When completing an application, read each part carefully. Note when and where it should be turned in. Check to see whether any payments or other paperwork should be included.

Reading Skill

When you fill out an application, you are reading to perform a task. The task is to provide correct and complete information. On some applications, the directions are numbered and written in sentences. On others, brief labels tell what information should be provided in each section. To complete an application, preview and review the text.

Preview: First, look over the directions and questions. Summarize the directions in your head to make sure that you can answer the questions.

Review: After you have filled out the application, review it. Make sure it is readable and that you have completed all the necessary sections.

Previewing an Application

1. What information is being asked for?

2. On which line should the information be placed?

3. Must the information be typed or printed?

4. What other documents or items should be included?

5. Which information is optional and which is required?

6. When is the application due? To whom should it be sent?

Madison County Public Library Card Application Form

The library requires I.D. and written proof of current address. All library transactions and information are strictly confidential.

Please print:

Today's Date_____   **Staff Use** Card #_____

Mr. _____   Mrs._____   Miss_____   Ms. _____   Dr. _____

Name _____
          Last   First   Middle

Current Address _____
                     Street (including house number) or PO box

City _____ State _____ Zip Code _____

Date of Birth _____

Home Telephone _____ Work Telephone_____

Patron Type—Circle One

A—Adult (age 18 & over)   YA—Young Adult (age 14–17)
J—Juvenile (age 0–13)   CS—College Student (any age)

Permanent Address (if different from current address):

_____
                     Street (including house number) or PO box

City _____ State _____ Zip Code _____

Parent/Legal Guardian's Name (if under age 14) _____

Driver's License or Social Security Number _____

E-mail Address (optional) _____

I understand that by signing this form and accepting this library card I am responsible for all materials checked out using this card and for charges that may be assessed to me. I agree to give prompt notice to the library of any address change. If I am signing as a parent or legal guardian, I accept responsibility for my child's use of the card and agree to pay any fines or other charges incurred by my child. As a parent, I am aware that the library permits children to have access to all materials and is not responsible for restricting or censoring the materials which children may select.

Cardholder Signature _____

Parent/Legal Guardian Signature _____

This line explains what is needed with the application.

The word *optional* means "not required." On an application, this means you can decide whether to provide certain information or not.

STUDENT POETRY CONTEST
North Carolina Poetry Society
Deadline for Receipt of Entries: January 8, 2004

Prizes to Be Awarded
All winning poems will also be published!
- **First Place: Trophy + Certificate + $25.00**
- **Second Place: Certificate + $15.00**
- **Third Place: Certificate + $10.00**
- **Honorable Mention: Certificate**

> Since this application is for a contest, it also describes the awards.

For Students of North Carolina Schools

Who may enter this contest?
Students in grades 3–12 and college undergraduates.

What are the types of entries and awards?
- The Travis Tuck Jordan Award is for students in grades 3–5.
- The Frances W. Phillips Award is for poems about the environment and is for students in grades 3–8.
- The Mary Chilton Award is for students in grades 6–8.
- The Marie Barringer Rogers Award is for students in grades 9–undergraduate.
- The Lyman Haiku Award is for students in grades 9–undergraduate.

Note: All poems except the Lyman Haiku entries may be in any form but must have no more than 32 lines per poem.

> The structure of this part points to certain information. It tries to answer possible questions students might have.

What are the rules and how do I enter the contest?
1. You may submit one poem for each category.
2. Send two typed copies of each poem on 8½ X 11 paper.
3. In the upper left corner of each copy, type the name of the award category you are entering. Do not put your name or address on these copies.
4. On a separate piece of paper, type or print
   - the name of the category and the title of the poem you are entering
   - your name, your home address and zip code, and your phone number
   - the name of your school, your grade, your school address and telephone number, and the name of your teacher
5. Your teacher must sign the paper (see item 4 above).
6. You must also sign the paper and write: I pledge that this is my original poem.

> In order to submit your entry correctly, you should follow these numbered steps carefully.

Note: The copies of your poems that you submit to this contest will not be returned to you, so please be sure to keep copies of your poems for yourself.

Monitor Your Progress

Directions Choose the letter of the best answer or write the answer using complete sentences.

1. Which of these is required in order to complete the library application?
   A proof of current address
   B an e-mail address
   C a permanent job
   D a fee of five dollars

2. According to the poetry contest application, in which form must the poems be submitted?
   A professionally printed
   B electronically produced
   C handwritten
   D typed

3. Which group is not allowed to enter the poetry contest?
   A students in grades 3–5
   B students in grades 6–8
   C high school teachers
   D college students

4. On the library application, which type of user requires the signature of a parent or guardian? What ages does this group include?

5. Why does the poetry contest ask people to pledge that their poems are original?

Writing on Your Own

Applications ask for information, but they often provide information as well. Use the information on the library application. Write a paragraph. Explain the rights and responsibilities that come with having a library card.

COMPARING LITERARY WORKS | Build Understanding

Alphabet   by Naomi Shihab Nye

Naomi Shihab Nye
1952–

About the Author

Naomi Shihab Nye was born to a Palestinian father and an American mother. She has lived in the United States and in the Middle East. Now she lives in Texas, but she travels often. In her writing—poems, short stories, and children's books— she draws on her travel experience.

Nye often writes about the tiny details of everyday life. She keeps a journal, where she jots down details to use in her work. Nye's poetry has won many awards. She has also edited several collections of poetry from around the world.

About the Selection

Nye explores history and home in her poem "Alphabet." This poem talks about changes that occur in the speaker's neighborhood. It tells of the losses that occur as elderly neighbors die.

As you read this poem, compare the language to that of "Wind and water and stone." Think about the senses that each appeals to and why.

COMPARING LITERARY WORKS | Build Skills

Literary Terms **Sensory language** is writing or speech that appeals to one or more of the five senses. Those senses are sight, sound, touch, taste, and smell. The use of sensory language creates clear images for the reader or listener. Here are some examples:

sensory language

> **sensory language** writing or speech that appeals to the five senses

- An icy wind blew in with an eerie moan. (appeals to touch and hearing)

- She sank her teeth into a juicy, sweet peach. (appeals to touch and taste)

- The fragrance of the fresh pink roses filled the room. (appeals to smell and sight)

Reading on Your Own Writers use sensory language to stir up memories in a reader's mind. As you read, look for sensory details. Think about how those details connect to your life. Think about the feelings that you have as you read those details.

Writing on Your Own Poems often describe a place that is important to the speaker. Write a short description of a place that is important to you. Explain what makes it special.

Vocabulary Focus The flower *narcissus* is associated with a Greek myth. A young man named Narcissus gazed lovingly at his own image in a pool of water. As a result, he was turned into the flower that now bears his name. Several English words come from characters in Greek myths. Look online or in the dictionary. Find the stories behind these words: *chaos*, *psyche*, and *titan*.

Think Before You Read How do neighbors make a neighborhood special?

One by one
the old people
of our neighborhood
are going up
5 into the air

their yards
still wear
small white **narcissus**
sweetening winter

10 their stones
glisten
under the sun
but one by one

we are losing
15 their **housecoats**
their formal **phrasings**
their cupcakes

When I string their names
on the long cord

narcissus heavily
scented bulb plant with
white or yellow flowers

housecoats ladies'
clothing for wearing at
home

phrasings ways of
speaking

300 *Unit 4 Part 2 Poetry*

Reading Strategy:
Visualizing
What image do you
"see" when you
read these lines?

Alphabet

20 when I think how
    there is almost no one left
    who remembers
    what stood in that
    brushy spot
25 ninety years ago

    when I pass their yards
    and the bare peach tree
    bends a little
    when I see their rusted chairs
30 sitting in the same spots

    what will be forgotten
    falls over me
    like the sky
    over our whole neighborhood

35 or the time my plane
    circled high above our street
    the roof of our house
    dotting the tiniest
    "i"

To what senses do
the words *rusted
chairs* appeal?

Alphabet   by Naomi Shihab Nye

Directions Choose the letter of the best answer or write the answer using complete sentences.

Comprehension: Identifying Facts

1. Which is NOT something the speaker says "we are losing"?
   A housecoats
   B formal phrasings
   C peach trees
   D cupcakes

2. Which words describe the tree that stands in the yard of the old people?

3. Name two things that still remain in the old people's yards.

Comprehension: Putting Ideas Together

4. What does the speaker mean by "the old people . . . are going up in the air"?
   A They are dying out.
   B They are taking trips.
   C They are flying around.
   D They are moving up.

5. Why can't these people and things be replaced?

6. What does the description of the peach tree tell you about the neighborhood?

Understanding Literature: Sensory Language

Sensory language appeals to the sense of sight, sound, touch, smell, or taste. Poets choose vivid adjectives to describe a scene so that the reader can "sense" it. For example, Bashō's "old silent pond" appeals to the senses of hearing and sight. Eve Merriam's willow, "sleek as a velvet-nosed calf," appeals to the sense of touch.

7. Compare "Alphabet" to "Wind and water and stone." Which uses more images that appeal to hearing? Which one appeals more to sight?

8. How do the images help you understand each poem's message about time?

Critical Thinking

9. Choose one poem from Part 2. Explain how the poet uses sensory language to appeal to the senses.

Thinking Creatively

10. Why is sensory language especially important to poetry? In what other kinds of literature might you find sensory language?

Grammar Check

In "Alphabet," the poet repeats the phrase "When I." Each group of words that follows is a dependent clause. It contains a subject and verb, but it cannot stand alone. Dependent clauses may be used as adjectives, adverbs, or nouns.

Adjective: I love poems <u>that tell about weather.</u>

Adverb: <u>After you finish</u>, explain the poem to me.

Noun: <u>What the poet means</u> is difficult to tell.

Name one adverb clause and one noun clause from "Alphabet."

 Vocabulary Builder

Synonyms are words that mean the same or nearly the same thing. For each word below, find a synonym in "Alphabet." Then use the synonym in a sentence of your own.

speech   sparkle   uncovered   smallest

 Writing on Your Own

Compare the use of sensory language in "Alphabet" and in one other poem from Part 2. Write a paragraph answering the following questions:

- Which images in the two poems are the clearest to you? Why?
- How does the sensory language in each poem help you understand the poet's meaning?
- Which poem uses sensory language more vividly?

   Listening and Speaking

Work with a partner. Summarize the poem "Alphabet" in your own words. Tell the main idea of the poem and give some supporting details. Ask your partner whether he or she agrees with your summary. Then listen to your partner's own summary of the poem.

Media and Viewing

Poetry is present in more places than just the pages of this book. We come across poetic devices every day in the media, especially advertising and music. Consider the following poetic devices: alliteration, simile, metaphor, rhythm, rhyme, and repetition. Find examples of these devices in the media. Look at newspapers, magazines, television, and the Internet. Take notes on your findings. Share your favorite example with the class.

Prefixes are word parts added to the beginning of base words. Suffixes are word parts added to the ends of words.

Master the Basics

The following will help you spell many words with prefixes and suffixes.

- The spelling of a base word does not change when a prefix is added.
- To add a suffix beginning with a consonant (*-ful, -tion, -ly*):
  - ❏ Change *y* to *i* in the base word, unless a consonant comes before the *y*.
  - ❏ Most other times, do not change the base word.
- To add suffixes beginning with a vowel (*-ion, -al, -able*):
  - ❏ Change *y* to *i* in the base word, unless a consonant comes before the *y*.

- ❏ Usually, drop the final *e* in the base word.
- ❏ Most other times, do not change the base word.

Practice

Use the Word List to complete:

1. Write three words with prefixes. Underline each prefix.

2. Write three words that have suffixes starting with vowels. Circle the word in which the spelling of the base word does not change.

3. Write four words that have suffixes starting with consonants. Circle the word that does not follow the guidelines.

Word List
disappoint
misspent
reelect
argument
announcement
joyous
stubbornness
pitiful
imitation
burial

" . . . and if you reelect me I promise to double the length of recess! "

CLASS PRESIDENTIAL DEBATE

Unit 4 SUMMARY

Unit 4 introduced poetry and poets from many places and times. You learned how poets use sound devices to add music to their words. You saw how figurative language makes language interesting and meaningful. You discovered that imagery and sensory language help a reader "sense" what the poet is describing.

Some of the poems in this unit use rhyme. Others do not. Some poems are in special forms. Haiku is an ancient form of poetry. Each of the three lines in haiku has a set number of syllables. Limericks are another old form of poetry. Their purpose is more humorous, but their form is strict. Concrete poetry is modern. Poets form their lines into shapes to tell more about the subject of their poems.

Every poem in this unit tells something about the poet. The poet is not always the speaker, but poetry is personal. The poet's thoughts and feelings flow into the poem, and out to you as you read. Poetry is a wonderful way to communicate. It requires a careful choice of words and an understanding of the power of language.

Selections
- "Adventures of Isabel" by Ogden Nash is a silly poem about a brave girl.

- "Ankylosaurus" by Jack Prelutsky is a humorous poem about a dinosaur.

- "Learning to Read" by Frances E. W. Harper tells of a former slave's desire to educate herself.

- "Simile: Willow and Ginkgo" by Eve Merriam compares two trees.

- "Fame Is a Bee" by Emily Dickinson likens fame to a small, powerful bee.

- "April Rain Song" by Langston Hughes describes a gentle April rain.

- "Dust of Snow" by Robert Frost tells of an image that lifts the speaker's mood.

- "Haiku" by Matsuo Bashō describes a sudden movement in a still pond.

- "Limerick" (anonymous) is a tongue twister about bugs stuck in a chimney.

- "The Sidewalk Racer" by Lillian Morrison explores skateboarding.

- "Camping Out in the Backyard" by Antonio Vallone shows how simple things become scary at twilight.

- "Wind and water and stone" by Octavio Paz presents an image of three elements working together.

- "The Sun Has Long Been Set" by William Wordsworth tells why the poet prefers simple pleasures.

- "Alphabet" by Naomi Shihab Nye explains the loss to a neighborhood as older neighbors die.

Directions Choose the letter of the best answer or write the answer using complete sentences.

Comprehension: Identifying Facts

1. How old is the speaker in "Learning to Read"?
   A around 10   **C** nearly 60
   B in her early 20s   **D** over 75

2. What happens to change the speaker's mood in "Dust of Snow"?

3. Of the haiku, the limerick, and the concrete poem, which uses rhyming lines?

4. Name two things that scare the boys in "Camping Out in the Backyard."

5. Which bird is loudest in "The Sun Has Long Been Set"?

Comprehension: Putting Ideas Together

6. What word might you use to describe the subject of "Ankylosaurus"?
   A daring   **C** playful
   B swift   **D** sturdy

7. Why does the poet's heart go to the gingko in "Simile: Willow and Ginkgo"?

8. What does Dickinson mean when she says that fame "has a wing"?

9. What is the "asphalt sea" in Morrison's "The Sidewalk Racer"?

10. Why does the speaker in "Alphabet" miss the neighbors' housecoats, formal phrasings, and cupcakes?

Understanding Literature: Sound Devices and Imagery

Poets use different ways of connecting with their readers. They add sound devices to their poetry to highlight key ideas. This also adds music to their words. Rhythm and rhyme can give a poem a sing-song feel. Alliteration and other kinds of repetition make words sound pleasing to the ear. Onomatopoeia brings certain familiar sounds to the reader's mind.

Poets also use imagery, which is language that describes. The poet's words combine with the reader's memory to create a picture.

11. List all the poems in this unit that use rhyming lines.

12. Name two examples of alliteration in "Adventures of Isabel."

13. Compare the pools in "April Rain Song" to the pond in Bashō's "Haiku." Use examples from the poems to describe each body of water.

14. Find an example of onomatopoeia in "Ankylosaurus." What does the onomatopoeia tell you about the subject of the poem?

15. Which imagery in "The Sun Has Long Been Set" do you think best describes the setting?

Critical Thinking

16. Use a Venn Diagram, described in Appendix A, to compare "The Sidewalk Racer" to "Camping Out in the Backyard." Tell how they are alike and different.

17. Is Dickinson's metaphor reasonable in "Fame Is a Bee"? Why or why not?

18. Which poem in this unit do you think uses sensory language best? Give some examples to support your opinion.

19. How would you describe the mood in "Alphabet"? Explain your answer.

Thinking Creatively

20. Do you agree with Octavio Paz that poetry is man's natural form of expression? Why or why not?

Speak and Listen

Work with a small group. Choose one poet from this unit about whom you will present a report to the class. Some group members can find other poems by that poet. Some can look for information about the life of that poet. Some can learn about the poet's style or influences. Meet together and decide how to organize your report. Then present it to the class.

Writing on Your Own

Choose a topic for a poem and decide on a style. Write two four-line stanzas. Get feedback on your poem from a classmate. Then edit the poem to improve alliteration or to add imagery. Share your finished work with the class.

Beyond Words

Choose one poem from this unit that paints a picture in your mind. Use the imagery and sensory language from the poem to sketch a picture. Use watercolors to add color to your sketch. Share your sketch with the class. Can your classmates tell which poem you illustrated?

Test-Taking Tip

Read test directions carefully. Do not assume that you know what you are supposed to do.

Exposition: Comparison-and-Contrast Essay

Comparisons often highlight what is similar between two things, while a contrast points out differences. A comparison-and-contrast essay uses details to tell how two or more subjects are alike and different. The essay may compare two candidates. It may compare two tomato soups. Either way, the purpose of the comparison should be clear. Follow the steps in this workshop to write a comparison-and-contrast essay.

Assignment Write a comparison-and-contrast essay in which you show how two subjects are alike and different.

What to Include Your comparison-and-contrast essay should feature the following elements:

- a topic involving two or more subjects that are alike and different in clear ways
- a structure that illustrates likenesses and differences
- a strong opening paragraph that grabs readers' interest
- facts, descriptions, and examples that show how the two subjects are alike and different

Using the Form
You may use elements of this form in these writing situations:
- Literary reviews
- Movie reviews
- Product comparisons

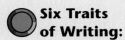 **Six Traits of Writing:**

Ideas message, details, and purpose

Prewriting
Choosing Your Topic

Choose subjects that are similar and different in important ways. Use one of these strategies to find a topic:

- **Quicklist** Make a three-column chart. In the first column, jot down people, places, and things that are interesting to you. In the second column, list an adjective to describe each one. Then, in the third column, provide a detail about each one. Review your list. Look for ideas that it suggests, such as two foods or two sports you enjoy. Choose a pair of such ideas as your topic.

- **Media Flip-Through** As you read a magazine or watch television, take notes. Jot down pairs of related subjects such as issues in the news, television programs, or films. Review your notes, and choose the most interesting topic.

Narrowing Your Topic

You could probably write an entire book comparing and contrasting Mexico and Spain. To make your broad topic easier to manage, divide it into smaller subtopics. Then choose one, such as Mexican and Spanish food, as the topic of your essay.

Gathering Details

Use a Venn Diagram. Gather facts, descriptions, and examples that you can use to make comparisons and contrasts. Organize your details in a Venn Diagram (see Appendix A) like the one shown. In the two outside sections, record details about how each subject is different. In the overlapping area, record how they are alike.

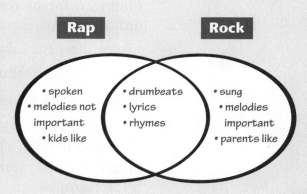

Rap | Rock

- spoken
- melodies not important
- kids like

- drumbeats
- lyrics
- rhymes

- sung
- melodies important
- parents like

Writing Your Draft

Shaping Your Writing

Decide how you will organize your essay. Choose one of these plans:

Six Traits of Writing:
Organization order, ideas tied together

Block Method: Present all the details about one subject first. Then present all the details about the second subject. This method works well when you are writing about more than two things. It works when you are covering many different types of details.

Point-by-Point Method: Discuss each feature of your subjects in turn. For example, suppose you are comparing two types of dinosaurs. You could first discuss the diets of each one, then the size, and so on.

Block	Point by Point
1. Introduction	1. Introduction
2. Tyrannosaurus: diet, size, and mobility	2. Diet of tyrannosaurus vs. velociraptor
3. Velociraptor: diet, size, and mobility	3. Size and mobility of tyrannosaurus vs. velociraptor
4. Conclusion	4. Conclusion

Plan your introduction. Begin your essay with a strong introductory paragraph that does the following:

- introduces the subjects you are comparing and contrasting
- identifies the features you will discuss
- states a main idea about your subjects

Providing Elaboration

Use exact details. The more clearly you show likenesses and differences, the more interesting your essay will be. Look at these examples.

General: holiday meal
Concrete: holiday breakfast of omelettes and cinnamon rolls

Use transitions. Use words and phrases to signal that you are discussing either a likeness or a difference. Words that show likenesses include *also, both,* and *like.* Words that show difference include *unlike, on the other hand, but,* and *however.*

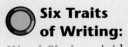
Six Traits of Writing:
Word Choice vivid words that "show, not tell"

Revising
Revising Your Overall Structure

Check organization and balance. Your essay should give equal space to each subject. It should be organized clearly. Reread your essay. Use a red marker. Underline or highlight all the features and details related to one subject. Then, use a yellow marker for the other subject.

If one color stands out, add more features and details related to the other subject.

Revising Your Word Choice

Check subject-verb agreement. Check your draft for subject-verb agreement. Make sure that sentences with singular subjects have singular verbs. Make sure that sentences with plural subjects have plural verbs.

Editing and Proofreading

Correct errors in spelling, grammar, and punctuation.

Focus on Double Comparisons: Comparison-and-contrast essays often contain adjectives that compare. Avoid using double comparisons. Never use *-er* or *-est* and *more* or *most* with the same adjective.

Six Traits of Writing:
Conventions correct grammar, spelling, and mechanics

Publishing and Presenting

Consider one of the following ways to share your writing:

Create a picture essay. Find photographs to illustrate the similarities and differences you have discussed. Then, share your illustrated essay with classmates.

Create an audiotape. Practice reading your essay aloud a few times. Read slowly and clearly. Give added weight to your key ideas. Then, record it and share it with a group of classmates.

Reflecting on Your Writing

Writer's Journal Jot down your ideas on writing a comparison-and-contrast essay. Begin by answering these questions:

- Do you view your topic differently now that you have looked at it thoroughly? Explain.

- What prewriting strategy would you use again? Why?

Theater Performance
Noma

Unit 5 Drama

Drama is a form of storytelling. It is meant to be performed by actors on a stage. The kinds of drama we usually see today began in ancient Greece. Then and now, playwrights—the writers of plays—tell stories through the words and actions of characters. Some plays are based on real life or history. Some are completely invented by the playwright.

In this unit, you will read a play that is based on a beloved children's book.

"And one of the nice things that happens . . . is that when you're writing a scene . . . you can get the feeling that all you're doing is eavesdropping, and the characters are doing the talking. And you're just jotting it down as fast as you can."

—Norton Juster, interview, 2001

Unit 5 About Drama

Elements of Drama

Drama is different from other forms of writing because it is written to be performed. When you read a drama, you should imagine that you see and hear the action of the play. However, like other forms of writing, drama includes **characters**—a person or animal in the story. It often also includes a **conflict,** or a problem between two characters or forces. Like other forms of writing, drama has a **theme,** or main idea.

The following parts help readers and performers make the magic of drama:

- An **act** is a major unit of action in a play. Acts are usually divided into scenes. A **scene** is a unit of action in a play that takes place in one setting.

- **Dialogue** is the conversation among characters in a story: the words that characters in a play speak. The characters speak from a **script.** A script is the written text of the play, used in production or performances. The words of each character in a script are next to the character's name.

- **Stage directions** are notes by playwrights describing such things as setting, lighting, sound effects, and how the actors are to look, behave, move, and speak.

- The **set** is the making of the stage that tells the time and place of the action.

- A **prop** is a piece of equipment used on stage during a play.

Types of Drama

Drama is a word used to tell that the play talks about something serious.

Comedy is a form of drama that has a happy ending. The fun often comes out of the characters' dialogue. Comedies can be written for fun or to talk about something serious.

Tragedy is a play that ends with the suffering or death of one or more of the main characters.

A drama is often written to be performed on a stage. However, a drama can be written for other reasons, too:

- **Screenplays** are scripts from which movies are made.

- **Teleplays** are types of screenplays written for television. Each of these has directions on where to put the camera. A teleplay usually has more scene changes than a stage play.

- **Radio plays** are written for radio. A radio play usually has sound effects, but not lighting or staging directions.

Part 1

Reading Strategy:
Summarizing

You learned about summarizing strategies in Unit 3. Continue to use those strategies as you read the selections in this unit. Ask yourself:

- Who or what is this about?

- What is the main thing being said about this topic?

If you are having trouble identifying the main idea, try rereading the text.

Literary Terms

playwright the author of a play

pun a joke formed by a play on words

drama a story told through the words and actions of characters, written to be performed

character a person or animal in a story, poem, or play

setting a story's time and place

plot the series of events in a story

dialogue the conversation among characters in a story or play

script the written text of a play

novel fiction that is book-length and has more characters and detail than a short story

dramatization the acting out in drama form of a real-life event or another form of literature

The Phantom Tollbooth, Act I   by Susan Nanus

About the Author

Susan Nanus has written many award-winning scripts for dramas, television miniseries, and movies. In 1997, she won the Writers Guild Award for the television drama *Harvest of Fire*.

Nanus sometimes adapts, or reworks, novels to create screenplays for movies. She based the screenplay for the television miniseries "A Will of Their Own" on the novel *Daughters of the New World* by Susan Richards Shreve. The novel tells about the struggles of women through four generations of Shreve's family. She was also on the writing team for a 1996 Academy Award-nominated screenplay.

Nanus has written several plays. Her script for *The Phantom Tollbooth* was adapted from a novel by Norton Juster. Nanus lives in Los Angeles, where she writes scripts for television and movies.

About the Selection

The original novel on which this play is based was published in England in 1961. This play was published 16 years later. The **playwright** was careful to keep the best-loved qualities of the original book. She included the **puns,** or jokes formed by plays on words, and the silly characters. She created the character of the Clock to help tell about some of the action.

Objectives

- To read and understand drama
- To recognize dialogue
- To identify characters, setting, and plot
- To read and understand stage directions

Before Reading **continued on next page**

The Phantom Tollbooth, Act I   by Susan Nanus

playwright the author of a play

pun a joke formed by a play on words

drama a story told through the words and actions of characters, written to be performed

character a person or animal in a story, poem, or play

setting the time and place in a story

plot the series of events in a story

dialogue the conversation among characters in a story or play

script the written text of a play

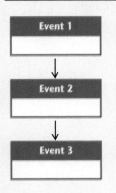

| Event 1 |
| Event 2 |
| Event 3 |

Literary Terms A **drama**, or a play, is a story that is written to be performed. Like short stories, dramas have **characters**, a **setting**, and a **plot**. A character is a person or animal in a story, poem, or play. Setting is a story's time and place. Plot is the series of events in a story. In dramas, however, these elements are developed mainly through **dialogue**, the conversation among characters in a story or play. In the **script**, or written text, of a drama, the characters' names appear before their dialogue. Paying attention to what the characters say will help you understand and enjoy the script of a drama.

Reading on Your Own A summary is a short statement about a piece of writing. It tells the main ideas and most important points of the writing. To summarize a drama, first reread it to identify main events. Include only major events that move the story forward. Then, arrange events in the order in which they happen. As you read, use a chart like the one shown to record major events.

Writing on Your Own Make a list of possible reasons why students your age might be bored. Then, add some possible cures. How do you get over being bored?

Vocabulary Focus In the play as well as the novel, the names of some characters and places describe their qualities.

• The Lethargarians are sleepy characters who spend their days lying around. Their name comes from the word *lethargy*. It means "slow-moving" or "lacking energy."

• Digitopolis is the place where all numbers come from. Its name combines the word *digit*, meaning "number," and the root *-polis*, meaning "city."

• Dictionopolis is the place where all words are born. Its name combines *diction*, meaning "language," and *-polis*.

Think Before You Read What does the title of the play mean? Write down your guess and why you think so. As you read, look for the points in the play where the title is explained.

The Phantom Tollbooth, Act I

Based on the Book by Norton Juster

CAST (in order of appearance)

THE CLOCK
MILO, a boy
THE WHETHER MAN
SIX LETHARGARIANS
TOCK, THE WATCHDOG (same as the clock)
AZAZ THE **UNABRIDGED**, KING OF DICTIONOPOLIS
THE MATHEMAGICIAN, KING OF DIGITOPOLIS
PRINCESS SWEET RHYME
PRINCESS PURE **REASON**
GATEKEEPER OF DICTIONOPOLIS
THREE WORD MERCHANTS
THE LETTERMAN (fourth word merchant)
SPELLING BEE
THE HUMBUG

THE DUKE OF DEFINITION
THE MINISTER OF MEANING
THE EARL OF **ESSENCE**
THE COUNT OF **CONNOTATION**
THE UNDERSECRETARY OF UNDERSTANDING
A PAGE
KAKAFONOUS A. DISCHORD, DOCTOR OF **DISSONANCE**
THE AWFUL DYNNE
THE DODECAHEDRON
MINERS OF THE NUMBERS MINE
THE EVERPRESENT WORDSNATCHER
THE TERRIBLE TRIVIUM
THE DEMON OF **INSINCERITY**
SENSES TAKER

The SET

1. MILO'S BEDROOM—with shelves, **pennants**, pictures on the wall, as well as suggestions of the characters of the Land of Wisdom.

2. THE ROAD TO THE LAND OF WISDOM—a forest, from which the Whether Man and the Lethargarians emerge.

3. DICTIONOPOLIS—a marketplace full of open air stalls as well as little shops. Letters and signs should abound.

4. DIGITOPOLIS—a dark, glittering place without trees or greenery, but full of shining rocks and cliffs, with hundreds of numbers shining everywhere.

5. THE LAND OF IGNORANCE—a gray, gloomy place full of cliffs and caves, with frightening faces. Different levels and heights should be suggested through one or two platforms or risers, with a set of stairs that lead to the castle in the air.

---

unabridged complete; not shortened

reason common sense

essence meaning

connotation the suggestion of meaning

dissonance disagreement

insincerity dishonesty

pennants banners or flags

Act I
Scene I

As you read, think about how you know what characters are speaking and what sets are in the play.

[The stage is completely dark and silent. Suddenly the sound of someone winding an alarm clock is heard, and after that, the sound of loud ticking is heard.]

[LIGHTS UP on the CLOCK, a huge alarm clock. The CLOCK reads 4:00. The lighting should make it appear that the CLOCK is suspended in mid-air (if possible). The CLOCK ticks for 30 seconds.]

Clock See that! Half a minute gone by. Seems like a long time when you're waiting for something to happen, doesn't it? Funny thing is, time can pass very slowly or very fast, and sometimes even both at once. The time now? Oh, a little after four, but what that means should depend on you. Too often, we do something simply because time tells us to. Time for school, time for bed, whoops, 12:00, time to be hungry. It can get a little silly, don't you think? Time is important, but it's what you do with it that makes it so. So my advice to you is to use it. Keep your eyes open and your ears perked. Otherwise it will pass before you know it, and you'll certainly have missed something!

Things have a habit of doing that, you know. Being here one minute and gone the next.

In the twinkling of an eye.

In a jiffy.

In a flash!

Reading Strategy: Summarizing

How would you summarize the point Clock is making?

I know a girl who yawned and missed a whole summer vacation. And what about that caveman who took a nap one afternoon, and woke up to find himself completely alone. You see, while he was sleeping, someone had invented the wheel and everyone had moved to the **suburbs.** And then of course, there is Milo. *[LIGHTS UP to reveal MILO's Bedroom. The CLOCK appears to be on a shelf in the room of a young boy—a room filled with books, toys, games, maps, papers, pencils, a*

suburbs
neighborhoods just
outside cities

bed, a desk. There is a dartboard with numbers and the face of the MATHEMAGICIAN, *a bedspread made from* KING AZAZ's *cloak, a kite looking like the spelling bee, a punching bag with the* HUMBUG's *face, as well as records, a television, a toy car, and a large box that is wrapped and has an envelope taped to the top. The sound of* FOOTSTEPS *is heard, and then enter* MILO **dejectedly**. *He throws down his books and coat, flops into a chair, and sighs loudly.*] Who never knows what to do with himself—not just sometimes, but always. When he's in school, he wants to be out, and when he's out, he wants to be in. [*During the following speech,* MILO *examines the various toys, tools, and other possessions in the room, trying them out and* **rejecting** *them.*] Wherever he is, he wants to be somewhere else—and when he gets there, so what. Everything is too much trouble or a waste of time. Books—he's already read them. Games—boring. T.V.—dumb. So what's left? Another long, boring afternoon. Unless he bothers to notice a very large package that happened to arrive today.

Milo [*Suddenly notices the package. He drags himself over to it, and disinterestedly reads the label.*] "For Milo, who has plenty of time." Well, that's true. [*Sighs and looks at it.*] No. [*Walks away.*] Well . . . [*Comes back. Rips open envelope and reads.*]

A Voice "One genuine turnpike tollbooth, easily assembled at home for use by those who have never traveled in lands beyond."

Milo Beyond what? [*Continues reading.*]

A Voice "This package contains the following items:" [MILO *pulls the items out of the box and sets them up as they are mentioned.*] One (1) genuine turnpike tollbooth to be erected according to directions. Three (3) **precautionary** signs to be used in a precautionary fashion. Assorted coins for paying tolls. One (1) map, strictly up to date, showing how to get from here to there. One (1) book of rules and traffic

A *turnpike* is a road that people pay a fee, or toll, to use. Long ago, long spears called pikes blocked the road. The pikes were turned aside only after travelers paid the fee. A *tollbooth* is the booth or gate at which tolls are collected.

dejectedly unhappily	**precautionary** protecting against possible danger
rejecting not using	

regulations which may not be bent or broken. Warning! Results are not **guaranteed.** If not perfectly satisfied, your wasted time will be **refunded.**"

Milo [*Skeptically.*] Come off it, who do you think you're kidding? [*Walks around and examines tollbooth.*] What am I supposed to do with this? [*The ticking of the* CLOCK *grows loud and impatient.*] Well . . . what else do I have to do. [MILO *gets into his toy car and drives up to the first sign.*]

Voice "HAVE YOUR DESTINATION IN MIND."

Milo [*Pulls out the map.*] Now, let's see. That's funny. I never heard of any of these places. Well, it doesn't matter anyway. Dictionopolis. That's a weird name. I might as well go there. [*Begins to move, following map. Drives off.*]

Clock See what I mean? You never know how things are going to get started. But when you're bored, what you need more than anything is a rude awakening.

[*The ALARM goes off very loudly as the stage darkens. The sound of the alarm is **transformed** into the honking of a car horn, and is then joined by the blasts, bleeps, roars and growls of heavy highway traffic. When the lights come up, MILO's bedroom is gone and we see a lonely road in the middle of nowhere.*]

Scene II The Road to Dictionopolis
[ENTER MILO *in his car.*]

Milo This is weird! I don't recognize any of this scenery at all. [*A SIGN is held up before* MILO, *startling him.*] Huh? [*Reads.*] WELCOME TO **EXPECTATIONS.** INFORMATION, **PREDICTIONS** AND ADVICE CHEERFULLY OFFERED. PARK HERE AND BLOW HORN. [MILO *blows horn.*]

How might such an unusual gift affect Milo's bored state of mind?

A *rude awakening* is something that happens suddenly and in a disturbing way. It can lead to the beginning of a new experience or way of thinking.

Reading Strategy:
Summarizing
Reread scene I to find and summarize the key events.

guaranteed promised	**skeptically** slow to believe	**expectations** hopes or possibilities
refunded paid back	**transformed** changed	**predictions** guesses about the future

Whether Man [*A little man wearing a long coat and carrying an umbrella pops up from behind the sign that he was holding. He speaks very fast and excitedly.*] My, my, my, my, my, welcome, welcome, welcome, welcome to the Land of Expectations, Expectations, Expectations! We don't get many travelers these days; we certainly don't get many travelers. Now what can I do for you? I'm the Whether Man.

Milo [*Referring to map.*] Uh . . . is this the right road to Dictionopolis?

Whether Man Well now, well now, well now, I don't know of any wrong road to Dictionopolis, so if this road goes to Dictionopolis at all, it must be the right road, and if it doesn't, it must be the right road to somewhere else, because there are no wrong roads to anywhere. Do you think it will rain?

Milo I thought you were the Weather Man.

Whether Man Oh, no, I'm the Whether Man, not the weather man. [*Pulls out a SIGN or opens a FLAP of his coat, which reads: "WHETHER."*] After all, it's more important to know whether there will be weather than what the weather will be.

Milo What kind of place is Expectations?

Whether Man Good question, good question! Expectations is the place you must always go to before you get to where you are going. Of course, some people never go beyond Expectations, but my job is to hurry them along whether they like it or not. Now what else can I do for you? [*Opens his umbrella.*]

Milo I think I can find my own way.

Whether Man Splendid, splendid, splendid! Whether or not you find your own way, you're bound to find some way. If you happen to find my way, please return it. I lost it years ago.

What do you learn about the Whether Man from his first speech?

I imagine by now it must be quite rusty. You did say it was going to rain, didn't you? [**Escorts** MILO *to the car under the open umbrella.*] I'm glad you made your own decision. I do so hate to make up my mind about anything, whether it's good or bad, up or down, rain or shine. Expect everything, I always say, and the unexpected never happens. Goodbye, goodbye, goodbye, good . . .

[*A loud CLAP of THUNDER is heard.*] Oh dear! [*He looks up at the sky, puts out his hand to feel for rain, and RUNS AWAY: MILO watches puzzledly and drives on.*]

How do Milo's words here move the plot along?

Milo I'd better get out of Expectations, but fast. Talking to a guy like that all day would get me nowhere for sure. [*He tries to speed up, but finds instead that he is moving slower and slower.*] Oh, oh, now what? [*He can barely move. Behind MILO, the LETHARGARIANS begin to enter from all parts of the stage. They are dressed to blend in with the scenery and carry small pillows that look like rocks. Whenever they fall asleep, they rest on the pillows.*] Now I really am getting nowhere. I hope I didn't take a wrong turn. [*The car stops. He tries to the start it. It won't move. He gets out and begins to tinker with it.*] I wonder where I am.

Lethargarian 1 You're . . . in . . . the . . . Dol . . . drums . . . [MILO *looks around.*]

How do the Lethargarians talk? How can you tell?

Lethargarian 2 Yes . . . the . . . Dol . . . drums . . . [*A YAWN is heard.*]

Milo [*Yelling.*] WHAT ARE THE **DOLDRUMS**?

Lethargarian 3 The Doldrums, my friend, are where nothing ever happens and nothing ever changes. [*Parts of the Scenery stand up or Six People come out of the scenery colored in the same colors of the trees or the road. They move very slowly and as soon as they move, they stop to rest again.*] Allow me to introduce all of us. We are the Lethargarians at your service.

---

escorts walks or goes with someone   **doldrums** a general feeling of boredom

Milo [*Uncertainly.*] Very pleased to meet you. I think I'm lost. Can you help me?

Lethargarian 4 Don't say think. [*He yawns.*] It's against the law.

Lethargarian 1 No one's allowed to think in the Doldrums. [*He falls asleep.*]

Lethargarian 2 Don't you have a rule book? It's local **ordinance** 175389-J. [*He falls asleep.*]

Milo [*Pulls out rule book and reads.*] **Ordinance** 175389-J: "It shall be unlawful, illegal and **unethical** to think, think of thinking, **surmise,** presume, reason, **meditate** or **speculate** while in the Doldrums. Anyone breaking this law shall be severely punished." That's a ridiculous law! Everybody thinks.

All The Lethargarians We don't!

Lethargarian 2 And most of the time, you don't, that's why you're here. You weren't thinking and you weren't paying attention either. People who don't pay attention often get stuck in the Doldrums. Face it, most of the time, you're just like us. [*Falls, snoring, to the ground.* MILO *laughs.*]

Lethargarian 5 Stop that at once. Laughing is against the law. Don't you have a rule book? It's local ordinance 574381-W.

Milo [*Opens rule book and reads.*] "In the Doldrums, laughter is frowned upon and smiling is permitted only on **alternate** Thursdays." Well, if you can't laugh or think, what can you do?

ordinance a law	**meditate** to consider	**alternate** every other; skipping one in-between
unethical wrong	**speculate** to wonder about	
surmise to suppose		

What does this dialogue tell you about the Lethargarians?

Lethargarian 6 Anything as long as it's nothing, and everything as long as it isn't anything. There's lots to do. We have a very busy schedule . . .

Lethargarian 1 At 8:00 we get up and then we spend from 8 to 9 daydreaming.

Lethargarian 2 From 9:00 to 9:30 we take our early midmorning nap . . .

Lethargarian 3 From 9:30 to 10:30 we **dawdle** and delay . . .

Lethargarian 4 From 10:30 to 11:30 we take our late early morning nap . . .

Lethargarian 5 From 11:30 to 12:00 we **bide** our time and then we eat our lunch.

Lethargarian 6 From 1:00 to 2:00 we **linger** and **loiter** . . .

Lethargarian 1 From 2:00 to 2:30 we take our early afternoon nap . . .

Lethargarian 2 From 2:30 to 3:30 we put off for tomorrow what we could have done today . . .

Lethargarian 3 From 3:30 to 4:00 we take our early late afternoon nap . . .

Lethargarian 4 From 4:00 to 5:00 we **loaf** and lounge until dinner . . .

Lethargarian 5 From 6:00 to 7:00 we **dilly-dally** . . .

Lethargarian 6 From 7:00 to 8:00 we take our early evening nap and then for an hour before we go to bed, we waste time.

Lethargarian 1 [*Yawning.*] You see, it's really quite **strenuous** doing nothing all day long, and so once a week, we take a holiday and go nowhere.

Ellipsis points— three spaced periods—can mean a pause or an unfinished thought. How does this punctuation tell you how this dialogue should be read?

dawdle to waste time	**loiter** to hang around	**dilly-dally** to waste time
bide to wait	**loaf** to not do anything	**strenuous** tiring, requiring much effort
linger to stay behind		

Lethargarian 5 Which is just where we were going when you came along. Would you care to join us?

Milo [*Yawning.*] That's where I seem to be going, anyway. [*Stretching.*] Tell me, does everyone here do nothing?

Lethargarian 3 Everyone but the terrible watchdog. He's always sniffing around to see that nobody wastes time. A most unpleasant character.

Milo The Watchdog?

Lethargarian 6 THE WATCHDOG!

All The Lethargarians [*Yelling at once.*] RUN! WAKE UP! RUN! HERE HE COMES! THE WATCHDOG! [*They all run off and ENTER a large dog with the head, feet, and tail of a dog, and the body of a clock, having the same face as the character* THE CLOCK.]

Watchdog What are you doing here?

Milo Nothing much. Just killing time. You see . . .

Watchdog KILLING TIME! [*His ALARM RINGS in fury.*] It's bad enough wasting time without killing it. What are you doing in the Doldrums, anyway? Don't you have anywhere to go?

Milo I think I was on my way to Dictionopolis when I got stuck here. Can you help me?

Watchdog Help you! You've got to help yourself. I suppose you know why you got stuck.

Milo I guess I just wasn't thinking.

Watchdog **Precisely.** Now you're on your way.

Milo I am?

Reading Strategy:
Summarizing

How would you summarize what the Lethargarians do all day?

Usually, a watchdog guards a place. How is this "watchdog" different? How is its name a play on words? In other words, how does this name suggest more than one meaning?

Reading Strategy:
Summarizing

Would you include the arrival of the Watchdog in a summary of this scene? Why or why not?

precisely exactly

Watchdog Of course. Since you got here by not thinking, it seems reasonable that in order to get out, you must start thinking. Do you mind if I get in? I love automobile rides. [*He gets in. They wait.*] Well?

Milo All right. I'll try. [*Screws up his face and thinks.*] Are we moving?

Watchdog Not yet. Think harder.

Milo. I'm thinking as hard as I can.

Watchdog Well, think just a little harder than that. Come on, you can do it.

How does Milo's dialogue with the Watchdog help you understand the problem here?

Milo All right, all right. . . . I'm thinking of all the planets in the solar system, and why water expands when it turns to ice, and all the words that begin with "q," and . . . [*The wheels begin to move.*] We're moving! We're moving!

Watchdog Keep thinking.

Milo. [*Thinking.*] How a steam engine works and how to bake a pie and the difference between Fahrenheit and Centigrade . . .

Watchdog Dictionopolis, here we come.

Milo Hey, Watchdog, are you coming along?

Tock You can call me Tock, and keep your eyes on the road.

What does this dialogue tell you about how the actors should move?

Milo What kind of place is Dictionopolis, anyway?

Tock It's where all the words in the world come from. It used to be a marvelous place, but ever since Rhyme and Reason left, it hasn't been the same.

Milo Rhyme and Reason?

Rhyme or *reason* is a term that means "good sense." To lack rhyme or reason is to be without common sense and order. What do the princesses' names tell you about the Land of Wisdom?

Tock The two princesses. They used to settle all the arguments between their two brothers who rule over the Land of Wisdom. You see, Azaz is the king of Dictionopolis and the Mathemagician is the king of Digitopolis and they almost never see eye to eye on anything. It was the job of the Princesses Sweet Rhyme and Pure Reason to solve the differences between the two kings, and they always did so

well that both sides usually went home feeling very satisfied. But then, one day, the kings had an argument to end all arguments. . . .

[*The LIGHTS DIM on* TOCK *and* MILO, *and come up on* KING AZAZ *of Dictionopolis on another part of the stage.* AZAZ *has a great stomach, a grey beard reaching to his waist, a small crown and a long robe with the letters of the alphabet written all over it.*]

Azaz Of course, I'll **abide** by the decision of Rhyme and Reason, though I have no doubt as to what it will be. They will choose words, of course. Everyone knows that words are more important than numbers any day of the week.

[*The* MATHEMAGICIAN *appears opposite* AZAZ. *The* MATHEMAGICIAN *wears a long flowing robe covered entirely with* **complex** *mathematical equations, and a tall pointed hat. He carries a long* **staff** *with a pencil point at one end and a large rubber eraser at the other.*]

---

abide obey   **complex** difficult   **staff** a pole

Reading Strategy: Summarizing
Briefly explain the argument between Azaz and the Mathemagician.

Mathemagician That's what you think, Azaz. People wouldn't even know what day of the week it is without numbers. Haven't you ever looked at a calendar? Face it, Azaz. It's numbers that count.

Azaz Don't be ridiculous. [*To audience, as if leading a cheer.*] Let's hear it for WORDS!

Mathemagician [*To audience, in the same manner.*] Cast your vote for NUMBERS!

Azaz A, B, C's!

Mathemagician 1, 2, 3's! [*A **FANFARE** is heard.*]

Azaz And Mathemagician [*To each other.*] Quiet! Rhyme and Reason are about to announce their decision.

[RHYME *and* REASON *appear.*]

Rhyme Ladies and gentlemen, letters and numerals, fractions and punctuation marks—may we have your attention, please. After careful consideration of the problem set before us by King Azaz of Dictionopolis [AZAZ *bows.*] and the Mathemagician of Digitopolis [MATHEMAGICIAN *raises his hands in a victory salute.*] we have come to the following conclusion:

Reason Words and numbers are of equal value, for in the cloak of knowledge, one is the warp and the other is the woof.

Rhyme It is no more important to count the sands than it is to name the stars.

Rhyme And Reason Therefore, let both kingdoms, Dictionopolis and Digitopolis, live in peace.

[*The sound of CHEERING is heard.*]

Azaz Boo! is what I say. Boo and Bah and Hiss!

The *warp* is the yarn that is arranged lengthwise in weaving. The *woof* is the yarn that crosses the warp. This crossing of the warp and woof is what gives strength to a woven object.

What conclusion do Rhyme and Reason reach?

fanfare a trumpet blast

Mathemagician What good are these girls if they can't even settle an argument in anyone's favor? I think I have come to a decision of my own.

Azaz So have I.

Azaz And Mathemagician [*To the* PRINCESSES.] You are hereby **banished** from this land to the Castle-in-the-Air. [*To each other.*] And as for you, KEEP OUT OF MY WAY! [*They* **stalk** *off in opposite directions.*]

[*During this time, the set has been changed to the Market Square of Dictionopolis. LIGHTS come UP on the* **deserted** *square.*]

Reading Strategy: Summarizing

Reread this section to summarize the events that led to Rhyme and Reason's banishment.

Tock And ever since then, there has been neither Rhyme nor Reason in this kingdom. Words are misused and numbers are mismanaged. The argument between the two kings has divided everyone and the real value of both words and numbers has been forgotten. What a waste!

Milo Why doesn't somebody rescue the Princesses and set everything straight again?

Tock That is easier said than done. The Castle-in-the-Air is very far from here, and the one path which leads to it is guarded by **ferocious** demons. But hold on, here we are. [*A Man appears, carrying a Gate and a small Tollbooth.*]

Gatekeeper AHHHHREMMMM! This is Dictionopolis, a happy kingdom, **advantageously** located in the foothills of Confusion and **caressed** by gentle breezes from the Sea of Knowledge. Today, by royal **proclamation,** is Market Day. Have you come to buy or sell?

Milo I beg your pardon?

Gatekeeper Buy or sell, buy or sell. Which is it? You must have come here for a reason.

banished sent away	**ferocious** wild and dangerous	**caressed** gently touched
stalk to stomp angrily		
deserted empty	**advantageously** well	**proclamation** announcement

Milo Well, I . . .

Gatekeeper Come now, if you don't have a reason, you must at least have an explanation or certainly an excuse.

Milo [*Meekly.*] Uh . . . no.

Gatekeeper [*Shaking his head.*] Very serious. You can't get in without a reason. [*Thoughtfully.*] Wait a minute. Maybe I have an old one you can use. [*Pulls out an old suitcase from the tollbooth and rummages through it.*] No . . . no . . . no . . . this won't do . . . hmmm . . .

Milo [*To* TOCK.] What's he looking for? [TOCK *shrugs.*]

What details about Dictionopolis does the Gatekeeper make known in his dialogue with Milo?

Gatekeeper Ah! This is fine. [*Pulls out a **Medallion** on a chain. Engraved in the Medallion is: "WHY NOT?"*] Why not. That's a good reason for almost anything . . . a bit used, perhaps, but still quite **serviceable.** There you are, sir. Now I can truly say: Welcome to Dictionopolis.

[*He opens the Gate and walks off.* CITIZENS *and* MERCHANTS *appear on all levels of the stage, and* MILO *and* TOCK *find themselves in the middle of a noisy marketplace. As some people buy and sell their wares, others hang a large banner which reads: WELCOME TO THE WORD MARKET.*]

Milo Tock! Look!

Merchant 1 Hey-ya, hey-ya, hey-ya, step right up and take your pick. Juicy tempting words for sale. Get your fresh picked "if's," "and's" and "but's"! Just take a look at these nice ripe "where's" and "when's."

Merchant 2 Step right up, step right up, fancy, best-quality words here for sale. **Enrich** your vocabulary and expand your speech with such elegant items as "quagmire," "flabbergast," or "upholstery."

Merchant 3 Words by the bag, buy them over here. Words by the bag for the more talkative customer. A pound of

---

medallion a large medal, often on a chain

serviceable useful

enrich to add to

"happy's" at a very reasonable price . . . very useful for "Happy Birthday," "Happy New Year," "happy days," or "happy-go-lucky." Or how about a package of "good's," always handy for "good morning," "good afternoon," "good evening," and "goodbye."

Milo I can't believe it. Did you ever see so many words?

Tock They're fine if you have something to say. [*They come to a Do-It-Yourself Bin.*]

Milo [*To* MERCHANT 4 *at the bin.*] Excuse me, but what are these?

Merchant 4 These are for people who like to make up their own words. You can pick any **assortment** you like or buy a special box complete with all the letters and a book of instructions. Here, taste an "A." They're very good. [*He pops one into MILO's mouth.*]

Milo [*Tastes it **hesitantly.***] It's sweet! [*He eats it.*]

Merchant 4 1 knew you'd like it. "A" is one of our best-sellers. All of them aren't that good, you know. The "Z," for instance—very dry and sawdusty. And the "X"? Tastes like a trunkful of stale air. But most of the others aren't bad at all. Here, try the "I."

Milo [*Tasting.*] Cool! It tastes icy.

Merchant 4 [*To* TOCK.] How about the "C" for you? It's as crunchy as a bone. Most people are just too lazy to make their own words, but take it from me, not only is it more fun, but it's also *de*-lightful, [*Holds up a "D."*] **e-lating,** [*Holds up an "E."*] and extremely *u*seful! [*Holds up a "U."*]

Milo But isn't it difficult? I'm not very good at making words.

[*The* SPELLING BEE, *a large colorful bee, comes up from behind.*]

What is sold in the Dictionopolis marketplace?

Reading Strategy:
Summarizing

Would you include the scene in the Word Market in a summary of scene II? Why or why not?

---

assortment a variety or collection

hesitantly in a cautious way

elating thrilling

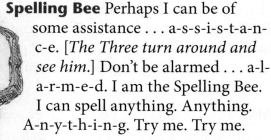

Spelling Bee Perhaps I can be of some assistance . . . a-s-s-i-s-t-a-n-c-e. [*The Three turn around and see him.*] Don't be alarmed . . . a-l-a-r-m-e-d. I am the Spelling Bee. I can spell anything. Anything. A-n-y-t-h-i-n-g. Try me. Try me.

Milo [*Backing off,* TOCK *on his guard.*] Can you spell goodbye?

Spelling Bee Perhaps you are under the **misapprehension** . . . m-i-s-a-p-p-r-e-h-e-n-s-i-o-n that I am dangerous. Let me assure you that I am quite peaceful. Now, think of the most difficult word you can, and I'll spell it.

Milo Uh . . . o.k. [*At this point,* MILO *may turn to the audience and ask them to help him choose a word or he may think of one on his own.*] How about . . . "Curiosity"?

Spelling Bee [*Winking.*] Let's see now . . . uh . . . how much time do I have?

Milo Just ten seconds. Count them off, Tock.

Spelling Bee [*As* TOCK *counts.*] Oh dear, oh dear. [*Just at the last moment, quickly.*] C-u-r-i-o-s-i-t-y.

Merchant 4 Correct! [ALL *Cheer.*]

Milo Can you spell anything?

Spelling Bee [*Proudly.*] Just about. You see, years ago, I was an ordinary bee minding my own business, smelling flowers all day, occasionally picking up part-time work in people's bonnets. Then one day, I realized that I'd never amount to anything without an education, so I decided that . . .

Humbug [*Coming up in a booming voice.*] **BALDERDASH**! [*He wears a **lavish** coat, striped pants, checked vest, **spats** and*

To have a "bee in one's bonnet" means to be excited or eager about something.

misapprehension misunderstanding	**lavish** splendid and costly	**spats** cloth coverings for the ankles and insteps
balderdash nonsense		

*a **derby** hat.*] Let me repeat . . . BALDERDASH! [*Swings his cane and clicks his heels in the air.*] Well, well, what have we here? Isn't someone going to introduce me to the little boy?

Spelling Bee [***Disdainfully.***] This is the Humbug. You can't trust a word he says.

Humbug NONSENSE! Everyone can trust a Humbug. As I was saying to the king just the other day . . .

Spelling Bee You've never met the king. [*To* MILO.] Don't believe a thing he tells you.

Humbug **Bosh,** my boy, pure bosh. The Humbugs are an old and noble family, honorable to the core. Why, we fought in the Crusades with Richard the Lionhearted, crossed the Atlantic with Columbus, blazed trails with the pioneers. History is full of Humbugs.

Spelling Bee A very pretty speech . . . s-p-e-e-c-h. Now, why don't you go away? I was just advising the lad of the importance of proper spelling.

Humbug BAH! As soon as you learn to spell one word, they ask you to spell another. You can never catch up, so why bother? [*Puts his arm around* MILO.] Take my advice, boy, and forget about it. As my great-great-great-grandfather George Washington Humbug used to say . . .

Spelling Bee You, sir, are an **impostor** i-m-p-o-s-t-o-r who can't even spell his own name!

Humbug What? You dare to doubt my word? The word of a Humbug? The word of a Humbug who has direct **access** to the ear of a King? And the king shall hear of this, I promise you . . .

Voice 1 Did someone call for the King?

The word *humbug* means "nonsense" or "trickery." How do the Humbug's words connect to his name?

What does the dialogue between the Humbug and the Spelling Bee show about their relationship?

---

derby a domelike man's hat

disdainfully with strong dislike

bosh foolish talk or activity

imposter a fake

access the ability to get close to

Voice 2 Did you mention the monarch?

Voice 3 Speak of the **sovereign?**

Voice 4 **Entreat** the Emperor?

Voice 5 Hail his highness?

[*Five tall, thin gentlemen **regally** dressed in silks and satins, plumed hats and buckled shoes appear as they speak.*]

Milo Who are they?

Spelling Bee The King's **advisors.** Or in more formal terms, his cabinet.

Minister 1 Greetings!

Minister 2 **Salutations!**

Minister 3 Welcome!

Minister 4 Good Afternoon!

Minister 5 Hello!

Milo Uh . . . Hi.

[*All the MINISTERS, from here on called by their numbers, unfold their scrolls and read in order.*]

Minister 1 By the order of Azaz the Unabridged . . .

Minister 2 King of Dictionopolis . . .

Minister 3 Monarch of letters . . .

Minister 4 Emperor of phrases, sentences, and **miscellaneous** figures of speech . . .

Minister 5 We offer you the **hospitality** of our kingdom . . .

Minister 1 Country

Minister 2 Nation

The ministers here are advisors in the king's cabinet, not members of a church.

3

sovereign a ruler	**advisors** assistants who give advice	**miscellaneous** various
entreat to ask (for)		
regally grandly	**salutations** greetings	**hospitality** welcome

Minister 3 State

Minister 4 Commonwealth

Minister 5 Realm

Minister 1 Empire

Minister 2 Palatinate

Minister 3 Principality.

Milo Do all those words mean the same thing?

Minister 1 Of course.

Minister 2 Certainly.

Minister 3 Precisely.

Minister 4 Exactly.

Minister 5 Yes.

Milo Then why don't you use just one? Wouldn't that make a lot more sense?

Minister 1 Nonsense!

Minister 2 Ridiculous!

Minister 3 Fantastic!

Minister 4 Absurd!

Minister 5 Bosh!

Minister 1 We're not interested in making sense. It's not our job.

Minister 2 Besides, one word is as good as another, so why not use them all?

Minister 3 Then you don't have to choose which one is right.

Minister 4 Besides, if one is right, then ten are ten times as right.

Minister 5 Obviously, you don't know who we are.

How does the dialogue of the five ministers show the importance of words in Dictionopolis?

[*Each presents himself and* MILO **acknowledges** *the introduction.*]

Minister 1 The Duke of Definition.

Minister 2 The Minister of Meaning.

Minister 3 The Earl of Essence.

Minister 4 The Count of Connotation.

Minister 5 The Undersecretary of Understanding.

All Five And we have come to invite you to the Royal Banquet.

Spelling Bee The banquet! That's quite an honor, my boy. A real h-o-n-o-r.

Humbug DON'T BE RIDICULOUS! Everybody goes to the Royal Banquet these days.

Spelling Bee [*To the* HUMBUG.] True, everybody does go. But some people are invited and others simply push their way in where they aren't wanted.

Humbug HOW DARE YOU? You buzzing little **upstart**, I'll show you who's not wanted . . . [*Raises his cane threateningly.*]

Spelling Bee You just watch it! I'm warning w-a-r-n-i-n-g you! [*At that moment, an ear-shattering blast of* TRUMPETS, *entirely off-key, is heard, and a* PAGE *appears.*]

Page King Azaz the Unabridged is about to begin the Royal banquet. All guests who do not appear promptly at the table will automatically lose their place. [*A huge Table is carried out with* KING AZAZ *sitting in a large chair, carried out at the head of the table.*]

Azaz Places. Everyone take your places. [*All the characters, including the* HUMBUG *and the* SPELLING BEE, *who forget their quarrel, rush to take their places at the table.* MILO *and* TOCK *sit near the* KING. AZAZ *looks at* MILO.] And just who is this?

acknowledges notices and responds to	**upstart** an unimportant person

Milo Your Highness, my name is Milo and this is Tock. Thank you very much for inviting us to your banquet, and I think your palace is beautiful!

Minister 1 Exquisite.

Minister 2 Lovely.

Minister 3 Handsome.

Minister 4 Pretty.

Minister 5 Charming.

Azaz SILENCE! Now tell me, young man, what can you do to entertain us? Sing songs? Tell stories? Juggle plates? Do tumbling tricks? Which is it?

Milo I can't do any of those things.

Azaz What an ordinary little boy. Can't you do anything at all?

Milo Well . . . I can count to a thousand.

Azaz AARGH, numbers! Never mention numbers here. Only use them when we absolutely have to. Now, why don't we change the subject and have some dinner? Since you are the guest of honor, you may pick the menu.

Milo Me? Well, uh . . . I'm not very hungry. Can we just have a light snack?

Azaz A light snack it shall be!

[AZAZ *claps his hands. Waiters rush in with covered trays. When they are uncovered, **Shafts** of Light pour out. The light may be created through the use of battery-operated flashlights which are **secured** in the trays and covered with a false bottom. The Guests help themselves.*]

Humbug Not a very **substantial** meal. Maybe you can suggest something a little more filling.

---

shafts beams	**secured** fastened	**substantial** large in amount

What does Milo mean by "a light snack"? What does he mean by "a square meal"?

Milo Well, in that case, I think we ought to have a square meal . . .

Azaz [*Claps his hands.*] A square meal it is! [*Waiters serve trays of Colored Squares of all sizes. People serve themselves.*]

Spelling Bee These are awful. [HUMBUG *coughs and all the Guests do not care for the food.*]

Azaz [*Claps his hands and the trays are removed.*] Time for speeches. [*To* MILO.] You first.

Milo [*Hesitantly.*] Your Majesty, ladies and gentlemen, I would like to take this opportunity to say that . . .

Azaz That's quite enough. Mustn't talk all day.

Milo But I just started to . . .

Azaz NEXT!

Humbug [*Quickly.*] Roast turkey, mashed potatoes, vanilla ice cream.

Spelling Bee Hamburgers, corn on the cob, chocolate pudding p-u-d-d-i-n-g. [*Each Guest names two dishes and a dessert.*]

Translated, the king ordered goose liver, onion soup, endive salad, cheese and fruit, and a cup of coffee.

Azaz [*The last.*] Pâté de foie gras, soupe à l'oignon, salade endives, fromage et fruits et demi-tasse. [*He claps his hands. Waiters serve each Guest his Words.*] Dig in. [*To* MILO.] Though I can't say I think much of your choice.

Milo I didn't know I was going to have to eat my words.

Azaz Of course, of course, everybody here does. Your speech should have been in better taste.

Minister 1 Here, try some somersault. It improves the flavor.

Minister 2 Have a rigamarole. [*Offers breadbasket.*]

Minister 3 Or a ragamuffin.

Minister 4 Perhaps you'd care for a synonym bun.

Rigmarole or *rigamarole* is confused or meaningless talk or processes. A *ragamuffin* is a ragged or lowly person. What other meaning might these words have here?

Minister 5 Why not wait for your just desserts?

Azaz Ah yes, the dessert. We're having a special treat today . . . freshly made at the half-bakery.

Milo The half-bakery?

Azaz Of course, the half-bakery! Where do you think half-baked ideas come from? Now, please don't interrupt. By royal command, the pastry chefs have . . .

Milo What's a half-baked idea?

[AZAZ *gives up the idea of speaking as a cart is wheeled in and the Guests help themselves.*]

Find one pun, or play on words, that adds humor to the dialogue here.

Humbug They're very tasty, but they don't always agree with you. Here's a good one. [HUMBUG *hands one to* MILO.]

Milo [*Reads.*] "The earth is flat."

Spelling Bee People swallowed that one for years. [*Picks up one and reads.*] "The moon is made of green cheese." Now, there's a half-baked idea.

[Everyone chooses one and eats. They include: "It Never Rains But Pours," "Night Air Is Bad Air," "Everything Happens for the Best," "Coffee **Stunts** Your Growth."]

Azaz And now for a few closing words. Attention! Let me have your attention! [*Everyone leaps up and Exits, except for* MILO, TOCK, *and the* HUMBUG.] Loyal subjects and friends, once again on this **gala** occasion, we have . . .

Milo Excuse me, but everybody left.

Azaz [*Sadly.*] I was hoping no one would notice. It happens every time.

Humbug They're gone to dinner, and as soon as I finish this last bite, I shall join them.

Milo That's ridiculous. How can they eat dinner right after a banquet?

Reading Strategy:
Summarizing
Briefly summarize the events at the banquet.

stunts slows up; holds back	**gala** event for celebrating

Azaz SCANDALOUS! We'll put a stop to it at once. From now on, by royal command, everyone must eat dinner before the banquet.

Milo But that's just as bad.

Humbug Or just as good. Things which are equally bad are also equally good. Try to look at the bright side of things.

Milo I don't know which side of anything to look at. Everything is so confusing, and all your words only make things worse.

Azaz How true. There must be something we can do about it.

Humbug Pass a law.

Azaz We have almost as many laws as words.

Humbug Offer a reward. [AZAZ *shakes his head and looks madder at each suggestion.*] Send for help? Drive a bargain? Pull the switch? Lower the boom? Toe the line?

[*As AZAZ continues to scowl, the HUMBUG loses confidence and finally gives up.*]

Milo Maybe you should let Rhyme and Reason return.

Azaz How nice that would be. Even if they were a bother at times, things always went so well when they were here. But I'm afraid it can't be done.

Humbug Certainly not. Can't be done.

Milo Why not?

Humbug [*Now siding with* MILO.] Why not, indeed?

Azaz Much too difficult.

Humbug Of course, much too difficult.

Milo You could, if you really wanted to.

Humbug By all means, if you really wanted to, you could.

---

scandalous shocking; inviting trouble

Azaz [*To* HUMBUG.] How?

Milo [*Also to* HUMBUG.] Yeah, how?

Humbug Why . . . uh, it's a simple task for a brave boy with a stout heart, a **steadfast** dog and a serviceable small automobile.

What major problem do Milo and Azaz discuss here?

Azaz Go on.

Humbug Well, all that he would have to do is cross the dangerous, unknown countryside between here and Digitopolis, where he would have to persuade the Mathemagician to release the Princesses, which we know to be impossible because the Mathemagician will never agree with Azaz about anything. Once achieving that, it's a simple matter of entering the Mountains of Ignorance from where no one has ever returned alive, an effortless climb up a two thousand foot stairway without railings in a high wind at night to the Castle-in-the-Air. After a pleasant chat with the Princesses, all that remains is a leisurely ride back through those **chaotic** crags where the frightening **fiends** have sworn to tear any **intruder** limb from limb and devour him down to his belt buckle. And finally after doing all that, a triumphal parade! If, of course, there is anything left to parade . . . followed by hot chocolate and cookies for everyone.

What purpose does this speech serve in the play's action?

Azaz I never realized it would be so simple.

Milo It sounds dangerous to me.

Tock And just who is supposed to make that journey?

Azaz A very good question. But there is one far more serious problem.

Milo What's that?

Azaz I'm afraid I can't tell you that until you return.

Milo But wait a minute, I didn't . . .

steadfast loyal	**fiends** evil people
chaotic messy; disorganized	**intruder** someone who breaks in

Azaz Dictionopolis will always be grateful to you, my boy, and your dog. [AZAZ *pats* TOCK *and* MILO.]

Tock Now, just one moment, sire . . .

Azaz You will face many dangers on your journey, but fear not, for I can give you something for your protection. [AZAZ *gives* MILO *a box.*] In this box are the letters of the alphabet. With them you can form all the words you will ever need to help you overcome the **obstacles** that may stand in your path. All you must do is use them well and in the right places.

Milo [*Miserably.*] Thanks a lot.

Azaz You will need a guide, of course, and since he knows the obstacles so well, the Humbug has cheerfully volunteered to accompany you.

Humbug Now, see here . . . !

Azaz You will find him dependable, brave, **resourceful** and loyal.

Humbug [*Flattered.*] Oh, your Majesty.

Milo I'm sure he'll be a great help. [*They approach the car.*]

Tock I hope so. It looks like we're going to need it.

[*The lights darken and the KING fades from view.*]

Azaz Good luck! Drive carefully! [*The three get into the car and begin to move. Suddenly a thunderously loud NOISE is heard. They slow down the car.*]

Milo What was that?

Tock It came from up ahead.

Humbug It's something terrible, I just know it. Oh, no. Something dreadful is going to happen to us. I can feel it in my bones. [*The NOISE is repeated. They all look at each other fearfully as the lights fade.*]

> Based on these lines, how does Azaz feel about the power of words?

> *Reading Strategy:* **Summarizing**
> Reread Scene II and summarize the main events.

---

obstacles things getting in the way   **resourceful** practical   **flattered** pleased by words of praise

Directions Choose the letter of the best answer or write the answer using complete sentences.

Comprehension: Identifying Facts

1. Where is Milo when the play begins?
   A in Dictionopolis
   B at the tollbooth
   C in his bedroom
   D on the turnpike

2. According to the Clock, what does Milo need "more than anything"?
   A a good night's sleep
   B a rude awakening
   C a trip around the world
   D a best friend

3. What happens as Milo tries to leave Expectations?

4. How do the Lethargarians spend their days?

5. What makes Tock angry with Milo when they first meet?

6. What two brothers rule the Land of Wisdom?

7. Who are Rhyme and Reason?

8. What is Milo served when he asks for a light snack?

9. How does the Humbug describe the journey that Milo must make?

10. What does King Azaz give Milo?

Comprehension: Putting Ideas Together

11. What is wrong with Milo as the play opens?
    A He is lonely.   C He is sick.
    B He is bored.   D He is lost.

12. How does Milo manage to get out of the Doldrums?
    A He starts thinking hard.
    B He shuts his eyes and drives.
    C He gives the wheel to Tock.
    D He reads his map carefully.

13. What effect does the princesses' absence have on Dictionopolis?

14. How does King Azaz's name fit his role?

15. Why might *Z* taste "dry and sawdusty" compared to *A*?

16. What does the Spelling Bee think of the Humbug?

17. What is the main responsibility of the ministers?

18. What does Azaz forbid Milo to mention? Why?

19. Why does Milo need to rescue the princesses?

20. Why does King Azaz believe that his gift will protect Milo?

After Reading **continued on next page**

Understanding Literature: Dialogue

A drama tells a story using dialogue. The back-and-forth speech among characters moves the story along. Unlike a novel, speech in a drama is not shown in quotation marks. One character is named, and his or her words follow. Then another character is named, and so on. The characters' words in a drama are very important. They give information about the characters' feelings and personalities. They tell the actors how to perform on stage.

21. What is the main purpose of the Clock's opening speech?

22. What makes the Whether Man's speech unusual?

23. Which characters in the play speak mostly in synonyms?

24. Name two characters whose dialogue shows a conflict between them.

25. Which character spends a lot of the time asking questions? Why do you think that is so?

Critical Thinking

26. Which character would you most like to meet? Explain.

27. What events would you include in a summary of Act I? Explain why they are the most important events.

28. Why are names like the "Humbug" and the "Spelling Bee" funny?

29. In Act II, Milo will start his journey. What do you think it will be like? Give three details from Act I to support your answer.

Thinking Creatively

30. If you had a booth at the Dictionopolis marketplace, what words would you sell? Why?

Grammar Check

A preposition is a word that connects a noun or pronoun to another word in the sentence. Prepositions include *in, between, by, from, on, with, at,* and *for.*

A prepositional phrase is a group of words that begins with a preposition and includes a noun or pronoun. The noun or pronoun that is being related to another word in the sentence is called the object of the preposition.

 Vocabulary Builder

A word root is the basic unit of meaning in a word. The Latin root *-scrib,* meaning "write," is part of the English words *script* and *scribble.*

Tell how the meaning of *-scrib* helps you understand each underlined word. Then, answer the questions.

1 What does a <u>description</u> offer?

2 How is a <u>script</u> used for a play?

 Writing on Your Own

Write a summary of Act I. Be sure to do the following:

- Include only important events, characters, and ideas.
- Tell about events in the order in which they occur.
- Leave out unimportant details to keep your summary brief.

 Listening and Speaking

Write and deliver a brief speech that Milo might have given at the banquet about his experiences so far. Practice the speech before presenting it. Use gestures and the tone of your voice to add force to your words.

 Research and Technology

Working with a small group, do research online. Using computers or other technology, prepare a presentation about the history of drama. Include these things:

- Facts about some part of the history of drama
- Printouts, slides, photos, or drawings
- Diagrams, time lines, or other graphics

Let each group member deliver part of the presentation.

from The Phantom Tollbooth, Milo   by Norton Juster

Norton Juster
1929–

About the Author

Norton Juster's first career was as an architect. He designed buildings and other structures. He took up creative writing in his spare time. He thought of it "as a relaxation" from architecture. When he began writing *The Phantom Tollbooth,* he thought it was just a short story for his own pleasure. Yet before long, Juster says, "it had created its own life, and I was hooked."

About the Selection

The novel, *The Phantom Tollbooth,* has become popular throughout the world. It has been translated into several foreign languages. It was also adapted for an animated film. Juster has even rewritten it as an opera!

In this selection, you will learn about the main character, Milo. Milo does not enjoy anything. He is never happy, because he does not think there is anything interesting to do. When a mysterious tollbooth is delivered to his bedroom, it leads him into a series of adventures. In this first chapter of the novel, Milo first finds the Phantom Tollbooth. As you read, compare this chapter to Act I, Scene I of the play on page 320.

Literary Terms A **novel** is written in prose. It is divided into chapters, and the chapters are presented in paragraphs. Words the characters say are set inside quotation marks. The story is told by a narrator. A **dramatization** takes a real event or another form of literature and changes it into a drama. In a dramatization of a novel, the story is told through words and actions of characters. There may or may not be a narrator.

Reading on Your Own As you read, use a Venn Diagram to compare and contrast the novel with Act I, Scene I of the play you just read. (See Appendix A for a description of this Graphic Organizer.) Think about the plot, the characters, and the way the story is presented.

novel fiction that is book-length and has more characters and detail than a short story

dramatization the acting out in drama form of a real-life event or another form of literature

Novel

• Milo is the main character

Both

• The clock speaks

Drama

Writing on Your Own Before you begin reading, write a quick summary of Act I, Scene I on pages 320–322. Use your summary to help you compare the novel with its dramatization.

Vocabulary Focus Adverbs are often used to tell how characters act and speak. The suffix -*ly* means "in this way." So the adverb *happily* means "in a happy way." *Happy* is the adjective from which *happily* is made. Look at these adverbs from the story. Write the adjective from which each one is made.

dejectedly   glumly   wistfully

Think Before You Read How do you think a novel is different from a drama? Why do you think so?

from The Phantom Tollbooth

MILO

Who is speaking in this opening paragraph?

There was once a boy named Milo who didn't know what to do with himself—not just sometimes, but always.

When he was in school he longed to be out, and when he was out he longed to be in. On the way he thought about coming home, and coming home he thought about going. Wherever he was he wished he were somewhere else, and when he got there he wondered why he'd bothered. Nothing really interested him—least of all the things that should have.

"It seems to me that almost everything is a waste of time," he remarked one day as he walked **dejectedly** home from school. "I can't see the point in learning to solve useless problems, or subtracting turnips from turnips, or knowing where Ethiopia is or how to spell February." And, since no one bothered to explain otherwise, he regarded the process of seeking knowledge as the greatest waste of time of all.

As he and his unhappy thoughts hurried along (for while he was never anxious to be where he was going, he liked to

dejectedly unhappily

get there as quickly as possible) it seemed a great wonder that the world, which was so large, could sometimes feel so small and empty.

"And worst of all," he continued sadly, "there's nothing for me to do, nowhere I'd care to go, and hardly anything worth seeing." He **punctuated** this last thought with such a deep sigh that a house sparrow singing nearby stopped and rushed home to be with his family.

Without stopping or looking up, Milo dashed past the buildings and busy shops that lined the street and in a few minutes reached home—dashed through the lobby—hopped onto the elevator—two, three, four, five, six, seven, eight, and off again—opened the apartment door—rushed into his room—flopped dejectedly into a chair, and grumbled softly, "Another long afternoon."

He looked **glumly** at all the things he owned. The books that were too much trouble to read, the tools he'd never learned to use, the small electric automobile he hadn't driven in months—or was it years?—and the hundreds of other games and toys, and bats and balls, and bits and pieces scattered around him. And then, to one side of the room, just next to the **phonograph,** he noticed something he had certainly never seen before.

Who could possibly have left such an enormous package and such a strange one? For, while it was not quite square, it was definitely not round and for its size it was larger than almost any other big package of smaller **dimension** that he'd ever seen.

Attached to one side was a bright-blue envelope which said simply: "FOR MILO, WHO HAS PLENTY OF TIME."

Of course, if you've ever gotten a surprise package, you can imagine how puzzled and excited Milo was; and if you've never gotten one, pay close attention, because someday you might.

> The playwright did not include this description of Milo's walk home from school. Why not?

> What parts of the drama's story do you see here?

---

punctuated interrupted

glumly in a sad way

phonograph a machine that plays records

dimension a measurement of size

"I don't think it's my birthday," he puzzled, "and Christmas must be months away, and I haven't been outstandingly good, or even good at all." (He had to admit this even to himself.) "Most probably I won't like it anyway, but since I don't know where it came from, I can't possibly send it back." He thought about it for quite a while and then opened the envelope, but just to be polite.

"ONE GENUINE TURNPIKE TOLLBOOTH," it stated— and then it went on:

"EASILY ASSEMBLED AT HOME, AND FOR USE BY THOSE WHO HAVE NEVER TRAVELED IN LANDS BEYOND."

"Beyond what?" thought Milo as he continued to read.

"THIS PACKAGE CONTAINS THE FOLLOWING ITEMS:

"One (1) genuine turnpike tollbooth to be erected according to directions.

"Three (3) precautionary signs to be used in a precautionary fashion.

"Assorted coins for use in paying tolls.

"One (1) map, up to date and carefully drawn by master **cartographers, depicting** natural and man-made features.

"One (1) book of rules and traffic regulations, which may not be bent or broken."

And in smaller letters at the bottom it concluded:

"RESULTS ARE NOT GUARANTEED, BUT IF NOT PERFECTLY SATISFIED, YOUR WASTED TIME WILL BE REFUNDED."

Following the instructions, which told him to cut here, lift there, and fold back all around, he soon had the tollbooth unpacked and set up on its stand. He fitted the windows in place and attached the roof, which extended out on both sides, and fastened on the coin box. It was very much like the tollbooths he'd seen many times on family trips, except of course it was much smaller and purple.

"What a strange present," he thought to himself. "The least they could have done was to send a highway with it, for it's terribly **impractical** without one." But since, at the time, there was nothing else he wanted to play with, he set up the three signs,

SLOW DOWN APPROACHING TOLLBOOTH
PLEASE HAVE YOUR FARE READY
HAVE YOUR DESTINATION IN MIND

and slowly unfolded the map.

How are the contents of the letter explained in the novel? How does the drama show the contents?

cartographers map-makers	**depicting** showing	**impractical** not useful

What clues tell you whether the narrator is inside or outside the story?

As the announcement stated, it was a beautiful map, in many colors, showing **principal** roads, rivers and seas, towns and cities, mountains and valleys, **intersections** and detours, and sites of outstanding interest both beautiful and historic.

The only trouble was that Milo had never heard of any of the places it indicated, and even the names sounded most peculiar.

"I don't think there really is such a country," he concluded after studying it carefully. "Well, it doesn't matter anyway." And he closed his eyes and poked a finger at the map.

"Dictionopolis," read Milo slowly when he saw what his finger had chosen. "Oh, well, I might as well go there as anywhere."

He walked across the room and dusted the car off carefully. Then, taking the map and rule book with him, he hopped in and, for lack of anything better to do, drove slowly up to the tollbooth. As he deposited his coin and rolled past he remarked **wistfully**, "I do hope this is an interesting game, otherwise the afternoon will be so terribly dull."

Reading Strategy: **Summarizing**

Summarize this chapter of the novel in a few sentences. Then go back to your summary of Act I, Scene I. How do the two compare?

| **principal** major | **intersections** where roads cross | **wistfully** in a hopeful but sad way |

COMPARING LITERARY WORKS | Apply the Skills

from *The Phantom Tollbooth, Milo*   by Norton Juster

Directions Choose the letter of the best answer or write the answer using complete sentences.

Comprehension: Identifying Facts

1. Where is Milo as the novel begins?
   A in his bedroom
   B walking home from school
   C riding his electric car
   D flopped in a chair

2. What is the main setting for both Act I, Scene I and the first chapter of the novel?
   A Milo's bedroom
   B Dictionopolis
   C a city street
   D a made-up highway

3. What character appears in Act I, Scene I but not in the novel?

4. Where does Milo wish he were when he is in school?

5. According to Milo, what is the greatest waste of time of all?

6. What does the outside of the blue envelope say?

7. What is included in the package? Are these things the same for the play as for the novel?

8. How is Milo's tollbooth different from others he has seen?

9. Where does Milo choose to go?

10. What does Milo say aloud at the end of the chapter?

Comprehension: Putting Ideas Together

11. How does Milo feel as both the play and the novel begin?
   A annoyed   **C** angry
   B uninterested   **D** frightened

12. About what time is it when the action of the novel begins?
   A 8:00 A.M.   **C** 3:00 P.M.
   B noon   **D** 7:00 P.M.

13. What does the author mean when he says that Milo "didn't know what to do with himself"?

14. To whom is the narrator speaking when he says, "pay close attention"?

15. What does Milo admit to himself?

16. Why is Milo puzzled about receiving a surprise package?

17. Why does the author write that the book of rules and traffic regulations may not be "bent or broken"?

18. What is so strange about the map that Milo receives?

Comparing continued on next page

19. How do you think Milo really feels as he begins his journey?

20. Why does Milo hope the game will be interesting?

Understanding Literature: Comparing a Novel to Its Dramatization

A novel is a story told in sentences and paragraphs. It may have a narrator who describes the scene and tells how the characters feel and act. A dramatization of a novel must tell the story by using dialogue. The dramatization uses the words of the characters to move the story along.

21. How does the novel introduce Milo to the reader? How does the drama introduce Milo to the reader?

22. What features in the novel help you to see and hear the characters, settings, and actions? What features in the drama do the same for you?

23. How do the pictures in the novel help you understand the story? How might they help someone who is designing the set for the drama?

24. At the end of Act I, Scene I, the Clock says, "But when you're bored, what you need more than anything is a rude awakening." Why do you think the playwright added this line?

25. Why did the playwright add a "Voice" to read the package directions aloud?

Critical Thinking

26. Why does the world seem "small and empty" to Milo?

27. Can you relate to the way Milo feels? Why or why not?

28. Why do you think Milo decides to put the tollbooth together?

29. Why does the author have Milo speak at the end of the chapter, even though he is alone? Why does the author have him speak in the play, even though he is alone?

Thinking Creatively

30. How does your imagination help you read each form of the story? Which do you prefer, the drama or the novel? Why?

Grammar Check

A participle is a form of a verb that acts as an adjective. A present participle is the *-ing* form of a verb: *relaxing* or *catching*. A participial phrase combines a participle with other words to make a phrase. This entire phrase acts as an adjective that modifies a noun.

Example: A house sparrow *singing nearby* stopped and rushed home.

Rewrite the sentence three times, each time using a different participial phrase.

A house sparrow _____ stopped and rushed home.

 Vocabulary Builder

Answer each question. Each uses vocabulary from *The Phantom Tollbooth*, Chapter 1. Explain your answer.

1 If you got a compliment, would you respond *glumly*?

2 Would you sit *dejectedly* if you won a contest?

3 If a good friend moved away, would you think of him or her *wistfully*?

4 Would markers be *impractical* tools for making a poster?

 Writing on Your Own

Choose the selection that you liked better. Write a short letter to Susan Nanus or to Norton Juster. Tell what you liked about what you read.

 Listening and Speaking

Work with a small group. Talk about novels you have read that might make good dramas. Decide on two novels that you would like to see made into plays or movies. Be able to explain why they would make good dramatizations. Share your choices with the class.

 Media and Viewing

A cartoon version of *The Phantom Tollbooth* was made in 1970. Imagine you were going to make a new cartoon version of the novel. Make a storyboard for the opening scenes. A storyboard is a poster with pictures that show the action in a story. In your storyboard, sketch the action. You may use stick figures if you like. Include details of the setting as well. Try to create a cartoon that the author would like. Share your storyboard with the class.

Indexes

In Part 1, you have learned about summarizing. When you summarize, you give the main idea, or topic, of what you are reading. You cut down a lot of words to a few that state the topic. Suppose you are looking for a single topic in a book. You may be able to use an index to find exactly what you need.

About Indexes

An index is a list of the topics in a book. The topics are listed in ABC order. The index gives the page number where each topic can be found. This may be presented as a single page or as a range of pages. It may be presented as several pages that are not connected.

An index often has main headings and subheadings. The subheadings always relate to the main headings.

Clocks

Alarm	245
Battery	245–246
Wall	247–249

In the example below, the main heading is "Clocks." Under that are three subheadings. The subheadings are in ABC order. You can find information about alarm clocks on page 245. You can find information about wall clocks on pages 247, 248, and 249.

The indexes on the next two pages are from a catalog and from a textbook. Notice how each one is organized to help you find information.

Reading Skill

To use an index, you must know how to scan. Scanning is moving your eyes quickly to find key letters or words. Suppose you want to find all the pages in a book that tell about telephones. You would find the *T* words in the index. Then you would run your eyes down the list until you found the word *telephone*.

If an index is organized well, it should be easy to scan. You must use your alphabetizing skills to help with your search.

Work Sharp Office Products Index

This listing tells you to look elsewhere in the index. You should find the C listings and look under "Clocks."

INDEX

In this index, key words are set in bold type.

A

Abolitionists, 164, 165
Adams, John, 136
Adams, Samuel, 134, 136
Africans
  achievements of, 75–76
  come to America, 75–78, 90–93, 163
  cultures of, 75–76, 114
Agriculture
  in Canada, 310, 452–453
  in Colombia, 299–300, 304–306
  in English colonies, 84, 86, 92, 97–98
  industrialism and, 260, 262, 281
Alaska, 158
Allen, Ethan, 137
Altitude, 435
Amazon River, 436–438, 439
American Revolution, 136–139
Andes Mountains, 298, 434, 441
Archaeology, 319
Arnold, Benedict, 137
Articles of Confederation, 140
Automobiles
  growth of cities and, 369, 398–399, 401
  invention of, 258
  laws about, 258
  pollution and, 286, 290–291, 404, 407, 422
  traffic problems and, 404–405, 407–408
Aztec Indians, 56–58, 66–67, 73, 318–327

B

Bering Strait, 42
Bill of Rights, 144, 203
Bolivar, Simon, 78, 83
Boone, Daniel, 150–151
Booth, John Wilkes, 169
Boston, Massachusetts, 133–135, 341, 343, 348–350
Boston Massacre, 133
Boston Tea Party, 134–135

B

Brazil, 69–71, 78, 435
Buffalo, 50–51, 150

C

Calendars, 55, 57
Campesinos, 299, 301, 305–306
Canada
  agriculture in, 310, 452–453
  cities in, 452–455
  history of, 82–83, 115–117
  industry in, 308–311
  people of, 115–119, 165, 310–311
Canals, 153–154, 363–364
Capital, 232, 250, 253–254, 306–307, 310
Carpetbaggers, 170–171
Cattle raising, 300, 306, 365, 367
Chicanos, 401
  See also **Mexican Americans.**
Child labor, 251, 278–280
Chinese Americans, 104–105, 113
Cities
  Canada in, 452–455
  colonial, 327–335, 341–356
  ghettos in, 392–395, 418–419, 421
  kinds of, 399–400
  markets in, 322, 324–325
  movement from, 395–397
  movement to, 333, 367, 375–378, 390–392
  planned, 327–328
  suburbs and, 334, 374–375, 396–397, 407–408
  transportation in, 372–374

Look for cross-references in an index. Some topics are listed in more than one place.

Indexes list names of people by last name first. First names follow after a comma. When two or more people share last names, their first names appear in ABC order.

Monitor Your Progress

Directions Choose the letter of the best answer or write the answer using complete sentences.

1. If you added the topic "Toner" to the Work Sharp index, where would it fit?
   A between "Tough Envelopes" and "Towels"
   B between "Towels" and "Trash Bags"
   C between "Thumbtacks" and "Tough Envelopes"
   D between "Televisions/VCRs" and "Thumbtacks"

2. On what page of the Work Sharp catalog would you find coin trays?
   A 61
   B 286
   C 351
   D You cannot tell from the information given.

3. Of these topics, which one has the most page references in the textbook?
   A Samuel Adams
   B Boston, Massachusetts
   C Agriculture in Colombia
   D Cities in Canada

4. Based on the topics in the index, what kind of textbook do you think this is?

5. "Agriculture in Canada" appears in two places in the textbook index. Explain where it appears and why.

Writing on Your Own

Tell a friend how to locate information about canals in the textbook index. Write a step-by-step explanation. Then follow your own steps to make sure your explanation is complete.

Part 2

Reading Strategy:
Questioning

Asking questions as you read will help you understand and remember more of the information. Questioning the text will also help you to be a more active reader. As you read, ask yourself these questions:

- What is my reason for reading this text?

- What decisions can I make about the facts and details in this text?

- What connections can I make between this text and my own life?

Literary Terms

stage directions notes by playwrights describing such things as setting, lighting, and sound effects; they also describe how the actors are to look, behave, move, and speak

prop a piece of equipment used onstage during a play

About the Author

Susan Nanus has earned several prizes for her writing, including the Christopher Award in 1988. In 1996, she was a part of the writing team nominated for an Academy Award for their work on *If These Walls Could Talk*. She has written several plays, as well as the 1998 screenplay for *A Will of Their Own*. The screenplay was based on the novel *Daughters of the New World* by Susan Richards Shreve.

Nanus currently lives in Los Angeles, where she continues to write scripts for television and movies.

About the Selection

In Act I, you read how Milo's boredom ended when he received a strange gift. After being transported to an unusual kingdom, he became tangled in a conflict over letters and numbers. Now he is on a mission to rescue the princesses who can help settle the conflict. In Act II you will read about Milo's rescue attempt and the demons he meets along the way.

Objectives

- To read and understand drama
- To recognize dialogue
- To identify characters, setting, and plot
- To read and understand stage directions

Before Reading **continued on next page**

stage directions
notes by playwrights describing such things as setting, lighting, and sound effects; they also describe how the actors are to look, behave, move, and speak

prop a piece of equipment used on stage during a play

Literary Terms **Stage directions** are notes by playwrights describing such things as setting, lighting, and sound effects. They also describe how the actors are to look, behave, move, and speak. Stage directions are the words in a drama that the characters do not say. They help readers picture the action, sounds, and scenery. They may also tell about **props**, the equipment used on stage during a play. Stage directions are usually printed in italics and set between brackets, as in this example:

CARLOS. [*To ISABEL.*] Remember, don't make a sound! [*He tiptoes offstage, holding the lantern high.*]

Reading on Your Own Asking questions as you read helps you understand and remember what you are reading. Questioning is part of being an active reader. As you read Act II, ask yourself the following questions:

• What is my purpose for reading?

• What do I think about the action?

• How does this connect to my own life?

Writing on Your Own In Act II, Milo thinks about the importance of words and numbers. Think about how you use words and numbers daily. Then, write two sentences about why words and numbers are important to you.

Vocabulary Focus Choose one of these words from Act II. Pick one whose definition you do not know. Look up the word in a dictionary. Write a sentence that uses the new word correctly.

dissonance   admonishing   iridescent

malicious   deficiency   pantomimes

Think Before You Read Find a partner. Discuss what the playwright did in Act I that makes you interested in reading Act II.

The Phantom Tollbooth, Act II

Based on the Book by Norton Juster

Review and Anticipate

In Act I, Milo is lifted from his boredom into a strange kingdom that is in conflict over the importance of letters and numbers. After traveling through Dictionopolis, he agrees to rescue the princesses who can settle the conflict. As Act II opens, Milo enters Digitopolis with Tock and Humbug—characters who will help him rescue the princesses.

Act II Scene I

*The set of Digitopolis glitters in the background, while Upstage Right near the road, a small colorful Wagon sits, looking quite deserted. On its side in large letters, a sign reads: "KAKAFONOUS A. DISCHORD Doctor of **Dissonance**." Enter MILO, TOCK, and HUMBUG, fearfully. They look at the wagon.*

Reading Strategy: Questioning

What questions do you want answered in Act II?

Tock There's no doubt about it. That's where the noise was coming from.

Humbug [*To MILO.*] Well, go on.

Milo Go on what?

Humbug Go on and see who's making all that noise in there. We can't just ignore a creature like that.

Upstage is the back part of the stage that is farthest from the audience. *Stage right* means the right side of the stage for an actor facing the audience.

dissonance
conflicting sounds; an
unpleasant noise

Milo Creature? What kind of creature? Do you think he's dangerous?

Humbug Go on, Milo. Knock on the door. We'll be right behind you.

Milo o.k. Maybe he can tell us how much further it is to Digitopolis.

What information about sound effects do you learn from these stage directions?

[MILO tiptoes up to the wagon door and KNOCKS timidly. The moment he knocks, a terrible CRASH is heard inside the wagon, and MILO and the others jump back in fright. At the same time, the Door Flies Open, and from the dark interior, a Hoarse VOICE inquires.]

Voice Have you ever heard a whole set of dishes dropped from the ceiling onto a hard stone floor? *[The Others are speechless with fright. MILO shakes his head. VOICE happily.]* Have you ever heard an ant wearing fur slippers walk across a thick wool carpet? *[MILO shakes his head again.]* Have you ever heard a blindfolded octopus unwrap a **cellophane**-covered bathtub? *[MILO shakes his head a third time.]* Ha! I knew it. *[He hops out, a little man, wearing a white coat, with a **stethoscope** around his neck, and a small mirror attached to his forehead, and with very huge ears, and a **mortar and pestle** in his hands. He stares at MILO, TOCK and HUMBUG.]* None of you looks well at all! Tsk, tsk, not at all. *[He opens the top or side of his Wagon, revealing a dusty interior resembling an old **apothecary** shop, with shelves lined with jars and boxes, a table, books, test tubes and bottles and measuring spoons.]*

Milo *[Timidly.]* Are you a doctor?

Dischord *[Voice.]* I am KAKAFONOUS A. DISCHORD, DOCTOR OF DISSONANCE! *[Several small explosions and a grinding crash are heard.]*

---

cellophane a thin, crinkly material used for wrapping

stethoscope a doctor's tool for listening to sounds in the body

mortar and pestle a bowl and rod used to grind materials

apothecary a person who prepares and sells medicines

Humbug *[Stuttering with fear.]* What does the "A" stand for?

Dischord AS LOUD AS POSSIBLE! *[Two screeches and a bump are heard.]* Now, step a little closer and stick out your tongues. *[DISCHORD examines them.]* Just as I expected. *[He opens a large dusty book and thumbs through the pages.]* You're all suffering from a severe lack of noise. *[DISCHORD begins running around, collecting bottles, reading the labels to himself as he goes along.]* "Loud Cries." "Soft Cries." "Bangs, Bongs, Swishes. Swooshes." "Snaps and Crackles." "Whistles and Gongs." "Squeeks, Squawks, and Miscellaneous Uproar." *[As he reads them off, he pours a little of each into a large glass **beaker** and stirs the mixture with a wooden spoon. The **concoction** smokes and bubbles.]* Be ready in just a moment.

Milo *[Suspiciously.]* Just what kind of doctor are you?

Reading Strategy: Questioning

How would you feel if you were Milo? Would you be suspicious, too? Why?

Dischord Well, you might say, I'm a **specialist**. I specialize in noises, from the loudest to the softest, and from the slightly annoying to the terribly unpleasant. For instance, have you ever heard a square-wheeled steamroller ride over a street full of hard-boiled eggs? *[Very loud CRUNCHING SOUNDS are heard.]*

Milo *[Holding his ears.]* But who would want all those terrible noises?

Dischord *[Surprised at the question.]* Everybody does. Why, I'm so busy I can hardly fill all the orders for noise pills, racket lotion, **clamor salve** and **hubbub tonic**. That's all people seem to want these days. Years ago, everyone wanted pleasant sounds and business was terrible. But then the cities were built and there was a great need for honking horns, screeching trains, clanging bells and all the rest of those wonderfully unpleasant sounds we use so much today. I've been working overtime ever since and my medicine here

beaker an open glass container	**specialist** one who works in one special area	**hubbub** noise
concoction a mixture, as of ingredients		**tonic** a medicine that refreshes or gives strength
	clamor loud noise	
	salve a soothing cream	

is in great demand. All you have to do is take one spoonful every day, and you'll never have to hear another beautiful sound again. Here, try some.

Humbug [*Backing away.*] If it's all the same to you, I'd rather not.

Milo I don't want to be cured of beautiful sounds.

Tock Besides, there's no such sickness as a lack of noise.

Dischord How true. That's what makes it so difficult to cure. [*Takes a large glass bottle from the shelf.*] Very well, if you want to go all through life suffering from a noise **deficiency**, I'll just give this to Dynne for his lunch. [*Uncorks the bottle and pours the liquid into it. There is a rumbling and then a loud explosion accompanied by smoke, out of which DYNNE, a smog-like creature with yellow eyes and a frowning mouth, appears.*]

Dynne [*Smacking his lips.*] Ahhh, that was good, Master. I thought you'd never let me out. It was really cramped in there.

Dischord This is my assistant, the awful Dynne. You must forgive his appearance, for he really doesn't have any.

Milo What is a Dynne?

Dischord You mean you've never heard of the awful Dynne? When you're playing in your room and making a great amount of noise, what do they tell you to stop?

Milo That awful din.

Dischord When the neighbors are playing their radio too loud late at night, what do you wish they'd turn down?

Tock That awful din.

Dischord And when the street on your block is being repaired and the drills are working all day, what does everyone complain of?

Humbug [*Brightly.*] The dreadful **row**.

Look at the stage directions. What do the Humbug's actions tell about his feelings?

How does this stage direction help you imagine what Dynne is like?

Dischord is a play on discord, which means "a clash of sounds." *Dynne* is a play on din, which means "a loud uproar."

deficiency a shortage or lack   **row** a noisy racket

Dynne The Dreadful Rauw was my grandfather. He perished in the great silence **epidemic** of 1712. I certainly can't understand why you don't like noise. Why, I heard an explosion last week that was so lovely, I groaned with appreciation for two days. *[He gives a loud groan at the memory.]*

Dischord He's right, you know! Noise is the most valuable thing in the world.

Milo King Azaz says words are.

Dischord NONSENSE! Why, when a baby wants food, how does he ask?

Dynne *[Happily.]* He screams!

Dischord And when a racing car wants gas?

Dynne *[Jumping for joy.]* It chokes!

Dischord And what happens to the dawn when a new day begins?

Dynne *[Delighted.]* It breaks!

Dischord You see how simple it is? *[To DYNNE.]* Isn't it time for us to go?

Milo Where to? Maybe we're going the same way.

Dynne I doubt it. *[Picking up empty sacks from the table.]* We're going on our collection rounds. Once a day, I travel throughout the kingdom and collect all the wonderfully horrible and beautifully unpleasant sounds I can find and bring them back to the doctor to use in his medicine.

Dischord Where are you going?

Milo To Digitopolis.

Dischord Oh, there are a number of ways to get to Digitopolis, if you know how to follow directions. Just take a look at the sign at the fork in the road. Though why you'd ever want to go there, I'll never know.

epidemic a
widespread disease

Milo We want to talk to the Mathemagician.

Humbug About the release of the Princesses Rhyme and Reason.

How do these stage directions help you understand what Dischord is doing?

Dischord Rhyme and Reason? I remember them. Very nice girls, but a little too quiet for my taste. In fact, I've been meaning to send them something that Dynne brought home by mistake and which I have absolutely no use for. [He rummages through the wagon.] Ah, here it is . . . or maybe you'd like it for yourself. [*Hands MILO a Package.*]

Milo What is it?

Dischord The sounds of laughter. They're so unpleasant to hear, it's almost unbearable. All those giggles and snickers and happy shouts of joy, I don't know what Dynne was thinking of when he collected them. Here, take them to the Princesses or keep them for yourselves, I don't care. Well, time to move on. Goodbye now and good luck! [*He has shut the wagon by now and gets in. LOUD NOISES begin to **erupt** as DYNNE pulls the wagon off-stage.*]

Milo [*Calling after them.*] But wait! The fork in the road . . . you didn't tell us where it is . . .

Tock It's too late. He can't hear a thing.

Humbug I could use a fork of my own, at the moment. And a knife and a spoon to go with it. All of a sudden, I feel very hungry.

Milo So do I, but it's no use thinking about it. There won't be anything to eat until we reach Digitopolis. [*They get into the car.*]

Humbug [*Rubbing his stomach.*] Well, the sooner the better is what I say. [*A SIGN suddenly appears.*]

---

erupt to explode outward

Reading Strategy: Questioning

How is this sign like signs you have seen while traveling? How is it different?

DIGITOPOLIS	5 miles
	1,600 Rods
	8,800 Yards
	26,400 Feet
	316,800 Inches
	633.600 Half Inches AND THEN SOME

Voice *[A strange voice from nowhere.]* But which way will get you there sooner? That is the question.

Tock Did you hear something?

Milo Look! The fork in the road and a signpost to Digitopolis! *[They read the Sign.]*

Humbug Let's travel by miles, it's shorter.

Milo Let's travel by half inches. It's quicker.

Tock But which road should we take? It must make a difference.

Milo Do you think so?

Tock Well, I'm not sure, but . . .

Humbug He could be right. On the other hand, he could also be wrong. Does it make a difference or not?

Voice Yes, indeed, indeed it does, certainly, my yes, it does make a difference.

*[The DODECAHEDRON appears, a 12-sided figure with a different face on each side, and with all the edges labeled with a small letter and all the angles labeled with a large letter. He wears a **beret** and peers at the others with a serious face. He **doffs** his cap and recites:]*

Dodecahedron *My angles are many.*
My sides are not few.
I'm the Dodecahedron.
Who are you?

---

beret a flat, soft cap   **doffs** takes off

Milo What's a Dodecahedron?

Dodecahedron [*Turning around slowly.*] See for yourself. Dodecahedron is a mathematical shape with 12 faces. [*All his faces appear as he turns, each face with a different expression. He points to them.*] I usually use one at a time. It saves wear and tear. What are you called?

Milo Milo.

Dodecahedron That's an odd name. [*Changing his smiling face to a frowning one.*] And you have only one face.

Milo [*Making sure it is still there.*] Is that bad?

Dodecahedron You'll soon wear it out using it for everything. Is everyone with one face called Milo?

Milo Oh, no. Some are called Billy or Jeffery or Sally or Lisa or lots of other things.

Dodecahedron How confusing. Here everything is called exactly what it is. The triangles are called triangles, the circles are called circles, and even the same numbers have the same name. Can you imagine what would happen if we named all the twos Billy or Jeffery or Sally or Lisa or lots of other things? You'd have to say Robert plus John equals four, and if the fours were named Albert, things would be hopeless.

Milo I never thought of it that way.

Dodecahedron [*With an **admonishing** face.*] Then I suggest you begin at once, for in Digitopolis, everything is quite **precise**.

Milo Then perhaps you can help us decide which road we should take.

Dodecahedron [*Happily.*] By all means. There's nothing to it. [*As he talks, the three others try to solve the problem on a Large Blackboard that is wheeled onstage for the occasion.*] Now, if a small car carrying three people at 30 miles an

Why would the information given here be important to a group performing the play?

Reading Strategy:
Questioning

What is the Dodecahedron saying about the difference between math and language? Do you agree with him?

---

admonishing	**precise** exact
disapproving	

hour for 10 minutes along a road 5 miles long at 11:35 in the morning starts at the same time as 3 people who have been traveling in a little automobile at 20 miles an hour for 15 minutes on another road exactly twice as long as half the distance of the other, while a dog, a bug, and a boy travel an equal distance in the same time or the same distance in an equal time along a third road in mid-October, then which one arrives first and which is the best way to go?

Humbug Seventeen!

Milo [*Still figuring frantically.*] I'm not sure, but . . .

Dodecahedron You'll have to do better than that.

Milo I'm not very good at problems.

Dodecahedron What a shame. They're so very useful. Why, did you know that if a beaver 2 feet long with a tail a foot and a half long can build a dam 12 feet high and 6 feet wide in 2 days, all you would need to build Boulder Dam is a beaver 68 feet long with a 51 foot tail?

Humbug [*Grumbling as his pencil snaps.*] Where would you find a beaver that big?

Dodecahedron I don't know, but if you did, you'd certainly know what to do with him.

Milo That's crazy.

Dodecahedron That may be true, but it's completely accurate, and as long as the answer is right, who cares if the question is wrong?

Tock [*Who has been patiently doing the first problem.*] All three roads arrive at the same place at the same time.

Dodecahedron Correct! And I'll take you there myself. [*The blackboard rolls off, and all four get into the car and drive off.*] Now you see how important problems are. If you hadn't done this one properly, you might have gone the wrong way.

Milo But if all the roads arrive at the same place at the same time, then aren't they all the right road?

Reading Strategy: Questioning

What are the two meanings of "problems" in this part of the drama? What can you learn from this play on words?

What do the stage directions tell you here about how the stage looks now?

Dodecahedron [*Glaring from his upset face.*] Certainly not! They're all the wrong way! Just because you have a choice, it doesn't mean that any of them has to be right.

[*Pointing in another direction.*] That's the way to Digitopolis and we'll be there any moment. [*Suddenly the lighting grows dimmer.*] In fact, we're here. Welcome to the Land of Numbers.

Humbug [*Looking around at the barren landscape.*] It doesn't look very inviting.

Milo Is this the place where numbers are made?

Dodecahedron They're not made. You have to dig for them. Don't you know anything at all about numbers?

Milo Well, I never really thought they were very important.

Dodecahedron NOT IMPORTANT! Could you have tea for two without the 2? Or three blind mice without the 3? And how would you sail the seven seas without the 7?

Milo All I meant was . . .

Dodecahedron [*Continues shouting angrily.*] If you had high hopes, how would you know how high they were? And did you know that narrow escapes come in different widths? Would you travel the whole world wide without ever knowing how wide it was? And how could you do anything at long last without knowing how long the last was? Why, numbers are the most beautiful and valuable things in the world. Just follow me and I'll show you. [*He motions to them and **pantomimes** walking through rocky **terrain** with*

---

pantomimes acts out silently   **terrain** the ground *the others in tow. A Doorway similar to the Tollbooth appears and the DODECAHEDRON opens it and motions the others to follow him through.]* Come along, come along. I can't wait for you all day. *[They enter the doorway and the lights are dimmed very low, as to **simulate** the interior of a cave. The SOUNDS of scrapings and tapping, scuffling and digging are heard all around them. He hands them Helmets with flashlights attached.]* Put these on.

Milo *[Whispering.]* Where are we going?

Dodecahedron We're here. This is the numbers mine. *[LIGHTS UP A LITTLE, revealing Little Men digging and chopping, shoveling and scraping.]* Right this way and watch your step. *[His voice echoes and **reverberates**. **Iridescent** and glittery numbers seem to sparkle from everywhere.]*

Milo *[Awed.]* Whose mine is it?

Voice of Mathemagician By the four million eight hundred and twenty-seven thousand six hundred and fifty-nine hairs on my head, it's mine, of course! *[ENTER the MATHEMAGICIAN, carrying his long staff which looks like a giant pencil.]*

Humbug *[Already **intimidated**.]* It's a lovely mine, really it is.

Mathemagician *[Proudly.]* The biggest number mine in the kingdom.

Milo *[Excitedly.]* Are there any precious stones in it?

Mathemagician Precious stones! *[Then softly.]* By the eight million two hundred and forty-seven thousand three hundred and twelve threads in my robe, I'll say there are. Look here. *[Reaches in a cart, pulls out a small object, polishes it **vigorously** and holds it to the light, where it sparkles.]*

Milo But that's a five.

> What information do these stage directions give about the action?

simulate to give the appearance of	**iridescent** showing different colors when seen from different angles	**intimidated** frightened
reverberates rings with repeated sound		**vigorously** quickly and with force

Mathemagician Exactly. As valuable a jewel as you'll find anywhere. Look at some of the others. *[Scoops up others and pours them into MILO's arms. They include all numbers from 1 to 9 and an **assortment** of zeros.]*

Dodecahedron We dig them and polish them right here, and then send them all over the world. Marvelous, aren't they?

Tock They are beautiful. *[He holds them up to compare them to the numbers on his clock body.]*

Milo So that's where they come from. *[Looks at them and carefully hands them back, but drops a few which smash and break in half.]* Oh, I'm sorry!

Mathemagician *[Scooping them up.]* Oh, don't worry about that. We use the broken ones for fractions. How about some lunch? *[Takes out a little whistle and blows it. Two miners rush in carrying an immense **cauldron** which is bubbling and steaming. The workers put down their tools and gather around to eat.]*

Humbug That looks delicious!

[TOCK and MILO also look hungrily at the pot.]

Mathemagician Perhaps you'd care for something to eat?

Milo Oh, yes, sir!

Tock Thank you.

Humbug *[Already eating.]* Ummm . . . delicious! *[All finish their bowls immediately.]*

Mathemagician Please have another portion. *[They eat and finish. MATHEMAGICIAN serves them again.]* Don't stop now. *[They finish.]* Come on, no need to be **bashful**. *[Serves them again.]*

Milo *[To TOCK and HUMBUG as he finishes again.]* Do you want to hear something strange? Each one I eat makes me a little hungrier than before.

---

assortment a variety or collection   **cauldron** a large iron pot   **bashful** shy

Mathemagician Do have some more. *[He serves them again. They eat frantically, until the MATHEMAGICIAN blows his whistle again and the pot is removed.]*

Humbug *[Holding his stomach.]* Uggghhh! I think I'm starving.

Milo Me, too, and I ate so much.

Dodecahedron *[Wiping the gravy from several of his mouths.]* Yes, it was delicious, wasn't it? It's the specialty of the kingdom . . . subtraction stew.

Tock *[Weak from hunger]* I have more of an appetite than when I began.

Mathemagician Certainly, what did you expect? The more you eat, the hungrier you get, everyone knows that.

Milo They do? Then how do you get enough?

Mathemagician Enough? Here in Digitopolis, we have our meals when we're full and eat until we're hungry. That way, when you don't have anything at all, you have more than enough. It's a very **economical** system. You must have been stuffed to have eaten so much.

Dodecahedron It's completely **logical**. The more you want, the less you get, and the less you get, the more you have. Simple arithmetic, that's all. *[TOCK, MILO and HUMBUG look at him blankly.]* Now, look, suppose you had something and added nothing to it. What would you have?

Milo The same.

Dodecahedron Splendid! And suppose you had something and added less than nothing to it? What would you have then?

Humbug Starvation! Oh, I'm so hungry.

Reading Strategy: Questioning
What seems to be happening to the characters? What questions do you have about the food that is being served?

Reading Strategy: Questioning
Does this system make sense to you? Why or why not?

economical money-saving	**logical** reasonable; following a step-by-step process	**starvation** terrible hunger

Dodecahedron Now, now, it's not as bad as all that. In a few hours, you'll be nice and full again . . . just in time for dinner.

Milo But I only eat when I'm hungry.

Mathemagician *[Waving the eraser of his staff.]* What a curious idea. The next thing you'll have us believe is that you only sleep when you're tired.

[The mine has disappeared as well as the Miners.]

Humbug Where did everyone go?

Mathemagician Oh, they're still in the mine. I often find that the best way to get from one place to another is to erase everything and start again. Please make yourself at home.

*[They find themselves in a **unique** room, in which all the walls, tables, chairs, desks, cabinets and blackboards are labeled to show their heights, widths, depths and distances to and from each other. To one side is a gigantic notepad on an artist's easel, and from hooks and strings hang a collection of rulers, measures, weights and tapes, and all other measuring devices.]*

Milo Do you always travel that way? *[He looks around in wonder.]*

A *plumb line* is a cord that has a lead weight on the end. This weight is often called a plumb or plumb bob. The weight keeps the line straight. This makes it a useful tool for measuring heights and straight lines.

Mathemagician No, indeed! *[He pulls a plumb line from a hook and walks.]* Most of the time I take the shortest distance between any two points. And of course, when I have to be in several places at once . . . [He writes 3 x 1 = 3 on the notepad with his staff.] I simply multiply. [THREE FIGURES looking like the MATHEMAGICIAN appear on a platform above.]*

Milo How did you do that?

Mathemagician And The Three There's nothing to it, if you have a magic staff. *[THE THREE FIGURES cancel themselves out and disappear.]*

unique one-of-a-kind

Humbug That's nothing but a big pencil.

Mathemagician True enough, but once you learn to use it, there's no end to what you can do.

Milo Can you make things disappear?

Mathemagician Just step a little closer and watch this. *[Shows them that there is nothing up his sleeve or in his hat. He writes:]* 4 + 9 – 2 x 16 + 1 = 3 x 6 – 67 + 8 x 2 – 3 + 26 – 1 – 34 + 3 – 7 + 2 – 5 = *[He looks up **expectantly**.]*

Humbug Seventeen?

Milo It all comes to zero.

Mathemagician Precisely. *[Makes a **theatrical** bow and rips off paper from notepad.]* Now, is there anything else you'd like to see? *[At this point, an appeal to the audience to see if anyone would like a problem solved.]*

Milo Well . . . can you show me the biggest number there is?

Mathemagician Why, I'd be delighted. *[Opening a closet door.]* We keep it right here. It took four miners to dig it out. *[He shows them a huge "3" twice as high as the MATHEMAGICIAN.]*

Milo No, that's not what I mean. Can you show me the longest number there is?

Mathemagician Sure. *[Opens another door]* Here it is. It took three carts to carry it here. *[Door reveals an "8" that is as wide as the "3" was high.]*

Milo No, no, that's not what I meant either. *[Looks helplessly at TOCK.]*

Tock I think what you would like to see is the number of the greatest possible **magnitude**.

---

expectantly with interest; eagerly   **theatrical** showy   **magnitude** size

How do these stage directions give choices to the actors?

Mathemagician Well, why didn't you say so? *[He busily measures them and all other things as he speaks, and marks it down.]* What's the greatest number you can think of? *[Here, an appeal can also be made to the audience or MILO may think of his own answers.]*

Milo Uh . . . nine trillion, nine hundred and ninety-nine billion, nine hundred ninety-nine million, nine-hundred ninety-nine thousand, nine hundred and ninety-nine *[He puffs.]*

Mathemagician *[Writes that on the pad.]* Very good. Now add one to it. *[MILO or audience does.]* Now add one again. *[MILO or audience does so.]* Now add one again. Now add one again. Now add . . .

Milo But when can I stop?

Mathemagician Never. Because the number you want is always at least one more than the number you have, and it's so large that if you started saying it yesterday, you wouldn't finish tomorrow.

Humbug Where could you ever find a number so big?

Mathemagician In the same place they have the smallest number there is, and you know what that is?

Milo The smallest number . . . let's see . . . one one-millionth?

Mathemagician Almost. Now all you have to do is divide that in half and then divide that in half and then divide that in half and then divide that . . .

Milo Doesn't that ever stop either?

Mathemagician How can it when you can always take half of what you have and divide it in half again? Look. *[Pointing offstage.]* You see that line?

Milo You mean that long one out there?

Mathemagician That's it. Now, if you just follow that line forever, and when you reach the end, turn left, you will find the Land of **Infinity**. That's where the tallest, the shortest, the biggest, the smallest and the most and the least of everything are kept.

Milo But how can you follow anything forever? You know, I get the feeling that everything in Digitopolis is very difficult.

Mathemagician But on the other hand, I think you'll find that the only thing you can do easily is be wrong, and that's hardly worth the effort.

Milo But . . . what bothers me is . . . well, why is it that even when things are correct, they don't really seem to be right?

Mathemagician [Grows sad and quiet.] How true. It's been that way ever since Rhyme and Reason were **banished**. [Sadness turns to fury.] And all because of that stubborn **wretch** Azaz! It's all his fault.

Milo Maybe if you discussed it with him . . .

Mathemagician He's just too unreasonable! Why just last month, I sent him a very friendly letter, which he never had the courtesy to answer. See for yourself. [Puts the letter on the easel. The letter reads:]

4738 1919,

667 394107 5841 62589 85371 14

39588 7190434 203 27689 57131 481206.

5864 98053,

62179875073

Milo But maybe he doesn't understand numbers.

Mathemagician Nonsense! Everybody understands numbers. No matter what language you speak, they always mean the same thing. A seven is a seven everywhere in the world.

infinity the quality of having no limit or end   **banished** sent away   **wretch** a shameful person

Milo [*To TOCK and HUMBUG.*] Everyone is so **sensitive** about what he knows best.

Tock With your permission, sir, we'd like to rescue Rhyme and Reason.

Mathemagician Has Azaz agreed to it?

Tock Yes, sir.

Mathemagician THEN I DON'T! Ever since they've been banished, we've never agreed on anything, and we never will.

Milo Never?

Mathemagician NEVER! And if you can prove otherwise, you have my permission to go.

Milo Well then, with whatever Azaz agrees, you disagree.

Mathemagician Correct.

Milo And with whatever Azaz disagrees, you agree.

Mathemagician [*Yawning, cleaning his nails.*] Also correct.

Milo Then, each of you agrees that he will disagree with whatever each of you agrees with, and if you both disagree with the same thing, aren't you really in agreement?

Mathemagician I'VE BEEN TRICKED! [*Figures it over, but comes up with the same answer.*]

Tock And now may we go?

Mathemagician [*Nods weakly.*] It's a long and dangerous journey. Long before you find them, the demons will know you're there. Watch out for them, because if you ever come face to face, it will be too late. But there is one other **obstacle** even more serious than that.

Milo [*Terrified.*] What is it?

What does this stage direction tell you about the Mathemagician's opinion of himself?

---

sensitive touchy; easily upset

obstacle something standing in the way; a difficulty

Mathemagician I'm afraid I can't tell you until you return. But maybe I can give you something to help you out. *[Claps hands. ENTER the DODECAHEDRON, carrying something on a pillow. The MATHEMAGICIAN takes it.]* Here is your own magic staff. Use it well and there is nothing it can't do for you. *[Puts a small, gleaming pencil in MILO's breast pocket.]*

Humbug Are you sure you can't tell about that serious obstacle?

Mathemagician Only when you return. And now the Dodecahedron will escort you to the road that leads to the Castle-in-the-Air. Farewell, my friends, and good luck to you. *[They shake hands, say goodbye, and the DODECAHEDRON leads them off.]* Good luck to you! *[To himself.]* Because you're sure going to need it. *[He watches them through a telescope and marks down the **calculations**.]*

Dodecahedron *[He re-enters.]* Well, they're on their way.

Mathemagician So I see. . . *[DODECAHEDRON stands waiting.]* Well, what is it?

Dodecahedron I was just wondering myself, your Numbership. What actually is the serious obstacle you were talking about?

Mathemagician *[Looks at him in surprise.]* You mean you really don't know?

BLACKOUT

Scene II The Land of Ignorance
LIGHTS UP on RHYME and REASON, in their castle, looking out two windows.

Rhyme *I'm worried sick, I must confess*
    I wonder if they'll have success
    All the others tried in vain,
    And were never seen or heard again.

BLACKOUT means that all the lights pointing to the stage are turned off. How does this add suspense here?

What effect does the stage direction *LIGHTS UP* have on the action?

calculations the work for solving problems

Reason Now, Rhyme, there's no need to be so **pessimistic**. Milo, Tock, and Humbug have just as much chance of succeeding as they do of failing.

Rhyme *But the demons are so deadly smart*
They'll stuff your brain and fill your heart
*With **petty** thoughts and selfish dreams*
And trap you with their nasty schemes.

Reason Now, Rhyme, be reasonable, won't you? And calm down, you always talk in **couplets** when you get nervous. Milo has learned a lot from his journey. I think he's a match for the demons and that he might soon be knocking at our door. Now come on, cheer up, won't you?

Rhyme I'll try.

[LIGHTS FADE on the PRINCESSES and COME UP on the little Car, traveling slowly.]

Milo So this is the Land of Ignorance. It's so dark. I can hardly see a thing. Maybe we should wait until morning.

Reading Strategy:
Questioning

Why might the Land of Ignorance be dark?

Voice They'll be mourning for you soon enough. *[They look up and see a large, soiled, ugly bird with a dangerous beak and a **malicious** expression.]*

Milo I don't think you understand. We're looking for a place to spend the night.

Bird *[Shrieking.]* It's not yours to spend!

Milo That doesn't make any sense, you see . . .

Bird Dollars or cents, it's still not yours to spend.

Milo But I don't mean . . .

Bird Of course you're mean. Anybody who'd spend a night that doesn't belong to him is very mean.

---

pessimistic negative; gloomy	**couplets** pairs of rhyming lines
petty small and unimportant	**malicious** having or showing evil plans

Tock Must you interrupt like that?

Bird Naturally, it's my job. I take the words right out of your mouth. Haven't we met before? I'm the Everpresent Wordsnatcher.

Milo Are you a demon?

Bird I'm afraid not. I've tried, but the best I can manage to be is a nuisance. *[Suddenly gets nervous as he looks beyond the three.]* And I don't have time to waste with you. *[Starts to Leave.]*

Tock What is it? What's the matter?

Milo Hey, don't leave. I wanted to ask you some questions . . . Wait!

Bird Weight? Twenty-seven pounds. Bye-bye. *[Disappears.]*

Milo Well, he was no help.

Man Perhaps I can be of some assistance to you? *[There appears a beautifully dressed man, very polished and clean.]* Hello, little boy. *[Shakes MILO's hand.]* And how's the faithful dog? *[Pats TOCK.]* And who is this handsome creature? *[Tips his hat to HUMBUG.]*

Humbug *[To others.]* What a pleasant surprise to meet someone so nice in a place like this.

Man But before I help you out, I wonder if first you could spare me a little of your time, and help me with a few small jobs?

Humbug. Why, certainly.

Tock Gladly.

Milo Sure, we'd be happy to.

Man Splendid, for there are just three tasks. First, I would like to move this pile of sand from here to there. *[Indicates through pantomime a large pile of sand.]* But I'm afraid that all I have is this tiny tweezers. *[Hands it to MILO, who begins moving the sand one grain at a time.]* Second, I would like to empty this well and fill that other, but I have no bucket, so you'll have to use this eyedropper. *[Hands it to TOCK, who begins*

How do these stage directions move the action along?

to work.] And finally, I must have a hole in this cliff, and here is a needle to dig it. *[HUMBUG eagerly begins. The man leans against a tree and stares vacantly off into space. The LIGHTS indicate the passage of time.]*

Milo You know something? I've been working steadily for a long time, now, and I don't feel the least bit tired or hungry. I could go right on the same way forever.

Man Maybe you will. *[He yawns.]*

Milo *[Whispers to TOCK.]* Well, I wish I knew how long it was going to take.

Tock Why don't you use your magic staff and find out?

Milo *[Takes out pencil and calculates. To MAN.]* Pardon me, sir, but it's going to take 837 years to finish these jobs.

Man Is that so? What a shame. Well then you'd better get on with them.

Milo But . . . it hardly seems **worthwhile**.

Man WORTHWHILE! Of course they're not worthwhile. I wouldn't ask you to do anything that was worthwhile.

Tock Then why bother?

Man Because, my friends, what could be more important than doing unimportant things? If you stop to do enough of them, you'll never get where you are going. *[Laughs **villainously**.]*

Milo *[Gasps.]* Oh, no, you must be . . .

Trivium is related to trivia, which means "unimportant, useless facts or matters."

Man Quite correct! I am the Terrible Trivium, demon of petty tasks and worthless jobs, ogre of wasted effort and monster of habit. *[They start to back away from him.]* Don't try to leave, there's so much to do, and you still have 837 years to go on the first job.

Milo But why do unimportant things?

worthwhile	villainously in a
meaningful; worth doing	tricky, evil way

Man Think of all the trouble it saves. If you spend all your time doing only the easy and useless jobs, you'll never have time to worry about the important ones which are so difficult. *[Walks toward them whispering.]* Now do come and stay with me. We'll have such fun together. There are things to fill and things to empty, things to take away and things to bring back, things to pick up and things to put down . . . *[They are **transfixed** by his soothing voice. He is about to **embrace** them when a VOICE screams.]*

Voice Run! Run! *[They all wake up and run with the TRIVIUM behind. As the voice continues to call out directions, they follow until they lose the TRIVIUM.]* RUN! RUN! This way! This way! Over here! Over here! Up here! Down there! Quick, hurry up!

Tock *[Panting.]* I think we lost him.

Voice Keep going straight! Keep going straight! Now step up! Now step up!

Milo Look out! *[They all fall into a Trap.]* But he said "up!"

Voice Well, I hope you didn't expect to get anywhere by listening to me.

Humbug We're in a deep pit! We'll never get out of here.

Voice That is quite an accurate **evaluation** of the situation.

Milo *[Shouting angrily.]* Then why did you help us at all?

Voice Oh, I'd do as much for anybody. Bad advice is my specialty. *[A Little Furry Creature appears.]* I'm the demon of

Reading Strategy: Questioning

What lesson can you learn from what the Terrible Trivium says here?

| **transfixed** without moving, as one under a spell | **embrace** put one's arms around someone or something | **evaluation** a judgment |

Insincerity. I don't mean what I say; I don't mean what I do; and I don't mean what I am.

Milo Then why don't you go away and leave us alone!

Insincerity *[VOICE]* Now, there's no need to get angry. You're a very clever boy and I have complete confidence in you. You can certainly climb out of that pit . . . come on, try . . .

Milo I'm not listening to one word you say! You're just telling me what you think I'd like to hear, and not what is important.

Insincerity Well, if that's the way you feel about it . . .

Milo That's the way I feel about it. We will manage by ourselves without any unnecessary advice from you.

Insincerity *[Stamping his foot.]* Well, all right for you! Most people listen to what I say, but if that's the way you feel, then I'll just go home. *[Exits in a **huff**.]*

Humbug *[Who has been quivering with fright.]* And don't you ever come back! Well, I guess we showed him, didn't we?

Milo You know something? This place is a lot more dangerous than I ever imagined.

Tock *[Who's been surveying the situation.]* I think I figured a way to get out. Here, hop on my back. *[MILO does so.]* Now, you, Humbug, on top of Milo. *[He does so.]* Now hook your umbrella onto that tree and hold on. *[They climb over HUMBUG, then pull him up.]*

Humbug *[As they climb.]* Watch it! Watch it, now. Ow, be careful of my back! My back! Easy, easy . . . oh, this is so difficult. Aren't you finished yet?

Tock *[As he pulls up HUMBUG.]* There. Now, I'll lead for a while. Follow me, and we'll stay out of trouble. *[They walk and climb higher and higher.]*

Humbug Can't we slow down a little?

> Notice the last stage direction for the Humbug. Compare it to the stage direction for Tock. How do the stage directions help show what the characters are like?

huff showing a bad temper

Tock Something tells me we better reach the Castle-in-the-Air as soon as possible, and not stop to rest for a single moment. *[They speed up.]*

Milo What is it, Tock? Did you see something?

Tock Just keep walking and don't look back.

Milo You did see something!

Humbug What is it? Another demon?

Tock Not just one, I'm afraid. If you want to see what I'm talking about, then turn around. *[They turn around. The stage darkens and hundreds of Yellow Gleaming Eyes can be seen.]*

Humbug Good grief! Do you see how many there are? Hundreds! The **Overbearing** Know-it-all, the **Gross Exaggeration**, the Horrible Hopping **Hindsight**, . . . and look over there! The Triple Demons of **Compromise**! Let's get out of here! *[Starts to scurry.]* Hurry up, you two! Must you be so slow about everything?

Milo Look! There it is, up ahead! The Castle-in-the-Air! *[They all run.]*

Humbug They're gaining!

Milo But there it is!

Humbug I see it! I see it!

*[They reach the first step and are stopped by a little man in a **frock coat**, sleeping on a worn **ledger**. He has a long quill pen and a bottle of ink at his side. He is covered with ink stains over his clothes and wears spectacles.]*

Tock Shh! Be very careful. *[They try to step over him, but he wakes up.]*

How is the way these new creatures make their entrance different from the way other characters appear on stage?

overbearing bossy **gross** major **exaggeration** an overstatement	**hindsight** the understanding that comes later **compromise** a solution that both sides of an argument agree to	**frock coat** a man's formal coat reaching to the knees **ledger** an account book

Senses Taker *[From sleeping position.]* Names? *[He sits up.]*

Humbug Well, I . . .

Senses Taker *NAMES?* *[He opens book and begins to write, splattering himself with ink.]*

Humbug Uh . . . Humbug, Tock and this is Milo.

Senses Taker Splendid, splendid. I haven't had an "M" in ages.

Milo What do you want our names for? We're sort of in a hurry.

Senses Taker Oh, this won't take long. I'm the official Senses Taker and I must have some information before I can take your sense. Now if you'll just tell me: *[Handing them a form to fill. Speaking slowly and **deliberately**.]* When you were born, where you were born, why you were born, how old you are now, how old you were then, how old you'll be in a little while . . .

Milo I wish he'd hurry up. At this rate, the demons will be here before we know it!

Senses Taker . . . Your mother's name, your father's name, where you live, how long you've lived there, the schools you've attended, the schools you haven't attended . . .

Humbug I'm getting **writer's cramp**.

Tock I smell something very evil and it's getting stronger every second. *[To SENSES TAKER.]* May we go now?

Senses Taker Just as soon as you tell me your height, your weight, the number of books you've read this year . . .

A census taker collects information about people who live in a place. This character's name is a pun—a joke formed by a play on words.

deliberately with purpose	writer's cramp stiffness in the fingers caused by too much writing

Milo We have to go!

Senses Taker All right, all right, I'll give you the short form. *[Pulls out a small piece of paper.]* Destination?

Milo But we have to . . . . .

Senses Taker DESTINATION?

Milo, Tock and Humbug The Castle-in-the-Air! *[They throw down their papers and run past him up the first few stairs.]*

Senses Taker Stop! I'm sure you'd rather see what I have to show you. *[Snaps his fingers; they freeze.]* A circus of your very own. *[CIRCUS MUSIC is heard. MILO seems to go into a trance.]* And wouldn't you enjoy this most wonderful smell? *[TOCK sniffs and goes into a trance.]* And here's something I know you'll enjoy hearing . . . [To HUMBUG. The sound of CHEERS and APPLAUSE for HUMBUG is heard, and he goes into a trance.]* There we are. And now, I'll just sit back and let the demons catch up with you.

[MILO accidentally drops his package of gifts. The Package of Laughter from DR. DISCHORD opens and the Sounds of Laughter are heard. After a moment, MILO, TOCK and HUMBUG join in laughing and the spells are broken.]

Milo There was no circus.

Tock There were no smells.

Humbug The applause is gone.

Senses Taker I warned you I was the Senses Taker. I'll steal your sense of Purpose, your sense of Duty, destroy your sense of Proportion—and but for one thing, you'd be helpless yet.

Milo What's that?

> Without these stage directions, would you be able to picture the action here? Explain.

---

trance a sleep-like state

Senses Taker As long as you have the sound of laughter, I cannot take your sense of Humor. Agh! That horrible sense of humor.

Humbug HERE THEY COME! LET'S GET OUT OF HERE! *[The demons appear in nasty **slithering hordes**, running through the audience and up onto the stage, trying to attack TOCK, MILO and HUMBUG. The three heroes run past the SENSES TAKER up the stairs toward the Castle-in-the-Air with the demons snarling behind them.]*

Milo Don't look back! Just keep going! *[They reach the castle. The two PRINCESSES appear in the windows.]*

Princesses Hurry! Hurry! We've been expecting you.

Milo You must be the Princesses. We've come to rescue you.

Humbug And the demons are close behind!

Tock We should leave right away.

Princesses We're ready anytime you are.

Milo Good, now if you'll just come out. But wait a minute— there's no door! How can we rescue you from the Castle-in-the-Air if there's no way to get in or out?

Humbug Hurry, Milo! They're gaining on us.

Reason Take your time, Milo, and think about it.

Milo Ummm, all right . . . just give me a second or two. *[He thinks hard.]*

Humbug I think I feel sick.

Milo I've got it! Where's that package of presents? *[Opens the package of letters.]* Ah, here it is. *[Takes out the letters and sticks them on the door, spelling:]* E-N-T-R-A-N-C-E. Entrance. Now, let's see. *[Rummages through and spells in smaller letters:]* P-u-s-h. Push. *[He pushes and a door opens. The*

Reading Strategy:
Questioning
Based on Milo's actions here, how has he changed since leaving his bedroom?

---

slithering slinking and sliding, like a snake   **hordes** great numbers; crowds

PRINCESSES come out of the castle. Slowly, the demons ascend the stairway.]

Humbug Oh, it's too late. They're coming up and there's no other way down!

Milo Unless . . . *[Looks at TOCK.]* Well . . . Time flies, doesn't it?

Tock Quite often. Hold on, everyone, and I'll take you down.

Humbug Can you carry us all?

Tock We'll soon find out. Ready or not, here we go! *[His alarm begins to ring. They jump off the platform and disappear. The demons, howling with rage, reach the top and find no one there. They see the PRINCESSES and the heroes running across the stage and bound down the stairs after them and into the audience. There is a mad chase scene until they reach the stage again.]*

Humbug I'm exhausted! I can't run another step.

Milo We can't stop now . . .

Tock Milo! Look out there! *[The armies of AZAZ and MATHEMAGICIAN appear at the back of the theater, with the Kings at their heads.]*

Azaz *[As they march toward the stage.]* Don't worry, Milo, we'll take over now.

Mathemagician Those demons may not know it, but their days are numbered!

Spelling Bee Charge! C-H-A-R-G-E! Charge! *[They rush at the demons and battle until the demons run off howling. Everyone cheers. The FIVE MINISTERS OF AZAZ appear and shake MILO's hand.]*

Minister 1 Well done.

Minister 2 Fine job.

Minister 3 Good work!

Minister 4 Congratulations!

Minister 5 CHEERS! *[Everyone cheers again. A fanfare interrupts. A PAGE steps forward and reads from a large scroll:]*

Page *Henceforth, and* **forthwith,**
   Let it be known by one and all,
   That Rhyme and Reason
   Reign *once more in Wisdom.*

[The PRINCESSES bow gratefully and kiss their brothers, the Kings.]

   And furthermore,
   The boy named Milo,
   The dog known as Tock,
   And the insect **hereinafter** *referred to as the Humbug*
   Are **hereby** *declared to be Heroes of the* **Realm.**

[All bow and salute the heroes.]

Milo But we never could have done it without a lot of help.

Reason That may be true, but you had the courage to try, and what you can do is often a matter of what you *will* do.

Azaz That's why there was one very important thing about your **quest** we couldn't discuss until you returned.

Milo I remember. What was it?

Azaz Very simple. It was impossible!

Mathemagician *Completely* impossible!

Humbug Do you mean . . . ? *[Feeling faint.]* Oh . . . I think I need to sit down.

Azaz Yes, indeed, but if we'd told you then, you might not have gone.

---

henceforth from now on

forthwith at once

reign to rule

hereinafter after this

hereby by means of this

realm a kingdom

quest a journey in search of something

Mathemagician And, as you discovered, many things are possible just as long as you don't know they're impossible.

Milo I think I understand.

Rhyme I'm afraid it's time to go now.

Reason And you must say goodbye.

Milo To everyone? *[Looks around at the crowd. To TOCK and HUMBUG.]* Can't you two come with me?

Humbug I'm afraid not, old man. I'd like to, but I've arranged for a lecture tour which will keep me occupied for years.

Tock And they do need a watchdog here.

Milo Well, O.K., then. *[MILO hugs the HUMBUG.]*

Humbug *[Sadly.]* Oh, bah.

Milo *[He hugs TOCK, and then faces everyone.]* Well, goodbye. We all spent so much time together, I know I'm going to miss you. *[To the PRINCESSES.]* I guess we would have reached you a lot sooner if I hadn't made so many mistakes.

Reason You must never feel badly about making mistakes, Milo, as long as you take the trouble to learn from them. Very often you learn more by being wrong for the right reasons than you do by being right for the wrong ones.

Milo But there's so much to learn.

Rhyme That's true, but it's not just learning that's important. It's learning what to do with what you learn and learning why you learn things that matters.

Milo I think I know what you mean, Princess. At least, I hope I do. *[The car is rolled forward and MILO climbs in.]* Goodbye! Goodbye! I'll be back someday! I will! Anyway, I'll try. *[As MILO drives the set of the Land of Ignorance begins to move offstage.]*

Azaz Goodbye! Always remember. Words! Words! Words!

Reading Strategy: **Questioning**

Do you think there are real-life situations in which the Mathemagician's statement might be true? Explain.

Reading Strategy: **Questioning**

Which piece of advice—Reason's or Rhyme's—seems more important to you? Why?

Mathemagician And numbers!

Azaz Now, don't tell me you think numbers are as important as words?

Mathemagician Is that so? Why I'll have you know . . . *[The set disappears, and MILO'S Room is seen onstage.]*

Milo *[As he drives on.]* Oh, oh, I hope they don't start all over again. Because I don't think I'll have much time in the near future to help them out. *[The sound of loud ticking is heard. MILO finds himself in his room. He gets out of the car and looks around.]*

The Clock Did someone mention time?

Milo Boy, I must have been gone for an awful long time. I wonder what time it is. *[Looks at clock.]* Five o'clock. I wonder what day it is. *[Looks at calendar]* It's still today! I've only been gone for an hour! *[He continues to look at his calendar, and then begins to look at his books and toys and maps and chemistry set with great interest.]*

Clock An hour. Sixty minutes. How long it really lasts depends on what you do with it. For some people, an hour seems to last forever. For others, just a moment, and so full of things to do.

Milo *[Looks at clock.]* Six o'clock already?

Clock In an instant. In a **trice**. Before you have time to blink. *[The stage goes black in less than no time at all.]*

Based on these stage directions, how do you think Milo now feels about time?

---

trice a very short time

AFTER READING THE SELECTION | Apply the Skills

The Phantom Tollbooth, Act II   by Susan Nanus

Directions Choose the letter of the best answer or write the answer using complete sentences.

Comprehension: Identifying Facts

1. Who is the ruler of Digitopolis?
  A King Azaz
  B the Lethargarian
  C the Mathemagician
  D the Terrible Trivium

2. Who is the first character Milo meets in Act II?
  A Tock   **C** Dodecahedron
  B the Humbug   **D** Dr. Dischord

3. What is unusual about the Dodecahedron's head?

4. Where do the workers of Digitopolis find numbers?

5. What happens when Milo, Tock, and the Humbug eat subtraction stew?

6. What does the Terrible Trivium want Milo, Tock, and Humbug to do?

7. How is the Senses Taker's spell broken?

8. How does Milo open the door of the castle?

9. Who gets Milo and the princesses from the castle to the ground?

10. In the end, who are declared Heroes of the Realm?

Comprehension: Putting Ideas Together

11. How are Azaz and the Mathemagician similar?
  A Both love numbers.
  B Both love letters.
  C Both believe their way of life is best.
  D Both are glad to be rid of Rhyme and Reason.

12. Whom does the Mathemagician blame for troubles in his kingdom?
  A Azaz   **C** Milo
  B Rhyme and   **D** the demons
      Reason

13. Why is Rhyme gloomy about Milo's chances of rescuing her and her sister?

14. How would you describe the Terrible Trivium's tasks?

15. When the Demon of Insincerity says "You're a very clever boy and I have complete confidence in you," what does he really mean?

16. What does Milo learn about humor from his meeting with the Senses Taker?

After Reading **continued on next page**

17. What is the goal of all the demons Milo meets?

18. How can you tell that Azaz and his brother have stopped fighting each other?

19. Reason says, "What you can do is often a matter of what you will do." What does this mean?

20. What lesson do Rhyme and Reason teach Milo as he leaves them?

Understanding Literature: Stage Directions

In scripts, stage directions tell actors and other stage crew how to present the drama. For example, stage directions may tell actors how to say a line. They may tell the lighting crew how to light the scene. They may tell the props manager what to provide for each actor. They may explain to a set designer how to create a setting on stage. For readers of a play, stage directions help show how a character acts and feels. They help the readers visualize the scene.

21. In the first stage direction in Act II, Scene I, what do you learn about Dr. Dischord's wagon?

22. As Act II, Scene I continues, how can you tell that Milo and the Humbug are afraid of Dr. Dischord?

23. When the Mathemagician enters, what prop does he have? What does it look like?

24. Describe one place in the play where stage directions are important for understanding the events.

25. Find one place in the play that has no stage directions. Using your imagination, write your own stage directions for that scene.

Critical Thinking

26. Of all the senses that the Senses Taker wants to steal, which do you think is most important? Why?

27. What lesson does Milo learn through his experience with the Terrible Trivium?

28. Pick a character from "The Phantom Tollbooth." Explain how this character's name describes his or her characteristics.

29. How do you think Milo's experience with the tollbooth has changed him?

Thinking Creatively

30. Do you agree that the speed of time depends on what you are doing? Support your answer with examples from your own life.

Grammar Check

A gerund is a verb form that ends in *-ing* and is used as a noun. A gerund phrase is a group of words containing a gerund and any related words.

Gerund: *Singing* is fun. I enjoy *reading.*

Gerund Phrase: *Singing that song* was fun.

Create a gerund by adding *-ing* to each verb below. Then, write a sentence that includes a gerund phrase.

1 cook   **3** answer
2 make   **4** dance

 ## Vocabulary Builder

Words in English may be "borrowed" from other languages. For example, people from Italy introduced a special pie to the English-speaking world. They also introduced its name, pizza.

Explain which language you think each word is borrowed from. Then, check your answers in a dictionary.

1 fiesta   **3** moose
2 quiche   **4** rodeo

 ## Writing on Your Own

Imagine you are a drama critic, and write a review of "The Phantom Tollbooth." Review Act I and Act II. Note parts you enjoyed and parts you did not enjoy. Note characters you liked the most and least. Begin by writing your overall opinion of the play. Then, use your notes to support your opinion.

 ## Listening and Speaking

With a group, hold a debate on this statement: *Numbers are more important and more fun than words.* Divide into two teams. One team will speak for numbers, and one will speak for words. Plan with your team how you will express your ideas and opinions. Use examples from the play and from your own experiences to support your ideas.

 ## Research and Technology

Use reference materials to prepare a math report on the idea of infinity. Find out what scientists believe to be the largest and smallest numbers. Display your findings in a chart, a diagram, or a group of illustrations. Prepare a written summary to go with your picture.

All words contain at least one syllable—a word part that is pronounced as a separate sound. In multisyllable words, an unstressed syllable vowel sound is pronounced as a schwa. A schwa is an open "uh" sound like the one you hear at the beginning of *ago*.

Sounds Like "Uh" to Me

Certain word combinations are used to spell most long and short vowel sounds. The schwa sound, however, can be spelled with almost any of the vowels. In a dictionary pronunciation, the schwa sound is represented with the symbol ə.

Practice

Each word from the list is broken into syllables. The syllables are out of order. Put the syllables in order. Spell each word correctly. Underline the unstressed syllable that contains the schwa sound.

1. ra cou geous
2. i cab net
3. gize a pol o
4. pi hos tal
5. ble la syl
6. po op site
7. rate sep a
8. en cal dar
9. gas line o
10. ve lope en

Word List
opposite
separate
cabinet
envelope
apologize
calendar
hospital
gasoline
courageous
syllable

DICTIONARY SPELLING DEPARTMENT

a   i   e

An uh sound . . . hmm . . . make it an e this time

Unit 5 introduced you to drama. You read the entire two-act play "The Phantom Tollbooth." This play is a dramatization of a famous novel. When you compare the drama to the novel, you can see the likenesses and differences. Like a novel, a drama has characters, settings, and a plot. Unlike a novel, a drama's story is told through dialogue alone. The script of a drama shows the characters' names and the words they speak. It also includes stage directions, which tell how the words should be spoken. Stage directions also tell about the settings and the props that are used to tell the story.

A drama is meant to be performed. For this reason, dramas do not describe everything that a novel would. Therefore, when you read a play, you must use your imagination to understand the story. Stage directions can help you do this. They can tell you how characters feel and act. They can give clues about how the set looks. This helps you visualize the scene. By using dialogue and stage directions, a playwright can create an entire world on stage.

Selections

- "The Phantom Tollbooth," Act I by Susan Nanus. In Act I, Milo, who is bored by everything, receives a strange gift and begins a surprising adventure.

- "Milo" from *The Phantom Tollbooth* by Norton Juster. Milo comes home from school to find a large box containing a tollbooth, a rulebook, and a map.

- "The Phantom Tollbooth," Act II by Susan Nanus. In Act II, Milo, the watchdog Tock, and the Humbug visit Digitopolis. They escape from the demons and rescue the princesses Rhyme and Reason.

Directions Choose the letter of the best answer or write the answer using complete sentences.

Comprehension: Identifying Facts

1. What is the setting of Act I, Scene II of "The Phantom Tollbooth"?
   A Milo's bedroom
   B the road to Digitopolis
   C the road to Dictionopolis
   D the land of Ignorance

2. What has happened to Rhyme and Reason as the story begins?

3. What does Dr. Dischord collect on his rounds?

4. What do Dodecahedron and the Mathemagician value more than anything?

5. As the novel chapter called "Milo" ends, what is Milo doing?

Comprehension: Putting Ideas Together

6. What element of style does the playwright use all throughout "The Phantom Tollbooth"?
   A one-word sentences
   B plays on words
   C Southern dialect
   D rhythm and rhyme

7. Which character serves as a narrator in the dramatized version of "The Phantom Tollbooth"?

8. Why does Milo need a "rude awakening"?

9. How do the demons interfere with Milo's trip?

10. Why are Rhyme and Reason so important to their brothers?

Understanding Literature: Dialogue and Stage Directions

Any line of dialogue may be said in many different ways. Actors use stage directions to get clues about how to say their words. Stage directions appear in brackets. They give actors and readers important information about how the characters feel, speak, and act.

Other stage directions have to do with the setting of the drama. Stage directions may explain the set, the lighting effects, or the use of colors. These directions allow a set designer to create a set that matches the playwright's vision.

11. What makes dialogue so important in a play?

12. How do stage directions help actors? How do they help readers?

13. Find an example of a stage direction that tells an actor how to say a line. Copy the stage direction. Explain what it tells the actor to do.

14. Find an example in Act II of dialogue that shows a conflict between two characters. Describe the dialogue in your own words.

15. Look at the last stage direction in the play. Is that direction meant more for the reader or for the lighting director? Explain your answer.

Critical Thinking

16. Which character changes the most over the course of the play? Explain your answer.

17. What real-life qualities do the princesses stand for? Why is it important to have them in the kingdom, or in real life?

18. How do the gifts that Milo is given move the plot of the play along?

19. How does the playwright add humor to the play? Would that kind of humor be easier for a reader or an audience member to understand? Why do you think so?

Thinking Creatively

20. After reading the dramatization of "Milo" in Act I, Scene I of the play, do you think Norton Juster would approve? Why or why not?

Speak and Listen

Work with two or three other students. Create a tableau based on a scene from the play. In a tableau, people pose as the characters in a scene, but they do not move. Ask your classmates to guess which scene you are showing. They may ask three questions about the scene before guessing.

Writing on Your Own

You know that dialogue is between two or more characters in a play. A monologue is a long speech by just one character. Write a monologue for Milo to perform at the end of the play. Tell how he feels about his adventure, and what he learned from it. You may perform your monologue for the class.

Beyond Words

Make a shoebox model of a stage setting for one scene from the play. You may use toy figures or make characters out of clay. Use stage directions from the play to decide how the set should look.

Test-Taking Tip

Answer all questions you are sure of first. Then go back and answer the others.

Exposition: Cause-and-Effect Essay

Almost anything that happens involves causes and effects. A cause-and-effect essay is a brief piece of expository—or explanatory—writing. It may explain the reasons something happens—these are the causes. It may also explain the results of an event—these are the effects. Follow the steps in this workshop to write your own cause-and-effect essay.

Assignment Write a cause-and-effect essay. Explain the reasons leading to an event or situation. Explain the results of the event or situation.

What to Include A good cause-and-effect essay has these parts:

- a statement about the causes and effects of a situation
- facts and details that support the statement
- facts in an order that shows the cause-and-effect relationships
- words such as *because* and *since* that make connections between ideas
- error-free writing, including a variety of sentence patterns

Prewriting
Choosing Your Topic

To choose a topic for your essay, try the following tips:

- **Brainstorming** In a group, discuss possible topics. You may want to begin with a general idea such as "historical events." You might try a fill-in-the-blank exercise such as "What causes X?" Review the results. Then, choose an idea from the list as your topic.

- **Browsing** Look through the newspaper or a favorite magazine for topics that interest you. Circle key words or ideas. Consider their causes or effects. Choose a topic based on what you find.

Using the Form

You may use elements of this essay form in these types of reports:

- history, social studies, or geography reports
- scientific lab reports
- news reports

Narrowing Your Topic

Use a topic web. Create a topic web like the one shown here to help you narrow your topic. First, write your topic inside a circle. Then, write connected ideas—subtopics—inside new circles around your topic. Label each idea "cause" or "effect." When you have finished, review your completed web. To narrow your topic, choose to write about only one of your subtopics.

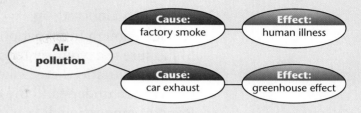

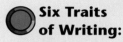

Six Traits of Writing:

Ideas message, details, and purpose

Gathering Details

Using a T-chart in research. To find details to explain the causes and effects, you may need to do research. Use a T-chart to organize—or put into order—your ideas. State your topic at the top. Below that, in side-by-side columns, list the causes and the matching effects.

Writing Your Draft
Shaping Your Writing

Organize details. You may have identified a single cause and a single effect. You may have found several causes for a single effect. This chart shows an example of a single cause with several effects. Organize a first draft, or example, of your essay based on one of these patterns.

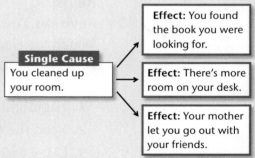

- **Many Causes/Single Effect** Does a number of unrelated events lead to a single result? Write a paragraph for each cause.

- **Single Cause/Many Effects** Does one cause produce several effects? Write a paragraph for each effect.

Focus or direct your writing to the topic by using a strong opening statement. Think about the cause-and-effect relationship you will discuss. Using your notes, write one sentence that states your main idea.

Providing Elaboration

Include enough information to build a link between ideas. Make sure that your sentences show readers exactly how the events or situations are linked. In other words, make sure readers can understand the cause-and-effect relationships. Provide supporting details that are clear and complete.

Unclear: If your skin is damaged, you are at risk for illness.

Clear: If you are fair-skinned and do not wear sunscreen, you are at risk for skin cancer.

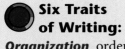

Six Traits of Writing:
Organization order, ideas tied together

Connect with transitions. Choose words and phrases that make cause-and-effect relationships clear to your readers.

To show a cause: Because of the flood, many homes were damaged.

To show an effect: As a result, people will have to rebuild their homes.

Revising

Revising Your Overall Structure

Watch for clear connections. Examine the connections between your paragraphs. Follow these steps to be sure the sentences in each paragraph support your main idea.

1. Highlight the topic sentence of each paragraph.
2. Read the topic sentences in the order in which they appear.
3. Label each connection to the topic as cause or effect.
4. Reorder sentences or paragraphs to make the essay clear.

Six Traits of Writing:
Word Choice vivid words that "show, not tell"

Revising Your Sentences

Confirm the link. Your essay should describe events that are connected by cause and effect. It should not simply list events in time order—it should show connections between events.

Time Order Only: We finished the test and the dismissal bell rang.

Cause and Effect: When I finished the test, I turned in my paper.

Peer Review: Share your essay with a partner. Ask your reader to tell you whether all of your cause-and-effect relationships are clear.

Check facts. Take another look at your research. Compare your notes to your draft. Make sure that your writing reports the facts correctly.

Editing and Proofreading
Review your draft to fix errors.

Focus on Verb Tenses: Review your draft to be sure you have written in a single verb tense. For example, you may have used only the past tense (I was). You may have used only the present tense (I am). Reread your draft. Do you find a change in tense that should not be there? Change it to fit with the rest of your draft.

Publishing and Presenting
Try using one of the following ways to share your writing:

Make a movie "pitch." Treat your cause-and-effect essay like a script for a short film. Create a storyboard that shows the images that you would choose. Try to persuade others to use your ideas to make a movie.

Give an oral presentation. Read your essay aloud to classmates or family members. Then invite their questions and discussion.

Reflecting on Your Writing
Writer's Journal Write your thoughts about writing a cause-and-effect essay. Begin by answering these questions:

Which tips did you find helpful for choosing a topic? Why?

Do you still think that topic was a good one? Why or why not?

Six Traits of Writing:
Conventions correct grammar, spelling, and mechanics

Human face in the tropics
Caren Loebel-Fried

Themes in Folk Literature

Long before there were books, there were stories. People tell stories to help them remember the past or just to pass the time. They also tell stories to explain the world around them. Long ago, most people did not know how to read and write. Instead, they handed stories down to their children by telling them over and over again. Such stories are called oral literature, or folk literature. After a while, people began to gather these stories together and write them down. Types of folk literature include folktales, fables, myths, legends, folk songs, and fairy tales. Many of these stories tell about great heroes, adventure, and magical powers.

"Each of us is a story seeking to be heard."

—Julius Lester

Unit 6   About Folk Literature

Characteristics of Folk Literature

Long before there were books, there were stories. These stories were passed along by word of mouth from one age group to the next. The passing along of stories in this way is called the **oral tradition.** Writing such as folktales, fables, myths, legends, folk songs, and fairy tales all started in the oral tradition. As you study the oral tradition, you will see the following in common:

- A **universal theme** is a message about life that can be understood by most people.

- **Fantasy** is imaginative fiction that often has strange settings and characters.

- **Personification** is giving characters such as animals or objects the characteristics or qualities of humans.

- **Irony** is the difference between what is expected to happen in a story and what does happen. Some folktales and fables have surprise, or ironic, endings because they do not turn out as you expect.

- **Hyperbole** is obvious and deliberate exaggeration not intended to be taken literally. Hyperboles are often used for dramatic or comic effect.

- **Dialect** is the speech of a particular part of a country, or a certain group of people. People who tell stories use dialect to make the characters more real.

- Local customs reflect the way people speak, dress, and behave in certain places. Details of local color help build the **setting**—the time and place in a story.

Frank and Ernest

The Oral Tradition in Print

Folktales are stories that have been handed down from one generation to another. They are told not only for fun, but also for groups of people to share. They are often about heroes, adventure, magic, or love. These stories were told over time and the stories changed each time they were told. Finally, the stories were gathered and written down.

Fables are brief stories or poems with a **moral** (lesson about life), often with animals who act like humans.

Myths are important stories, often part of a culture's religion, that explain how the world came to be or why natural events happen. Myths usually include gods, goddesses, or unusually powerful human beings. A collection of myths is called **mythology.**

Legends are usually based on fact. They are traditional stories that were at one time told orally and handed down from one generation to another. Sometimes a legend becomes the part of an allusion. An allusion is something referring to a historical event, a person, a place, or a work of literature.

Part 1

Reading Strategy:
Predicting

When readers make predictions, they make guesses about what will happen next. The details in the text help readers make their predictions. In Part 1, you will read some selections that contain cause and effect.

■ A *cause* is the reason something happens.

■ An *effect* is what happens as a result.

As you read, make predictions based on the causes and effects of events. Remember, you can change your predictions as you learn more information.

Literary Terms

fable a story or poem with a lesson about life, often with animals acting like humans

folktale a story that has been handed down from one generation to another

character a person or animal in a story, poem, or play

moral a message or lesson about life

hero the leading male character in a story, novel, play, or film

myth an important story, often part of a culture's religion, that explains how the world came to be or why natural events happen, usually including gods, goddesses, or unusually powerful human beings

plot the series of events in a story

fantasy an imaginative story that often has strange settings and characters

setting the time and place in a story

dialogue the conversation among characters in a story or play

The Tiger Who Would Be King | *The Ant and the Dove*

About the Authors

Growing up in Columbus, Ohio, James Thurber wrote for his high school and college newspapers. He also wrote plays and songs for the Ohio State University drama club. Before long, Thurber was writing columns for his hometown newspaper, *The Columbus Dispatch.* Thurber left college during World War I to join the U.S. military. He was unable to complete his training because of a childhood eye injury. After the war, he became famous for his funny stories and cartoons. Much of his early work appeared in *The New Yorker* magazine. Unfortunately, failing eyesight forced him to give up drawing. Thurber went on writing his very popular funny stories for many more years.

James Thurber
1894–1961

Leo Tolstoy was born into a wealthy family in Russia. At age 19, young Tolstoy found himself owning the family estate. There he wrote some of the world's most famous novels. His greatest works include *Anna Karenina* and *War and Peace.* As he grew older, Tolstoy began to seek a simpler life. He gave up the rights to many of his works and gave away his property. This world-famous writer died alone in a train station in Russia.

Leo Tolstoy
1828–1910

Ivan E. Repin, Portrait of Leo Tolstoy. Tretyakov Gallery, Moscow, Russia. TASS/Sovfoto.

About the Selections

"The Tiger Who Would Be King" is a story that teaches an important lesson. Although the characters are all animals, they think and act very much like people. The fable shows us that in some fights, nobody wins.

"The Ant and the Dove" is a retelling of a Russian tale. A dove does a kind deed for an ant. In the end, the ant repays the dove's kindness in a most surprising way.

Before Reading continued on next page

Objectives

◆ To read and understand a fable and a folktale

◆ To define character and hero

◆ To explain the moral of a story

fable a story or poem with a lesson about life, often with animals acting like humans

folktale a story that has been handed down from one generation to another

character a person or animal in a story, poem, or play

moral a message or lesson about life

hero the leading male character in a story, novel, play, or film

Literary Terms **Fables** and **folktales** are stories that have been passed along by word of mouth. Fables usually use animal **characters** to teach a lesson, or **moral.** Most folktales tell about **heroes** (the leading male characters), adventure, and magical powers. These stories amuse us while teaching a lesson. They often have surprising endings that do not turn out as one might expect.

Reading on Your Own A cause is an event, action, or feeling that leads to a result. The result is called an effect. Sometimes an effect is the result of more than one cause. To find the link between events and causes, carefully reread important parts of the story. As you read, record the events and actions that result in an effect.

Writing on Your Own "The Tiger Who Would Be King" and "The Ant and the Dove" are stories that teach a lesson. Write about a story you have read or heard that taught a lesson. As you write, talk about causes and effects in the story. Consider how these relationships move the story along.

Vocabulary Focus Good writers use lively and colorful language to paint pictures with words. As you read these stories, watch for the interesting words that make them come alive. Use a dictionary to look up any words you do not know.

Think Before You Read Make a prediction about the story "The Tiger Who Would Be King." What lesson do you think the tiger in this modern fable might learn?

The Tiger Who Would Be King

One morning the tiger woke up in the jungle and told his mate that he was king of beasts.

"Leo, the lion, is king of beasts," she said.

"We need a change," said the tiger. "The creatures are crying for a change."

The tigress listened but she could hear no crying, except that of her cubs.

"I'll be king of beasts by the time the moon rises," said the tiger. "It will be a yellow moon with black stripes, in my honor."

"Oh, sure," said the tigress as she went to look after her young, one of whom, a male, very like his father, had got an imaginary thorn in his paw.

The tiger prowled through the jungle till he came to the lion's den. "Come out," he roared, "and greet the king of beasts! The king is dead, long live the king!"

Inside the den, the lioness woke her mate. "The king is here to see you," she said.

As you read, think about the elements that make this story a fable.

Tigress means "a female tiger," and *lioness* means "a female lion."

Reading Strategy:
Predicting

What do you predict the lion will do to protect his role?

"What king?" he inquired, sleepily.

"The king of beasts," she said.

"I am the king of beasts," roared Leo, and he charged out of the den to defend his crown against the pretender.

It was a terrible fight, and it lasted until the setting of the sun. All the animals of the jungle joined in, some taking the side of the tiger and others the side of the lion. Every creature from the aardvark to the zebra took part in the struggle to overthrow the lion or to **repulse** the tiger, and some did not know which they were fighting for, and some fought for both, and some fought whoever was nearest, and some fought for the sake of fighting.

"What are we fighting for?" someone asked the aardvark.

"The old order," said the aardvark.

"What are we dying for?" someone asked the zebra.

"The new order," said the zebra.

Reading Strategy:
Predicting

How does the ending compare to the prediction you made earlier in the story?

When the moon rose, fevered and **gibbous,** it shone upon a jungle in which nothing stirred except a **macaw** and a **cockatoo,** screaming in horror. All the beasts were dead except the tiger, and his days were numbered and his time was ticking away. He was **monarch** of all he surveyed, but it didn't seem to mean anything.

MORAL:

You can't very well be king of beasts
if there aren't any.

repulse to drive back	**macaw** a large, bright-colored parrot	**monarch** a king or ruler
gibbous mostly, but not fully, lit up	**cockatoo** a kind of parrot with mostly white feathers	

The Ant and the Dove
Russian Folktale

A thirsty ant went to the stream to drink. Suddenly it got caught in a **whirlpool** and was almost carried away.

At that moment a dove was passing by with a twig in its beak. The dove dropped the twig for the tiny insect to grab hold of. So it was that the ant was saved.

A few days later a hunter was about to catch the dove in his net. When the ant saw what was happening, it walked right up to the man and bit him on the foot. **Startled,** the man dropped the net. And the dove, thinking that you never can tell how or when a kindness may be **repaid,** flew away.

whirlpool spinning water that pulls in objects

startled surprised

repaid paid back

Directions Choose the letter of the best answer or write the answer using complete sentences.

Comprehension: Identifying Facts

1. Which two animals fight to rule in "The Tiger Who Would Be King?"
   A the lion and the lioness
   B the tiger and the tigress
   C the lion and the tiger
   D the aardvark and the zebra

2. How long does the terrible fight among the animals last?

3. What does the dove in "The Ant and the Dove" do for the ant?

Comprehension: Putting Ideas Together

4. What humanlike qualities do the animals show in "The Tiger Who Would Be King"?
   A They are happy, smart, and kind.
   B They are selfish, sly, and clever.
   C They are foolish, cruel, and too eager to fight.
   D They are cheerful, helpful, and friendly.

5. What is surprising about the ending of "The Tiger Who Would Be King"?

6. In "The Ant and the Dove," why does the ant bite the man?

Understanding Literature: Folk Literature

As you have seen, folk literature comes in different forms. Most folktales amuse the reader while teaching an important lesson. The characters in a fable are often talking animals.

7. Explain why "The Tiger Who Would Be King" can be called a fable.

8. What lesson about life is taught in "The Ant and the Dove"?

Critical Thinking

9. Which of these two stories do you think teaches a more important lesson? Why?

Thinking Creatively

10. The tiger in Thurber's story wants to be king of beasts. In real life, what happens when people fight for power?

Grammar Check

A clause is a group of words with its own subject and verb. An independent clause can stand alone as a complete sentence. A subordinate clause cannot stand alone as a complete sentence. A comma can be used to link a subordinate clause to an independent clause.

Example: When the moon rose, the battle was over.

Independent clause: The battle was over.

Subordinate clause: When the moon rose

Add to each subordinate clause below to make a complete sentence.

1 in case it begins to rain
2 because the boys arrive tomorrow
3 the bridge will be

 Vocabulary Builder

The words *fought* and *battled* are synonyms. They have the same basic meaning. You can use either word in most sentences without changing the meaning. For example:

The animals *fought* until the setting of the sun.

The animals *battled* until the setting of the sun.

 Writing on Your Own

Write a fable that teaches the same lesson as "The Tiger Who Would Be King" or "The Ant and the Dove."

- For your fable, create different characters and change the plot.
- Show the causes and effects of each event. The action of the story should lead to the lesson at the end.

 Listening and Speaking

Prepare an oral report on the life of either James Thurber or Leo Tolstoy. Use pictures or timelines to make the information easier to understand. End with a short reading from one of the author's other works.

 Media and Viewing

Imagine you are going to create a cartoon based on one of these fables. List the events of the story. What kind of music would you choose to go with these events? What kind of colors would you use to bring the story to life? Draw or paint your favorite scene.

Arachne   by Olivia E. Coolidge

Olivia E. Coolidge
1908–

Objectives

◆ To read and understand a myth
◆ To define plot
◆ To use context clues to figure out unfamiliar words

About the Author

Born in England, Olivia Ensor Coolidge has lived in both Europe and the United States. Coolidge has taught English, Latin, and Greek, but is best known as a writer. She especially enjoys writing stories about Greek mythology and life in the American colonies. Coolidge is careful to get the facts straight when she tells stories based on history. Her first book for children and young adults was *Greek Myths*. She believes that ancient legends and myths teach lessons that are still important today.

About the Selection

Arachne is a young woman famous for her weaving skills. When people say she must have been taught by the goddess Athene, Arachne grows angry. She insists that she learned her skill through practice and hard work. Arachne dares Athene to weave a finer cloth. Athene accepts the dare, and Arachne finally meets her match. In the end, Arachne is punished for her pride in an unusual way.

Literary Terms Like fables, **myths** are one of the oldest forms of stories. Myths tell about the actions of gods or heroes. The hero may be a god or a special human with great strength and power. The **plot,** or events in the story, tells what happens to the hero.

Reading on Your Own A cause is an event, action, or feeling that makes something happen. An effect is what happens. Sometimes an effect can become the cause of another event. For example, seeing someone lift a heavy object can cause you to offer help. Your help can then cause that person to feel good. As you read, look for clue words such as *because, so,* and *as a result.* These words suggest a link between cause and effect. Ask yourself questions such as "What happened?" and "Why did this happen?" These questions will help you match up causes and effects.

Writing on Your Own In "Arachne," a young woman is punished for thinking she is better than anyone else. As much as we may learn at school, we learn even more from life experience. Think about the lessons you have learned from your own life experiences. Write a few sentences to explain one of the lessons you have learned.

Vocabulary Focus Use context clues to help figure out the meaning of unfamiliar words. Context clues are found in the words and sentences that surround the unfamiliar word. They may be words with the same or the opposite meaning.

Think Before You Read Arachne, the main character in this myth, is a skilled weaver. *Arachnida* is the name of the class of creatures that includes spiders. What prediction can you make about the story based on this information?

> **myth** an important story, often part of a culture's religion, that explains how the world came to be or why natural events happen
>
> **plot** the series of events in a story

Arachne

Greek Myth

As you read, think about how pride in her skill might get Arachne into trouble.

What causes Arachne's work to be known all over Greece?

Arachne was a **maiden** who became famous throughout Greece, though she was neither **wellborn** nor beautiful and came from no great city. She lived in an **obscure** little village, and her father was a humble dyer of wool. In this he was very skillful, producing many **varied** shades, while above all he was famous for the clear, bright scarlet which is made from **shellfish,** and which was the most glorious of all the colors used in ancient Greece. Even more skillful than her father was Arachne. It was her task to spin the fleecy wool into a fine, soft thread and to weave it into cloth on the high, standing loom within the cottage.

Arachne was small and pale from much working. Her eyes were light and her hair was a dusty brown, yet she was quick and graceful, and her fingers, roughened as they were, went so fast that it was hard to follow their **flickering** movements. So soft and even was her thread, so fine her cloth, so gorgeous her embroidery, that soon her products were known all over Greece. No one had ever seen the like of them before.

At last Arachne's fame became so great that people used to come from far and wide to watch her working. Even the graceful nymphs would **steal** in from stream or forest and peep shyly through the dark doorway, watching in wonder the white arms of Arachne as she stood at the loom and threw

In the Greek tradition, *nymphs* were nature goddesses who lived in rivers, trees, and mountains. *Athene* was the Greek goddess of wisdom, skills, and warfare.

maiden an unmarried girl or woman

wellborn born in a family of wealth

obscure not well known, hidden

varied various

shellfish an animal with no bones that has a shell, such as a crab or shrimp

flickering fluttering

steal to go

the **shuttle** from hand to hand between the hanging threads, or drew out the long wool, fine as a hair, from the **distaff** as she sat spinning. "Surely Athene herself must have taught her," people would murmur to one another. "Who else could know the secret of such marvelous skill?"

Arachne was used to being wondered at, and she was immensely proud of the skill that had brought so many to look on her. Praise was all she lived for, and it displeased her greatly that people should think

Arachne (detail), **Arvis Stewart**

anyone, even a goddess, could teach her anything. Therefore when she heard them murmur, she would stop her work and turn round **indignantly** to say, "With my own ten fingers I gained this skill, and by hard practice from early morning till night. I never had time to stand looking as you people do while another maiden worked. Nor if I had, would I give

Why would Arachne get upset when people say Athene must have taught her to spin?

shuttle an instrument used in weaving to carry thread back and forth	**distaff** a stick used to hold wool for spinning	**indignantly** in a proud, angry way

Reading Strategy: Predicting

What do you predict will happen as a result of this boast?

Athene credit because the girl was more skillful than I. As for Athene's weaving, how could there be finer cloth or more beautiful embroidery than mine? If Athene herself were to come down and compete with me, she could do no better than I."

One day when Arachne turned round with such words, an old woman answered her, a gray old woman, bent and very poor, who stood leaning on a staff and peering at Arachne **amid** the crowd of onlookers. "Reckless girl," she said, "how dare you claim to be equal to the **immortal** gods themselves? I am an old woman and have seen much. Take my advice and ask pardon of Athene for your words. Rest content with your fame of being the best spinner and weaver that mortal eyes have ever beheld."

"Stupid old woman," said Arachne indignantly, "who gave you a right to speak in this way to me? It is easy to see that you were never good for anything in your day, or you would not come here in poverty and rags to gaze at my skill. If Athene resents my words, let her answer them herself. I have challenged her to a contest, but she, of course, will not come. It is easy for the gods to avoid matching their skill with that of men."

At these words the old woman threw down her staff and stood erect. The wondering onlookers saw her grow tall and fair and stand clad in long robes of dazzling white. They were terribly afraid as they realized that they stood in the presence of Athene. Arachne herself flushed red for a moment, for she had never really believed that the goddess would hear her. Before the group that was gathered there she would not give in; so pressing her pale lips together in **obstinacy** and pride, she led the goddess to one of the great looms and set herself before the other. Without a word both began to thread the long woolen strands that hang from the rollers, and between

What context clues help you figure out what *obstinacy* means?

| **amid** among | **immortal** living forever | **obstinacy** stubbornness |

which the shuttle moves back and forth. Many skeins lay heaped beside them to use, bleached white, and gold, and scarlet, and other shades, varied as the rainbow. Arachne had never thought of giving credit for her success to her father's skill in dyeing, though in actual truth the colors were as remarkable as the cloth itself.

Soon there was no sound in the room but the breathing of the **onlookers**, the whirring of the shuttles, and the creaking of the wooden frames as each pressed the thread up into place or tightened the pegs by which the whole was held straight. The excited crowd in the doorway began to see that the skill of both in truth was very nearly equal, but that, however the cloth might turn out, the goddess was the quicker of the two. A pattern of many pictures was growing on her loom. There was a border of **twined** branches of the olive, Athene's favorite tree, while in the middle, figures began to appear. As they looked at the glowing colors, the **spectators** realized that Athene was weaving into her pattern a last warning to Arachne. The central figure was the goddess herself competing with Poseidon for possession of the city of Athens; but in the four corners were mortals who had tried to **strive** with gods and pictures of the awful fate that had overtaken them. The goddess ended a little before Arachne and stood back from her marvelous work to see what the maiden was doing.

Poseidon is the Greek god of the sea.

Never before had Arachne been matched against anyone whose skill was equal, or even nearly equal to her own. As she stole glances from time to time at Athene and saw the goddess working swiftly, calmly, and always a little faster than herself, she became angry instead of frightened, and an evil thought came into her head. Thus as Athene stepped back a pace to watch Arachne finishing her work, she saw that the maiden had taken for her design a pattern of scenes which showed

onlookers witnesses

twined twisted together

spectators people who are watching

strive to struggle in contest with

evil or unworthy actions of the gods, how they had deceived fair maidens, **resorted** to trickery, and appeared on earth from time to time in the form of poor and humble people. When the goddess saw this insult glowing in bright colors on Arachne's loom, she did not wait while the cloth was judged, but stepped forward, her gray eyes blazing with anger, and tore Arachne's work across. Then she struck Arachne across the face. Arachne stood there a moment, struggling with anger, fear, and pride. "I will not live under this insult," she cried, and seizing a rope from the wall, she made a noose and would have hanged herself.

The goddess touched the rope and touched the maiden. "Live on, wicked girl," she said. "Live on and spin, both you and your descendants. When men look at you they may remember that it is not wise to strive with Athene." At that the body of Arachne **shriveled** up, and her legs grew tiny, **spindly**, and **distorted**. There before the eyes of the spectators hung a little dusty brown spider on a slender thread.

All spiders descend from Arachne, and as the Greeks watched them spinning their thread wonderfully fine, they remembered the contest with Athene and thought that it was not right for even the best of men to claim equality with the gods.

Why is Athene upset by Arachne's design?

Reading Strategy: **Predicting**

What do you predict Arachne will do about Athene's anger?

What characteristics of spiders does this myth explain?

---

resorted gone back to   **shriveled** dried up   **distorted** twisted out of normal shape or size

spindly long and thin

Arachne   by Olivia E. Coolidge

Directions Choose the letter of the best answer or write the answer using complete sentences.

Comprehension: Identifying Facts

1. Why was Arachne famous all over Greece?
   A She came from a great city.
   B Her father was a dyer of wool.
   C She was a wonderful weaver.
   D She was very beautiful.

2. Arachne had
   A dark eyes and black hair
   B blue eyes and golden hair
   C green eyes and red hair
   D light eyes and brown hair

3. How do people think Arachne learned her skill?

4. How does Arachne explain her skill?

5. What does the old woman tell Arachne to do?

6. What does Arachne do when she hears the old woman's words?

7. Who does the old woman turn out to be?

8. Why does Arachne's face turn red for a moment?

9. What does Athene do when she sees what Arachne has woven?

10. What happens to Arachne at the end of the story?

Comprehension: Putting Ideas Together

11. Which pair of words best describes Arachne?
    A rich and beautiful
    B proud and boastful
    C lazy and dull
    D calm and patient

12. Athene punishes Arachne because
    A Arachne does not show respect for the gods
    B Arachne is a very poor weaver
    C Arachne does not treat her father well
    D Athene is jealous of Arachne's skill

13. How does Arachne compare to her father?

14. How can you tell that Arachne was a very good weaver?

15. Why isn't Arachne pleased by all the praise she is given?

16. Why does Arachne grow angry at the old woman?

17. How does Athene compare to Arachne as a weaver?

After Reading **continued on next page**

18. Why does Arachne want to hang herself?

19. What words best describe Athene?

20. In what ways is Arachne like a spider?

Understanding Literature: Myths

Myths are stories that tell about the actions of gods or heroes. People all over the world have created, told, and believed in myths. Myths often have a message about life, just as fables do. A myth can do one or more of the following:

• tell how the world began or how it will end

• explain something in nature, such as thunder or earthquakes

• teach a lesson

• express a value, such as courage or honesty

21. What scene has Athene woven into her cloth?

22. What does Arachne's design suggest about her opinion of the gods?

23. What part of nature does this myth explain?

24. What lesson about life does this myth teach?

25. Why is this story called a myth and not a fable?

Critical Thinking

26. Should Arachne have gotten so upset when people thought she learned weaving from Athene? Explain your opinion.

27. Would you have spoken to the old woman the way Arachne did? Explain.

28. Would the ending be different if Arachne had woven a different scene? Explain.

29. Was it fair of Athene to turn Arachne into a spider? Why or why not?

Thinking Creatively

30. Do you think someone like Arachne would make a good friend? Explain.

Grammar Check

Compound sentences are sentences that contain more than one subject and more than one verb. For example: "She lived in an obscure little village, and her father was a humble dyer of wool." The two subjects are *she* and *father*. The two verbs are *lived* and *was*. Find three other compound sentences in "Arachne." Write them down, underlining their subjects and verbs.

 Vocabulary Builder

As you read, you might find words whose meanings you do not know. Try using the words around the unknown word to figure out what the word means. This is called using *context clues*. For example: Arachne embroidered beautiful pictures into the cloth.

The context clues *beautiful pictures* and *into the cloth* help you guess that *embroidered* means "decorated with needlework."

 Writing on Your Own

You can learn important lessons from reading as well as from your own experiences. Jot down notes about the main lesson of "Arachne." Then jot down notes about lessons you have learned from your own life experiences. Write an essay in which you compare these two different ways of learning.

 Listening and Speaking

In a group, prepare an oral report about spiders. How many different kinds of spiders are there? What do they look like? Where do they live? What do they eat? Present your findings to the class. Include pictures in your report. Try to answer any questions your classmates may have.

 Research and Technology

Learn all you can about one of the ancient Greek gods or goddesses. Use the Internet and other library materials to do your research. Then prepare a written report and share your findings with classmates. Put your reports together to make a class book about Greek myths.

Cause-and-Effect Articles

In Part 1, you are learning about cause and effect in literature. Understanding cause and effect is also important when you read informational texts. Informational articles are often found in magazines, newspapers, and textbooks. They explain how one event leads to another. For example, the article "Our Changing Climate" shows how everyday behavior can cause climate change.

A cause-and-effect article tells how events are connected. In other words, it shows the reason that things happen the way they do. Facts and figures may be used to show both causes and effects.

Reading Skill

As you read, ask, "How are the ideas connected to one another?" You might find that they are arranged to show cause and effect. Cause is the reason behind an event. Effect is the result of the cause. Causes and effects usually do not stand alone. An effect may become a cause for another effect. A cause of one event may be the effect of an earlier cause.

As you read a cause-and-effect article, first find the main event or effect. Then look for other causes and effects presented by the writer. Words that signal cause and effect include *result, because, when, if/then,* and *leads to.*

Read the following article. Use a chart like the one below to help you track causes and effects.

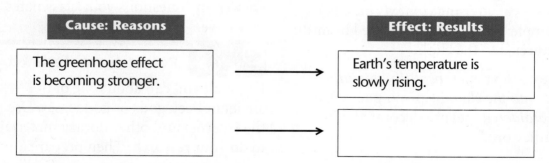

Cause: Reasons — The greenhouse effect is becoming stronger. → Effect: Results — Earth's temperature is slowly rising.

Our Changing Climate

The Earth is slowly getting warmer, and nobody is exactly sure why.

This change in our planet's climate is called *global warming*. Until fairly recently, changes in climate have always taken place gradually over periods of thousands of years. Why the Earth's average temperature has risen significantly in just the past 100 years is a mystery that climate scientists are working very hard to solve.

Our planet is surrounded by a thin layer of gases called the *atmosphere*. As sunlight passes through the atmosphere, energy is absorbed by the Earth's surface. Some of this energy escapes back into space, but much of it is trapped by the gases that blanket the Earth. Like the glass plates of a greenhouse, gases such as water vapor, carbon dioxide, and methane let sunlight in while preventing heat from escaping. Because of the way they help warm our world, we call these gases *greenhouse gases*. Without the so-called *greenhouse effect* to keep it warm, our planet would be too cold to sustain life.

But sometimes there can be too much of a good thing! As the greenhouse effect becomes stronger, the Earth's temperature is slowly rising. Global warming upsets the delicate balance of rainfall and temperature that plants and animals rely upon for survival. In fact, the Earth's glaciers have already begun to melt and sea levels have begun to rise. Over the past 100 years, sea levels have risen by more than six inches worldwide. If global warming continues at this

> Sometimes the cause of an event is not known for sure. In that case, the writer may suggest possible causes.

> The writer presents possible effects that may result because of global warming.

rate, we may expect to see coastal flooding, worsening air pollution, and dangerous changes in our food and water supplies.

Who is to blame for this impending global crisis? Sadly, the fault lies largely with ourselves. Most scientists agree that human activity is responsible for sending more and more greenhouse gases into the air. We produce these gases when we burn fossil fuels like coal and oil to make electricity; when we send our trash to decompose in landfills; when we run our cars and trucks; and when we operate our factories. The more energy we consume, the stronger the greenhouse effect grows.

Fortunately, there are steps we can all take to help slow down global warming. The key, of course, is to conserve energy. By using less gasoline, not wasting electricity, and recycling our trash, we decrease the amount of greenhouse gases being released into the atmosphere. No one knows for sure what the future holds for our planet, but we must all play our part in slowing down the destructive effects of global warming.

> The writer finishes with details that are themselves causes and effects.

Monitor Your Progress

Directions Choose the letter of the best answer or write the answer using complete sentences.

1. What is the thin layer of gases surrounding the Earth called?
   A the biosphere
   B the atmosphere
   C the greenhouse effect
   D global warming

2. What is one effect of global warming?
   A an increased need for gasoline
   B the production of more greenhouse gases
   C a rise in the sea level
   D a cooling of the Earth's surface

3. How do greenhouse gases keep the Earth warm?

4. How is the use of energy connected to global warming?

5. What can people do to slow down global warming?

Writing on Your Own

Sometimes a single cause results in several effects. Explain how one cause presented in the article has more than one effect.

Mowgli's Brothers   by Rudyard Kipling

**Rudyard Kipling
1865–1936**

Objectives

- ◆ To read and understand a fantasy
- ◆ To explore how setting and dialogue add to the reading experience

About the Author

Rudyard Kipling was born in India to British parents. When he was very young, his Indian nurses told him folktales about talking animals. These stories stirred his imagination. Later, he would make up stories of his own with talking animals as the characters. The most famous of these was *The Jungle Book,* in which "Mowgli's Brothers" appears. This book was later made into many movies, one of which was animated.

As a young boy, Kipling was sent to school in England. He returned to India at age 16 to work as a newspaper reporter. Before long, he became famous around the world for his stories and poems. In 1907, he was presented with the Nobel Prize in Literature.

About the Selection

"Mowgli's Brothers" takes place in the jungles of India. The Seeonee hills in the story refer to what is known as the Seoni district. The Waingunga River runs through this north central part of India.

Even though the setting is real, this story is fiction. It is about a boy who lives among wolves. One evening in the jungle, Father Wolf finds the child near his cave. He brings the boy inside and places him with the pups. Mother Wolf names the child Mowgli. She knows that she cannot keep him unless the pack agrees. Meanwhile, the dangerous tiger Shere Khan claims the boy as his own.

Both "The Tiger Who Would Be King" and "Mowgli's Brothers" are stories about talking animals. In each story, a tiger thinks of himself as king of the jungle. The animals in both stories argue and fight. However, the reader feels very different when reading these two stories. One seems more true to life, while the other is more like make-believe.

Literary Terms **Fantasy** is imaginary writing that contains features not found in real life. Stories about singing donkeys, undersea kingdoms, or magic skateboards are examples of fantasy. Like most stories, fantasies have characters, a **setting**, and a plot. Some of these story parts may seem real. Others do not. Both "The Tiger Who Would Be King" and "Mowgli's Brothers" are set in the jungle. However, the characters we meet within this real setting are talking animals. The conversation among the characters is called **dialogue.**

Reading on Your Own The plot is the chain of events that make up a story. As you read "Mowgli's Brothers," think about how its plot is similar to Thurber's fable. In what ways are the plots alike? In what ways are they different?

Writing on Your Own "Mowgli's Brothers" is about a child who grows up among wolves in the jungle. What would it be like to live without human companions? Write a paragraph or two about how you think it would feel. What would you miss most? Why?

Vocabulary Focus A suffix is a word ending that changes the meaning of the word. Use your knowledge of suffixes to figure out the meaning of words you might not recognize. For example, read this sentence: The wolves moved on noiseless feet. The suffix -*less* means "without." The wolves were moving without making noise.

Think Before You Read "Mowgli's Brothers" is a fantasy, but parts of it seem very true to life. Make a prediction based on what you already know about the story. What parts of the story do you think will seem true to life?

fantasy
an imaginative story that often has strange settings and characters

setting the time and place in a story

dialogue the conversation among characters in a story or play

Mowgli's Brothers

*Now Chil the **Kite** brings home the night*
That Mang the Bat sets free—
*The herds are shut in **byre** and hut*
For loosed till dawn are we.
This is the hour of pride and power,
***Talon** and **tush** and claw.*
Oh hear the call!—Good hunting all
That keep the Jungle Law!
—Night-Song in the Jungle

It was seven o'clock of a very warm evening in the Seeonee hills when Father Wolf woke up from his day's rest, scratched himself, yawned, and spread out his paws one after the other to get rid of the sleepy feeling in their tips. Mother Wolf lay with her big gray nose dropped across her four tumbling,

kite a bird of the hawk family	**byre** a cow barn	**tush** a tusk
	talon a bird's claw	

squealing cubs, and the moon shone into the mouth of the cave where they all lived. "Augrh!" said Father Wolf, "it is time to hunt again"; and he was going to spring downhill when a little shadow with a bushy tail crossed the **threshold** and whined: "Good luck go with you, O Chief of the Wolves; and good luck and strong white teeth go with the noble children, that they may never forget the hungry in this world."

As you read, think about what parts of the story show that it is a fantasy.

It was the jackal—Tabaqui the Dishlicker—and the wolves of India **despise** Tabaqui because he runs about making mischief, and telling tales, and eating rags and pieces of leather from the village rubbish-heaps. But they are afraid of him too, because Tabaqui, more than anyone else in the jungle, is **apt** to go mad, and then he forgets that he was ever afraid of anyone, and runs through the forest biting everything in his way. Even the tiger runs and hides when little Tabaqui goes mad, for madness is the most disgraceful thing that can overtake a wild creature. We call it hydrophobia, but they call it *dewanee*—the madness—and run.

Hydrophobia is the disease we call rabies.

"Enter, then, and look," said Father Wolf, stiffly; "but there is no food here."

"For a wolf, no," said Tabaqui; "but for so mean a person as myself a dry bone is a good feast. Who are we, the Gidur log [the jackal-people], to pick and choose?" He scuttled to the back of the cave, where he found the bone of a buck with some meat on it, and sat cracking the end merrily.

"All thanks for this good meal," he said, licking his lips. "How beautiful are the noble children! How large are their eyes! And so young too! Indeed, indeed, I might have remembered that the children of Kings are men from the beginning."

Now, Tabaqui knew as well as anyone else that there is nothing so unlucky as to compliment children to their faces; and it pleases him to see Mother and Father Wolf look uncomfortable.

threshold an opening or doorway   **despise** to hate   **apt** likely to

Tabaqui sat still, rejoicing in the mischief that he had made: then he said spitefully:

"Shere Khan, the Big One, has shifted his hunting-grounds. He will hunt among these hills for the next moon, so he has told me."

Shere Khan was the tiger who lived near the Waingunga River, twenty miles away.

"He has no right!" Father Wolf began angrily—"By the Law of the Jungle he has no right to change his **quarters** without due warning. He will frighten every head of game within ten miles, and I—I have to kill for two, these days."

"His mother did not call him Lungri [the Lame One] for nothing," said Mother Wolf, quietly. "He has been lame in one foot from his birth. That is why he has only killed cattle. Now the villagers of the Waingunga are angry with him, and he has come here to make our villagers angry. They will **scour** the Jungle for him when he is far away, and we and our children must run when the grass is set **alight**. Indeed, we are very grateful to Shere Khan!"

"Shall I tell him of your gratitude?" said Tabaqui.

"Out!" snapped Father Wolf. "Out and hunt with thy master. Thou hast done harm enough for one night."

"I go," said Tabaqui, quietly. 'Ye can hear Shere Khan below in the thickets. I might have saved myself the message."

Father Wolf listened, and below in the valley that ran down to a little river, he heard the dry, angry, snarly, singsong whine of a tiger who has caught nothing and does not care if all the Jungle knows it.

"The fool!" said Father Wolf. "To begin a night's work with that noise! Does he think that our buck are like his fat Waingunga **bullocks**?"

"H'sh! It is neither bullock nor buck he hunts tonight," said Mother Wolf. "It is Man." The whine had changed to a sort of humming purr that seemed to come from every quarter of the compass. It was the noise that bewilders woodcutters and

Why do the wolves dislike Tabaqui?

Some of the dialogue in this story uses old forms of English speech. For example, *thy* means "your" and *thou hast* means "you have." *Ye* means "you" and *wilt* means "will."

quarters an area where one lives	**scour** to search or go through	**alight** on fire
		bullocks steers

gypsies sleeping in the open, and makes them run sometimes into the very mouth of the tiger.

"Man!" said Father Wolf, showing all his white teeth. "Faugh! Are there not enough beetles and frogs in the tanks that he must eat Man and on our ground too!"

The Law of the Jungle, which never orders anything without a reason, forbids every beast to eat Man except when he is killing to show his children how to kill, and then he must hunt outside the hunting-grounds of his pack or tribe. The real reason for this is that man-killing means, sooner or later, the arrival of white men on elephants, with guns, and hundreds of brown men with **gongs** and rockets and torches. Then everybody in the jungle suffers. The reason the beasts give among themselves is that Man is the weakest and most defenseless of all living things, and it is unsportsmanlike to touch him. They say too—and it is true—that man-eaters become **mangy**, and lose their teeth.

The purr grew louder, and ended in the full-throated "Aaarh!" of the tiger's charge.

Then there was a howl—an untigerish howl—from Shere Khan. "He has missed," said Mother Wolf. "What is it?"

Father Wolf ran out a few paces and heard Shere Khan muttering and mumbling savagely, as he tumbled about in the **scrub**.

"The fool has had no more sense than to jump at a wood-cutter's campfire, and has burned his feet," said Father Wolf, with a grunt. "Tabaqui is with him."

"Something is coming up hill," said Mother Wolf, twitching one ear. "Get ready."

The bushes rustled a little in the thicket, and Father Wolf dropped with his **haunches** under him, ready for his leap. Then, if you had been watching, you would have seen the most wonderful thing in the world—the wolf checked in

> How does the jungle setting add to the action in the story?

gongs large cymbals that make a heavy sound

mangy having mange, a skin disease in animals that causes sores and hair loss

scrub a small tree or bush

haunches hind legs

mid-spring. He made his bound before he saw what it was he was jumping at, and then he tried to stop himself. The result was that he shot up straight into the air for four or five feet, landing almost where he left ground.

"Man!" he snapped. "A man's cub. Look!"

Directly in front of him, holding on by a low branch, stood a naked brown baby who could just walk—as soft and as **dimpled** a little atom as ever came to a wolf's cave at night. He looked up into Father Wolf's face, and laughed.

"Is that a man's cub?" said Mother Wolf. "I have never seen one. Bring it here."

A wolf accustomed to moving his own cubs can, if necessary, mouth an egg without breaking it, and though Father Wolf's jaws closed right on the child's back not a tooth even scratched the skin, as he laid it down among the cubs.

"How little! How naked, and—how bold!" said Mother Wolf, softly. The baby was pushing his way between the cubs to get close to the warm hide. "Ahai! He is taking his meal with the others. And so this is a man's cub. Now, was there ever a wolf that could boast of a man's cub among her children?"

"I have heard now and again of such a thing, but never in our Pack or in my time," said Father Wolf. "He is altogether without hair, and I could kill him with a touch of my foot. But see, he looks up and is not afraid."

dimpled having a small dent

The moonlight was blocked out of the mouth of the cave, for Shere Khan's great square head and shoulders were thrust into the entrance. Tabaqui, behind him, was squeaking: "My lord, my lord, it went in here!"

"Shere Khan does us great honor," said Father Wolf, but his eyes were very angry. "What does Shere Khan need?"

"My **quarry**. A man's cub went this way," said Shere Khan. "Its parents have run off. Give it to me."

Shere Khan had jumped at a woodcutter's campfire, as Father Wolf had said, and was furious from the pain of his burned feet. But Father Wolf knew that the mouth of the cave was too narrow for a tiger to come in by. Even where he was, Shere Khan's shoulders and **forepaws** were cramped for want of room, as a man's would be if he tried to fight in a barrel.

"The Wolves are a free people," said Father Wolf. "They take orders from the Head of the Pack, and not from any striped cattle-killer. The man's cub is ours—to kill if we choose."

"Ye choose and ye do not choose! What talk is this of choosing? By the bull that I killed, am

quarry anything that is hunted

forepaws the front feet of an animal

I to stand nosing into your dog's den for my fair dues? It is I, Shere Khan, who speak!"

The tiger's roar filled the cave with thunder. Mother Wolf shook herself clear of the cubs and sprang forward, her eyes, like two green moons in the darkness, facing the blazing eyes of Shere Khan.

"And it is I, Raksha [The Demon], who answer. The man's cub is mine, Lungri—mine to me! He shall not be killed. He shall live to run with the Pack and to hunt with the Pack; and in the end, look you, hunter of little naked cubs—frog-eater—fish-killer—he shall hunt thee! Now get **hence**, or by the Sambhur that I killed (I eat no starved cattle), back thou goest to thy mother, burned beast of the Jungle, lamer than ever thou camest into the world! Go!"

Father Wolf looked on amazed. He had almost forgotten the days when he won Mother Wolf in fair fight from five other wolves, when she ran in the Pack and was not called The Demon for compliment's sake. Shere Khan might have faced Father Wolf, but he could not stand up against Mother Wolf, for he knew that where he was she had all the advantage of the ground, and would fight to the death. So he backed out of the cave-mouth growling, and when he was clear he shouted:

"Each dog barks in his own yard! We will see what the Pack will say to this **fostering** of man-cubs. The cub is mine, and to my teeth he will come in the end, O bushtailed thieves!"

Mother Wolf threw herself down panting among the cubs, and Father Wolf said to her gravely:

"Shere Khan speaks this much truth. The cub must be shown to the Pack. Wilt thou still keep him, Mother?"

"Keep him!" she gasped. "He came naked, by night, alone and very hungry; yet he was not afraid! Look, he has pushed one of my babies to one side already. And that lame butcher would have killed him and would have run off to the Waingunga while the villagers here hunted through all our lairs in revenge! Keep him? Assuredly I will keep him.

Reading Strategy:
Predicting

Do you think that the wolves will have to give up the child? Explain.

A *sambhur,* or sambur, is a large Asian deer found in India.

What does this dialogue tell you about Mother Wolf?

hence away	**fostering** taking care of

Lie still, little frog. O thou Mowgli—for Mowgli the Frog I will call thee—the time will come when thou wilt hunt Shere Khan as he has hunted thee."

"But what will our Pack say?" said Father Wolf. The Law of the Jungle lays down very clearly that any wolf may, when he marries, withdraw from the Pack he belongs to; but as soon as his cubs are old enough to stand on their feet he must bring them to the Pack Council, which is generally held once a month at full moon, in order that the other wolves may identify them. After that inspection the cubs are free to run where they please, and until they have killed their first buck no excuse is accepted if a grown wolf of the Pack kills one of them. The punishment is death where the murderer can be found; and if you think for a minute you will see that this must be so.

Father Wolf waited till his cubs could run a little, and then on the night of the Pack Meeting took them and Mowgli and Mother Wolf to the Council Rock—a hilltop covered with stones and boulders where a hundred wolves could hide. Akela, the great gray Lone Wolf, who led all the Pack by strength and cunning, lay out at full length on his rock, and below him sat forty or more wolves of every size and color, from badger-colored **veterans** who could handle a buck alone, to young black three-year-olds who thought they could. The Lone Wolf had led them for a year now. He had fallen twice into a wolf-trap in his youth, and once he had been beaten and left for dead; so he knew the manners and customs of men. There was very little talking at the Rock. The cubs tumbled over each other in the center of the circle where their mothers and fathers sat, and now and again a senior wolf would go quietly up to a cub, look at him carefully, and return to his place on noiseless feet. Sometimes a mother would push her cub far out into the moonlight, to be sure that he had not been overlooked. Akela from his rock would cry: "Ye know the

> What about the Law of the Jungle seems real? What about it makes it more like fantasy?

veterans people with lots of experience

Reading Strategy: Predicting

What do you predict the wolf pack will decide to do with Mowgli?

In what ways is this gathering of wolves like a gathering of people?

Law—ye know the Law. Look well, O Wolves!" and the anxious mothers would take up the call: "Look—look well, O Wolves!"

At last—and Mother Wolf's neck-bristles lifted as the time came—Father Wolf pushed "Mowgli the Frog," as they called him, into the center, where he sat laughing and playing with some pebbles that glistened in the moonlight.

Akela never raised his head from his paws, but went on with the **monotonous** cry: "Look well!" A muffled roar came up from behind the rocks—the voice of Shere Khan crying: "The cub is mine. Give him to me. What have the Free People to do with a man's cub?" Akela never even twitched his ears: all he said was: "Look well, O Wolves! What have the Free People to do with the orders of any save the Free People? Look well!"

There was a chorus of deep growls, and a young wolf in his fourth year flung back Shere Khan's question to Akela: "What have the Free People to do with the man's cub?" Now the Law of the Jungle lays down that if there is any dispute as to the right of a cub to be accepted by the Pack, he must be spoken for by at least two members of the Pack who are not his father and mother.

"Who speaks for this cub?" said Akela. "Among the Free People who speaks?" There was no answer, and Mother Wolf got ready for what she knew would be her last fight, if things came to fighting.

Then the only other creature who is allowed at the Pack Council—Baloo, the sleepy brown bear who teaches the wolf cubs the Law of the Jungle: old Baloo, who can come and go where he pleases because he eats only nuts and roots and honey—rose up on his hind quarters and grunted.

"The man's cub—the man's cub?" he said. "I speak for the man's cub. There is no harm in a man's cub. I have no gift of words, but I speak the truth. Let him run with the Pack, and be entered with the others. I myself will teach him."

monotonous with little or no change

"We need yet another," said Akela. "Baloo has spoken, and he is our teacher for the young cubs. Who speaks besides Baloo?"

A black shadow dropped down into the circle. It was Bagheera the Black Panther, inky black all over, but with the panther marking showing up in certain lights like the pattern of watered silk. Everybody knew Bagheera, and nobody cared to cross his path; for he was as cunning as Tabaqui, as bold as the wild buffalo, and as reckless as the wounded elephant. But he had a voice as soft as wild honey dripping from a tree, and a skin softer than down.

"O Akela, and ye the Free People," he purred, "I have no right in your assembly; but the Law of the Jungle says that if there is a doubt which is not a killing matter in regard to a new cub, the life of that cub may be bought at a price. And the Law does not say who may or may not pay that price. Am I right?"

"Good! good!" said the young wolves, who are always hungry. "Listen to Bagheera. The cub can be bought for a price. It is the Law."

How is Bagheera
different from
Shere Khan?
How is he similar?

Reading Strategy:
Predicting

Do you think
Mowgli will be able
to live among the
wolves? Why or
why not?

"Knowing that I have no right to speak here, I ask your leave."

"Speak then," cried twenty voices.

"To kill a naked cub is shame. Besides, he may make better sport for you when he is grown. Baloo has spoken in his behalf. Now to Baloo's word I will add one bull, and a fat one, newly killed, not half a mile from here, if ye will accept the man's cub according to the Law. Is it difficult?"

There was a **clamor** of scores of voices, saying: "What matter? He will die in the winter rains. He will **scorch** in the sun. What harm can a naked frog do us? Let him run with the Pack. Where is the bull, Bagheera? Let him be accepted." And then came Akela's deep bay, crying: "Look well—look well, O Wolves!"

Mowgli was still deeply interested in the pebbles, and he did not notice when the wolves came and looked at him one by one. At last they all went down the hill for the dead bull, and only Akela, Bagheera, Baloo, and Mowgli's own wolves were left. Shere Khan roared still in the night, for he was very angry that Mowgli had not been handed over to him.

"Ay, roar well," said Bagheera, under his whiskers; "for the time comes when this naked thing will make thee roar to another tune, or I know nothing of man."

"It was well done," said Akela. "Men and their cubs are very wise. He may be a help in time."

"Truly, a help in time of need; for none can hope to lead the Pack forever," said Bagheera.

Akela said nothing. He was thinking of the time that comes to every leader of every pack when his strength goes from him and he gets feebler and feebler till at last he is killed by the wolves and a new leader comes up—to be killed in his turn.

"Take him away," he said to Father Wolf, "and train him as befits one of the Free People."

And that is how Mowgli was entered into the Seeonee wolf-pack at the price of a bull and on Baloo's good word.

---

clamor loud noise   **scorch** to burn severely

Directions Choose the letter of the best answer or write the answer using complete sentences.

Comprehension: Identifying Facts

1. How do the wolves of India feel about Tabaqui?
   A They find him funny.
   B They think he brings good luck.
   C They enjoy his stories.
   D They hate and fear him.

2. What type of animal is Shere Khan?
   A panther   **C** jackal
   B tiger   **D** lion

3. Why did Shere Khan's mother call him Lungri, The Lame One?

4. When does the Law of the Jungle allow animals to eat people?

5. What is the real reason that killing people is not allowed?

6. What does Mowgli do the first time he looks up at Father Wolf?

7. Why doesn't Shere Khan enter the wolves' cave?

8. Who is Akela?

9. Why is Baloo welcome among the wolves?

10. What do the wolves think will happen to Mowgli before long?

Comprehension: Putting Ideas Together

11. What do the tigers in "Mowgli's Brothers" and "The Tiger Who Would Be King" have in common?
    A They are loved by all the other animals.
    B They make trouble for the other animals.
    C They fight with lions.
    D They want to take something from the wolves.

12. In which story does a mother look after her cubs?
    A only in "Mowgli's Brothers"
    B only in "The Tiger Who Would Be King"
    C in both stories
    D in neither story

13. Why does Tabaqui praise the wolf cubs?

14. How does Mowgli get along with the wolf cubs?

15. How does Mother Wolf show her courage?

16. How does Father Wolf feel about the Law of the Jungle? How do you know?

17. Is Akela a good leader? Explain.

Comparing continued on next page

Mowgli's Brothers   by Rudyard Kipling

18. Why does Bagheera pay the price for Mowgli?

19. Why are the wolves so eager to accept the man's cub into the pack?

20. In what ways is Shere Khan different from the tiger in Thurber's fable?

Understanding Literature: Fantasy Literature

A fantasy is a story about things that cannot happen in real life. This is also true of a fable. However, the main purpose of most fantasies is to amuse. Fables are written to teach a lesson.

21. Does Kipling's fantasy seem more or less true to life than Thurber's fable? Explain.

22. Which character in "Mowgli's Brothers" seems most real to you? Explain.

23. Which character in "Mowgli's Brothers" seems least real? Support your answer with details from the story.

24. Would the animals in "Mowgli's Brothers" ever behave like the animals in Thurber's fable? Explain.

25. If Kipling had written "Mowgli's Brothers" as a fable, what lesson might it teach?

Critical Thinking

26. How does the wolf pack make its decisions? Is this the way people decide things in real life?

27. How is Mowgli like the wolf cubs? How is he different?

28. Who would make a better friend: Baloo or Bagheera? Explain.

29. Would Thurber's fable have ended differently if Mowgli had lived in that jungle? Explain.

Thinking Creatively

30. In what ways might "The Tiger Who Would Be King" be different if Kipling had written it?

Grammar Check

Nouns are the names of people, animals, places, things, or ideas. The words *Mowgli, tiger, jungle, claws,* and *truth* are all nouns. Find 10 other nouns in "Mowgli's Brothers" that are things, places, or ideas. Note whether each one names a thing, place, or idea.

 Vocabulary Builder

Use each of these words from the story in a sentence of your own. Look the words up in a dictionary if you are unsure of their meaning.

threshold   gratitude   rejoicing
inspection   feebler

 Writing on Your Own

Think about which you like better— a fantasy or a story based on real life. Write an essay explaining how they are different and which you enjoy reading more. Why do you enjoy the type of story you chose? Which kind of story do you think would be harder to write?

 Listening and Speaking

The animals in Kipling's story speak to each other. This is done through dialogue. Pick a partner or two and read aloud some of the dialogue from the story. Try to make the words flow as if you were really speaking as the characters. After you read, talk about what you did. What might you do with your voice to make your reading sound more lively and natural?

  Media and Viewing

Several different movies and cartoons have been based on *The Jungle Book.* Two of the best-known are the 1967 cartoon and the 1942 live-action movie. Watch one of these films and compare it to Kipling's story. Do you think the cartoon would have been better without the songs? Do you think the actor who plays Mowgli in the live-action movie does a good job? After viewing the movie, discuss it with classmates who watched the same one.

Part 2

Reading Strategy:
Text Structure

The organization of a text helps readers figure out which parts are most important. Readers can also use text structure to help identify a purpose for reading. Two of the main reasons for reading a text are for entertainment and for information. As you read, ask yourself what is the purpose of the reading. Read each selection carefully so that you remember the information.

Literary Terms

personification giving characters such as animals or objects the characteristics or qualities of humans

figurative language writing or speech not meant to be understood exactly as written

simile a figure of speech that makes a comparison using the words *like* or *as*

theme the main idea of a story or play

conflict the struggle of the main character against himself or herself, another person, or nature

foreshadowing clues or hints that a writer gives about something that has not yet happened

flashback a look into the past at some point in a story

BEFORE READING THE SELECTION | Build Understanding

Why the Tortoise's Shell Is Not Smooth by Chinua Achebe

About the Author

Chinua Achebe grew up in the African nation of Nigeria. He likes to retell stories that were first told long ago in his native land. Achebe writes, "Our ancestors created their myths and legends and told their stories for a purpose. . . . Any good story, any good novel, should have a message."

Achebe went to the local mission school where his father taught. He then went to University College in Ibadan, Nigeria, and later studied in London.

In 1958, Achebe wrote *Things Fall Apart,* a famous novel about changing times in Africa. He has since written poetry and essays as well as many other books and articles. Achebe now lives and teaches in the United States.

About the Selection

A *tortoise* is a type of turtle. This African folktale about a tortoise was told orally before it was written down. Here the tale is told as a story within a story. Like a fable, it teaches a lesson about not believing everything you hear. Like a myth, it also offers an amusing explanation for the markings on a tortoise's shell.

Tortoise hears that all the birds go to a great feast in the sky. He tricks the birds into lending him some feathers so that he can join them. He makes trouble for the birds, but they get revenge in the end.

Chinua Achebe
1930–

Objectives

- ◆ To read and understand folktales
- ◆ To recognize personification, figurative language, and simile

Before Reading **continued on next page**

Why the Tortoise's Shell Is Not Smooth   *by Chinua Achebe*

personification
giving characters
such as animals
or objects the
characteristics or
qualities of humans

**figurative
language**
writing or speech
not meant to be
understood exactly
as written

simile a figure of
speech that makes
a comparison using
the words *like* or *as*

Literary Terms As you know, folktales are stories that
were first passed along by word of mouth. Many folktales, like
"Why the Tortoise's Shell Is Not Smooth," were later preserved
in writing. Such oral literature may change greatly as stories
are told and retold throughout the years. Folktales often
use **personification** to teach a lesson or explain something
in nature. Personification gives animals or nonliving
things human characteristics such as the ability to speak.
Personification is a type of **figurative language**—writing
or speech not meant to be understood exactly as written.

Reading on Your Own Before you begin to read, think
about your purpose for reading. Your purpose is the reason
for reading a particular piece of writing. Sometimes you
choose a text based on a purpose you already have. Other
times your purpose is based on the kind of text you are
reading. Setting a purpose helps you focus your reading.
You might read to learn about something, to take an action,
or simply to enjoy yourself.

Writing on Your Own Not long ago, folktales were only
passed along by "word of mouth"—oral retellings. Today,
folktales from around the world have been written down
and collected into books. Write a paragraph explaining the
importance of writing down folktales from different cultures.

Vocabulary Focus Writers use figurative language to
compare things in new and surprising ways. A **simile** shows
how things are alike using the words *like* or *as*. Here is an
example from "Why the Tortoise's Shell Is Not Smooth":
"His body rattled like a piece of dry stick in his empty shell."

Think Before You Read Before you begin to read, look at
the pictures. Read the title and author's name. Now make a
prediction. What kind of story do you think this is going to be?

Why the Tortoise's Shell Is Not Smooth

Low voices, broken now and again by singing, reached Okonkwo from his wives' huts as each woman and her children told folk stories. Ekwefi and her daughter, Ezinma, sat on a mat on the floor. It was Ekwefi's turn to tell a story.

"Once upon a time," she began, "all the birds were invited to a feast in the sky. They were very happy and began to prepare themselves for the great day. They painted their bodies with red cam wood and drew beautiful patterns on them with dye.

"Tortoise saw all these preparations and soon discovered what it all meant. Nothing that happened in the world of the animals ever escaped his notice; he was full of cunning. As soon as he heard of the great feast in the sky his throat began to itch at the very thought. There was a **famine** in those days and Tortoise had not eaten a good meal for two moons. His body rattled like a piece of dry stick in his empty shell. So he began to plan how he would go to the sky."

"But he had no wings," said Ezinma.

"Be patient," replied her mother. "That is the story. Tortoise had no wings, but he went to the birds and asked to be allowed to go with them.

" 'We know you too well,' said the birds when they had heard him. 'You are full of cunning and you are ungrateful. If we allow you to come with us you will soon begin your mischief.'

famine a great shortage of food

Reading Strategy: Text Structure

As you read, think about the purpose of the story. What is a good reason for reading this folktale?

Red cam wood is a hard West African wood that makes red dye.

How does this description of his body help you understand what Tortoise looked like?

Why might the author create a character like Ekwefi to tell the story?

What does it mean to say "Tortoise had a sweet tongue"?

" 'You do not know me,' said Tortoise. 'I am a changed man. I have learned that a man who makes trouble for others is also making it for himself.'

"Tortoise had a sweet tongue, and within a short time all the birds agreed that he was a changed man, and they each gave him a feather, with which he made two wings.

"At last the great day came and Tortoise was the first to arrive at the meeting place. When all the birds had gathered together, they set off in a body. Tortoise was very happy as he flew among the birds, and he was soon chosen as the man to speak for the party because he was a great **orator**.

" 'There is one important thing which we must not forget,' he said as they flew on their way. 'When people are invited to a great feast like this, they take new names for the occasion. Our hosts in the sky will expect us to honor this age-old custom.'

"None of the birds had heard of this custom but they knew that Tortoise, in spite of his failings in other directions, was a widely traveled man who knew the customs of different peoples. And so they each took a new name. When they had all taken, Tortoise also took one. He was to be called *All of you*.

Why do you think Tortoise chose such an odd name for himself?

"At last the party arrived in the sky and their hosts were very happy to see them. Tortoise stood up in his many-colored **plumage** and thanked them for their invitation. His speech was so **eloquent** that all the birds were glad they had brought him, and nodded their heads in approval of all he said. Their hosts took him as the king of the birds, especially as he looked somewhat different from the others.

Kola nuts, yams, palm wine, and *palm oil* are common foods in West Africa.

"After kola nuts had been presented and eaten, the people of the sky set before their guests the most **delectable** dishes Tortoise had ever seen or dreamed of. The soup was brought out hot from the fire and in the very pot in which it had been cooked. It was full of meat and fish. Tortoise began to sniff

---

orator a person who is skilled at public speaking

plumage feathers

eloquent well-spoken

delectable delicious

aloud. There was pounded yam and also yam **pottage** cooked with palm oil and fresh fish. There were also pots of palm wine. When everything had been set before the guests, one of the people of the sky came forward and tasted a little from each pot. He then invited the birds to eat. But Tortoise jumped to his feet and asked: 'For whom have you prepared this feast?'

" 'For all of you,' replied the man.

"Tortoise turned to the birds and said: 'You remember that my name is *All of you*. The custom here is to serve the spokesman first and the others later. They will serve you when I have eaten.'

"He began to eat and the birds grumbled angrily. The people of the sky thought it must be their custom to leave all the food for their king. And so Tortoise ate the best part of the food and then drank two pots of palm wine, so that he was full of food and drink and his body grew fat enough to fill out his shell.

Crawling Turtle II,
Barry Wilson

pottage a thick soup or stew

"The birds gathered round to eat what was left and to peck at the bones he had thrown all about the floor. Some of them were too angry to eat. They chose to fly home on an empty stomach. But before they left, each took back the feather he had lent to Tortoise. And there he stood in his hard shell full of food and wine but without any wings to fly home. He asked the birds to take a message for his wife, but they all refused. In the end Parrot, who had felt more angry than the others, suddenly changed his mind and agreed to take the message.

What human quality does Parrot show?

" 'Tell my wife,' said Tortoise, 'to bring out all the soft things in my house and cover the **compound** with them so that I can jump down from the sky without very great danger.'

"Parrot promised to deliver the message, and then flew away. But when he reached Tortoise's house he told his wife to bring out all the hard things in the house. And so she brought out her husband's hoes, **machetes**, spears, guns, and even his cannon. Tortoise looked down from the sky and saw his wife bringing things out, but it was too far to see what they were. When all seemed ready he let himself go. He fell and fell and fell until he began to fear that he would never stop falling. And then like the sound of his cannon he crashed on the compound."

"Did he die?" asked Ezinma.

"No," replied Ekwefi. "His shell broke into pieces. But there was a great medicine man in the neighborhood. Tortoise's wife sent for him and he gathered all the bits of shell and stuck them together. That is why Tortoise's shell is not smooth."

Reading Strategy: Text Structure

Did you achieve your purpose for reading this folktale?

| **compound** grounds surrounded by buildings | **machetes** large heavy knives for cutting sugarcane |

Why the Tortoise's Shell Is Not Smooth   by Chinua Achebe

Directions Choose the letter of the best answer or write the answer using complete sentences.

Comprehension: Identifying Facts

1. Why does Tortoise need wings?
  A to stay warm
  B to fly to the great feast in the sky
  C to look more handsome
  D to get a new shell

2. Why do the birds not want Tortoise to join them?

3. How do the birds help Tortoise to fly?

Comprehension: Putting Ideas Together

4. Tortoise angers the birds by
  A refusing to go to the feast with them
  B making them taste the food first
  C stealing their feathers
  D eating the best part of the food

5. How does Tortoise's new name allow him to eat before the birds?

6. What lesson do the birds learn about Tortoise?

Understanding Literature: Personification

Animal characters in some stories can think, speak, and act like humans. Writers often use personification to make a point about how humans treat one another.

7. In what ways does Tortoise act like some people?

8. In what ways do the birds act as if they were human?

Critical Thinking

9. Do you think Tortoise got what he deserved? Explain.

Thinking Creatively

10. Think about what you know of tortoises and turtles. What other characteristics of these animals could be explained in a story?

After Reading continued on next page

Why the Tortoise's Shell Is Not Smooth *by Chinua Achebe*

 Grammar Check

A comma is used to separate words or groups of words in a list. Commas signal readers to pause. They also help make the meaning of sentences clear. This chart shows the correct use of commas to separate things in a list.

Incorrect	Correct
We brought pencils paper and books to school.	We brought pencils, paper, and books to school.
To find the library go up the stairs and down the hallway.	To find the library, go up the stairs and down the hallway.

Write three sentences of your own using commas correctly.

 Vocabulary Builder

In an analogy, two pairs of words are linked together in the same way. To complete an analogy, figure out what the two sets of words have in common. Complete these analogies using vocabulary words from the story.

1 *speech* is to *speaker* as *oration* is to _____

2 *fur* is to *bears* as _____ is to *birds*

3 *dull* is to *boring* as *well-spoken* is to _____

 Writing on Your Own

Imagine the people of the sky have asked you to invite guests to their feast. Plan the letter you would write. Begin with a paragraph telling what will be served at the feast. Mention the date, time, and place, as well as directions.

 Listening and Speaking

Work with a group. Choose a scene from the story in which the characters are speaking. Then present a reading of the scene to the class. Act out the parts of the characters as you read. Use your voice to express the characters' feelings. Remember, Tortoise should not sound like the birds!

 Research and Technology

Use the Internet and the library to find folktales from different countries. With a group, prepare a presentation of two folktales from different lands. Use keyword searches to find different ways that each story has been told.

Editorials

In Part 2, you are learning how to set a purpose for reading. This skill is useful in reading informational materials such as editorials. You read folktales to learn what was important to people who lived long ago. Editorials help you learn about things that are important to people today.

About Editorials

Newspapers and magazines print editorials to express the ideas and opinions of the editors. Editorials do these things:

- They state a point of view about something the editors believe is important.
- They try to get readers to believe something or take action.
- They use facts and reasons to support opinions.

Reading Skill

Whenever you read, adjust your speed of reading to match your purpose for reading. Skim, or glance quickly through a work, to get the general idea. Scan, or quickly read through a work, to locate the information you need to find. You might scan your history book to find a certain name or date. Then you would read closely for more information about the person or event.

The chart will help you skim and scan for different purposes.

To identify the main idea of a work	**Skim** title, headings, and pictures
To answer questions about when something happened	**Scan** for mention of days, months, or years
To answer questions about a person or group	**Scan** for the name of the person or group

Portsmouth
Herald

This editorial appeared in the *Portsmouth Herald,* a New Hampshire newspaper.

Music for All

Traip music students' effort is commendable

The headline sums up what the editorial is about.

And the band played on.

This past Tuesday night, Traip Academy students were eloquent when asking the School Committee not to bring the curtain down on the town's music program.

Pied piper refers to a folktale about a musician who leads a town's children away.

First, the students noted, a good high school education should go beyond reading, writing and arithmetic. We all learn differently and for some, music will be the pied piper leading them on a path to higher learning. The students also noted that the band is more than an academic endeavor, it is a part of town life that everyone can enjoy. Finally, the students pointed out that teenagers who are busy rehearsing and playing music are not out getting into trouble.

Clearly, the Kittery School Committee heard the message of these commendable students and decided to discuss the matter in greater detail at a public meeting on Feb. 26 with the goal of finding some other way to hold the line on education spending in town.

We understand that the Town Council does not have an endless pot of gold and cannot fund everything at the levels residents might desire. When money gets tight, tough choices have to be made.

But we would encourage the School Committee to look at the music program as essential, in many ways just as important as math, science and literature. Cuts to the program should be viewed with the same horror as we would view cuts to core curriculum.

Music is not a frill. It is one of mankind's greatest accomplishments and, at times, it can teach and inspire in a way that words and equations cannot.

We hope 2004 will not be the year the music dies in Kittery.

Facts and reasons support a particular viewpoint in the editorial.

The writer clearly states the editor's opinion in these two paragraphs. More reasons are presented.

The editorial ends by urging the School Committee not to cut the music program.

Monitor Your Progress

Directions Choose the letter of the best answer or write the answer using complete sentences.

1. What is this editorial mainly about?
   A the Kittery School Committee's Town Council
   B the reading, writing, and arithmetic programs in Portsmouth
   C the music program at Traip Academy in Portsmouth
   D something that is wrong

2. What is the editorial's opinion about the music program at Traip Academy?
   A Music is just as important as math, science, and literature.
   B The music program is not as important as other subjects.
   C Interest in music should not go beyond the classroom.
   D Money can be better spent by the School Committee.

3. When will the Kittery School Committee meet again?
   A Tuesday
   B February 19
   C 2004
   D none of the above

4. According to the editorial, why is a music program important to learning?

5. Explain how a school music program can help a town.

Writing on Your Own

Write a letter to the School Committee. Tell why you think it should either keep or cut the music program at your school. If you think the program should be kept, explain how the program could be improved. If you suggest cutting the music program, how should the extra money be used? Use information from the editorial to support your position.

The Three Wishes   by Ricardo E. Alegría

Ricardo E. Alegría
1921–

About the Author

Ricardo E. Alegría was born in San Juan, Puerto Rico. He was a pioneer in the study of Puerto Rico's native people. Alegría has worked long and hard to preserve Puerto Rican history, customs, and language. He has a special interest in the folktales of his homeland. In 1976, Alegría opened the Center of Advanced Studies of Puerto Rico and the Caribbean. In 1992, he started the Museum of the Americas. On his 75th birthday, he received the James Smithson Medal of the Smithsonian Institution. He still lives in San Juan.

About the Selection

Folktales are passed along by word of mouth. They often travel from one place to another. Storytellers may change parts of the story based on their own experience. Different versions, or expressions, of "The Three Wishes" can be found around the world. The point of the story is always the same. A poor couple is given three wishes and they foolishly waste the first two. The way they use their final wish offers a message about what is really important. In tales such as this, greed always leads to unhappiness.

Objectives

◆ To read and understand a folktale

◆ To understand theme and conflict

◆ To set a purpose for reading

***Before Reading* continued on next page**

The Three Wishes   by Ricardo E. Alegría

theme the main idea of a story or play

conflict the struggle of the main character against himself or herself, another person, or nature

Literary Terms The **theme** is the main idea of a story, play, or poem. It can express an important message or idea about life and human nature. Universal themes are ideas that appear often in different places and times. Examples are the importance of courage, the power of love, and the danger of greed. To understand the theme, think about the **conflict,** or struggle, faced by the main character. How is this character affected by the conflict?

Reading on Your Own Always set a purpose for reading. One general purpose is to make connections. Find the link between what you read and your own experience. Look for universal themes about big ideas such as friendship or courage. Notice ways of life that are different from your own. Recognize ways in which the ideas in the story connect with your own life.

Writing on Your Own You may already know a few "three wishes" tales. Think about the lessons you can learn from these stories. Then write a few sentences about the good and bad parts of making wishes.

Vocabulary Focus Verbs tell readers what actions take place. Verb tenses can show when the action takes place. For example, "her ears *grew* larger" means her ears already changed. "Her ears *will grow* larger" means they have not yet changed. "Her ears *are growing* larger" means it is happening now. Each verb describes action at a different time. Some verbs change their form when telling about a past action. Look for verbs in this folktale that tell about past actions. What letter combination makes up their endings?

Think Before You Read Why might it help to know a writer's history before reading his or her work? How can knowing about the writer's life help you understand their purpose for writing?

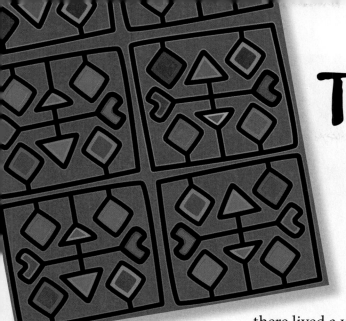

The Three Wishes

Puerto Rican Folktale

As you read, ask yourself what universal theme is expressed in this folktale.

Many years ago, there lived a woodsman and his wife. They were very poor but very happy in their little house in the forest. Poor as they were, they were always ready to share what little they had with anyone who came to their door. They loved each other very much and were quite content with their life together. Each evening, before eating, they gave thanks to God for their happiness.

One day, while the husband was working far off in the woods, an old man came to the little house and said that he had lost his way in the forest and had eaten nothing for many days. The woodsman's wife had little to eat herself, but, as was her custom, she gave a large portion of it to the old man. After he had eaten everything she gave him, he told the woman that he had been sent to test her and that, as a reward for the kindness she and her husband showed to all who came to their house, they would be granted a special grace. This pleased the woman, and she asked what the special grace was.

The old man answered, "Beginning immediately, any three wishes you or your husband may wish will come true."

When she heard these words, the woman was overjoyed and exclaimed, "Oh, if my husband were only here to hear what you say!"

The last word had scarcely left her lips when the woodsman appeared in the little house with the ax still in his hands. The first wish had come true.

Reading Strategy: Text Structure

Based on how the story begins, what do think is going to happen next? How do you know?

Martinique Landscape, 11887, **Paul Gauguin**

The woodsman couldn't understand it at all. How did it happen that he, who had been cutting wood in the forest, found himself here in his house? His wife explained it all as she **embraced** him. The woodsman just stood there, thinking over what his wife had said. He looked at the old man who stood quietly, too, saying nothing.

Suddenly he realized that his wife, without stopping to think, had used one of the three wishes, and he became very annoyed when he remembered all of the useful things she might have asked for with the first wish. For the first time, he became angry with his wife. The desire for riches had turned

embraced held in the arms fondly

his head, and he scolded his wife, shouting at her, among other things, "It doesn't seem possible that you could be so stupid! You've wasted one of our wishes, and now we have only two left! May you grow ears of a donkey!"

He had no sooner said the words than his wife's ears began to grow, and they continued to grow until they changed into the pointed, furry ears of a donkey.

When the woman put her hand up and felt them, she knew what had happened and began to cry. Her husband was very ashamed and sorry, indeed, for what he had done in his temper, and he went to his wife to comfort her.

The old man, who had stood by silently, now came to them and said, "Until now, you have known happiness together and have never quarreled with each other. Nevertheless, the mere knowledge that you could have riches and power has changed you both. Remember, you have only one wish left. What do you want? Riches? Beautiful clothes? Servants? Power?"

The woodsman tightened his arm about his wife, looked at the old man, and said, "We want only the happiness and joy we knew before my wife grew donkey's ears."

No sooner had he said these words than the donkey ears disappeared. The woodsman and his wife fell upon their knees to ask forgiveness for having acted, if only for a moment, out of **covetousness** and greed. Then they gave thanks for all their happiness.

The old man left, but before going, he told them that they had **undergone** this test in order to learn that there can be happiness in poverty just as there can be unhappiness in riches. As a reward for their **repentance**, the old man said that he would **bestow** upon them the greatest happiness a married couple could know. Months later, a son was born to them. The family lived happily all the rest of their lives.

> What problem does the couple have to solve?

> What experience in your own life has taught you the same lesson?

covetousness wanting what another person has	**repentance** changing one's ways after doing something wrong
undergone gone through	**bestow** to give as a gift

Directions Choose the letter of the best answer or write the answer using complete sentences.

Comprehension: Identifying Facts

1. What does the old man do after the woman feeds him?
   - **A** He runs away and hides.
   - **B** He tells her a secret about her husband.
   - **C** He offers her three wishes.
   - **D** He helps her clean the house.

2. How does the couple use the first two wishes?

3. How is the couple rewarded at the end of the story?

Comprehension: Putting Ideas Together

4. How were the woodsman and his wife before they met the old man?
   - **A** rich and unhappy
   - **B** poor and unhappy
   - **C** rich and happy
   - **D** poor and happy

5. What do their wishes say about the woodsman and his wife?

6. How does the couple's life change from the beginning of the story to the end?

Understanding Literature: Theme

A theme, or main idea, is often a lesson about life. Universal themes are found in stories from many different places and periods of time. People everywhere have always had to deal with the same kinds of problems. It is not surprising that their stories tell about the shared human condition.

7. How does the couple change when they are given the chance to make wishes?

8. What lesson does the couple learn from this experience?

Critical Thinking

9. Would it have been better for the couple if the old man had never come? Why or why not?

Thinking Creatively

10. Did you ever have a wish come true with surprising results? Tell about your experience.

Grammar Check

A semicolon connects two independent clauses that are close in meaning. A semicolon can also separate things in a list when commas have already been used.

Example: The family visited Houston, Texas; Santa Fe, New Mexico; and Phoenix, Arizona.

A colon is used after an independent clause to introduce a list of things. A colon is also used to show time or at the beginning of a business letter.

Example: They needed only three things: a warm home, an ax, and a child to love.

 Vocabulary Builder

An antonym is a word that is opposite in meaning to another word. Antonyms help show how things are different. For example: The woodsman and his wife were poor, but their neighbors were rich. *Poor* and *rich* are antonyms. Antonyms are used to show how the woodsman and his wife are unlike their neighbors.

 Writing on Your Own

Plan a story based on the same universal theme as "The Three Wishes." First, state the theme. What lesson about life did the characters in the story learn? Then think of characters and a plot to use in a story of your own. Write a few sentences about the events that would show the theme of your story.

 Listening and Speaking

Present the theme of "The Three Wishes" aloud to a group of your classmates. As you plan your speech, clearly state the story's theme. Tell whether you agree or disagree with the story's message. Use examples from other stories or from your own experience. Arrange your ideas in a way that makes sense.

When you finish writing, practice your speech. Make sure your message is clear. When you are ready, present your ideas to a small group. Be sure to speak slowly and clearly.

 Research and Technology

The setting for this folktale is a forest in Puerto Rico. Learn more about the forests, rivers, plants, animals, and climate of Puerto Rico. Use the Internet and other library resources to prepare a written report. Use maps and pictures to make your findings clear. Then present your findings to the class.

Why the North Star Stands Still   retold by William R. Palmer

Objectives

◆ To read and understand an American Indian myth

◆ To identify foreshadowing and flashback

About the Author

This myth comes from the Paiute, or Pahute, people of the western United States. Long ago, these American Indians lived mainly by hunting, fishing, and digging for roots. Their homes were small round huts called *wickiups.* Today there are over 11,000 Paiute in the United States. They live mostly in Arizona, California, Nevada, Oregon, and Utah. This retelling of a Paiute myth was written by William R. Palmer. Palmer was a leading member of the Utah State Historical Society. He was active in trying to preserve Paiute history, legends, music, and dance.

About the Selection

The North Star, also called Polaris, marks the end of the Little Dipper. Unlike other stars, Polaris does not appear to move across the sky. People all over the world have told stories about this unusual star. The ancient Chinese called it the Emperor Star. To the Navajo people, it is the Fire Star. This Paiute myth tells how a brave mountain sheep was turned into the North Star. Although the main character is a talking animal, this is not a fable. Its main purpose is not to teach a lesson but to explain something in nature. Use these ideas to compare this story to "Why the Tortoise's Shell Is Not Smooth." As you read, look for clues about what will happen next.

Literary Terms Storytellers often use **foreshadowing** and **flashback** to tell their stories. Foreshadowing gives the reader a hint about something that has not yet happened. A flashback looks into the past at some point in the story. The reader learns something about earlier events that helps explain what is happening now.

Reading on Your Own One purpose for reading myths is to understand how different people viewed the world. Many myths express a universal theme that is shared by people all over the world. As you read, think about what this story explains. Try to identify a universal theme that many people would understand even today.

Writing on Your Own This Paiute myth explains why the North Star stands still in the sky. The African folktale you read explains why the tortoise has a rough shell. Think of something in nature that might be explained with an interesting story. Write a few sentences about the myth you would make up.

Vocabulary Focus Every word has a strict dictionary definition. This is called the word's *denotation*. The way a word makes us feel is called its *connotation*. For example, the main character in this story is said to be *determined*. Most people admire someone who is determined. The word *stubborn*, on the other hand, has a very different connotation. Someone who is stubborn does not know when to give up. As you read, think about why the writer chooses words with certain connotations.

Think Before You Read How are myths different from fables? Think about the purpose for each and the way each is written.

---

foreshadowing clues or hints that a writer gives about something that has not yet happened

flashback a look into the past at some point in a story

WHY THE NORTH STAR STANDS STILL

The Pahutes, an ancient people, once large and prosperous, lived mostly in what is now the state of Utah. To the Pahutes, the supreme gods are two brothers, Tobats and Shinob.

Reading Strategy:
Text Structure
How does the first paragraph help you set your purpose for reading?

The Eagle, Buffalo, Deer, and Horse here are all references to different constellations—groups of stars that are believed to form patterns or designs.

The storyteller uses foreshadowing to tell you what will happen to Na-gah. The rest of the story is a flashback that explains the North Star.

The sky is full of living things. The Pahute call them *poot-see* and others call them stars. They are as restless as the Pahutes themselves, travelling around the universe and leaving trails all over the sky. Some of the stars are birds who go away for a time to winter in warmer **climes**; some are animals hunting for better grass—Quan-ants the Eagle, Cooch the Buffalo, Tu-ee the Deer and Cab-i the Horse. The sky is their happy hunting ground; they travel in search of food and follow the good weather.

Yet there is one who does not travel. He is Qui-am-i Wintook, the North Star. He cannot travel, since there is no place he can go. Once he was Na-gah, the mountain sheep on earth.

He was daring, brave and sure-footed. Shinob, the Great Spirit, was so proud of him that he hung great earrings on the sides of his head to make him look more grand.

Always Na-gah would be climbing, climbing, climbing. He hunted in the roughest, and highest mountains, and there he lived and was happy.

Once in the long-ago time, Na-gah found a high mountain with steep smooth sides, ending in a high sharp peak reaching up into the clouds. He looked up at that peak and said:

"I wonder what is up there? I will climb to the very top."

climes climates

He set out to find a way up. Around the mountain he walked, seeking a path; yet there was none—nothing but sheer cliffs all the way round. It was the very first mountain he could not climb.

He thought and thought; and the more he thought the more determined he was to find a way to the top. Shinob would surely be proud to see him standing on the very peak of such a mountain.

    After searching for an age, he finally found a crack in the rock; but the crack went down into the earth, not up. So down he went; there was no other choice. He had not gone far when he came to a path that turned upwards, and he began to climb. Soon it grew so dark that he could not see: he stumbled into rocks which broke loose and rolled down beneath his feet. A terrible crashing rang through the mountain as the rolling rocks dashed themselves to pieces at the bottom. In the blackness he often slipped and cut his knees, and his courage began to **waver**. He had never experienced such blackness before.

waver to feel doubt

Na-gah was soon very tired and decided to turn back.

"Upon the open cliffs I am not afraid," he said to himself. "But this dark hole fills me with fear. I must find a way out."

But when he turned to go back down he found that loose rocks blocked his way; he could not return the way he had come. There was only one way to go—and that was up. He had to continue climbing until he emerged into the light.

After a long time he was able to make out a faint light above him; and he knew he was safe. When he finally emerged into the open, he found himself on the very top of the mountain. He could see great cliffs below him, all the way round. He had only a small platform to move around on, and to gaze down from this great height made him dizzy. Nowhere could he climb down on the outside; and the way back was blocked on the inside.

"Here I must die," he sighed. "But at least I have climbed the mountain."

He found a little grass growing out of the **crevices** and some water in the rock holes. After he had eaten and drunk, he felt better.

About this time, Shinob was out walking across the sky and was surprised to see Na-gah stranded on the mountain peak.

"I will turn him into a *poot-see*," said Shinob, "and he can stand there and shine for everyone to see. He will be a guide for all living things on earth and in the sky."

And so it was. Na-gah became a star that every living thing can see and the only star that will always be found in the same place. Travellers can find their way by him, since unlike the other stars, he stands quite still. And because he is in the north sky, the people call him Qui-am-i Wintook Poot-see, the North Star.

There are other mountain sheep in the sky. They have seen Na-gah on top of the high mountain and try to join him; so they are always moving round and round the mountain, seeking the trail that leads to the top.

What might the darkness surrounding Na-gah be foreshadowing as he climbs?

What do Na-gah's words tell you about him? How is he different from the Tortoise in the African folktale?

Reading Strategy: **Text Structure**

How did setting a purpose for reading help you to better understand the story?

crevices narrow openings

Why the North Star Stands Still   retold by William R. Palmer

Directions Choose the letter of the best answer or write the answer using complete sentences.

Comprehension: Identifying Facts

1. What was Qui-am-i Wintook, the North Star, before becoming a star?
   - **A** Na-gah, the mountain sheep
   - **B** Cooch, the Buffalo
   - **C** Quan-ants, the Eagle
   - **D** Cab-i, the Horse

2. Why can't Na-gah escape from the hole the same way he came in?

3. What does Shinob decide to do when he sees Na-gah on the mountain peak?

Comprehension: Putting Ideas Together

4. What do both Na-gah in the myth and Tortoise in the folktale do?
   - **A** trick other animals
   - **B** hope to enjoy a feast
   - **C** have trouble coming down from a high place
   - **D** become stars in the sky

5. Why doesn't Na-gah climb down from the top of the mountain?

6. How does Na-gah's attitude about his struggles differ from Tortoise's?

Understanding Literature: Foreshadowing

Writers use foreshadowing to give readers a peek into future events in a story. Foreshadowing makes the reader wonder what will happen next. A good example is in "Why the Tortoise's Shell Is Not Smooth." When the birds say Tortoise will make mischief, the reader wonders what he will do.

7. How does the first sentence tell you what you will learn about the North Star?

8. At what point in the story are you first told what will happen to Na-gah?

Critical Thinking

9. How did foreshadowing add to or take away from your enjoyment of this story?

Thinking Creatively

10. Would you behave as Na-gah did if you were facing the same kind of difficulty? Explain.

Grammar Check

All nouns are either common or proper. A common noun names any of a group of people, places, or things. A proper noun names a particular person, place, or thing. Proper nouns are always capitalized. Common nouns are only capitalized in a title or at the beginning of a sentence.

- Common nouns:
  nation   sheep   spirit
- Proper nouns:
  Pahute   Nah-gah   Shinob

Find at least two other common nouns and proper nouns in the story. Write these nouns on a sheet of paper.

 Vocabulary Builder

Synonyms are words that have the same meaning as other words. Use a thesaurus to find a synonym for each of these words from the story.

  brave   sheer   determined
  crevices   stranded

Write the word and its definition on a sheet of paper.

 Writing on Your Own

In this myth, Na-gah is rewarded for his daring climb. In "Why the Tortoise's Shell Is Not Smooth," Tortoise is punished for his actions. What would have been different if Na-gah was punished instead? Try telling the myth of the North Star from a different point of view. In your retelling, have Shinob be angry at Na-gah for climbing the mountain.

 Listening and Speaking

What tone of voice would you use to tell someone this myth? How would you make your voice sound? Would changing the tone depend on the age of your audience? Explain how your tone might affect the people who are listening to you.

 Media and Viewing

What scene from "Why the North Star Stands Still" is most vivid in your mind? What was your favorite scene in "Why the Tortoise's Shell Is Not Smooth"? Picture these scenes in your mind. Then find a way to create pictures of these scenes. Share your pictures with your classmates. In what ways are your pictures alike? In what ways are they different?

Words that have the same root make up a word family. Many English word families are built around Greek roots. Often these roots keep the same spelling in all the words of the word family.

What Can You Learn from the Greek Language?

The words below are part of very common word families built on Greek roots. The Greek root *–tele–* means "far," *–auto–* means "self," and *–cyc–* means "wheel" or "ring." The spelling of these forms does not change from word to word. Keep this in mind when spelling words in the same word families correctly.

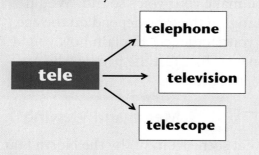

Practice

Read the clues. Then, on your paper write the word from the Word List that matches each clue.

1. a two-wheeler
2. what you might want from a movie star
3. a program shown on a screen
4. the kind of screen you would show the program on
5. works by itself
6. hurricane
7. a way to talk to friends
8. four wheels and a gas pedal
9. reuse
10. something you use to look at the stars

Word List
autograph
automatic
automobile
bicycle
cyclone
recycle
telecast
telephone
telescope
television

Unit 6 introduced you to themes in folk literature. Folk literature began before people could read or write. No one knows who first told these stories. They were passed along through the years by word of mouth. This passing along of stories is called the oral tradition. Folk literature often changes as it passes from place to place and time to time. You may have heard some of the stories in this unit told in different ways.

In this unit you read fables, myths, folktales, and fantasy. Many of these stories told about talking animals, adventure, and magical events. They used personification to make animals and objects seem human. Some taught important lessons about life. Universal themes are messages about life that are understood by most people around the world. Some of these stories tried to explain something about nature. Some of them may have even made you laugh.

Selections

■ "The Tiger Who Would Be King" by James Thurber is a modern fable. Its characters are talking animals, and it ends with a moral.

■ "The Ant and the Dove" by Leo Tolstoy is a retelling of a Russian folktale. Like a fable, it ends with an important lesson about life.

■ "Arachne" by Olivia E. Coolidge retells an ancient Greek myth. It explains where spiders came from.

■ "Mowgli's Brothers" by Rudyard Kipling is an example of fantasy. It tells how a boy ends up growing up among animals in the jungle.

■ "Why the Tortoise's Shell Is Not Smooth" by Chinua Achebe is an African folktale. It presents a funny explanation for something in nature.

■ "The Three Wishes" by Ricardo E. Alegría is a folktale from Puerto Rico. It teaches that greed leads to unhappiness.

■ "Why the North Star Stands Still" is a Paiute myth. It tells how a mountain sheep was turned into the motionless North Star.

Directions Choose the letter of the best answer or write the answer using complete sentences.

Comprehension: Identifying Facts

1. Which story is a myth?
   A "The Tiger Who Would Be King"
   B "The Three Wishes"
   C "Mowgli's Brothers"
   D "Arachne"

2. What lesson does the tiger learn in "The Tiger Who Would Be King"?

3. In Tolstoy's fable, how does the ant help the dove?

4. How does Athene punish Arachne?

5. In "Mowgli's Brothers," who are the Free People?

Comprehension: Putting Ideas Together

6. Which is understood by all kinds of people and gives a message about life?
   A a folktale
   B an example of personification
   C a myth
   D a universal theme

7. In ancient times, what lessons might the story of Arachne have taught the Greeks?

8. Why didn't the birds help Tortoise return home safely?

9. What universal theme is expressed in "The Three Wishes"?

10. In "Why the North Star Stands Still," how does Na-gah serve others after his long climb?

Understanding Literature: Personification

Personification lets nonhuman things speak, think, and act like human beings. In folk literature, animals are often allowed to act like people. Writers may make fun of human foolishness by using animal characters in their stories.

11. Which animal character is punished for tricking others?

12. In what way do the animals in Thurber's fable act like people?

13. Do the wolves in "Mowgli's Brothers" act like humans? Explain.

14. Which animal character is curious and brave but frightened by the dark?

15. In which story do you think the animals act most like people? Why?

Critical Thinking

16. What might world leaders learn from the moral in Thurber's fable?

17. What lesson about real life can be learned from the myth of Arachne?

18. In what important ways are Father Wolf and Shere Khan different?

19. In "Why the Tortoise's Shell Is Not Smooth," do you admire Tortoise for his cleverness? Why or why not?

Thinking Creatively

20. Which story do you think offers the most important message? Explain your choice.

Speak and Listen

Choose a story that might be fun to act out. Work in a group to prepare an oral presentation of the story. Figure out how many actors you need for your presentation. Give the actors time to practice reading their parts together aloud. Then present the story to the class.

Writing on Your Own

Write a fable to express one of the following morals:

- *Look before you leap.*
- *The early bird gets the worm.*
- *Don't count your chickens before they hatch.*
- *Treat others as you would have them treat you.*

When your work is complete, share it with the class.

Beyond Words

Make a collage to show a scene from the story you liked best. Use pictures and words from magazines, the Internet, and your own drawings to complete this project.

Test-Taking Tip

After you have finished a test, reread the questions and your answers. Ask yourself: Do my answers show that I understood the questions?

Research: Research Report

A research report presents information gathered from several trustworthy sources. Sources might include newspapers, books, informational Web sites, and magazines. A research report includes a bibliography—a list of all sources that were used. Follow the steps in this workshop to write your own research report.

Assignment Write a research report to gain more knowledge about a topic that interests you.

What to Include To succeed, your research report should:

- be about a topic that is narrow enough to cover well
- have a strong beginning that clearly states the topic
- use examples and explanations from trustworthy sources to support the main ideas
- be well organized
- include a clear and complete listing of all sources
- show proper grammar, spelling, and punctuation

Prewriting

Choosing Your Topic

- **Browsing** Browse through reference books at a library, such as an encyclopedia. Jot down each person, place, object, or event that interests you. Then scan your notes and circle any words or phrases that suggest a good topic.

- **Make a List** Jot down a few examples of interesting people, historic events, inventions, and places. Then, choose a topic from this list.

Narrowing Your Topic

Use a graphic organizer. Make sure that your topic is not too broad to cover well. Narrow your topic by using a graphic organizer like the Structured Overview. The top row should state the general topic. Each row below that should contain smaller and smaller parts of your general topic.

Using the Form
Research skills are useful in these writing situations:

- history and science reports
- newspaper or magazine articles
- informative essays and speeches

Six Traits of Writing:

Ideas message, details, and purpose

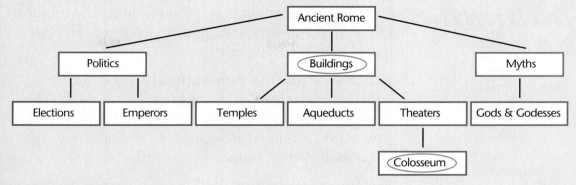

Gathering Details

Take notes from several different sources. Try to use some primary sources. These are firsthand accounts of information, such as speeches, photographs, newspaper articles, and interviews. Secondary sources, such as encyclopedia articles, are based on primary sources.

Use source cards and note cards to keep track of the information you gather.

- On each source card, write the title, author, publication date and place, and page numbers.

- On each note card, write down information to use in your report. Use quotation marks when you copy words exactly. Note the page number on which the quotation appears. In most cases, use your own words.

Writing Your Draft

Shaping Your Writing

Organize your research report. Arrange your notes into groups to break your topic into subtopics. For example, if you are writing about the Colosseum, you might use these topics in your outline: *architecture, construction, events held, spectators.*

Six Traits of Writing:
Organization order, ideas tied together

I. Introduction
II. Architecture of
    Colosseum
    A. measurements
    B. building material

III. Construction of
    Colosseum
    A. beginning date
    B. workers

IV. Conclusion

Use Roman numerals (I, II, III) to number the subtopics. Use at least two letters (A, B) to show details and facts included in each subtopic.

Match your draft to your outline. A good outline will guide you through the writing of your draft. The headings with Roman numerals are the main sections of your report. You may need to write several paragraphs to cover each Roman numeral topic fully.

Providing Elaboration

Support main ideas with facts. Using your outline, write sentences to express each main idea in your report. Use the information on your note cards to fill in the details.

Prepare to cite your sources. Use your own words to write the ideas you found in your sources. Do not plagiarize, or present another person's work as your own. As you write, circle ideas that come from your sources. Note the author's last name and the page numbers of the material used. You can use this information later when you list your sources.

Revising
Revising Your Paragraphs

Now that you have explored ideas and written a draft, it is time to revise. During this step, you will rewrite parts of your report. All good writing goes through many drafts. Each paragraph of your report should have:

- a topic sentence (T) stating the paragraph's main idea
- a restatement (R) of the topic sentence
- strong illustrations (I), including facts, examples, or details about the main idea

Look over your draft. Mark each of your sentences a *T*, *R*, or *I*. A paragraph containing a group of *I*'s should have a strong *T* that they support. If you find a *T* by itself, add *I*'s to support it.

Revising Your Word Choice

Help your readers to understand and enjoy your report.
Explain difficult words or add context clues to make these
words easier to understand.

Difficult: A popular show at the Roman Colosseum featured
gladiators.

Context Clue: A popular show at the Roman Colosseum
featured gladiators. These trained fighters often faced other
men or even wild animals.

Editing and Proofreading

Review your report and correct mistakes in spelling and
grammar.

Check the facts: Review the names of the authors that you
quote. Also check the names of the books, articles, or other
sources that you used.

Publishing and Presenting

Consider one of these ways to publish and present your
report:

Create a bibliography or works-cited list. A works-cited page
gives readers complete information on each source you used.
Follow the format your teacher prefers and check that each
entry is complete.

Create a mini-lesson. Use your report to plan a short lesson
on your topic. Present your lesson to a group of classmates.

Reflecting on Your Writing

Writer's Journal Jot down a few notes on writing a research
report. Begin by answering these questions:

- What was the most interesting thing that you learned about
  your topic?
- Which source gave you the most useful information?

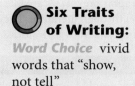

**Six Traits
of Writing:**
Word Choice vivid
words that "show,
not tell"

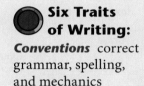

**Six Traits
of Writing:**
Conventions correct
grammar, spelling,
and mechanics

Appendix A: Graphic Organizers

Graphic organizers are like maps. They help guide you through literature. They can also help you plan or "map out" your own stories, research, or presentations.

1. Character Analysis Guide

This graphic organizer helps you learn more about a character in a selection.

To use: Choose a character. List four traits of that character. Write down an event from the selection that shows each character trait.

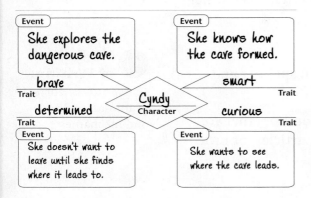

2. Story Map

This graphic organizer helps you summarize a story that you have read or plan your own story.

To use: List the title, setting, and characters. Describe the main problem of the story and the events that explain the problem. Then write how the problem is solved.

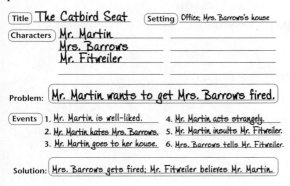

3. Main Idea Graphic (Umbrella)

This graphic organizer helps you determine the main idea of a selection or of a paragraph in the selection.

To use: List the main idea of a selection. Then, write the details that show or support the main idea of the story.

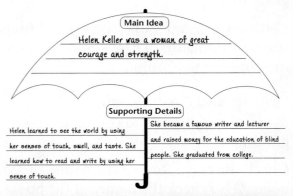

4. Main Idea Graphic (Table)

This graphic organizer is another way to determine the main idea of a selection or of a paragraph in the selection. Just like a table is held up by four strong legs, a main idea is held up or supported by many details.

To use: Write the main idea of a selection or paragraph on the tabletop. Then, write the details that show or support the main idea of the selection or paragraph on the table legs.

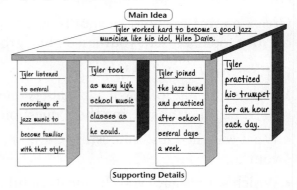

5. Main Idea Graphic (Details)

This graphic organizer is also a way to determine the main idea of a selection or of a paragraph in the selection. If the main idea of a selection or paragraph is not clear, add the details together to find it.

To use: First, list the supporting details of the selection or paragraph. Then, write one sentence that summarizes all the events. That is the main idea of the story.

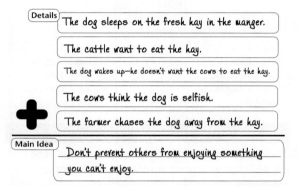

Details
- The dog sleeps on the fresh hay in the manger.
- The cattle want to eat the hay.
- The dog wakes up—he doesn't want the cows to eat the hay.
- The cows think the dog is selfish.
- The farmer chases the dog away from the hay.

Main Idea
Don't prevent others from enjoying something you can't enjoy.

6. Venn Diagram

This graphic organizer can help you compare and contrast two stories, characters, events, or topics.

To use: List the things that are common to both stories, events, characters, and so on in the "similarities" area between the circles. List the differences on the parts that do not overlap.

What is being compared? _____

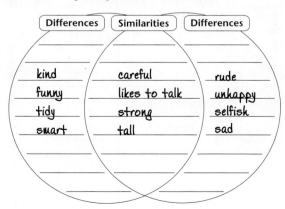

Differences	Similarities	Differences
kind	careful	rude
funny	likes to talk	unhappy
tidy	strong	selfish
smart	tall	sad

7. Sequence Chain

This graphic organizer outlines a series of events in the order in which they happen. This is helpful when summarizing the plot of a story. This graphic organizer may also help you plan your own story.

To use: Fill in the box at the top with the title of the story. Then, in the boxes below, record the events in the order in which they happen in the story. Write a short sentence in each box and only include the major events of the story.

Sequence Chain for: __Cinderella__

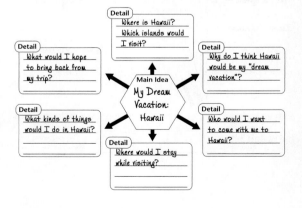

1. Cinderella lives with her father and evil stepmother and stepsisters.

2. She is ordered to do chores and to wait on her stepmother and stepsisters all day.

8. The Prince searches the kingdom looking for the owner of the glass slipper.

9. The Prince finds that the slipper belongs to Cinderella, and they marry.

8. Concept Map

This graphic organizer helps you to organize supporting details for a story or research topic.

To use: Write the topic in the center of the graphic organizer. List ideas that support the topic on the lines. Group similar ideas and details together.

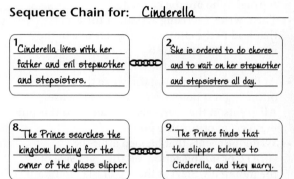

Detail
Where is Hawaii? Which islands would I visit?

Detail
What would I hope to bring back from my trip?

Detail
Why do I think Hawaii would be my "dream vacation"?

Main Idea
My Dream Vacation: Hawaii

Detail
What kinds of things would I do in Hawaii?

Detail
Who would I want to come with me to Hawaii?

Detail
Where would I stay while visiting?

9. Plot Mountain

This graphic organizer helps you organize the events of a story or plot. There are five parts in a story's plot: the exposition, the rising action, the climax, the falling action, and the resolution (or denouement). These parts represent the beginning, middle, and end of the selection.

To use:

- Write the exposition, or how the selection starts, at the left base of the mountain. What is the setting? Who are the characters?
- Then, write the rising action, or the events that lead to the climax, on the left side of the mountain. Start at the base and list the events in time order going up the left side.
- At the top of the mountain, write the climax, or the highest point of interest or suspense. All events in the rising action lead up to this one main event or turning point.
- Write the events that happen after the climax, or falling action, on the right side of the mountain. Start at the top of the mountain, or climax, and put the events in time order going down the right-hand side.
- Finally, write the resolution, or denouement, at the right base of the mountain. The resolution explains how the problem, or conflict, in the story is solved or how the story ends.

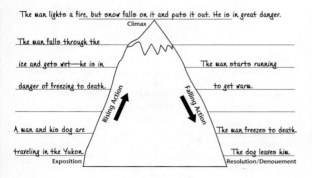

10. Structured Overview

This graphic organizer shows you how a main idea branches out in a selection.

To use: Write the main idea of a selection in the top box. Then, branch out and list events and details that support the main idea. Continue to branch off more boxes as needed to fill in the details of the story.

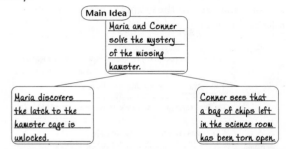

11. Semantic Table

This graphic organizer can help you understand the differences among words that have similar meanings.

To use: Choose a topic. List nouns for that topic in the top row. Put adjectives that describe your topic in the first column. Then, fill in the rest of the grid by checking those adjectives that are appropriate for the nouns. That way, in your writing, you can use words that make sense for your story.

Topic: __Homes__

Adjectives Nouns→	apartment	4-bedroom home	cabin
large	—	✔	—
expensive	—	✔	—
quiet	—	✔	✔

12. Prediction Guide

This graphic organizer can be used to predict, or try to figure out, how a selection might end. Before finishing a selection, fill in this guide.

To use: List the time, place, and characters in the selection. Write what the problem, or conflict, is in the story. Then, try to predict possible endings or solutions. Compare your predictions with others.

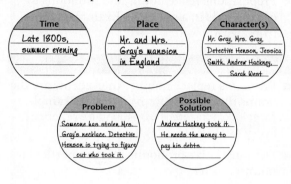

Time	Place	Character(s)
Late 1800s, summer evening	Mr. and Mrs. Gray's mansion in England	Mr. Gray, Mrs. Gray, Detective Henson, Jessica Smith, Andrew Hackney, Sarah West

Problem	Possible Solution
Someone has stolen Mrs. Gray's necklace. Detective Henson is trying to figure out who took it.	Andrew Hackney took it. He needs the money to pay his debts.

13. Semantic Line

This graphic organizer can help you think of synonyms for words that are used too often in writing.

To use: At the end of each line, write two overused words that mean the opposite. Then, fill in the lines with words of similar meaning. In the example below, the opposite words are *beautiful* and *ugly*. Words that are closer in meaning to beautiful are at the top. Words that are closer in meaning to ugly are at the bottom. The word *plain* falls in the middle.

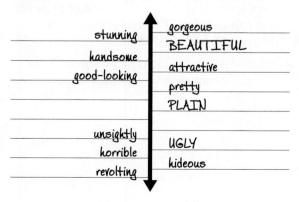

stunning	gorgeous
	BEAUTIFUL
handsome	
good-looking	attractive
	pretty
	PLAIN
unsightly	
horrible	UGLY
revolting	hideous

14. KWL Chart

This graphic organizer can help you learn about a topic before you start reading a selection or conducting research.

To use: Before you start reading a selection or conducting research, fill in the organizer. Write the topic on the line. In the first column, write what you already *know* (K) about your topic. Next, list what you *want* (W) to know about your topic in the next column. Then, as you start reading a selection or conducting research, write down what you *learn* (L) in the last column.

Topic: __Mount Everest__

K What I Know	W What I Want to Know	L What I Have Learned
It's a tall mountain in Asia. People may have tried to climb it. It's part of a larger mountain chain. It's one of the most famous mountains in the world.	How tall is it? Is it the tallest? What mountain chain is it part of?	It is the tallest in the world. It is part of the Himalayas. People have climbed it before. Some people have died trying.

Appendix B: Grammar

Parts of Speech

Adjectives

- Adjectives describe nouns and pronouns. They answer *What kind? Which one? How many?* or *How much?* Example: The *new* book costs *five* dollars.

- Comparative adjectives compare two nouns and usually end in *–er*. Example: *newer*

- Superlative adjectives compare three or more nouns and usually end in *–est*. Example: *newest*

Adverbs

- Adverbs modify verbs, adjectives, and other adverbs. They answer *When? How? How often?* and *How long?* Many adverbs end in *–ly*. Example: She laughed *loudly*.

Conjunctions

- Conjunctions connect parts of a sentence.

- Coordinating conjunctions connect two equal parts of a sentence using words like *and, but, nor, or, for, yet, so,* and *as well as.* Example: Do you want milk *or* water?

- Correlative conjunctions are used in pairs and connect equal parts of a sentence. Correlative conjunctions are *both/and, neither/nor, either/or, but/also.* Example: The teenagers had *neither* the time *nor* the money.

- Subordinating conjunctions connect two unequal parts of a sentence using words like *after, although, before, because, since, if, unless, while.* Example: *Since* you are arriving late, we will eat dinner at 7 p.m.

Interjections

- Interjections are words or phrases that show strong feeling, often followed by exclamation points. Examples: Wow! Ouch! Oops!

Nouns

- A noun names a person, place, thing, or idea.

- Proper nouns are names that are capitalized. Examples: Susan, New York

Prepositions

- Prepositions relate nouns and pronouns to other words in a sentence. Examples: above, from, with

Pronouns

- Pronouns replace nouns. Antecedents are the nouns that the pronouns replace. Example: Jorge takes karate lessons, and *he* practices every week.

- Demonstrative pronouns identify particular nouns: *this* hat, *those* shoes

- Indefinite pronouns do not refer to particular nouns. Examples: all, everyone, none

- Interrogative pronouns begin questions. Examples: who, which, what

- Personal pronouns refer to people or things. Examples: I, me, you, it, he, she, we, us, they, him, her, them

- Possessive pronouns show ownership. Examples: my, mine, his, hers, its, our, yours, their, ours, theirs

- Reflexive pronouns follow a verb or preposition and refer to the noun or pronoun that comes before. Examples: myself, themselves, himself, herself

- Relative pronouns introduce a subordinate clause. Examples: who, whom, whose, which, that, what

Verbs

- Verbs show action or express states of being.

- If the verbs are *transitive*, they link the action to something or someone. Example: John *hit* the ball. Action verbs that are *intransitive* do not link the action to something or someone. Example: The ball *flew*.

- Linking verbs connect a subject with a word or words that describe it. Some linking verbs are *am, are, was, were, is,* and *be*. Example: Susan *is* student council president.

Grammar Glossary

Active and Passive Voice

- Active voice is when the subject is *doing* the action. A sentence written in active voice is often shorter and easier to understand. Example: Jane drove the car to school.

- Passive voice is when the subject *receives* the action. A sentence written in passive voice can be awkward. Use a passive sentence only when the doer is unknown or unnecessary. Example: The car was driven by Jane.

Antecedent

- An antecedent is the noun or pronoun that a pronoun refers to in a sentence. Example: *Kevin* ran for Student Council so that *he* could help improve the school. *Kevin* is the antecedent for the pronoun *he*.

Appositives

- An appositive is a noun or pronoun that follows another noun or pronoun. An appositive renames or adds detail about the word. Example: Mr. Smith, *our principal*, is a great leader.

Clauses

- A clause is a group of words that contains a subject and a verb. There are independent and dependent clauses.

- An independent clause can stand alone because it expresses a complete thought. Example: Our dog eats twice a day. She also walks two miles a day. Two independent clauses can also be joined to form one sentence by using a comma and a coordinating conjunction, such as *and, but, nor, or, for, yet, so,* and *as well as.* Example: Our dog eats twice a day, *and* she walks two miles a day.

- A dependent clause cannot stand alone because it does not express a complete thought. Example: Because exercise is good for pets. This is a fragment or incomplete sentence. To fix this, combine a dependent clause with an independent clause. Example: Our dog walks two miles a day because exercise is good for pets.

Complements

- A complement completes the meaning of a verb. There are three types of complements: direct objects, indirect objects, and subject complements.

- A direct object is a word or group of words that receives the action of the verb. Example: Jane set the table. (*The table* is the complement or direct object of the verb *set*.)

- An indirect object is a word or group of words that follow the verb and tell for whom or what the action is done. An indirect object always comes before a direct object in a sentence. Example: Setting the table saved her mother some time. (*Her mother* is the complement or indirect object of the verb *saved*.)

- A subject complement is a word or group of words that further identify the subject of a sentence. A subject complement always follows a linking verb. Example: Buddy is the best dog. (The word *dog* is the complement of the subject *Buddy*.)

Contractions

- A contraction is two words made into one by replacing one or more letters with an apostrophe. Examples: *didn't* (did not), *you're* (you are)

Double Negatives

- A double negative is the use of two negative words, such as *no* or *not*, in a sentence. To fix a double negative, make one word positive. Incorrect: She *did not* get *no* dessert after dinner. Correct: She did not get *any* dessert after dinner.

Fragments

- A fragment is not a complete sentence. It may have a subject and verb, but it does not express a complete thought. Incorrect: The leaves that fell in the yard. Correct: The leaves that fell in the yard needed to be raked.

Gerunds

- A gerund is a verb with an *–ing* ending. It is used as a noun. Example: *Golfing* is fun! Here, *golfing* is a noun and the subject of the sentence.

Infinitives

- An infinitive is the word *to* plus the present tense of a verb. An infinitive can be a noun, adjective, or adverb in a sentence. Example: *To write* was her dream job. Here, *To write* is the infinitive, and it serves as a noun.

Modifiers

- A modifier is a word or group of words that change the meanings of other words in the sentence. Adjectives and adverbs are modifiers.

- A dangling or misplaced modifier is a group of descriptive words that is not near the word it modifies. This confuses the reader. Incorrect: Tucked up in the closet, Sarah found her grandma's photographs. *Tucked up in the closet* modifies Sarah. However, the photographs, not Sarah, are tucked up in the closet! Correct: Sarah found her grandma's photographs tucked up in the closet.

Parallel Structure

- Parallel structure is the use of words to balance ideas that are equally important. Incorrect: In the winter, I love to skate, snowmen, and to ski. Correct: In the winter, I love *to skate*, *to make* snowmen, and *to ski*.

Phrases

- A phrase is a group of words that does not have both a subject and a verb. Types of phrases include gerund phrases, infinitive phrases, and participial phrases.

- A gerund phrase has a gerund plus any modifiers and complements. The entire phrase serves as a noun. Example: Playing basketball with his friends was Trevor's favorite pastime. *Playing basketball with his friends* is the gerund phrase.

- An infinitive phrase has an infinitive plus any modifiers and complements. The entire phrase serves as a noun, adjective, or adverb in a sentence. Example: My mother liked to bake cookies on the weekend. *To bake cookies on the weekend* is the infinitive phrase.

- A participial phrase has a participle (a verb in its present form [*–ing*] or past form [*–ed or –en*]) plus all of its modifiers and complements. The entire phrase serves as an adjective in a sentence. Example: Wearing the robes of a king, Luis read his lines perfectly during play tryouts. *Wearing the robes of a king* is the participial phrase, and it modifies or describes the subject, Luis.

Plural Nouns

- A plural shows more than one of a particular noun. Use the following rules to create the plural form. Remember that there are exceptions to many spelling rules that you must simply memorize.

- Add –s to most singular nouns. Example: table/tables

- Add –es to a noun if it ends in –ch, –sh, –s, –x, and –z. Example: chur<u>ch</u>/churches

- If a noun ends with a vowel and a –y, add an –s to make the plural. Example: donk<u>ey</u>/donkeys

- If a noun ends with a consonant and a –y, drop the –y and add an –ies to make the plural. Example: pup<u>py</u>/puppies

- If a noun ends in an –f or –fe, change the –f or –fe to a v and add –es. Example: kni<u>fe</u>/knives

- If a noun ends in an –o, sometimes you add –es and sometimes you add –s. Look in a dictionary to find out. Examples: potat<u>o</u>/potatoes, rad<u>io</u>/radios

Possessives

- A possessive noun shows ownership of an object, action, or idea. A possessive noun ends in 's. Example: Susan's book

- A possessive pronoun also shows ownership of an object, action, or idea. Example: his glove

Pronoun–Antecedent Agreement

- Pronoun-antecedent agreement occurs when the pronoun matches the antecedent (the word it refers to) in gender and number.

- To agree in gender:
  –Replace the name of a male person with a masculine pronoun. Example: *Jake* ran down the field, and *he* scored.

  –Replace the name of a female person with a feminine pronoun. Example: *Ana* read "The Most Dangerous Game," and *she* loved it.

  –Replace singular names with *it* or *its*. Example: The *kitten* ran through the room, and *it* pounced on the ball.

  –Replace plural names with *they, them,* or *their.* Example: The *tenth graders* came into the gym, and *they* played volleyball.

- To agree in number:

  –Make the pronoun singular if its antecedent is singular. Example: *Michael* told *himself* that he did the right thing.

  –Make the pronoun plural if its antecedent is plural. Example: The hungry *teenagers* ordered sandwiches for *themselves*.

Run-on Sentences

- A run-on sentence is the combination of two or more sentences without proper punctuation.

- To correct a run-on sentence, you can break it into two or more sentences by using capital letters and periods. Incorrect: The house was built in 1960 it needs new windows. Correct: The house was built in 1960. It needs new windows.

- You can also correct a run-on sentence by adding a comma and a coordinating conjunction to separate the sentences. Correct: The house was built in 1960, *so* it needs new windows.

- Another way to correct a run-on sentence is by adding a semicolon between the sentences. A semicolon should stand alone and should not have a coordinating conjunction after it. Correct: The house was built in 1960; it needs new windows.

Sentence Construction

- A simple sentence has one independent clause that includes a subject and a predicate. Example: The afternoon was warm and sunny.

- A compound sentence has two or more independent clauses joined by a comma and a coordinating conjunction or joined by a semicolon. Example: The afternoon was warm and sunny, so we decided to drive to the beach.

- A complex sentence has one independent clause and one or more dependent clauses. Example: We are going to the beach if you want to come along.

- A compound–complex sentence has two or more independent clauses joined by a comma and a coordinating conjunction. It has at least one dependent clause. Example: Although the morning was cold and damp, the afternoon was warm and sunny, so we decided to drive to the beach.

Sentence Types

- You can use a declarative sentence, an exclamatory sentence, an imperative sentence, or an interrogative sentence in writing.

- A declarative sentence tells us something about a person, place, or thing. This type of sentence ends with a period. Example: Martin Luther King Jr. fought for civil rights.

- An exclamatory sentence shows strong feeling or surprise. This type of sentence ends with an exclamation point. Example: I can't believe the price of gasoline!

- An imperative sentence gives commands. This type of sentence ends with a period. (Note: The subject of an imperative sentence is the implied "you.") Example: Please read chapter two by next Monday.

- An interrogative sentence asks a question. This type of sentence ends with a question mark. Example: Will you join us for dinner?

Subjects and Predicates

- The subject of a sentence names the person or thing doing the action. The subject contains a noun or a pronoun. Example: The students created posters and brochures. The subject of this sentence is *The students*. The predicate of this sentence (see definition below) is *created posters and brochures*.

- The predicate of a sentence tells what the person or thing is doing. The predicate contains a verb. Example: The fans waited for the hockey game to begin. The predicate of this sentence is *waited for the hockey game to begin*. The subject of this sentence is *The fans*.

Punctuation Guidelines

Apostrophe

- Shows ownership (possessive nouns): Kelly's backpack

- Shows plural possessive nouns: The five students' success was due to hard work.

- Shows missing letters in contractions: that's (that is)

Colon

- Introduces a list after a complete sentence: We learned about planets: Mars, Venus, and Jupiter.

- Adds or explains more about a complete sentence: Lunch was one option: pizza.

- Follows the salutation in a formal letter or in a business letter: Dear Mr. Jackson:
- Separates the hour and the minute: 2:15
- Introduces a long quotation: Lincoln wrote: "Four score and seven years ago . . ."

Comma

- Separates three or more items in a series: We planted corn, squash, and tomatoes.
- Joins two independent clauses when used with a coordinating conjunction: Sam and Raul did their homework, and then they left.
- Separates a city and state: Los Angeles, California
- Separates a day and year: October 15, 2006
- Follows the salutation and closing in a friendly letter: Dear Shanice, Love always,
- Follows the closing in a business letter: Sincerely,
- Sets off a restrictive phrase clause: Angela, the youngest runner, won the race.
- Sets off an introductory phrase or clause: Before he started the experiment, Jason put on safety glasses.

Dash

- Sets off an explanation in a sentence: The three poets—Langston Hughes, Robert Frost, and William Carlos Williams—are modernist poets.
- Shows a pause or break in thought: After years away, I returned—and found lots had changed.

Ellipses

- Show that words have been left out of a text: Our dog dove into the lake . . . and swam to shore.

Exclamation Point

- Shows emotion: Our team won!

Hyphen

- Divides a word at the end of a line: We enjoyed the beaches.
- Separates a compound adjective before a noun to make its meaning clearer: much-loved book
- Separates a compound number: thirty-three.
- Separates a fraction when used as an adjective: two-thirds full

Period

- Marks the end of a statement or command: July is the warmest month.
- Follows most abbreviations: Mrs., Dr., Inc., Jr.

Question Mark

- Marks the end of a question: How many eggs are left?

Quotation Marks

- Enclose the exact words of a speaker: He said, "I'll buy that book."
- Enclose the titles of short works: "Dover Beach," "America the Beautiful"

Semicolon

- Separates items in a series when commas are within the items: We went to Sioux Falls, South Dakota; Des Moines, Iowa; and Kansas City, Kansas.
- Joins two independent clauses that are closely related: We went to the movie; they came with us.

Capitalization Guidelines

Capitalize:

- the first word of a sentence: The teacher asked her students to read.
- the first word and any important words in a title: *To Kill a Mockingbird*
- all proper nouns: Marlon Smith, Atlanta, March
- the pronoun *I*
- languages: English, French
- abbreviations: Mrs., Sgt., FDR, EST

Commonly Confused Words

accept, except

- *Accept* (verb) means "to receive." Example: The children will *accept* ice cream.
- *Except* (preposition) means "leaving out." Example: The children enjoyed all flavors *except* strawberry.

affect, effect

- *Affect* (verb) means "to have an effect on." Example: This storm will *affect* our town.
- *Effect* (noun) means "a result or an outcome." Example: The *effect* was a struggling local economy.

its, it's

- *Its* (adjective) is the possessive form of "it." Example: Our hamster liked to run on the wheel inside *its* cage.
- *It's* is a contraction for "it is." Example: *It's* a long time before lunch.

lie, lay

- *Lie* (verb) means "to rest." Example: Jenny had a headache, so she needed to *lie* down.
- *Lay* (verb) means "to place." Example: Jamal went to *lay* his baseball glove on the bench.

lose, loose

- *Lose* (verb) means "to misplace or not find something." Example: I always *lose* my sunglasses when I go to the beach.
- *Loose* (adjective) means "free or without limits." Example: Someone let Sparky *loose* from his leash.

than, then

- *Than* (conjunction) shows a comparison. Example: You are older *than* I am.
- *Then* (adverb) means "at that time." Example: Will turned the doorknob and *then* slowly opened the door.

their, there, they're

- *Their* (pronoun) shows possession. Example: This is *their* house.
- *There* (adverb) means "place." Example: Sit over *there*.
- *They're* is a contraction for "they are." Example: *They're* coming over for dinner.

to, too, two

- *To* (preposition) shows purpose, movement, or connection. Example: We drove *to* the store.
- *Too* (adverb) means "also or more than wanted." Example: I, *too*, felt it was *too* hot to go outside.
- *Two* is a number. Example: Ava has *two* more years of high school.

your, you're

- *Your* (adjective) shows possession and means "belonging to you." Example: Take off *your* hat, please.
- *You're* is a contraction for "you are." Example: *You're* the best artist in the school.

Types of Writing

Before you can begin the writing process, you need to understand the types, purposes, and formats of different types of writing.

Descriptive Writing

Descriptive writing covers all writing genres. Description can be used to tell a story, to analyze and explain research, or to persuade. Descriptive writing uses images and colorful details to "paint a picture" for the reader.

Five Senses in Descriptive Writing

Consider the five senses in your descriptive writing: sight, smell, touch, sound, and taste. Using your senses to help describe an object, place, or person makes your writing more interesting. Before you begin, ask yourself the following:

- How does something look? Describe the color, size, and/or shape. What is it like?

- What smell or smells are present? Describe any pleasant or unpleasant smells. Compare the smells to other smells you know.

- How does something feel? Think about textures. Also think about emotions or feelings that result from the touching.

- What sounds do you hear? Describe the volume and the pitch. Are the sounds loud and shrill, or quiet and peaceful? What do the sounds remind you of?

- What does something taste like? Compare it to a taste you know, good or bad.

Expository Writing

Expository writing explains and informs through essays, articles, reports, and instructions. Like descriptive writing, it covers all writing genres. The purpose of this type of writing is to give more information about a subject. This can be done in many ways. The two most common formats in the study of literature are the compare and contrast paper and the cause and effect paper.

- Compare and Contrast Paper—This paper shows the similarities and differences of two or more characters, objects, settings, situations, writing styles, problems, or ideas.

- Cause and Effect Paper—This paper explains why certain things happen or how specific actions led to a result. A cause and effect paper can be set up by writing about the result (effect) first, followed by the events that led up to it (causes). Or, the paper can trace the events (causes), in order, that lead up to the result (effect).

Narrative Writing

Narrative writing tells a story. The story can be true (nonfiction) or made up (fiction). Narratives entertain or inform readers about a series of events. Poetry, stories, diaries, letters, biographies, and autobiographies are all types of narrative writing.

Key Elements in Narrative Writing

Think about the type of narrative you want to write and these key elements of your story:

- Characters: Who are the major and minor characters in the story? What do they look like? How do they act?

- Dialogue: What conversations take place among the characters? How does the dialogue show the reader something about the personalities of the characters?

- Setting: Where and when do the events take place? How does the setting affect the plot?

- Plot: What events happen in the story? In what order do the events occur? What is the problem that the main character is struggling with? How is the problem solved?

There are two common ways to set up your narrative paper. You can start at the beginning and tell your story in chronological order, or in the order in which the events happened. Or, you can start at the ending of your story and, through a flashback, tell what events led up to the present time.

Persuasive Writing

Persuasive writing is used when you want to convince your reader that your opinion on a topic is the right one. The goal of this paper is to have your reader agree with what you say. To do this, you need to know your topic well, and you need to give lots of reasons and supporting details. Editorials (opinion writing) in the newspaper, advertisements, and book reviews are all types of persuasive writing.

Key Elements of Persuasive Writing

Choosing a topic that you know well and that you feel strongly about is important for persuasive writing. The feelings or emotions that you have about the topic will come through in your paper and make a stronger argument. Also, be sure that you have a good balance between appealing to the reader's mind (using facts, statistics, experts, and so on) and appealing to the reader's heart (using words that make them feel angry, sad, and so on). Think about these key elements:

- Topic: Is your topic a good one for your audience? Do you know a lot about your topic? Is your topic narrow enough so that you can cover it in a paper?

- Opinion: Is your opinion clear? Do you know enough about the opposite side of your opinion to get rid of those arguments in your paper?

- Reasons: Do you have at least three reasons that explain why you feel the way you do? Are these reasons logical?

- Supporting details or evidence: Do you have facts, statistics, experts, or personal experience that can support each reason?

- Opposing arguments: Can you address the opposite side and get rid of their arguments?

- Conclusion: Can you offer a solution or recommendation to the reader?

- Word choice: Can you find words that set the tone for your opinion? Will these words affect your readers emotionally?

There are two common ways to set up this paper. The first format is a six-paragraph paper: one paragraph for your introduction, three paragraphs for each of your three reasons, one paragraph for the opposing arguments and your responses to them, and one paragraph for your conclusion. Or you can write a five-paragraph paper where you place the opposing arguments and responses to each of your three reasons within the same paragraphs.

Research Report

A research report is an in-depth study of a topic. This type of writing has many uses in all subjects. It involves digging for information in many sources, including books, magazines, newspapers, the Internet, almanacs, encyclopedias, and other places of data. There are many key elements in writing a research report. Choosing a thesis statement, finding support or evidence for that thesis, and citing where you found your information are all important.

There are several uses of a research report in literature. You can explore a writer's life, a particular writing movement, or a certain writer's style. You could also write about a selection.

Business Writing

Business writing has many forms: memos, meeting minutes, brochures, manuals, reports, job applications, contracts, college essays. No matter what the format, the goal of business writing is clear communication. Keep the following key elements in mind when you are doing business writing:

- Format: What type of writing are you doing?

- Purpose: What is the purpose of your writing? Is the purpose clear in your introduction?

- Audience: Are your words and ideas appropriate for your audience?

- Organization: Are your ideas well-organized and easy to follow?

- Style: Are your ideas clearly written and to the point?

The Writing Process

The writing process is a little different for each writer and for each writing assignment. However, the goals of writing never change: Writers want to:

- have a purpose for their writing

- get their readers' attention and keep it

- present their ideas clearly

- choose their words carefully

To meet these goals, writers need to move through a writing process. This process allows them to explore, organize, write, revise, and share their ideas. There are five steps to this writing process: prewriting; drafting; revising; editing and proofreading; and publishing and evaluating.

Use the following steps for any writing assignment:

Step 1: Prewriting

Prewriting is where you explore ideas and decide what to write about. Here are some approaches.

Brainstorming

Brainstorming is fast, fun, and full of ideas. Start by stating a topic. Then write down everything you can think of about that topic. Ask questions about the topic. If you are in a group, have one person write everything down. Think of as many words and ideas as you can in a short time. Don't worry about neatness, spelling, or grammar. When you are finished, group words that are similar. These groups may become your supporting ideas.

Graphic Organizers

Graphic organizers are maps that can lead you through your prewriting. They provide pictures or charts that you fill in. Read the descriptions of these organizers in Appendix A, and choose the ones that will help you organize your ideas.

Outline

An outline can help you organize your information. Write your main ideas next to each Roman numeral. Write your supporting details next to the letters under each Roman numeral. Keep your ideas brief and to the point. Here's an example to follow:

Topic for persuasive paper: Lincoln High School should have a swimming pool.

I. Health benefits for students
   A. Weight control
   B. Good exercise
II. Water safety benefits for students
   A. Learn-to-swim programs
   B. Water safety measures to help others
III. School benefits
   A. Swim team
   B. Added rotation for gym class
IV. Community benefits
   A. More physically fit community members
   B. More jobs for community members

Narrowing Your Topic

Narrowing your topic means to focus your ideas on a specific area. You may be interested in writing about Edgar Allan Poe, but that is a broad topic. What about Poe interests you? Think about your purpose for writing. Is your goal to persuade, to explain, or to compare? Narrowing your scope and knowing your purpose will keep you focused.

Note-Taking and Research

Refer to the "How to Use This Book" section at the beginning of this textbook and Appendix D for help with note-taking and research skills.

Planning Your Voice

Your voice is your special way of using language in your writing. Readers can get to know your personality and thoughts by your sentence structure, word choice, and tone. How will your writing tell what you want to say in your own way? How will it be different from the way others write?

Step 2: Drafting

In the drafting step, you will write your paper. Use your brainstorming notes, outline, and graphic organizers from your prewriting stage as your guide. Your paper will need to include an introduction, a body, and a conclusion.

Introduction

The introduction states your topic and purpose. It includes a *thesis statement,* which is a sentence that tells the main idea of your entire paper. The last line of your introduction is a good place for your thesis statement. That way, your reader has a clear idea of the purpose of your paper before starting to read your points.

Your introduction should make people want to read more. Think about what your audience might like. Try one of these methods:

- asking a question
- sharing a brief story
- describing something
- giving a surprising fact
- using an important quotation

When you begin drafting, just write your introduction. Do not try to make it perfect the first time. You can always change it later.

Body

The body of your paper is made up of several paragraphs. Each paragraph also has a topic sentence, supporting details, and a concluding statement or summary. Remember, too, that each paragraph needs to support your thesis statement in your introduction.

- The topic sentence is usually the first sentence of a paragraph. It lets the reader know what your paragraph is going to be about.

- The supporting details of a paragraph are the sentences that support or tell more about your topic sentence. They can include facts, explanations, examples, statistics, and/or experts' ideas.

- The last sentence of your paragraph is a concluding statement or summary. A concluding statement is a judgment. It is based on the facts that you presented in your paragraph. A summary briefly repeats the main ideas of your paragraph. It repeats your idea or ideas in slightly different words. It does not add new information.

Conclusion

The conclusion ties together the main ideas of the paper. If you asked a question in your introduction, the conclusion answers it. If you outlined a problem, your conclusion offers solutions. The conclusion should not simply restate your thesis and supporting points.

Title of the Paper

Make sure to title your paper. Use a title that is interesting, but relates well to your topic.

Step 3: Revising

Now that you've explored ideas and put them into a draft, it's time to revise. During this step, you will rewrite parts or sections of your paper. All good writing goes through many drafts. To help you make the necessary changes, use the checklists below to review your paper.

Overall Paper

- ☑ Do I have an interesting title that draws readers in?
- ☑ Does the title tell my audience what my paper is about?
- ☑ Do I have an introduction, body, and conclusion?
- ☑ Is my paper the correct length?

Introduction

- ☑ Have I used a method to interest my readers?
- ☑ Do I have a thesis statement that tells the main idea of my paper?
- ☑ Is my thesis statement clearly stated?

Body

- ☑ Do I start every paragraph on a new line?
- ☑ Is the first line of every paragraph indented?
- ☑ Does the first sentence (topic sentence) in every paragraph explain the main idea of the paragraph? Does it attract my readers' attention?
- ☑ Do I include facts, explanations, examples, statistics, and/or experts' ideas that support the topic sentence?
- ☑ Do I need to take out any sentences that do not relate to the topic sentence?
- ☑ Do the paragraphs flow in a logical order? Does each point build on the last one?
- ☑ Do good transition words lead readers from one paragraph to the next?

Conclusion

- ☑ Does the conclusion tie together the main ideas of my paper?
- ☑ Does it offer a solution, make a suggestion, or answer any questions that the readers might have?

Writing Style

- ☑ Do I use words and concepts that my audience understands?
- ☑ Is the tone too formal or informal for my audience?
- ☑ Are my sentences the right length for my audience?
- ☑ Do I have good sentence variety and word choice?

Step 4: Editing and Proofreading

During the editing and proofreading step, check your paper or another student's paper for errors in grammar, punctuation, capitalization, and spelling. Use the following checklists to help guide you. Read and focus on one sentence at a time. Cover up everything but the sentence you are reading. Reading from the end of the paper backward also works for some students. Note changes using the proofreader marks shown on the following page. Check a dictionary or style manual when you're not sure about something.

Grammar

- ☑ Is there a subject and a verb in every sentence?
- ☑ Do the subject and verb agree in every sentence?
- ☑ Is the verb tense logical in every sentence?
- ☑ Is the verb tense consistent in every sentence?
- ☑ Have you used interesting, lively verbs?
- ☑ Do all pronouns have clear antecedents?
- ☑ Can repeated or unnecessary words be left out?
- ☑ Are there any run-on sentences that need to be corrected?
- ☑ Does sentence length vary with long and short sentences?

Punctuation

☑ Does every sentence end with the correct punctuation mark?

☑ Are all direct quotations punctuated correctly?

☑ Do commas separate words in a series?

☑ Is there a comma and a coordinating conjunction separating each compound sentence?

☑ Is there a comma after an introductory phrase or clause?

☑ Are apostrophes used correctly in contractions and possessive nouns?

Capitalization

☑ Is the first word of every sentence capitalized?

☑ Are all proper nouns and adjectives capitalized?

☑ Are the important words in the title of the paper capitalized?

Spelling

☑ Are words that sound alike spelled correctly (such as *to, too,* and *two*)?

☑ Is every plural noun spelled correctly?

☑ Are words with *ie* or *ei* spelled correctly?

☑ Is the silent *e* dropped before adding an ending that starts with a vowel?

☑ Is the consonant doubling rule used correctly?

If the paper was typed, make any necessary changes and run the spell-check and grammar-check programs one more time.

Proofreading Marks

Below are some common proofreading marks. Print out your paper and use these marks to correct errors.

Symbol	Meaning
¶	Start new paragraph
◠	Close up
#	Add a space
∏	Switch words or letters
≡	Capitalize this letter
/	Lowercase this letter
ℓ	Omit space, letter, mark, or word
∧	Insert space, mark, or word
⊙	Insert a period
⌄	Insert a comma
◯ sp	Spell out
. . . . stet	Leave as is (write dots under words)

Step 5: Publishing and Presenting

Once you have made the final text changes, make sure that the overall format of your paper is correct. Follow the guidelines that were set up by your teacher. Here are some general guidelines that are commonly used.

Readability

■ Double space all text.

■ Use an easy-to-read font such as Times Roman, Comic Sans, Ariel, or New York.

■ Use a 12-point type size.

■ Make sure that you have met any word, paragraph, or page count guidelines.

Format

- Make at least a one-inch margin around each page.

- Place the title of the paper, your name, your class period, and the date according to your teacher's guidelines. If you need a title page, make sure that you have a separate page with this information. If you do not need a title page, place your name, class period, and date in the upper right-hand corner of the first page. Center the title below that.

- Check to see if your pages need to be numbered. If so, number them in the upper right-hand corner or according to your teacher's guidelines.

- Label any charts and graphics as needed.

- Check that your title and any subheads are in boldface print.

- Check that your paragraphs are indented.

Citations

- Cite direct quotations, paraphrases, and summaries properly. Refer to the Modern Language Association (MLA) or American Psychological Association (APA) rules.

- Punctuate all citations properly. Refer to MLA or APA rules.

Bibliographies

- Include a list of books and other materials you reviewed during your research. This is a reference list only. Below are examples of how you would list a book, magazine article, and Web site using MLA style:

Book:
Author's Last Name, Author's First Name. *Book Title*. Publisher's City: Publisher's Name, Year.

London, Jack. *The Call of the Wild*. New York: Scholastic, 2001.

Magazine:
Author's Last Name, Author's First Name. "Article Title." Magazine Title. Volume Date: Page numbers.

Young, Diane. "At the High End of the River." *Southern Living*. June 2000: 126–131.

Web Site:
Article Title. Date accessed. URL

Circle of Stories. 25 Jan. 2006. <http://www.pbs.org/circleofstories/>

Six Traits of Writing

Good writing is not a miracle. It is not an accident either. Good writing is part science and part art. It is the result of careful thinking and choices. To write well, you need to know about six different traits that determine the quality of writing.

 **Six Traits of Writing:**

Ideas message, details, and purpose

What message do you want to get across? What details are important to get your message across clearly? Ideas are the heart of any writing. So begin the writing process by developing strong, clear ideas. Set off your ideas with details that stand out and catch attention.

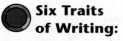 **Six Traits of Writing:**

Organization order, ideas tied together

A piece of writing has a structure or pattern, just like a building. Organize your ideas into a structure that makes sense and fits the ideas well. For example, you may tell about events or steps in order. You may compare two things or explain a solution or an effect. Organization holds writing together and gives shape to ideas.

 **Six Traits of Writing:**

Voice the writer's own language

Your writing should "sound like you." It should capture your thoughts and your point of view. This is your "voice." In writing, your voice shows that you are interested in and understand the subject. Your voice also gives a personal tone to your writing that is yours alone.

Six Traits of Writing:

Word Choice vivid words that "show, not tell"

Choose your words so that they are clear and interesting. Name things exactly. Use strong action verbs and specific adjectives. Good word choice helps you say exactly what you want to say. It helps your readers create a mental picture of what you want them to understand.

Six Traits of Writing:

Sentence Fluency smooth rhythm and flow

Well-made sentences make your writing easy to read. Aim for sentences that have the natural rhythms of speech. Vary sentence length and style. Then your sentences will flow. They will move your readers through your writing with ease.

Six Traits of Writing:

Conventions correct grammar, spelling, and mechanics

Once you have written something, ask yourself: Could this be published in a newspaper? Make sure your writing is free from mistakes in spelling, grammar, and mechanics. Mechanics includes things such as correct capitalization and punctuation.

Appendix D: Research

Planning and Writing a Research Report

⬇️ *Use the following steps to guide you in writing a research report.*

Step 1: Planning the Report

Choose a subject. Then narrow your topic. You may be interested in the poetry of Robert Frost, but that subject is too broad. Narrow your focus. The graphic organizers in Appendix A may help you narrow your topic and identify supporting details.

Step 2: Finding Useful Information

Go to the library and browse the card catalog for books. Check almanacs, encyclopedias, atlases, and other sources in the reference section. Also review *The Reader's Guide to Periodical Literature* for magazines.

Draw from primary sources. Primary sources are first-hand accounts of information, such as speeches, observations, research results, and interviews. Secondary sources interpret and analyze primary sources.

Use the Internet to further explore your topic. Be careful; some Internet sources are not reliable. Avoid chat rooms, news groups, and personal Web sites. Check the credibility of sites by reviewing the site name and sponsor. Web sites whose URL ends with .org, .gov, and .edu are typically good sources.

Step 3: Logging Information

Use index cards to take notes. Include this information for each source:

- name of author or editor
- title of book or title of article and magazine
- page numbers

- volume numbers
- date of publication
- name of publishing company
- Web site information for Internet sources
- relevant information or direct quotations

Step 4: Getting Organized

Group your cards by similar details and organize them into categories. Find a system that works for you in organizing your cards. You can color-code them, use different-colored index cards for different sections, label them, and so on. Do not use any note cards that do not fit the categories that you have set up. Make conclusions about your research. Write a final topic outline.

Step 5: Writing Your Report

Follow the writing process in Appendix C to write your report. Use your own words to write the ideas you found in your sources (paraphrase). Do not plagiarize—steal and pass off another's words as your own. Write an author's exact words for direct quotations, and name the author or source.

Step 6: Preparing a Bibliography or Works Cited Page

Use the information on your note cards to write a bibliography or works cited page. If you are writing a bibliography, put your note cards in alphabetical order by *title*. If you are writing a works cited page, put your note cards in alphabetical order by *author*.

See *Bibliographies* in Appendix C.

Research Tools

Almanac
An annual publication containing data and tables on politics, religion, education, sports, and more

American Psychological Association (APA) Style
A guide to proper citation to avoid plagiarism in research papers for the social sciences

Atlas
A bound collection of maps of cities, states, regions, and countries including statistics and illustrations

Audio Recording
Recordings of speeches, debates, public proceedings, interviews, etc.

The Chicago Manual of Style
Writing, editing, proofreading, and revising guidelines for the publishing industry

Database
A large collection of data stored electronically and able to be searched

Dictionary
A reference book of words, spellings, pronunciations, meanings, parts of speech, and word origins

Experiment
A series of tests to prove or disprove something

Field Study
Observation, data collection, and interpretation done outside of a laboratory

Glossary
A collection of terms and their meanings

Government Publications
A report of a government action, bill, handbook, or census data usually provided by the Government Printing Office

Grammar Reference
Explanation and examples of parts of speech, sentence structure, and word usage

History
A chronological record that explains past events

Information Services
A stored collection of information organized for easy searching

Internet/World Wide Web
A worldwide network of connected computers that share information

Interview
A dialogue between a subject and a reporter or investigator to gather information

Journal
A type of magazine offering current information on certain subjects such as medicine, the economy, and current events

Microfiche
Historical, printed materials saved to small, thin sheets of film for organization, storage, and use

Modern Language Association (MLA) Handbook
A guide to proper citation to avoid plagiarism in research papers for the humanities

News Source
A newspaper or a radio, television, satellite, or World Wide Web sending of current events and issues presented in a timely manner

Periodical
A magazine, newspaper, or journal

The Reader's Guide to Periodical Literature
A searchable, organized database of magazines, newspapers, and journals used for research

Speech
A public address to inform and to explain

Technical Document
A proposal, instruction manual, training manual, report, chart, table, or other document that provides information

Thesaurus
A book of words and their synonyms, or words that have almost the same meanings

Vertical File
A storage file of original documents or copies of original documents

Appendix E: Speaking

Types of Public Speaking

Public speaking offers a way to inform, to explain, and to entertain. Here are some common types of public speaking:

Debate

A debate is a formal event where two or more people share opposing arguments in response to questions. Often, someone wins by answering questions with solid information.

Descriptive Speech

A descriptive speech uses the five senses of sight, smell, touch, taste, and sound to give vivid details.

Entertaining Speech

An entertaining speech relies on humor through jokes, stories, wit, or making fun of oneself. The humor must be appropriate for the audience and purpose of the speech.

Expository Speech

An expository speech provides more detailed information about a subject. This can be done through classification, analysis, definition, cause and effect, or compare and contrast.

Group Discussion

A group discussion allows the sharing of ideas among three or more people. A group discussion may be impromptu (without being planned) or may include a set topic and list of questions.

Impromptu Speech

An impromptu speech happens at a moment's notice without being planned. The speaker is given a random topic to discuss within a given time period.

Interview

An interview is a dialogue between a subject and a reporter or investigator. An interview draws out information using a question-and-answer format.

Literature Recitation

A literature recitation is the act of presenting a memorized speech, poem, story, or scene in its entire form or with chosen excerpts.

Literature Response

A literature response can serve many purposes. A speaker can compare and contrast plots or characters. An analysis of the work of one author can be presented. Writing style, genre, or period can also be shared.

Narrative

A narrative is a fiction or nonfiction story told with descriptive detail. The speaker also must use voice variation if acting out character dialogue.

Reflective Speech

A reflective speech provides thoughtful analysis of ideas, current events, and processes.

Role Playing

Role playing is when two or more people act out roles to show an idea or practice a character in a story. Role playing can be an effective tool for learning.

Preparing Your Speech

⏬ *Use the following steps to prepare your speech:*

Step 1: Defining Your Purpose

Ask yourself:

- Do I want to inform?
- Do I want to explain something?
- Do I want to entertain?
- Do I want to involve the audience through group discussion, role playing, or debate?
- Do I want to get the audience to act on a subject or an issue?

Step 2: Knowing Your Audience

Ask yourself:

- What information does my audience already know about the topic?
- What questions, concerns, or opinions do they have about the topic?
- How formal or informal does my presentation need to be?
- What words are familiar to my audience? What needs explanation?
- How does my audience prefer to get information? Do they like visuals, audience participation, or lecture?

Step 3: Knowing Your Setting

Ask yourself:

- Who is my audience?
- Is the room large enough to need a microphone and a projector?

- How is the room set up? Am I on stage with a podium or can I interact with the audience?
- Will other noises or activity distract the audience?

Step 4: Narrowing Your Topic

Ask yourself:

- What topic is right for the event? Is it timely? Will it match the mood of the event?
- Is there enough time to share it?
- What topic is right for me to present? Is it something I know and enjoy? Is it something people want to hear from me?

Step 5: Prewriting

Ask yourself:

- What examples, statistics, stories, or descriptions will help me get across my point?
- If telling a story, do I have a sequence of events that includes a beginning, middle, and end?

Step 6: Drafting Your Speech

Your speech will include an introduction, a body, and a conclusion.

The introduction states your topic and purpose. It includes a thesis statement that tells your position. Your introduction should also establish your credibility. Share why you are the right person to give that speech based on your experiences. Lastly, your introduction needs to get people's attention so they want to listen. At the top of the next page are some possible ways to start your speech.

- Ask a question.
- Share a story.
- Describe something.
- Give a surprising fact.
- Share a meaningful quotation.
- Make a memorable, purposeful entrance.

The body of your speech tells more about your main idea and tries to prevent listener misunderstandings. It should include any of the following supporting evidence:

- facts
- details
- explanations
- reasons
- examples
- personal stories or experiences
- experts
- literary devices and images

The conclusion of your speech ties your speech together. If you asked a question in your introduction, the conclusion answers it. If you outlined a problem, your conclusion offers solutions. If you told a story, revisit that story. You may even want to ask your audience to get involved, take action, or become more informed on your topic.

Step 7: Selecting Visuals

Ask yourself:

- Is a visual aid needed for the audience to better understand my topic?
- What visual aids work best for my topic?
- Do I have access to the right technology?

The size of your audience and the setting for your speech will also impact what you select. Remember that a projection screen and overhead speakers are necessary for large groups. If you plan on giving handouts to audience members, have handouts ready for pickup by the entrance of the room. A slide show or a video presentation will need a darkened room. Be sure that you have someone available to help you with the lights.

Practicing and Delivering Your Speech

Giving a speech is about more than simply talking. You want to look comfortable and confident.

Practice how you move, how you sound, and how you work with visuals and the audience.

Know Your Script

Every speaker is afraid of forgetting his or her speech. Each handles this fear in a different way. Choose the device that works for you.

- Memorization: Know your speech by heart. Say it often so you sound natural.
- Word-for-word scripts: Highlight key phrases to keep you on track. Keep the script on a podium, so you are not waving sheets of paper around as you talk. Be careful not to read from your script. The audience wants to see your eyes.
- Outlines: Write a sentence outline of your main points and supporting details that you want to say in a specific way. Transitions and other words can be spoken impromptu (without being planned).

- Key words: Write down key words that will remind you what to say, like "Tell story about the dog."

- Put your entire speech, outline, or key words on note cards to stay on track. They are small and not as obvious as paper. Number them in case they get out of order.

Know Yourself

Your voice and appearance are the two most powerful things you bring to a speech. Practice the following, so you are comfortable, confident, and convincing:

- Body language: Stand tall. Keep your feet shoulder-width apart. Don't cross your arms or bury your hands in your pockets. Use gestures to make a point. For example, hold up two fingers when you say, "My second point is . . ." Try to relax; that way, you will be in better control of your body.

- Eye contact: Look at your audience. Spend a minute or two looking at every side of the room and not just the front row. The audience will feel as if you are talking to them.

- Voice strategies: Clearly pronounce your words. Speak at a comfortable rate and loud enough for everyone to hear you. Vary your volume, rate, and pitch when you are trying to emphasize something. For example, you could say, "I have a secret. . . ." Then, you could lean toward the audience and speak in a loud, clear whisper as if you are telling them a secret. This adds dramatic effect and engages the audience.

- Repetition of key phrases or words: Repetition is one way to help people remember your point. If something is important, say it twice. Use transitions such as, "This is so important it is worth repeating" or "As I said before, we must act now."

Appendix F: Listening

Listening Strategy Checklist

Here are some ways you can ensure that you are a good listener.

Be an Active Listener

- ☑ Complete reading assignments that are due prior to the presentation.
- ☑ Focus on what is being said.
- ☑ Ask for definitions of unfamiliar terms.
- ☑ Ask questions to clarify what you heard.
- ☑ Ask the speaker to recommend other readings or resources.

Be a Critical Listener

- ☑ Identify the thesis or main idea of the speech.
- ☑ Try to predict what the speaker is going to say based on what you already know.
- ☑ Determine the speaker's purpose of the speech.
- ☑ Note supporting facts, statistics, examples, and other details.
- ☑ Determine if supporting detail is relevant, factual, and appropriate.
- ☑ Form your conclusions about the presentation.

Be an Appreciative Listener

- ☑ Relax.
- ☑ Enjoy the listening experience.
- ☑ Welcome the opportunity to laugh and learn.

Be a Thoughtful and Feeling Listener

- ☑ Understand the experiences of the speaker.
- ☑ Value the emotion he or she brings to the subject.
- ☑ Summarize or paraphrase what you believe the speaker just said.
- ☑ Tell the speaker that you understand his or her feelings.

Be an Alert Listener

- ☑ Sit up straight.
- ☑ Sit near the speaker and face the speaker directly.
- ☑ Make eye contact and nod to show you are listening.
- ☑ Open your arms so you are open to receiving information.

Analyze the Speaker

- ☑ Does the speaker have the experiences and knowledge to speak on the topic?
- ☑ Is the speaker prepared?
- ☑ Does the speaker appear confident?
- ☑ Is the speaker's body language appropriate?
- ☑ What do the speaker's tone, volume, and word choices show?

Identify the Details

- ☑ Listen for the tendency of the speaker to favor or oppose something without real cause.
- ☑ Be aware of propaganda—someone forcing an opinion on you.
- ☑ Don't be swayed by the clever way the speaker presents something.
- ☑ After the speech ask about words that you don't know.

Identify Fallacies of Logic

A fallacy is a false idea intended to trick someone. Here are some common fallacies:

- *Ad hominem*: This type of fallacy attacks a person's character, lifestyle, or beliefs. Example: Joe should not be on the school board because he skipped classes in college.

- False causality: This type of fallacy gives a cause–effect relationship that is not logical. This fallacy assumes that something caused something else only because it came before the consequence. Example: Ever since that new family moved into the neighborhood, our kids are getting into trouble.

- Red herring: This type of fallacy uses distractions to take attention away from the main issue. Example: Since more than half of our nation's people are overweight, we should not open a fast-food restaurant in our town.

- Overgeneralization: This type of fallacy uses words such as *every*, *always*, or *never*. Claims do not allow for exceptions to be made. Example: People who make more than a million dollars a year never pay their fair share of taxes.

- Bandwagon effect: This type of fallacy appeals to one's desire to be a part of the crowd. It is based on popular opinion and not on evidence. Example: Anyone who believes that our town is a great place to live should vote for the local tax increase.

Take Notes

- Write down key messages and phrases, not everything that is said.

- Abbreviate words.

- Listen for cues that identify important details, like "Here's an example" or "To illustrate what I mean."

- Draw graphs, charts, and diagrams for future reference.

- Draw arrows, stars, and circles to highlight information or group information.

- Highlight or circle anything that needs to be clarified or explained.

- Use the note-taking strategies explained in "How to Use This Book" at the beginning of this textbook.

Appendix G: Viewing

Visual aids can help communicate information and ideas. The following checklist gives pointers for viewing and interpreting visual aids.

Design Elements

Colors

☑ What colors stand out?

☑ What feelings do they make you think of?

☑ What do they symbolize or represent?

☑ Are colors used realistically or for emphasis?

Shapes

☑ What shapes are created by space or enclosed in lines?

☑ What is important about the shapes? What are they meant to symbolize or represent?

Lines

☑ What direction do the lines lead you?

☑ Which objects are you meant to focus on?

☑ What is the importance of the lines?

☑ Do lines divide or segment areas? Why do you think this is?

Textures

☑ What textures are used?

☑ What emotions or moods are they meant to affect?

Point of View

Point of view shows the artist's feelings toward the subject. Analyze this point of view:

☑ What point of view is the artist taking?

☑ Do you agree with this point of view?

☑ Is the artist successful in communicating this point of view?

Graphics

Line Graphs

Line graphs show changes in numbers over time.

☑ What numbers and time frame are represented?

☑ Does the information represent appropriate changes?

Pie Graphs

Pie graphs represent parts of a whole.

☑ What total number does the pie represent?

☑ Do the numbers represent an appropriate-sized sample?

Bar Graphs

Bar graphs compare amounts.

☑ What amounts are represented?

☑ Are the amounts appropriate?

Charts and Tables

Charts and tables organize information for easy comparison.

☑ What is being presented?

☑ Do columns and rows give equal data to compare and contrast?

Maps

☑ What land formations are shown?

☑ What boundaries are shown?

☑ Are there any keys or symbols on the map? What do they mean?

Appendix H: Media and Technology

Forms of Media

Television, movies, and music are some common forms of media that you know a lot about. Here are some others.

Advertisement

An advertisement selling a product or a service can be placed in a newspaper or magazine, on the Internet, or on television or radio.

Broadcast News

Broadcast news is offered on a 24-hour cycle through nightly newscasts, all-day news channels, and the Internet.

Documentary

A documentary shares information about people's lives, historic events, objects, or places. It is based on facts and evidence.

Internet and World Wide Web

This worldwide computer network offers audio and video clips, news, reference materials, research, and graphics.

Journal

A journal records experiences, current research, or ideas about a topic for a target audience.

Magazine

A magazine includes articles, stories, photos, and graphics of general interest.

Newspaper

A newspaper most often is printed daily or weekly.

Photography

Traditionally, photography has been the art or process of producing images on a film surface using light. Today, digital images are often used.

The Media and You

The media's role is to entertain, to inform, and to advertise. Media can help raise people's awareness about current issues. Media also can give clues about the needs and beliefs of the people.

Use a critical eye and ear to sort through the thousands of messages presented to you daily. Be aware of the media's use of oversimplified ideas about people, decent and acceptable language, and appropriate messages. Consider these questions:

- Who is being shown and why?
- What is being said? Is it based on fact?
- How do I feel about what and how it is said?

Technology and You

Technology can improve communication. Consider the following when selecting technology for research or presentations:

Audio/Sound

Speeches, music, sound effects, and other elements can set a mood or reinforce an idea.

Computers

- Desktop publishing programs offer tools for making newsletters and posters.
- Software programs are available for designing publications, Web sites, databases, and more.
- Word processing programs feature dictionaries, grammar-check and spell-check programs, and templates for memos, reports, letters, and more.

Multimedia

Slide shows, movies, and other electronic media can help the learning process.

Visual Aids

Charts, tables, maps, props, drawings, and graphs provide visual representation of information.

Handbook of Literary Terms

A

alliteration (ə lit ə rā′ shən) repeating sounds by using words whose beginning sounds are the same (p. 288)

anecdote (an′ ik dōt) a short account of an interesting event in someone's life (p. 220)

author's purpose (o′ thərs pėr′ pəs) the reason(s) for which the author writes: to entertain, to inform, to express opinions, or to persuade (pp. 26, 207)

autobiography (o tə bī og′ rə fē) a person's life story, written by that person (p. 188)

B

biography (bī og′ rə fē) a person's life story told by someone else (pp. 38, 195)

C

character (kar′ ik tər) a person or animal in a story, poem, or play (pp. 84, 318, 414)

character trait (kar′ ik tər trāt) a character's way of thinking, behaving, or speaking (p. 84)

characterization (kar ik tər ə zā′ shən) the way a writer develops character qualities and personality traits (p. 84)

chronological order (kron′ ə loj′ ə kəl or′dər) a plot that moves forward in order of time (p. 188)

climax (klī′ maks) the high point of interest or suspense in a story or play (pp. 6, 99)

concrete image (kon′ krēt im′ ij) people and things that can be seen or touched (p. 99)

concrete poem (kon′ krēt pō′ əm) a poem shaped to look like its subject (p. 282)

D

conflict (kon′ flikt) the struggle of the main character against himself or herself, another person, or nature (pp. 6, 99, 195, 464)

dialogue (dī′ ə log) the conversation among characters in a story or play (pp. 164, 318, 435)

drama (drä′ mə) a story told through the words and actions of characters, written to be performed (p. 318)

dramatization (dram′ ə tīz ā shən) the acting out in drama form of a real-life event or another form of literature (p. 349)

E

essay (es′ ā) a written work that shows a writer's opinions on some basic or current issue (p. 188)

exaggeration (eg zaj′ ə rā′ shən) a use of words to make something seem more than it is; stretching the truth to a great extent (p. 84)

exposition (ek spə zish′ ən) introduction of the setting, characters, and basic situation (p. 6)

F

fable (fā′ bəl) a story or poem with a lesson about life, often with animals acting like humans (p. 414)

falling action (fol′ ing ak′ shən) events that follow the climax in a story (p. 6)

fantasy (fan′ tə sē) an imaginative story that often has strange settings and characters (p. 435)

fiction (fik′ shən) writing that is imaginative and designed to entertain (p. 6)

figurative language (fig′ yər ə tiv lang′ gwij) writing or speech not meant to be understood exactly as it is written (pp. 130, 270, 452)

first person (fėrst pėr′ sən) a point of view where the narrator is also a character, using the pronouns *I* and *we* (pp. 14, 130)

flashback (flash′ bak) a look into the past at some point in a story (p. 471)

folktale (fōk′ tāl) a story that has been handed down from one generation to another (p. 414)

foreshadowing (fôr shad′ ō ing) clues or hints that a writer gives about something that has not yet happened (p. 471)

G

genre (zhän′ rə) a specific type, or kind, of literature (p. 220)

H

haiku (hī′ kü) a form of Japanese poetry having three lines with five syllables in the first, seven in the second, and five in the third (p. 282)

hero (hir′ ō) the leading male character in a story, novel, play, or film (p. 414)

image (im′ ij) a word or phrase that appeals to the senses and allows the reader to picture events (pp. 231, 276)

I

imagery (im′ ij rē) pictures created by words; the use of words that appeal to the five senses (p. 276)

L

legend (lej′ ənd) a story from folklore that features characters who actually lived, or real events or places (p. 62)

letter (let′ ər) impressions and feelings written to a specific person (p. 237)

limerick (lim′ ər ik) a humorous five-line poem in which the first, second, and fifth lines, and the third and fourth lines, rhyme (p. 282)

M

memoir (mem′ wär) writing based on a personal experience (p. 220)

metaphor (met′ ə fôr) a figure of speech that makes a comparison but does not use *like* or *as* (p. 270)

mood (müd) the feeling that writing creates (pp. 231, 276)

moral (môr′ əl) a message or lesson about life (p. 414)

motive (mō′ tiv) the reason a character does something (p. 84)

myth (mith) an important story, often part of a culture's religion, that explains how the world came to be or why natural events happen (p. 421)

N

narrative (nar′ ə tiv) a story, usually told in chronological order (p. 188)

narrator (nar′ ā tər) one who tells a story (pp. 14, 116)

a	hat	e	let	ī	ice	ô	order	ù	put	sh	she	ə	a	in about
ā	age	ē	equal	o	hot	oi	oil	ü	rule	th	thin		e	in taken
ä	far	ėr	term	ō	open	ou	out	ch	child	₮H	then		i	in pencil
â	care	i	it	ó	saw	u	cup	ng	long	zh	measure		o	in lemon
													u	in circus

nonfiction (non fik´ shən) writing about real people and events (pp. 26, 188)

novel (nov´ əl) fiction that is book-length and has more characters and detail than a short story (p. 349)

O

onomatopoeia (on ə mat ə pē´ ə) using words that sound like their meaning (p. 288)

P

personification (pər son ə fə kā´ shən) giving characters such as animals or objects the characteristics or qualities of humans (pp. 270, 452)

playwright (plā´ rīt) the author of a play (p. 318)

plot (plot) the series of events in a story (pp. 6, 99, 318, 421)

point of view (point ov vyü) the position from which the author or storyteller tells the story (pp. 14, 116, 207)

prop (prop) a piece of equipment used on stage during a play (p. 364)

pun (pun) a joke formed by a play on words (p. 318)

R

repetition (rep ə tish´ ən) using a word, phrase, or image more than once, for emphasis (p. 288)

resolution (rez ə lü´ shən) the act of solving the conflict in a story (pp. 6, 99)

rhyme (rīm) words that end with the same or similar sounds (p. 258)

rhythm (riŦH´ əm) a pattern created by the stressed and unstressed syllables in a line of poetry (p. 258)

rising action (rīz´ ing ak´ shən) the buildup of excitement in a story (pp. 6, 99)

S

script (skript) the written text of a play (p. 318)

sensory language (sen´ sər ē lang´ gwij) writing or speech that appeals to the five senses (p. 299)

setting (set´ ing) the time and place in a story (pp. 84, 318, 435)

short story (shôrt stôr´ ē) a brief work of prose fiction that includes plot, setting, characters, point of view, and theme (p. 84)

simile (sim´ ə lē) a figure of speech that makes a comparison using the words *like* or *as* (pp. 270, 452)

sound devices (sound di vī´ sez) words that create musical sounds in poetry (p. 288)

stage directions (stāj də rek´ shəns) notes by playwrights describing such things as setting, lighting, and sound effects; they also describe how the actors are to look, behave, move, and speak (p. 364)

style (stīl) an author's way of writing (p. 237)

suspense (sə spens´) a quality in a story that makes the reader uncertain or nervous about what will happen next (p. 144)

symbol (sim´ bəl) something that represents something else (p. 62)

symbolism (sim´ bə liz əm) the larger meaning of a person, place, or object (p. 62)

T

theme (thēm) the main idea of a literary work (pp. 130, 464)

third person (thėrd pėr´ sən) a point of view where the narrator is not a character, and refers to characters as *he* or *she* (pp. 14, 116)

tone (tōn) the attitude an author takes toward a subject (pp. 48, 237)

a	hat	e	let	ī	ice	ô	order	u̇	put	sh	she		a	in about
ā	age	ē	equal	o	hot	oi	oil	ü	rule	th	thin	ə	e	in taken
ä	far	ėr	term	ō	open	ou	out	ch	child	ᵗʜ	then		i	in pencil
â	care	i	it	ȯ	saw	u	cup	ng	long	zh	measure		o	in lemon
													u	in circus

Glossary

A

abide (ə bīd´) obey (p. 329)

abreast (ə brest´) alongside (p. 154)

abruptly (ə brupt´ lē) quickly or suddenly (p. 151)

absentminded (ab sənt mīn´ did) forgetful (p. 39)

access (ak´ ses) the ability to get close to (p. 335)

accumulated (ə kyü´ myə lā tid) built up little by little (p. 210)

acknowledges (ak nol´ ij əz) notices and responds to (p. 338)

adjoining (ə joi´ ning) next to (p. 146)

admonishing (ad mon´ ish ing) disapproving (p. 372)

adolescents (ad les´ ntz) teenagers (p. 28)

advancement (ad vans´ mənt) forward movement (p. 208)

advantageously (ad vən tā´ jəs lē) well (p. 331)

advisors (ad vī´ zərz) assistants who give advice (p. 336)

affectionate (ə fek´ shə nit) warm; loving (p. 51)

agin' (ə gen´) against (p. 261)

alarmed (ə lärmd´) very disturbed, as to send a warning (p. 31)

alight (ə līt´) on fire (p. 438)

alternate (ôl´ tər nāt) every other; skipping one in-between (p. 325)

ambition (am bish´ ən) an important goal for the future (p. 169)

amid (ə mid´) among (p. 424)

anatomy (ə nat´ ə mē) body (p. 30)

anguished (ang´ gwisht) as if suffering (p. 89)

antics (an´ tikz) wild actions (p. 154)

apothecary (ə poth´ ə ker ē) a person who prepares and sells medicines (p. 366)

apt (apt) likely to (pp. 41, 437)

arbors (är´ bərz) groups of trees (p. 233)

assortment (ə sôrt´ mənt) a variety or collection (pp. 333, 376)

attorney (ə tėr´ nē) lawyer (pp. 198, 209)

audible (ô´ də bəl) able to be heard (p. 30)

B

balderdash (bôl´ dər dash) nonsense (p. 334)

banished (ban´ ishd) sent away (pp. 331, 381)

barriers (bar´ ē ərz) things that block the way (p. 191)

bashful (bash´ fəl) shy (p. 376)

battalion (bə tal´ yən) a military unit (p. 64)

beaker (bē´ kər) an open glass container (p. 367)

beret (bə rā´) a flat, soft cap (p. 371)

bestow (bi stō´) to give as a gift (p. 467)

bickered (bik´ ərd) argued (p. 87)

bide (bīd) to wait (p. 326)

billiards (bil´ yərdz) a certain kind of game played on a pool table (p. 40)

blisses (blis´ əz) delights (p. 291)

bosh (bosh) foolish talk or activity (p. 335)

brandishing (bran´ dish ing) holding and waving (p. 65)

brine (brīn) very salty water (p. 120)

brutally (brü´ tl lē) in a very cruel manner (p. 198)

brute (brüt) an animal (p. 154)

buffing (buf´ ing) polishing (p. 17)

bullocks (bul´ əkz) steers (p. 438)

byre (bīr) a cow barn (p. 436)

C

calculations (kal kyə lā´ shənz) the work for solving problems (p. 383)

calico (kal´ ə kō) a type of simple cotton fabric (p. 145)

capsized (kap sīzd´) overturned (p. 151)

caress (kə res´) to touch lightly or gently (p. 32)

caressed (kə resd´) gently touched (p. 331)

caroming (kar´ əm ing) striking something so that it returns; hitting something else (p. 92)

cartographers (kär tog´ rə fərz) mapmakers (p. 353)

Caucasians (kô kā´ zhənz) white people (p. 209)

cauldron (kôl´ drən) a large iron pot (p. 376)

cavernous (kav´ ər nəs) vast and deep (p. 259)

cellophane (sel´ ə fān) a thin, crinkly material used for wrapping (p. 366)

chaotic (kā o´ tik) completely confused (p. 52); messy; disorganized (p. 343)

christening (kris´ n ing) giving a name to (p. 240)

chrome (krōm) bright metal trim (p. 17)

cinderblock (sin´ dər blok) a block made of concrete and burned coal (p. 7)

clamor (klam´ ər) loud noise (pp. 367, 446)

clashed (klashd) had a conflict (p. 196)

clasped (klaspd) held together tightly (p. 133)

cleft (kleft) split into two parts (p. 102)

climes (klīmz) climates (p. 472)

clods (klodz) lumps (p. 120)

cockatoo (kok ə tü´) a kind of parrot with mostly white feathers (p. 416)

cogs (kogz) the teeth around a wheel or gear (p. 117)

collided (kə līd´ əd) ran into each other (p. 92)

commencement (kə mens´ mənt) graduation (p. 53)

commissioner (kə mish´ ə nər) an official in charge of something (p. 148)

compatible (kəm pat´ ə bəl) suited well for each other (p. 88)

complex (kəm pleks´) difficult (p. 329)

complexion (kəm plek´ shən) the feel and color of the skin (p. 39)

complicated (kom´ plə kā tid) difficult (pp. 28, 53)

composed (kəm pōzd´) made up (p. 238)

compound (kom´ pound) grounds surrounded by buildings (p. 456)

a	hat	e	let	ī	ice	ò	order	ù	put	sh	she	ə {	a	in about
ā	age	ē	equal	o	hot	oi	oil	ü	rule	th	thin		e	in taken
ä	far	ėr	term	ō	open	ou	out	ch	child	ᴛʜ	then		i	in pencil
â	care	i	it	ȯ	saw	u	cup	ng	long	zh	measure		o	in lemon
													u	in circus

compromise (kom´ prə mīz) a solution that both sides of an argument agree to (p. 389)

compute (kəm pyüt´) to figure out using math (p. 221)

concocter (kon kokt´ ər) one who creates something by mixing things together (p. 260)

concoction (kon kok´ shən) a mixture, as of ingredients (p. 367)

confiscated (kon´ fə skā tid) took by force (p. 233)

confounding (kon found´ ing) confusing or mixing things up (p. 190)

connotation (kon´ ə tā´ shən) the suggestion of meaning (p. 319)

consequently (kon´ sə kwent lē) as a result (p. 40)

consumed (kən sümd´) burned away (p. 42)

contemporaries (kən tem´ pə rer ēz) peers (p. 239)

contradiction (kon trə dik´ shən) something that is both true and false (p. 27)

convent (kon´ vent) the place where nuns live (p. 63)

convoluted (kon və lü´ tid) confusing (p. 53)

corporations (kôr pə rā´ shənz) large companies (p. 199)

couplets (kup´ litz) pairs of rhyming lines (p. 384)

courthouse (kôrt´ hous) a building in which courts of law are held (p. 209)

covetousness (kuv´ ə təs nəss) wanting what another person has (p. 467)

cowardice (kou´ ər dis) failure to show courage (p. 65)

crescents (kres´ ntz) moon-shaped curved pieces (p. 16)

crevices (krev´ is əz) narrow openings (p. 475)

crock (krok) a clay pot used to store food items (p. 120)

crude (krüd) simple and rough (p. 271)

cuckoo (kü´ kü) a long-tailed bird with a two-note call (p. 291)

cudgel (kuj´ əl) a club (p. 260)

custody (kus´ tə dē) care or protection over another (p. 197)

D

dally (dal´ ē) to waste time (p. 122)

dawdle (dô´ dl) to waste time (p. 326)

defensive (di fen´ siv) ready to protect oneself (p. 32)

deficiency (di fish´ ən sē) a shortage or lack (p. 368)

deforested (dē fôr´ ist əd) cleared of trees or forests (p. 233)

degraded (di grā´ did) lowered in quality (p. 221)

deity (dē´ ə tē) a god or goddess (p. 41)

dejectedly (di jek´ tid lē) unhappily (pp. 321, 350)

delectable (di lek´ tə bəl) delicious (p. 454)

deliberately (di lib´ ər it lē) with purpose (p. 390)

demise (di mīz´) death (p. 221)

demolished (di mol´ ishd) torn down (p. 66)

depart (di pärt´) to leave (p. 31)

depicting (di pikt´ ing) showing (p. 353)

derby (dėr´ bē) a domelike man's hat (p. 335)

deserted (di zėr´ təd) empty (p. 331)

despairingly (di sper´ ing lē) in a hopeless way (p. 40)

despise (di spīz´) to hate (p. 437)

detect (di teckt´) to discover (p. 132)

devastated (dev´ ə stāt əd) very upset; destroyed (p. 197)

dilly-dally (dil´ ē dal ē) to waste time (p. 326)

dilution (də lü´ shən) process of weakening by mixing with something else (p. 221)

dimension (də men´ shən) a measurement of size (p. 351)

dimpled (dim´ pəld) having a small dent (p. 440)

disabled (dis ā´ bəld) not having certain abilities (p. 198)

discomfort (dis kum´ fərt) not at ease (p. 190)

disdainfully (dis dān´ fəl lē) with strong dislike (p. 335)

dispersed (dis pėrsd´) sent off in many directions (p. 290)

dissonance (dis´ n əns) disagreement (p. 319); conflicting sounds; an unpleasant noise (p. 365)

distaff (dis´ taf) a stick used to hold wool for spinning (p. 423)

distorted (dis tôr´ təd) twisted out of normal shape or size (p. 426)

divinely (də vīn´ lē) in a very good way (p. 30)

documentation (dok yə men tā´ shən) supporting evidence (p. 238)

doffs (dofz) takes off (p. 371)

doldrums (dol´ drəmz) a general feeling of boredom (p. 324)

domesticate (də mes´ tə kāt) to tame (p. 27)

dribbling (drib´ əl ing) to fall in drops little by little (p. 16)

drone (drōn) a continuous humming sound (p. 135)

dynamo (dī´ nə mō) a forceful person with a lot of energy (p. 93)

E

eaves (ēvz) the lower edges of a roof (p. 7)

economical (ē kə nom´ ə kəl) money-saving (p. 377)

eddies (ed´ ēz) currents of air moving in circular motions like little whirlwinds (p. 102)

efficiency (ə fish´ ən sē) doing things without wasting time or energy (p. 239)

elating (i lāt´ ing) thrilling (p. 333)

elevated (el´ ə vā tid) made greater (p. 27)

eloquent (el´ ə kwənt) well-spoken (p. 454)

embrace (em brās´) put one's arms around someone or something (p. 387)

embraced (em brāsd´) held in the arms fondly (p. 466)

emigrated (em´ ə grā tid) left one's own country to move to another (p. 196)

a	hat	e	let	ī	ice	ô	order	ù	put	sh	she	ə {	a	in about
ā	age	ē	equal	o	hot	oi	oil	ü	rule	th	thin		e	in taken
ä	far	ėr	term	ō	open	ou	out	ch	child	ᴛʜ	then		i	in pencil
â	care	i	it	ȯ	saw	u	cup	ng	long	zh	measure		o	in lemon
													u	in circus

emotional (i mō′ shə nəl) producing strong feelings (p. 196)

empathically (em fat′ ik ə lē) done with the understanding of another person (p. 85)

enchantment (en chant′ mənt) a state of delight (p. 28)

encounter (en koun′ tər) to run into (p. 117)

energetically (en ər jet′ ik lē) with a lot of energy (p. 170)

enforce (en fôrs′) to cause something to be carried out (p. 212)

engulfing (en gulf′ ing) surrounding completely (p. 232)

enrich (en rich′) to add to (p. 332)

enroll (en rōl′) to sign up for (p. 138)

entreat (en trēt′) to ask (for) (p. 336)

epidemic (ep ə dem′ ik) a widespread disease (p. 369)

erupt (i rupt′) to explode outward (p. 370)

escorts (es′ kôrtz) walks or goes with someone (p. 324)

essence (es′ ns) meaning (p. 319)

etching (ech′ ing) a print of a drawing made on metal, glass, or wood (p. 271)

ethnicity (eth nis′ ə tē) belonging to a group with the same appearance and customs (p. 51)

evaluation (i val yü ā′ shən) a judgment (p. 387)

evolved (i volvd′) developed (p. 28)

exaggeration (eg zaj ə rā′ shən) an overstatement (p. 389)

exotic (eg zot′ ik) unusual (p. 52)

expectantly (ek spek′ tənt lē) with interest; eagerly (p. 379)

expectations (ek spek tā′ shənz) hopes or possibilities (p. 322)

exquisite (ek′ skwi zit) of the highest quality (p. 232)

extinction (ek stingk′ shən) not living anymore (p. 221)

extraordinarily (ek strôr′ də ner ə lē) more than what is usual (p. 39)

exuded (eg züd′ əd) gave off (p. 103)

F

famine (fam′ ən) a great shortage of food (pp. 41, 453)

fanfare (fan′ fer) a trumpet blast (p. 330)

fateful (fāt′ fəl) bringing some significant event (p. 199)

feature (fē′ chər) something offered as special or important; a movie (p. 18)

ferocious (fə rō′ shəs) wild and dangerous (p. 331)

fester (fes′ tər) to decay or rot (p. 238)

fiends (fēndz) evil people (p. 343)

filter (fil′ tər) a screen that stops unwanted materials from passing through (p. 17)

financial (fə nan′ shəl) having to do with money (p. 166)

flank (flangk) the part of an animal or person that is on the side between the ribs and hip (p. 29)

flattered (flat′ ərd) gave many compliments (p. 28); pleased by words of praise (p. 344)

flaw (flô) a break or crack (p. 283)

flexed (fleksd) bent (p. 32)

flickering (flik′ ər ing) fluttering (p. 422)

florid (flôr′ id) fancy (p. 53)

floundering (floun´ dər ing) struggling to move in an awkward way (p. 152)

flue (flü) a passage for smoke or hot air, as in a chimney (p. 283)

forepaws (fôr´ pôz) the front feet of an animal (p. 441)

forthwith (fôrth with´) at once (p. 394)

fostering (fô´ stər ing) taking care of (p. 442)

fragments (frag´ məntz) pieces broken off (p. 190)

frock coat (frok kōt) a man's formal coat reaching to the knees (p. 389)

G

gait (gāt) a way of walking (p. 41)

gala (gā´ lə) an event for celebrating (p. 341)

galvanized (gal´ və nīzd) coated with the metal zinc to prevent rusting (p. 133)

gibbous (gib´ əs) mostly, but not fully, lit up (p. 416)

glazed (glāzd) having a glassy look (pp. 89, 102)

glint (glint) sparkle (p. 124)

glinting (glint´ ing) sparkling (p. 17)

glumly (glum´ lē) in a sad way (p. 351)

gongs (gôngz) large cymbals that make a heavy sound (p. 439)

granaries (gran´ ər ēz) bins for storing grains (p. 27)

grandeurs (gran´ jərz) the state of being grand (p. 42)

grille (gril) a grate on a car (p. 17)

gristle (gris´ əl) a tough, stringy tissue found in meat (p. 260)

gross (grōs) major (p. 389)

grudgingly (gruj´ ing lē) in an unwilling or resentful way (p. 8)

guaranteed (gar ən tēd´) promised (p. 322)

H

hacked (hakd) chopped; slashed (p. 289)

halfwit (haf´ wit) a foolish person (p. 239)

harmonious (här mō´ nē əs) having similar feelings or ideas (p. 87)

haste (hāst) a hurry (p. 152)

haunches (hônch´ əz) hind legs (p. 439)

hemlock (hem´ lok) an evergreen tree in the pine family (p. 277)

hence (hens) away (p. 442)

henceforth (hens fôrth´) from now on (p. 394)

hereby (hir bī´) by means of this (p. 394)

hereinafter (hir in af´ tər) after this (p. 394)

heritage (her´ ə tij) one's background, usually of family ties (p. 52); what is inherited from one's ancestors (p. 199)

hesitantly (hez´ ə tənt lē) in a cautious way (p. 333)

hindsight (hīnd´ sīt) the understanding that comes later (p. 389)

Hispanic (hi span´ ik) having Latin American ancestors (p. 51)

a	hat	e	let	ī	ice	ô	order	u̇	put	sh	she	ə	a	in about
ā	age	ē	equal	o	hot	oi	oil	ü	rule	th	thin		e	in taken
ä	far	ėr	term	ō	open	ou	out	ch	child	ᵺ	then		i	in pencil
â	care	i	it	ȯ	saw	u	cup	ng	long	zh	measure		o	in lemon
													u	in circus

hoarding (hôr´ ding) storing up and hiding from others (p. 289)

hops (hopz) a type of grain with a bitter flavor (p. 145)

horde (hôrd) a large crowd (p. 66)

hordes (hôrdz) great numbers; crowds (p. 392)

horsemanship (hôrs´ mən ship) the art or skill of riding on horseback (p. 239)

hospitality (hos pə tal´ ə tē) welcome (p. 336)

housecoats (hous´ kōtz) ladies' clothing for wearing at home (p. 300)

hubbub (hub´ ub) noise (p. 367)

huff (huf) showing a bad temper (p. 388)

humanity (hyü man´ ə tē) human beings as a group (p. 198)

humiliated (hyü mil´ ē āt id) shamed; disgraced (p. 233)

humiliating (hyü mil´ ē āt ing) causing one to feel embarrassed (p. 93)

hummocks (hum´ əkz) rises or ridges in a field of ice (p. 152)

humorist (hyü´ mər ist) one whose writing contains much humor (p. 42)

hypnosis (hip nō´ sis) a dream-like state (p. 89)

I

illuminated (i lü´ mə nāt əd) lighted (p. 63)

immigration (im ə grā´ shən) a government agency that checks people in when they enter a country (p. 49)

immortal (i môr´ tl) living forever (p. 424)

impertinent (im pėrt´ n ənt) showing a lack of proper respect (p. 238)

implies (im plīz´) quietly suggests (p. 240)

imposter (im pos´ tər) a fake (p. 335)

impractical (im prak´ tə kəl) not useful (p. 353)

incessantly (in ses´ nt lē) without stopping (p. 40)

indignantly (in dig´ nənt lē) in a proud, angry way (p. 423)

industrial (in dus´ trē əl) big enough for a factory (p. 17)

industrious (in dus´ trē əs) hard-working (p. 146)

inedible (in ed´ ə bəl) not fit to be eaten (p. 260)

inevitably (in ev´ ə tə bəl lē) not to be avoided (p. 52)

infinity (in fin´ ə tē) the quality of having no limit or end (p. 381)

initiate (i nish´ ē āt) to start (p. 28)

inscribed (in skrībd´) written on (p. 53)

inscription (in skrip´ shən) carved writing, such as in stone (p. 63)

insincerity (in sin ser´ ə tē) dishonesty (p. 319)

instinctively (in stingk´ tiv lē) done without thinking (p. 135)

intersections (in tər sek´ shənz) where roads cross (p. 354)

intimidated (in tim´ ə dā tid) frightened (p. 375)

intimidating (in tim´ ə dāt ing) to cause others to be frightened (p. 212)

intruder (in trüd´ ər) someone who breaks in (p. 343)

iridescent (ir ə des´ nt) showing different colors when seen from different angles (p. 375)

ironically (ī ron´ ə kel lē) oddly enough; in a different way than expected (p. 50)

irritating (ir´ ə tāt ing) annoying or bothersome (p. 93)

J

jabbed (jabd) poked quickly or suddenly (p. 120)

jalopy (jə lop´ ē) an old car in bad condition (p. 132)

jotted (jo´ təd) took a quick, short note (p. 135)

K

keen (kēn) sharp (p. 150)

kite (kīt) a bird of the hawk family (p. 436)

L

lavish (lav´ ish) splendid and costly (p. 334)

lawsuit (lô´ süt) a case in a law court between two people (p. 211)

leaves (lēvz) pages (p. 261)

ledger (lej´ ər) an account book (p. 389)

legacy (leg´ ə sē) that which is handed down from previous generations (p. 199)

liable (lī´ ə bəl) likely to do something; likely to happen (p. 147)

lieutenant (lü ten´ ənt) a military officer (p. 64)

linger (ling´ gər) to stay behind (p. 326)

linguistics (ling gwis´ tiks) the science of speech and language (p. 198)

literacy (lit´ ər ə sē) the ability to read and write (p. 208)

loaf (lōf) to not do anything (p. 326)

logical (loj´ ə kəl) reasonable; following a step-by-step process (p. 377)

loiter (loi´ tər) to hang around (p. 326)

loupe (lüp) a type of magnifying glass worn close to the eye (p. 122)

lure (lùr) to draw attention to (p. 30)

luscious (lush´ əs) highly pleasing (p. 30)

M

macaw (mə kô´) a large, bright-colored parrot (p. 416)

machetes (mə she´ tēz) a large heavy knife for cutting sugarcane (p. 456)

magnitude (mag´ nə tüd) size (p. 379)

mahogany (mə hog´ ə nē) a type of reddish-brown wood (p. 40)

maiden (mād´ n) an unmarried girl or woman (p. 422)

malicious (mə lish´ əs) having or showing evil plans (p. 384)

mangy (mān´ jē) having mange, a skin disease in animals that causes sores and hair loss (p. 439)

marrow (mar´ ō) the tissue inside of bones (p. 41)

masquerading (mas kə rād´ ing) dressing up, especially in costume (p. 291)

a	hat	e	let	ī	ice	ȯ	order	u̇	put	sh	she	ə	a	in about
ā	age	ē	equal	o	hot	oi	oil	ü	rule	th	thin		e	in taken
ä	far	ėr	term	ō	open	ou	out	ch	child	ᵺ	then		i	in pencil
â	care	i	it	ȯ	saw	u	cup	ng	long	zh	measure		o	in lemon
													u	in circus

medallion (mə dal´ yən) a large medal, often on a chain (p. 332)

meditate (mē´ dē āt) to consider (p. 325)

mere (mir) only; no more than (p. 90)

methods (meth´ ədz) ways of doing something (p. 222)

mimicked (mim´ ikd) imitated (p. 86)

minuscule (min´ ə skyül) very small (p. 260)

misapprehension (mis ap ri hen´ shən) misunderstanding (p. 334)

miscellaneous (mis ə lā´ nē əs) various (p. 336)

misery (miz´ ər ē) a great sorrow (p. 238)

moderately (mod´ ər it lē) somewhat; kind of (p. 30)

momentarily (mō´ mən ter ə lē) for a short time (p. 85)

monarch (mon´ ərk) a king or ruler (p. 416)

monotonous (mə not´ n əs) with little or no change; boring (pp. 93, 444)

mortar and pestle (môr´ tər and pes´ tl) a bowl and rod used to grind materials (p. 366)

mortified (môr´ tə fīd) feeling a great sense of shame (p. 94)

murdered (mėr´ dərd) killed by another (p. 198)

mute (myüt) silent (p. 289)

mutt (mut) a dog that is made up of at least two breeds (p. 10)

N

narcissus (när sis´ əs) heavily scented bulb plant with white or yellow flowers (p. 300)

nauseous (nô´ shəs) feeling sick to one's stomach (p. 87)

niche (nich) a cut out or indented shelf in a wall (p. 63)

nymph (nimf) a goddess of nature, thought of as a beautiful maiden (p. 271)

O

obscure (əb skyúr´) not well known, hidden (p. 422)

obsessed (əb sesd´) having all one's attention taken by one thing (p. 90)

obstacle (ob´ stə kəl) something standing in the way; a difficulty (p. 382)

obstacles (ob´ stə kəlz) things getting in the way (p. 344)

obstinacy (ob´ stə nə sē) stubbornness (p. 424)

onlookers (ôn´ lük ər) witnesses (p. 425)

orator (ôr´ ə tər) a person who is skilled at public speaking (p. 454)

ordinance (ôrd´ n əns) a law (p. 325)

original (ə rij´ ə nəl) first (p. 132)

ornithologists (ôr nə thol´ ə jistz) people who study birds (p. 221)

outlets (out´ letz) ways of expressing oneself (p. 199)

overbearing (ō vər ber´ ing) bossy (p. 389)

P

pantomimes (pan´ tə mīmz) acts out silently (p. 374)

passionate (pash´ ə nit) showing strong feeling (p. 190)

pauper (pô´ pər) a very poor person (p. 42)

pendulum (pen´ jə ləm) the part of a clock that hangs down and swings (p. 117)

penetrated (pen´ ə trā td) passed into (p. 102)

pennants (pen´ əntz) banners or flags (p. 319)

perilously (per´ ə ləs lē) dangerously (p. 150)

persisted (pər sis tid´) refused to give up (p. 190)

pessimistic (pes ə mis´ tik) negative; gloomy (p. 384)

pestilence (pes´ tl əns) a fast-spreading disease (p. 41)

petty (pet´ ē) small and unimportant (p. 384)

phenomenon (fe nom´ ə non) a very unusual event or thing (p. 89)

phonograph (fō´ nə graf) a machine that plays records (p. 351)

phrasings (frāz´ ingz) ways of speaking (p. 300)

pitch (pich) tar (p. 259)

plumage (plü´ mij) feathers (p. 454)

poising (poiz´ ing) balancing (p. 150)

poll (pōl) an expression of opinion in voting (p. 210)

populated (pop´ yə lā təd) inhabited (p. 134)

pot-liquor (pot lik´ ər) the liquid in which meat has been cooked (p. 261)

pottage (pot´ ij) a thick soup or stew (p. 455)

precautionary (pri kô´ shə ner ē) protecting against possible danger (p. 321)

precise (pri sīs´) exact (p. 372)

precisely (pri sīs´ lē) exactly (p. 327)

predators (pred´ ə tər) animals or people that feed upon others (p. 222)

predicted (pri dik´ təd) guessed about the future (p. 53)

predictions (pri dik´ shənz) guesses about the future (p. 322)

preferably (pref´ ər ə blē) if possible (p. 29)

preferences (pref´ ər əns əz) things that are wanted most (p. 169)

prelude (prel´ yüd) the lead-in to a main event (p. 15)

pried (prīd) used force to draw out (p. 123)

principal (prin´ sə pəl) major (p. 354)

privacy (prī´ və sē) a state of being away from others (p. 86)

probed (prōbd) searched into (p. 122)

proclamation (prok lə mā´ shən) announcement (p. 331)

prodded (prod´ əd) poked (p. 122)

proposition (prop ə zish´ ən) an offer (p. 165)

a	hat	e	let	ī	ice	ô	order	u̇	put	sh	she	ə	a in about
ā	age	ē	equal	o	hot	oi	oil	ü	rule	th	thin		e in taken
ä	far	ėr	term	ō	open	ou	out	ch	child	ᴴʜ	then		i in pencil
â	care	i	it	ȯ	saw	u	cup	ng	long	zh	measure		o in lemon
													u in circus

psychological (sī kə loj´ ə kəl) having to do with the mind (p. 199)

psychologist (sī kol´ ə jist) a person who has studied behavior patterns (p. 87)

pulsating (pul´ sāt ing) moving up and down quickly (p. 16)

punctuated (pungk´ chü ā tid) interrupted (p. 351)

puns (punz) jokes made of plays on words (p. 88)

pursue (pər sü´) to look for, go after (p. 50)

pursuers (pər sü´ ərz) persons chasing someone (p. 151)

Q

quarry (kwôr´ ē) anything that is hunted (p. 441)

quarters (kwôr´ tərz) an area where one lives (p. 438)

quartz (kwôrtz) a crystal-like mineral (p. 146)

quest (kwest) a journey in search of something (p. 394)

R

racist (rā´ sist) one who shows hatred toward a particular group of people (p. 211)

rancor (rang´ kər) bitter hate or ill will (p. 259)

ravenous (rav´ ə nəs) greedily hungry (p. 259)

reactionary (rē ak´ shə ner ē) a person who favors a return to a past state of affairs (p. 211)

realm (relm) a kingdom (p. 394)

reason (rē´ zn) common sense (p. 319)

rebellion (ri bel´ yən) a great struggle against power (p. 198)

recognition (rek əg nish´ ən) special attention (p. 42)

refunded (ri fund´ əd) paid back (p. 322)

regally (rē´ gəl lē) grandly (p. 336)

registrars (rej´ ə strärz) officials who keep records or lists (p. 210)

registration (rej´ ə strā´ shən) the act of signing up on a list or record (p. 208)

reign (rān) to rule (p. 394)

rejecting (ri jekt´ ing) not accepting (p. 196); not using (p. 321)

reluctantly (ri luk´ tənt lē) unwillingly (p. 233)

renew (ri nü´) start again (p. 190)

repaid (ri pād´) paid back (p. 417)

repentance (ri pen´ təns) changing one's ways after doing something wrong (pp. 191, 467)

reprimanded (rep´ rə mand əd) scolded (p. 65)

repulse (ri puls´) to drive back (p. 416)

resolved (ri zolvd´) made the decision (p. 147)

resorted (ri zôr´ təd) gone back to (p. 426)

resourceful (ri sôrs´ fəl) practical (p. 344)

restrain (ri strān´) to hold down (p. 31)

retroactive (ret rō ak´ tiv) influencing what has already happened (p. 210)

reveal (ri vēl´) to show (p. 42); to make known (p. 50)

revealed (ri vēld´) showed; made known (p. 123)

reverberates (ri vėr´ bə rātz) rings with repeated sound (p. 375)

roost (rüst) a perch where birds rest (p. 221)

routine (rü tēn´) the normal order of activity (p. 87)

row (rō) a noisy racket (p. 368)

rudimentary (rü də men´ tər ē) basic or undeveloped (p. 240)

rued (rüd) regretted (p. 277)

run-ins (run´ inz) unpleasant meetings or discussions with someone (p. 214)

S

salutations (sal yə tā´ shənz) greetings (p. 336)

salve (salv) a soothing cream (p. 367)

salved (salvd) calmed (p. 121)

satisfactorily (sat is fak´ tər i lē) in a way that fulfills a need or a goal (p. 166)

savoring (sā´ vər ing) enjoying (p. 136)

scandalous (skan´ dl əs) shocking; inviting trouble (p. 342)

scholarship (skol´ ər ship) quality of knowledge and learning (p. 239)

scorch (skôrch) to burn severely (p. 446)

scour (skour) to search or go through (p. 438)

scrub (skrub) a small tree or bush (p. 439)

sculpted (skulp´ təd) carved (p. 290)

secured (si kyürd´) fastened (p. 339)

segregation (seg rə gā´ shən) forced separation from others (p. 212)

self-reliant (self ri lī´ ənt) able to take care of oneself (p. 259)

self-sufficient (self sə fish´ ənt) able to take care of oneself (p. 27)

sensitive (sen´ sə tiv) careful and uneasy (p. 8); touchy; easily upset (p. 382)

sentiment (sen´ tə mənt) a gentle feeling (p. 190)

serviceable (sėr´ vi sə bəl) useful (p. 332)

shafts (shaftz) beams (p. 339)

sheepishly (shē´ pish lē) in an embarrassed way (p. 65)

shellfish (shel´ fish) an animal with no bones that has a shell, such as a crab or shrimp (p. 422)

shriveled (shriv´ əld) dried up (p. 426)

shuttle (shut´ l) an instrument used in weaving to carry thread back and forth (p. 423)

siblings (sib´ lingz) brothers and sisters (p. 87)

simulate (sim´ yə lāt) to give the appearance of (p. 375)

skeptically (skep´ tə kəl lē) slow to believe (p. 322)

slithering (sliᴛʜ´ ər ing) slinking and sliding, like a snake (p. 392)

sliver (sliv´ ər) a thin, sometimes sharp piece of a material (p. 118)

sluggish (slug´ ish) slow-moving (p. 222)

smirked (smėrkd) smiled in a self-satisfied way (p. 92)

a	hat	e	let	ī	ice	ȯ	order	u̇	put	sh	she	ə	a in about
ā	age	ē	equal	o	hot	oi	oil	ü	rule	th	thin		e in taken
ä	far	ėr	term	ō	open	ou	out	ch	child	ᴛʜ	then		i in pencil
â	care	i	it	ȯ	saw	u	cup	ng	long	zh	measure		o in lemon
													u in circus

smock (smok) a loose piece of clothing worn to protect the clothes underneath it (p. 119)

solitary (sol´ ə ter ē) alone (p. 29)

soprano (sə pran´ ō) one who uses the highest singing voice of women or boys (p. 271)

sovereign (sov´ rən) above all others; superior (p. 291); a ruler (p. 336)

spats (spatz) cloth coverings for the ankles and insteps (p. 334)

specialist (spesh´ ə list) one who works in one special area (p. 367)

specified (spes´ ə fīd) gave exact detail (p. 52)

spectators (spek´ tā tərz) people who are watching (p. 425)

speculate (spek´ yə lāt) to wonder about (p. 325)

spindly (spind´ lē) long and thin (p. 426)

spontaneous (spon tā´ nē əs) happening naturally, without planning (p. 88)

spraddle (sprad´ l) spread out or stretched wide apart (p. 223)

staff (staf) a pole (p. 329)

stalk (stôk) to stomp angrily (p. 331)

startled (stär´ tld) surprised (p. 417)

starvation (stär vā´ shən) a health problem due to lack of food (p. 10); terrible hunger (p. 377)

steadfast (sted´ fast) loyal (p. 343)

steal (stēl) to go (p. 422)

stepwell (step´ wel) an opening for stairs (p. 212)

stethoscope (steth´ ə skōp) a doctor's tool for listening to sounds in the body (p. 366)

strenuous (stren´ yü əs) tiring, requiring much effort (p. 326)

stricken (strik´ ən) knocked down (p. 42)

strive (strīv) struggle in contest with (p. 425)

strove (strōv) tried very hard (p. 149)

stubby (stub´ ē) short and thick (p. 260)

studious (stü´ dē əs) having to do with studying (p. 43)

stunts (stuntz) slows up; holds back (p. 341)

subsided (səb sīd´ əd) became less (p. 121)

substantial (səb stan´ shəl) large in amount (p. 339)

suburbs (sub´ ėrbz) neighborhoods just outside cities (p. 320)

sulking (sulk´ ing) to be moody and silent (p. 29)

summit (sum´ it) highest part (p. 153)

surmise (sər mīz´) to suppose (p. 325)

surnames (sėr´ nāmz) last names (p. 52)

surplus (sėr´ pləs) the amount that remains after needs are met (p. 133)

survives (sər vīvz´) carries on; continues to live (p. 271)

swerve (swėrv) to turn sharply (p. 284)

switch (swich) a thin, flexible whip (p. 43)

T

taint (tānt) a small amount (p. 222)

talon (tal´ ən) a bird's claw (p. 436)

termites (tėr´ mītz) winged insects that eat the wood in trees and buildings (p. 134)

terrain (te rān´) the ground (p. 374)

theatrical (thē at´ rə kəl) showy (p. 379)

thickset (thik´ set´) thick in form or build (p. 212)

threshold (thresh´ ōld) an opening or doorway (p. 437)

thrushes (thrush əz) robin-sized, brown birds (p. 291)

tickled (tik´ əld) greatly pleased or delighted (p. 169)

tidier (tī´ dē ər) neater (p. 16)

tonic (ton´ ik) a medicine that refreshes or gives strength (p. 367)

traditional (trə dish´ ə nəl) based on long-held customs (p. 196)

tragedy (traj´ ə dē) a very sad event; a disaster (p. 197)

trance (trans) a sleep-like state (p. 391)

transfixed (tran sfiksd´) without moving, as one under a spell (p. 387)

transformed (tran sfôrmd´) changed (p. 322)

translated (tran slā´ təd) changed to or from another language (p. 123)

treacheries (trech´ ər ēz) harmful acts against another (p. 233)

trice (trīs) a very short time (p. 396)

trilling (tril´ ing) rolling (p. 49)

trowel (trou´ əl) small hand-shovel for gardening (p. 16)

truce (trüs) a peaceful end to fighting (p. 29)

tumor (tü´ mər) a clump of growing tissue (p. 197)

tush (tush) a tusk (p. 436)

twined (twīnd) twisted together (p. 425)

U

unabridged (un ə brijd´) complete; not shortened (p. 319)

uncomprehending (un kom pri hend´ ing) not understanding the real meaning of (p. 189)

undergone (un dər gôn´) gone through (p. 467)

unethical (un eth´ ə kəl) wrong (p. 325)

unique (yü nēk´) one-of-a-kind (p. 378)

unveiled (un vāld´) made known (p. 66)

upstart (up´ stärt) an unimportant person (p. 338)

ushered (ush´ ərd) directed to a place (pp. 52, 117)

V

valise (və lēs´) a traveling bag (p. 117)

varied (ver´ ēd) various (p. 422)

verge (vėrj) the edge or border (p. 88)

veterans (vet´ ər ənz) people with lots of experience (p. 443)

vigilance (vij´ ə ləns) watchfulness (p. 223)

vigorously (vig´ ər əs lē) quickly and with force (pp. 18, 375)

villa (vil´ ə) a country home (p. 233)

villainously (vil´ ə nəs lē) in a tricky, evil way (p. 386)

virtue (vėr´ chü) goodness (p. 238)

vouch (vouch) to give proof of a fact (p. 208)

a	hat	e	let	ī	ice	ô	order	ù	put	sh	she	ə	a in about
ā	age	ē	equal	o	hot	oi	oil	ü	rule	th	thin		e in taken
ä	far	ėr	term	ō	open	ou	out	ch	child	ŦH	then		i in pencil
â	care	i	it	ò	saw	u	cup	ng	long	zh	measure		o in lemon
													u in circus

W

wage (wāj) to carry on (p. 29)

waver (wā´ vər) to feel doubt (p. 474)

wellborn (wel´ bôrn´) born in a family of wealth (p. 422)

whirlpool (hwėrl´ pül) spinning water that pulls in objects (p. 417)

whirring (hwėr´ ing) moving with a buzzing sound (p. 284)

winced (winsd) drew back slightly, as if in pain (pp. 17, 121)

wistfully (wist´ fəl lē) in a hopeful but sad way (p. 354)

witchery (wich´ ər ē) to act as though casting magical spells (p. 30)

wooed (wüd) sweet-talked (p. 28)

worthwhile (wėrth´ hwīl´) meaningful; worth doing (p. 386)

wretch (rech) a shameful person (p. 381)

writer's cramp (rī´ tərz kramp) stiffness in the fingers caused by too much writing (p. 390)

Y

yawing (yôn´ ing) swinging from side to side (p. 154)

Z

zwieback (swī´ bak) a dry, toastlike cracker (p. 260)

Index of Fine Art

Index of Authors and Titles

Index

detail identification, 512
dialogues, 97, 243, 449
dramatic reading, 225
feedback, 173
group discussions, 69, 357
interviews, 264
logic fallacies, 513
making judgments, 127
monologues, 110
note-taking and, 513
oral reports, 286, 419, 429
outlining, 158
poem reading, 274, 293
poetry analysis, 279
role-playing, 142
selling, 201
speaker analysis, 513
speeches, 347, 469
speech making, 217
speech writing, 12, 35, 56
strategy checklist for,
    512–13
summarizing, 303
teaching, 193
tone, 477
Literary terms, defined, xv
Literature
    recitations, 508
    responses, 508
Logic, fallacies of, 513
London, Jack, 143
Lose, loose, 497
Lyric poems, 255

M

Magazines, 515
Main Idea Graphic
    (Details), 487
Main Idea Graphic (Table),
    486
Main Idea Graphic
    (Umbrella), 486

Maps, 514
Mazer, Norma Fox, 83
Media accounts, 185
Media and Viewing, 515
    body language, 97
    cartoon creating, 419
    collages, 201
    compare and contrast, 449
    drawing and illustrating,
        477
    Internet research, 142
    moods, 235
    music for movies, 173
    online, 515
    poem recordings, 279
    poetic devices, 303
    posters, 20
    researching, 193
    slide shows, 56
    storyboards, 357
Memoirs, 224
    defined, 220
Merriam, Eve, 269
Metacognition, xviii
Metaphors, 254
    defined, 270
Mini-books, 264
Modifiers, 492
Monologues, 110
Moods, 234, 235, 246, 276,
    278
    defined, 231
Morals, defined, 414
Mori, Toshio, 163
Morrison, Lillian, 281
Motives, 172
    defined, 84
Movies
    books and, 449
    music and, 173
"Mowgli's Brothers," 434–49

Multimedia presentations,
    515
Music, movies and, 173
"My Papa, Mark Twain,"
    37–46
Myths, 411, 421, 428
    defined, xi

N

"Names/Nombres," 47–56
Nanus, Susan, 317, 363
Narration, autobiographical,
    74–77
Narrative poems, 255
Narratives, 497, 509
    autobiographical, 74–77
    defined, 188
    personal, 158
Narrative writing, 185, 497,
    509
Narrator, 2, 116
    defined, 14
Nash, Ogden, 257
Newspapers, 515
Nonfiction, 2, 26, 188, 192,
    245
    defined, xi
Nonfiction, characteristics, 2
    author's purpose, 2
    point of view, 2
    tone, 2
Nonfiction, types
    autobiography, 3
    biography, 3
    diary, 3
    essay, 3
    informational text, 3
    journal, 3
    letter, 3
    speech, 3
Nonfiction writing, elements
    author's influences, 184

Acknowledgments

Grateful acknowledgment is made to the following for copyrighted material:

Pages 7–10: "Stray" by Cynthia Rylant from *Every Living Thing.* Copyright © 1985 by Cynthia Rylant. Reprinted with permission by Atheneum Books for Young Readers, an imprint of Simon & Schuster Children's Publishing Division.

Pages 15–18: "The Drive-In Movies" by Gary Soto from *A Summer Life,* copyright © 1990 by University Press of New England, Hanover, N.H. Reprinted with permission by The University Press of New England.

Pages 22–23: "Website: Animaland" by Staff from *www.animaland.org.* Copyright © 2005 by The American Society for the Prevention of Cruelty to Animals. Reprinted with permission of the ASPCA.

Pages 27–32: "How to Talk to Your Cat" by Jean Craighead George from *How to Talk to Your Cat.* Text copyright © 2000 by Jean Craighead George. Illustrations copyright © 2000 by Paul Meisel. Used by permission of HarperCollins Publishers, Inc.

Pages 39–43: "My Papa Mark Twain" by Susy Clemens from *Small Voices.* Copyright © 1966 by Josef and Dorothy Berger. Reproduced by permission of Paul S. Eriksson, Publisher.

Pages 49–53: "Names/Nombres" by Julia Alvarez from *Nuestro, March, 1985.* Copyright © 1985 by Julia Alvarez. First published in *Nuestro,* March, 1985. All rights reserved. Reprinted by permission of Susan Bergholz Literary Services, New York.

Pages 63–66: "The Laughing Skull" retold by Lulu Delacre from *Golden Tales: Myths, Legends And Folktales From Latin America.* Scholastic Inc./Scholastic Press. Copyright © 1996 by Lulu Delacre. Used by permission of Scholastic, Inc.

Pages 85–94: "Cutthroat" by Norma Fox Mazer from *Ultimate Sports: Short Stories by Outstanding Writers for Young Adults.* Used by permission of The Elaine Markson Literary Agency, Inc.

Pages 100–107: "Zlateh the Goat" by Isaac Bashevis Singer from *Zlateh the Goat and Other Stories.* Text copyright © 1966 by Isaac Bashevis Singer, copyright © renewed 1994 by Alma Singer. Used by permission of HarperCollins Publishers, Inc.

Pages 112–113: "Poland: Tradition and Change" by Staff from *Prentice Hall World Explorer: Europe and Russia.* Copyright © 2003 by Pearson Education, Inc., publishing as Pearson Prentice Hall. Used by permission by Pearson Education, Inc., publishing as Pearson Prentice Hall.

Pages 117–124: "Lillian and Grand-père" by Sharon Hart Addy from *Cricket Magazine.* Used by permission of Sharon Addy.

Pages 131–139: "The Circuit" by Francisco Jiménez from *America Street: A Muliticultural Anthology of Stories.* Copyright © Francisco Jiménez. Reprinted with permission of Francisco Jiménez.

Pages 165–170: "Business at Eleven" by Toshio Mori from *America Street: A Multicultural Anthology of Stories.* Reproduced by permission of The Caxton Printers, Ltd.

Pages 189–191: "Water" by Helen Keller from *The Story of My Life.* Copyright © 1965 by Airmont Publishing Company, Inc. Reprinted by permission of Airmont Publishing Company, Inc.

Pages 196–199: "Amy Tan" by Kathy Ishizuka from *Asian American Literature.* Copyright © 2000 by Kathy Ishizuka. Published by Enslow Publshers, Inc., Berkeley Heights, NJ. All rights reserved. [Text only.] Used by permission of Enslow Publishers, Inc.

Pages 208–214: "from Rosa Parks: My Story" by Rosa Parks from *Rosa Parks: My Story,* copyright © 1992 by Rosa Parks. All rights reserved. Used by permission of Dial Books for Young Readers, A Division of Penguin Young Readers Group, A Member of Penguin Group (USA) Inc., 345 Hudson Street, New York, NY 10014.

Pages 221–223: "Turkeys" by Bailey White from *Mama Makes Up Her Mind* (Addison-Wesley, 1993.) Used by permission of The Lazear Agency, Inc.

Pages 232–233: "La Leña Buena," by John Phillip Santos from *Places Left Unfinished at the Time of Creation,* copyright © 1999 by John Phillip Santos. Used by permission of Viking Penguin, a division of Penguin Group (USA) Inc.

Pages 238–240: "Letter to Scottie" by F. Scott Fitzgerald from *F. Scott Fitzgerald: A Life In Letters.* Copyright © 1994 by The Trustees, Under Agreement Dated July 3, 1975, Created by Frances Scott Fitzgerald Smith. Reprinted with permission of Scribner, an imprint of Simon & Schuster Adult Publishing Group.

Pages 259–260: "Adventures of Isabel" by Ogden Nash from *Parents Keep Out.* Copyright © 1936 by Ogden Nash, renewed. All rights reserved. Reprinted by permission of Curtis Brown, Ltd.

Page 260: "Ankylosaurus" by Jack Prelutsky from *Tyrannosaurus Was A Beast.* Text copyright © 1988 by Jack Prelutsky. Used by permission of HarperCollins Publishers, Inc.

Page 271: "Simile: Willow and Gingko" by Eve Merriam from *A Sky Full of Poems.* Copyright © 1964, 1970, 1973, 1986 by Eve Merriam. All rights reserved. Reprinted by permission of Marian Reiner, Literary Agent, for the author.

Page 272: "Fame is a bee" by Emily Dickinson from *The Poems of Emily Dickinson.* Copyright © 1951, 1955, 1979,

1983 by the President and Fellows of Harvard College. Reprinted by permission of the publishers and the Trustees of Amherst College, Thomas H. Johnson, ed., Cambridge, Mass: The Belknap Press of Harvard University Press.

Page 272: "April Rain Song" by Langston Hughes from *The Collected Poems of Langston Hughes*, copyright © 1994 by The Estate of Langston Hughes. Used by permission of Alfred A. Knopf, a division of Random House, Inc.

Page 277: "Dust of Snow" by Robert Frost from *The Poetry of Robert Frost* edited by Edward Connery Lathem. Copyright © 1923, 1969 by Henry Holt & Company. Copyright © 1951 by Robert Frost. Reprinted by permission of Henry Holt and Company, LLC.

Page 283: "Haiku ("An old silent pond...")" by Matsuo Bashō from *Cricket Songs: Japanese Haiku*, translated by Harry Behn. Copyright © 1964 by Harry Behn; Copyright © renewed 1992 Prescott Behn, Pamela Behn Adam and Peter Behn. All rights reserved. Reprinted by permission of Marian Reiner, Literary Agent, for the author.

Page 284: "The Sidewalk Racer or On the Skateboard" by Lillian Morrison from *The Sidewalk Racer and Other Poems of Sports and Motion*. Copyright © 1965, 1967, 1968, 1977, 2001 by Lillian Morrison. All rights reserved. Reprinted by permission of Marian Reiner, Literary Agent, for the author.

Page 289: "Camping Out in the Backyard" by Antonio Vallone from *Roots and Flowers: Poets and Poems on Family*, copyright © 1998 by Antonio Vallone. Reprinted by permission of Antonio Vallone.

Page 290: "Wind and water and stone" by Octavio Paz, translated by Mark Strand, from *A Draft of Shadows*. Copyright © 1979 by The New Yorker Magazine, Inc. Reprinted by permission of New Directions Publishing Corp.

Pages 295–296: "Madison County Public Library Card Application Form" by Staff from *Madison County Public Library*. Used by permission of The Madison County Public Library (Kentucky.) "North Carolina Poetry Society Student Poetry Contest" by Staff from *www.sleepycreek.net/poetry/submissionsstudent.htm*. Used by permission of The North Carolina Poetry Society.

Pages 300–301: "Alphabet" by Naomi Shihab Nye from *Fuel*. Copyright © 1998 by Naomi Shihab Nye. All rights reserved. Reprinted by permission of BOA Editions Ltd., www.BOAEditions.org.

Pages 319–344 and 365–396: "The Phantom Tollbooth" by Susan Nanus and Norton Juster from *The Phantom Tollbooth: A Children's Play in Two Acts*. Copyright © 1977 by Susan Nanus and Norton Juster. <u>CAUTION</u>: Professionals and amateurs are hereby warned that "The Phantom Tollbooth," being fully protected under the copyright laws of the United States of America, the British Commonwealth countries, including Canada, and the other countries of the Copyright Union, is subject to royalty. All rights, including professional, amateur, motion picture, recitation, lecturing, public reading, radio, television and cable broadcasting, and the rights of translation into foreign languages, are strictly reserved. Any inquiry regarding the availability of performance rights, or the purchase of individual copies of the authorized acting edition, must be directed to Samuel French, Inc., 45 West 25th Street, NY, NY 10010 with other locations in Hollywood and Toronto, Canada. Reprinted by permission of Samuel French, Inc.

Pages 350–354: "Milo" by Norton Juster from *The Phantom Tollbooth*. Illustrations and text from *The Phantom Tollbooth* by Norton Juster illustrated by Jules Feiffer, copyright © 1961 and renewed 1989 by Norton Juster; Illustrations copyright © 1961 and renewed 1989 by Jules Feiffer. Used by permission of Alfred A. Knopf, a division of Random House, Inc.

Pages 415–416: "The Tiger Who Would Be King" by James Thurber from *Further Fables for Our Time*. Copyright © James Thurber. All rights reserved. Used by permission of The Barbara Hogenson Agency, Inc.

Page 417: "The Ant and the Dove" by Leo Tolstoy from *Fables and Folktales Adapted from Tolstoy*, adapted by Maristella Maaggie. The publisher wishes to thank Jean Grasso Fitzpatrick, translator, for granting permission for this use.

Pages 422–426: "Arachne" by Olivia E. Coolidge from *Greek Myths*. Copyright © 1949 by Olivia E. Coolidge; copyright © renewed 1977 by Olivia E. Coolidge. All rights reserved. Reprinted by permission of Houghton Mifflin Company.

Pages 453–456: "Why the Tortoise's Shell Is Not Smooth" by Chinua Achebe from *Things Fall Apart*. Copyright © 1959 by Chinua Achebe. Reprinted with permission of Harcourt Education.

Pages 465–467: "The Three Wishes" selected and adapted by Ricardo E. Alegría from *The Three Wishes: A Collection of Puerto Rican Folktales*. Copyright © 1969 by Ricardo E. Alegría. Reprinted by permission of Ricardo E. Alegria.

Pages 472–475: "Why the North Star Stands Still" by William R. Palmer from *The Songs My Paddle Sings*. Copyright © 1973 by Zion Natural History Association, Springdale. Used by permission of The Zion Natural History Association.

Note: Every effort has been made to locate the copyright owner of material reproduced in this component. Omissions brought to our attention will be corrected in subsequent editions.

Photo Credits

Cover image © Digital Vision/Getty Images; page x middle © Andres Rodriguez/Shutterstock; page x bottom © Anna Chelnokova/Shutterstock; page xx top © PhotoDisc Volumes Education 2 41307; page xx middle © Blend Images/SuperStock; page xxiv © Blue Lantern Studio/CORBIS All Rights Reserved; page 3 www.CartoonStock.com; page 5 Courtesy of Cynthia Rylant; page 7 © Zig Leszczynski/Animals Animals; page 8 © Robert Comport/Animals Animals; page 13 © Prentice Hall School Division; page 15 © Dave Bartruff/CORBIS All Rights Reserved; page 25 © Jean Craighead George; pages 27, 28, 30, 31, 32 © Paul Meisel/Harper Collins; pages 37, 40, 43 © The Mark Twain House, Hartford, CT; page 47 © Daniel Cima; page 49 © Pete Seaward/Getty Images Inc.—Stone Allstock; page 53 © Collage, 1992, Juan Sanchez, Courtesy of Juan Sanchez and Guarighen, Inc. NYC; page 58 © Map Resources; page 61 © Lulu Delacre; page 63 © Thinkstock/CORBIS; page 65 © Thinkstock/CORBIS; page 78 © Newberry Library/SuperStock; page 81 © "PEANUTS" reprinted by permission of United Feature Syndicate, Inc.; page 83 © Norma Fox Mazer/Elaine Markson Agency; pages 85, 86, 87, 88, 89, 90, 91, 92, 93, 94 Kazuko Collins; page 98 © Robert Maass/Corbis/Bettmann; page 107 top left © Suslov Nikolay Vladimirovich/Shutterstock; page 107 top right © M.E. Mulder/Shutterstock; page 107 bottom left © Dumitrescu Ciprian-Florin/Shutterstock; page 107 bottom right © Pixelman/Shutterstock; page 112 © Skjold Photographs; page 113 © Dorling Kindersley; page 115 © Brayer Photography; page 119 © Lynette Hemmant/Carus Publishing; page 123 © Lynette Hemmant/Carus Publishing; page 129 © Francisco Jiménez; page 131 © *My Brother*, 1942, Guayasamin (Oswaldo Guayasamin Calero), Oil on wood, 15 ⅞ x 12 ¾". The Museum of Modern Art/Licensed by Scala-Art Resource, NY. Inter-American Fund. Museo Fundacion Guayasamin, Quito, Ecuador; page 134 © Jim Sugar/CORBIS All Rights Reserved; page 137 © Nik Wheeler CORBIS All Rights Reserved; page 143 © Brown Brothers, Sterling, PA; page 145 © C Squared Studios/Getty Images, Inc.—Photodisc; page 148 The Granger Collection, New York; page 153 © PEMCO—Webster & Stevens Collection; Museum of History and Industry, Seattle/CORBIS All Rights Reserved; page 155 © Prentice Hall School Division; page 163 © Caxton Press; page 165 © SuperStock, Inc./SuperStock; page 167 left © Bettman/CORBIS; page 167 middle © Stapleton Collection/CORBIS All Rights Reserved; page 167 right © Time & Life Pictures/Getty Images; page 182 © Images.com/CORBIS; page 185 CALVIN AND HOBBES © 1992 Watterson. Reprinted with permission of UNIVERSAL PRESS SYNDICATE. All rights reserved.; page 187 © Bettmann/CORBIS All Rights Reserved; page 189 © Bettmann/CORBIS All Rights Reserved; page 191 © Photofest; page 197 © Renars Jurkovskis/Shutterstock; page 199 © Jim McHugh/Vistalux; page 206 © Reuters/CORBIS; page 208 © Bettmann/CORBIS; page 211 © Flip Schulke/CORBIS; page 213 © Bettmann/CORBIS; page 219 Courtesy of New Georgia Encyclopedia; page 221 © PhotoDisc Nature, Wildlife and the Environment 2 Volume 044 44170; page 223 © Animals Animals/Earth Scenes; page 226 © Bettman/CORBIS; page 230 © Photo: Mike Minehan, Berlin; page 232 © Ken Samuelsen/Getty Images, Inc.—Photodisc; page 236 © Brown Brothers, Sterling, PA; page 240 © Culver Pictures, Inc.; page 252 © Lou Wall/CORBIS; page 255 LUCKY COW © 2003 Mark Pett. Dist. by UNIVERSAL PRESS SYNDICATE. Reprinted with permission. All rights reserved.; page 257 top left © UPI/CORBIS/BETTMANN; page 257 top right © Random House; page 257 middle © CORBIS; pages 259, 260 top © Johanna Hantel/Images.com; page 260 bottom © Natural History Museum, London; page 262 © Falko Matte/Shutterstock; pages 266, 267 © Ingram Publishing Food and Beverage (runner beans, turnip, aubergine, burgandy pepper, artichoke, avocado, large tomato, cherry, pineapple, filled taco shells, lettuce, cauliflower, bunch of radishes, celery); page 269 top left © Photo by Bachrach. Used by permission of Marian Reiner.; page 269 top right © Amherst College Archives and Special Collections, by permission of the Trustees of Amherst College; page 269 middle © Getty Images, Inc.; page 271 © Richard Hamilton Smith/CORBIS All Rights Reserved; page 272 © J. Brackenbury/Peter Arnold, Inc.; page 275 The Granger Collection, New York; page 277 © David Macias/Photo Researchers, Inc.; page 281 top © The British Library/HIP/The Image Works; page 281 middle © Marian Reiner; page 283 (both images) © Christie's Images/CORBIS; page 284 © Mike & Elvan Habicht/Animals Animals; page 287 top left © Antonio Vallone; page 287 top right © Time Life Pictures/Getty Images; page 287 middle © Hulton-Deutsch Collection/CORBIS All Rights Reserved; page 289 © Robert Llewellyn/CORBIS; page 290 Fotosearch; page 291 © WizData/Images.com; page 298 © 1998 James McGoon; page 300 © Jim Vecchi/CORBIS; page 312 © Images.com/CORBIS; page 315 ZIGGY © 1998 ZIGGY AND FRIENDS, INC. Reprinted with permission of UNIVERSAL PRESS SYNDICATE. All rights; pages 325, 329, 334 Courtesy of Maureen Mahoney-Barraclough; page 348 © John Martin;

550 *Photo Credits*

pages 350, 352 © Random House; pages 367, 374, 377, 387, 390 Courtesy of Maureen Mahoney-Barraclough; page 408 © Caren Loebel-Fried/Images.com; page 411 © 2003 by Thaves Reprinted with permission. All rights reserved.; page 413 top © Bettmann/CORBIS; page 413 middle © Ivan E. Repin, Portrait of Leo Tolstoy. Tretyakov Gallery, Moscow, Russia. TASS/Sovfoto.; page 415 © PhotoDisc Nature, Wildlife and the Environment 2 Volume 044 44022; page 417 © Caren Loebel-Fried/Images.com; page 420 Courtesy of Houghton Mifflin Company; page 423 © Pearson Education/PH College; page 434 © Corbis/ Bettmann; pages 436, 440, 441, 445 Judy King; page 451 © Corbis/Reuters America LLC; page 455 *Crawling Turtle II,* Barry Wilson/SuperStock; page 460 © Prentice Hall School Division; page 463 © Ricardo E. Alegría; page 466 © Giraudon/Art Resource, NY; page 470 © Charles O'Rear/ CORBIS; page 473 © Wendy Nero/Shutterstock; page 474 © Amygdala Imagery/Shutterstock.

Staff Credits

Rosalyn Arcilla, Melania Benzinger, Carol Bowling, Laura Chadwick, Kazuko Collins, Nancy Condon, Barbara Drewlo, Kerry Dunn, Marti Erding, Sara Freund, Sue Gulsvig, Daren Hastings, Laura Henrichsen, Brian Holl, Bev Johnson, Julie Johnston, Patrick Keithahn, Marie Mattson, Daniel Milowski, Stephanie Morstad, Carrie O'Connor, Jeffrey Sculthorp, Julie Theisen, LeAnn Velde, Daniela Velez, Amber Wegwerth, Charmaine Whitman, Sue Will